The Nedbank American Express

South African Wine Buyer's Guide

1993 EDITION

DAVE HUGHES

STRUIK

Struik Publishers (Pty) Ltd
(A member of the Struik Group (Pty) Ltd)
Cornelis Struik House
80 McKenzie Street
Cape Town 8001

Reg. No.: 54/00965/07

First published 1986
Second edition 1987
Third edition 1988
Fourth edition 1989
Fifth edition 1990
Sixth edition 1991
Seventh edition 1992

Editor Hilda Hermann
Cover Design Neville Poulter
Designer Neville Poulter
DTP Suzanne Fortescue, Struik DTP
Reproduction BellSet cc, Cape Town
Printing and binding National Book Printers, Goodwood

ISBN 1 86825 303 1

Contents

Foreword

Nedbank American Express is pleased to be associated with the doyen of the wine industry, Dave Hughes, in this the seventh edition of the *South African Wine Buyer's Guide*.

The wine industry is well known and well respected locally; beyond our borders South African wines are receiving well deserved acclaim.

Our support for this industry, as well as our involvement in the related food and entertainment markets, has prompted us to continue working with Dave Hughes to bring out another top quality guide.

The feedback that we have had over the years indicates that this pocket-size review of more than 4 000 wines and vintages is highly regarded, and we are delighted to sponsor it.

May the wine industry grow from strength to strength and achieve much success in its future endeavours. In addition, we hope that you, the reader, will enjoy making use of this guide.

Gail Kelly

General Manager
Nedcor Bank Card Division

Preface

In the world of wine and spirits recent changes have been quite dramatic. Who, at this time last year, would have thought that KWV would drop its quota system? Well it has, and this should have far-reaching effects. The progressive vineyards and cellars, like Neethlingshof, took immediate advantage of the opportunity and wasted no time in preparing their high quality area for more plantings which the quota system had prevented them from doing. Development will be further stimulated when the KWV drops its guaranteed price system – then we will have a true free-market system which will be uncomfortable for many; only the best will survive.

Around the world changes are on the cards, and some European Common Market indicators will have definite ramifications for South Africa – some apparently very odd and generally unacceptable: keeping cellars cobweb-free and not allowing dirt floors in maturation cellars. We will have to see how the bureaucrats sort it all out.

Up-to-date information is a necessity, but you may well query how 'current' wine information can be when it takes five to seven years from soil preparation to getting grapes off the vines for wine making. But new wine cellars abound in the Cape and well-established ones undergo change: wine makers move and every vintage offers new wines and new labels. Although a guide like this is 'dated' from the time it goes to print, from the reaction I continually receive, many folk seem to find all the tasting I do in the course of a year and the notes I make of value when purchasing wine. Remember this is a *guide to wine*, not the wine maker, cellars etc. It concentrates on the wine, its potential and how wines that have been left to mature for a few years, or longer, are developing.

South African wines are under the international spotlight and will have to perform in terms of quality and price to be accepted in a world of over-supply. Our wines have received accolades on the international wine scene, and our top quality has been recognized with Beyers Truter of Kanonkop being awarded the Robert Mondavi Trophy for the Winemaker of the Year in 1991, at the International Wine and Spirit Competition.

Locally the cost of drinking continues to rise, but it is encouraging to see how many cellars have held their prices, while others have introduced new reds at more affordable prices. Price is where the battle will lie, especially in the highly competitive, popular-price area.

The wine scene is developing in every way: wine makers' skills, marketing methods, governing laws, and drinking fashions. With all the changes, we can only hope that the future of South African wine will bring even more affordable, good quality local wines and the opportunity to compare them with imported wines.

Many folk have mentioned to me how useful previous *Wine Buyer's Guides* have been, and I hope you find this year's edition just as useful. My sincere thanks go to Hilda Hermann, whose unenviable job it has been to edit and produce the *Guide* this year.

Dave Hughes
Stellenbosch, 1992

How to use this book

For easy reference, the book is divided into the wine assessments, a listing of wine according to star rating and a wine index. The listing will group wines in sections based on the different categories: Bordeaux Blends, Dry White Blends, Blanc de Noir Wines, etc. and list them in these groups according to star rating. This grouping will also enable the reader to compare ratings with price at a glance. The index is a list of the wines presented alphabetically according to the producer and will provide the reader with brief, concise information concerning a particular wine. Each wine appears with its star rating and price symbol and the page on which you will find the assessment. The wine index also includes wines that are available on the market but have not been assessed. The wine assessments provide more detailed descriptions and are divided into six broad categories: Red, White, Blanc de Noir/Rosé, Nouveau, Sparkling, Perlé, and Fortified. Within these sections you will find further divisions into cultivars, types and styles of wine. The wines in each section are then presented alphabetically together with their star rating and indication of price.

I have given my indication of quality on a scale of 0 to 5 stars. One must remember that wine is a living entity, and changes with the vintage are perfectly natural. Also, if a wine is not correctly cared for it might not be at its best when you try it and if you are not at your best, a wine might seem different from when you tried it last.

no stars	an unremarkable or poorly made wine
★	a sound wine without any special attributes
★★	a well-made wine of average quality
★★★	a good wine
★★★★	an excellent wine
★★★★★	a masterpiece, a tribute to the wine makers' art.

In instances where I have felt the wine to be worthy of slightly more than, say, three stars but not quite the standard of a four-star wine, I have included a fourth star in brackets; for example, Simonsig Cabernet Sauvignon★★★(★). Similarly a rating of ★★★★(★) indicates more than four stars but not quite five.

To give a firm retail price for the wines in the book would be foolhardy, but as an indication I have included with each assessment a symbol to indicate roughly the price range within which that wine falls. The symbols are based on bottle-store prices at the coast and I stress that the following is an indication only and in no way should be seen as fixed:

A = Less than R4,99 a bottle
B = R5,00 – R9,99 a bottle
C = R10,00 – R14,99 a bottle
D = R15,00 – R19,99 a bottle
E = R20,00 – R29,99 a bottle
F = more than R30,00 a bottle

In some instances I have included a vintage guide, to indicate the readiness of particular vintages for consumption.

Cultivars

The big, fleshy grapes one eats at the table do not usually produce good wine and in most cases the small, juicy, wine-making grapes have far more flavour than the table varieties. The most commonly used cultivars for wine, and in South Africa the only ones permitted by law, are those of the species *Vitis vinifera*. The grape is the basic ingredient of wine. It is from the juice of ripe grapes that wine is made and a wine maker can only make good wine from good grapes. The following represent the better-known grape varieties used.

White Cultivars

Chenin Blanc (Steen)
Pride of place goes to this remarkably versatile white grape. It is the most widely planted of all our wine cultivars, making up more than 31,9% of the area under vine. Good quality Steen makes fine, fruity, dry wines as well as wines of any degree of sweetness right through to the fullest botrytis wines. It makes our best sherries and is used in most of our finer sparkling wines. It is also used for sweet fortified wines and in brandy production. Grown in all the producing areas, it is an early mid-season ripening grape. Vines produce medium-sized, compact bunches with small, oval, thinnish-skinned berries.

White French (Palomino)
Known locally as White French or Fransdruif, this is the same cultivar used in Spain for sherry production and is known there as Palomino. Locally, it is rapidly declining in popularity owing to its vulnerability to the disease anthracnose. White French vineyards produce 9,7% of the area under vine. Vines produce large, loose bunches with medium-sized, round berries with tough skins. It is an early mid-season ripener.

Clairette Blanche
A late-maturing grape giving a low acid wine which is much appreciated in the making of sparkling wines. The vines produce medium-sized, loose bunches of medium-sized, long, oval, tough-skinned grapes which ripen right at the end of the vintage. Clairette Blanche represents 3,8% of national plantings.

Cape Riesling (South African Riesling) CRUCHEN BLANC
This grape made Riesling synonymous with top quality, dry, white wines in South Africa. The cultivar, however, represents only 3,6% of the national crop and is grown mainly in the Coastal Region. Vines produce medium-sized, compact bunches with round or slightly oval, thin-skinned berries. GASCONY MED QUALITY

Weisser Riesling (Rhine Riesling)
This variety is a relative newcomer to South Africa and produces a more fragrant wine than our traditional Cape Riesling which, incidentally, is a totally unrelated variety. It is grown mainly in the Coastal Region with scattered plantings in the Breede River Valley Region. Short, cylindrical, compact bunches are produced with medium-sized berries having medium-thick skins. It represents less than 1% of the national plantings.

Colombar (often spelled Colombard)
Originally grown for brandy production, this cultivar has in recent

years been used to produce very attractive, fruity wines especially in the Breede River Valley Region. It is also grown in the Coastal Region and in total now represents 6,2% of the national plantings. It ripens late mid-season and has medium-sized, conical bunches with short, oval berries.

Sémillon (Green Grape)

One of the grapes which was very popular in the early days of South African wine making and is the variety used in France for dry Graves and sweet Sauternes wines. Locally its use is dwindling and it now represents only 1,5% of national plantings. It ripens early mid-season. Medium-sized, compact bunches comprise soft-skinned, short, oval berries.

Gewürztraminer

This important variety of Alsace in Europe does not always develop the true 'gewürz' (spicey) flavour in our growing conditions. Grown mostly in the Coastal Region, including Tulbagh, it does in some localities, however, produce wines of good spice, as proven in recent international competitions. It makes up only a fraction (0,3%) of the total national plantings. The fairly short and mostly compact bunches have slightly pinkish berries, round to short oval and with tough skins. Gewürztraminer is an early season ripener.

Bukettraube

Introduced to South Africa only in the 1970s, this vigorous grower now comprises some 0,4% of all plantings, giving wines with slight Muscat aroma. Medium to large, fairly compact bunches are produced with medium-large, firm, thin- but tough-skinned berries. The variety is an early season ripener.

Kerner

Though introduced at the same time as Bukettraube, plantings of this variety represent only 0,1% of the national crop. It gives a distinctive if somewhat stern wine. It is an early ripener, bearing medium-large, compact bunches of medium-large, round, thick-skinned berries.

Sauvignon Blanc

A remarkable variety which, when used with Sémillon and Muscadel in Bordeaux in France, produces some of the most exceptional wines, including the driest Graves and sweetest Sauternes. It is also famous on the upper Loire for the striking wines of Sancerre. Although once popular in South Africa, it fell from favour but has now made a reappearance and recent efforts have shown some most encouraging wines. The variety has been planted in large quantities in recent years and now makes up almost 3,6% of the national plantings and produces medium-large, compact bunches with medium-large, round, thick-skinned grapes.

Chardonnay

The grape of the famous white wines of Burgundy, Chablis and Champagne in France, and now responsible for some of the finest wines in California. At this stage it is grown only in minimal quantities locally (1,04% of the total national crop), mainly in the Coastal Region and on a few farms in the Breede River Valley Region. The small, compact bunches have small, round, tough-skinned berries.

Chenel

This cross of Chenin Blanc and Trebbiano produced by Professor Chris Orffer of the University of Stellenbosch already represents over 0,7% of the national crop. The medium-sized, cylindrical bunches have short, oval, medium-sized, thin- but tough-skinned grapes. It is grown mostly in the high production inland areas, with much lesser amounts in the Coastal Region.

Muscat d'Alexandrie (Hanepoot)

One of the world's oldest cultivated grape varieties and definitely South Africa's favourite grape flavour. It is planted in a higher percentage in local vineyards than anywhere else in the world and currently produces 5,7% of the national plantings. Grown in all areas, its large, loose bunches have large, obovoid, thin- but tough-skinned berries. The grapes ripen in late mid-season and the wines have unmistakable Muscat character.

Raisin Blanc/Servan Blanc

These two names refer to the same grape which has been grown in the Cape over a long period. It is grown mainly in the Klein Karoo Region and later in the Worcester and Robertson districts. It is not a good quality wine grape and is better suited to brandy distillation. It represents 1,7% of the total crop.

Fernão Pires

This Portuguese cultivar was introduced to South Africa in the 1970s. It appears to be suited to the Cape (where 0,2% of the national crop is grown) and some good wines are now being made from it. It is an early ripener.

Red Cultivars

Cabernet Sauvignon

'King' Cabernet produces a great deal of the best Bordeaux wines and has been transplanted to the vineyards of the New World probably more successfully than any other noble variety. In Bordeaux its greatest successes are in blends in varying proportions with Cabernet Franc, Malbec, Merlot and Verdot. Cabernet Sauvignon makes very distinctive wines of remarkable range in style and individuality. It contributes 2,6% to national plantings and produces small, fairly loose, conical bunches of small, round, thick-skinned, dark berries.

Cinsaut

Formerly known as Hermitage, and although reducing in popularity, it is still by far the most widely planted red grape in South Africa, making up 7% of national plantings. Today it is not one of the fashionable varieties, nevertheless most of South Africa's red wine is made from it, albeit wine sold in the lower price range. It is grown in all areas but mainly in the Coastal Region. Cinsaut vines produce large conical bunches with large, oval berries which ripen early mid-season.

Pinotage

South Africa's first commercially successful crossing, this variety was produced by Professor A.I. Perold in 1925 from Pinot Noir and Hermitage, as Cinsaut was then known. It makes wines with a very distinct 'Pinotage ester' nose when young, but which age into good, soft reds. Pinotage vineyards, mainly in the Coastal Region, produce about 2% of the national crop. The variety is experiencing a revival and new plantings are expected. It has medium-sized, compact bunches with small, oval, tough, thick-skinned, dark berries.

Pinot Noir
This is the great red cultivar of Burgundy and Champagne, but it has not transplanted well in the New World and locally it is grown only in small amounts in the Coastal Region where it makes up about 0,3% of national plantings. The small, fairly compact bunches have small, round, fairly thick and tough-skinned, dark violet-blue berries which ripen early mid-season.

Shiraz
One of the major grapes of the Rhône Valley in Europe, this variety is believed to have originated in Persia. It makes well-flavoured wines with a peculiar nose described as 'smokey'. It makes up 0,9% of national plantings almost all of which are in the Coastal Region but with some notable exceptions in the Breede River Valley Region. Shiraz vines bear medium-sized, fairly loose bunches with small, oval berries which ripen in mid-season.

Merlot
There is not much Merlot yet in the Cape but encouraging quantities are being planted. Its ability to age more quickly makes it a great asset in softening the harder wines made from Cabernet Sauvignon hence its importance in Bordeaux-style blends. It produces soft, full, attractive wines. It makes up 0,5% of the national crop.

Cabernet Franc
Belonging to the same family as Cabernet Sauvignon, its wine is occasionally not easily identified from its relation; they are generally softer, however, and so make ideal blending partners. Cabernet Franc makes up only a small fraction of the national crop.

Gamay Noir
Second in importance only to Pinot Noir in Burgundy, this is the great grape of Beaujolais. Producing excellent, full-flavoured wine ready for early drinking in the Nouveau style, it can also produce very acceptable wines for ageing. Gamay Noir makes up only a small fraction of the national crop.

The South African Wine of Origin System

Legislation came into force on 1 September 1973, providing for one of the most advanced and comprehensive wine control systems in the world. It draws from the best features of wine legislation in France and Germany and is geared for our specific requirements. It is also recognized by the authorities of the European Economic Community (EEC). It encompasses the following elements which form the 'Wine of Origin Seal' appearing on the capsule of many bottles of wine.

Estate To qualify for the description 'Estate' a wine must be made from grapes grown and produced on a proclaimed Estate. It need not, however, be bottled on the Estate.

Origin (Blue band)

The legislation has divided the wine-producing areas into clearly defined Regions which are further divided into Districts which in some cases are made up of smaller Wards. The last-mentioned are still being determined and each year more are added to the list.

Cultivar (Green band)

If the type of grape used to make the wine is stated on the label the wine must contain a minimum 75% of that cultivar.

Vintage (Red band)

This refers to the year in which the grapes are harvested and at least 75% must be derived from the vintage stated.

During the course of 1990 Superior certification fell away. This certificate was given to wines of exceptional quality. The Wine of Origin law will, however, continue to guarantee vintage, cultivar, origin and Estate, but not superior quality.

The South African winelands in terms of Regions, Districts and Wards:

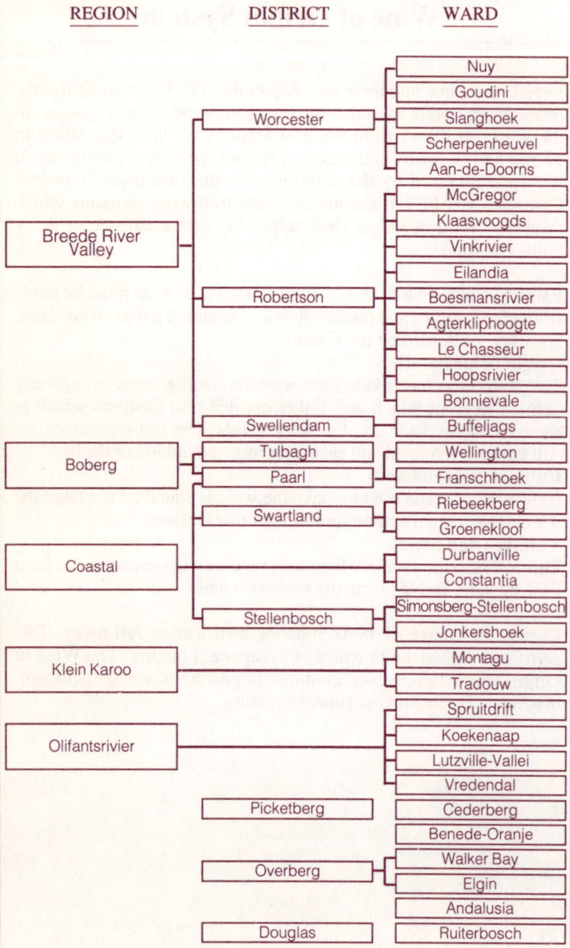

1. The Ward of Bonnievale now lies entirely in the Robertson District.
2. The Ward of Klaasvoogds has been determined in the Robertson District.
3. The Boberg Region is only recognized for fortified wines.
4. Tulbagh, excluding Wolseley, is included in the Coastal Region. Wolseley is included in the Breede River Valley.
5. Buffeljags is a Ward in the Swellendam District.
6. Wellington is a Ward in the Paarl District.
7. Durbanville and Constantia are Wards in the Coastal Region.
8. Elgin and Ruiterbosch are new Wards on their own.
9. Tradouw is a new Ward in the Klein Karoo region

Wine Producers

Aan-de-Doorns Co-op PO Box 235, Worcester 6849. Tel: (0231) 72301. Wine maker: Alwyn Mostert. Open weekdays 07h30 – 12h00 and 13h00 – 17h30; Saturdays 09h00 – 12h00.
Agterkliphoogte Co-op PO Box 267, Robertson 6705. Tel: (02351) 61103. Wine maker: Helmard Hanekom. Open weekdays 08h00 – 12h00, 13h30 – 17h00.
Allesverloren Estate PO Box 23, Riebeek-West 6800. Tel: (02246) 320. Wine maker: Fanie Malan. Visitors by appointment only.
Alphen *see* **Kleine Zalze**
Alto Estate PO Box 184, Stellenbosch 7599. Tel: (02231) 93884. Wine maker: Hempies du Toit. Visitors by appointment only.
Altydgedacht Estate PO Box 213, Durbanville 7550. Tel: (021) 961295. Wine maker: Oliver Parker. Vineyards: John Parker. Open Wednesdays 14h00 – 18h00; Saturdays 09h00 – 12h00.
Ashton Co-op PO Box 40, Ashton 6715. Tel: (0234) 51135. Fax: (0234) 51284. Manager: Willem Joubert. Wine maker: Kas Huisamen. Open weekdays 08h00 – 12h30, 13h30 – 17h30; Saturdays 08h30 – 12h30.
Aufwaerts Co-op PO Box 51, Rawsonville 6845. Tel: (0231) 91196. Wine maker: Hennie de Villiers. Visitors by appointment only.
Avontuur Estate PO Box 1128, Somerset West 7130. Tel: (024) 553450. Fax: (024) 554600. Wine maker: Jean-Luc Sweerts. General Manager: Manie Kloppers. Open weekdays 08h30 – 17h00 and Saturdays 09h00 – 13h00.
Backsberg Estate PO Box 1, Klapmuts 7625. Tel: (02211) 5141. Fax: (02211) 5144. Sydney Back. Wine maker: Hardy Laubser. Vineyards: Michael Back. Open weekdays 08h00 – 17h30; Saturdays and public holidays 08h00 – 13h00.
Badsberg Co-op Grootvlakte, PO Box 72, Rawsonville 6845. Tel: (0231) 91120. Wine maker: Gerrit van Zyl. Open Mondays to Fridays 08h00 – 17h00.
Barrydale Co-op PO Box 59, Barrydale 6750. Tel: (02972) 12. Fax: (02972) 314. Wine maker: Bob de Villiers. Open Mondays to Thursdays 08h30 – 17h30; open Fridays 08h30 – 17h00; Saturdays 08h30 – 13h00.
Belcher Wine Farm PO Box 541, Suider Paarl 7624. Tel: (02211) 631458. Fax: (02211) 632076. Proprietor: Ronnie Belcher. Wine maker: Ernst Gous.
Bellingham PO Box 246, Wellington 7655. Tel: (02211) 31001. Wine maker: Charles Hopkins. December to April four tastings per day at 09h30, 10h30, 14h30, 15h30 and Saturdays at 10h30. Closed to public during the rest of the season.
Bergkelder Private Bag X5001, Stellenbosch 7599. Tel: (02231) 73480. Fax: (02231) 75769. Cellar master: Dr Julius Laszlo. Regular cellar tours offered at 10h00 and 15h00, or by special arrangement.
Bergsig Estate PO Box 15, Breërivier 6858. Tel: (02324) 603. Fax: (02324) 658. Proprietor: B W (Prop) Lategan. Wine maker: De Wet Lategan. Open weekdays 08h45 – 16h45; Saturdays 09h00 – 12h00. Cellar tours by appointment.
Bertrams Wines/Gilbey Distillers & Vintners PO Box 137, Stellenbosch 7599. Tel: (02231) 70300. Fax: (02231) 70539. Operations

Manager: Martin van der Merwe. Wine maker: Leo Burger. Not open to the public.
Beyerskloof PO Box 107, Koelenhof 7605. Tel: (02231) 92376. Wine maker: Beyers Truter. Visits by appointment only.
Blaauwklippen PO Box 54, Stellenbosch 7599. Tel: (02231) 900133/4. Fax: (02231) 901250. Wine maker: Jacques Kruger. Open weekdays 09h00 – 17h00; Saturdays 09h00 – 13h00.
Bloemendal Estate PO Box 466, Durbanville 7550. Tel: (021) 962682. Wine maker: Jackie Coetzee. Open Wednesdays 13h00 – 18h00; Saturdays 09h00 – 12h00.
Bodega Farm Joostenbergvlakte 7570. Tel: (021) 9882929. Owners/Wine makers: Eddie and Julianne Barlow.
Bolandse Co-op Daljosaphat cellar: PO Box 2, Huguenot 7645. Tel: (02211) 626190/626191. Fax: (02211) 625379. Wine maker: Anthony de Jager. General Manager: Altus le Roux. Noorder Paarl cellar: PO Box 7007, Noorder Paarl, 7623. Tel: (02211) 21747/21748/21766. Fax: (02211) 23866. Wine maker: Jacques du Toit. General Manager: Altus le Roux. Open weekdays 08h00 – 13h00, 13h30 – 17h00; Saturdays 08h30 – 12h00.
Bon Courage Estate PO Box 589, Robertson 6705. Tel: (02351) 4178/4170. Fax: (02351) 3581. Wine maker: André Bruwer. Open weekdays 09h00 – 17h00; Saturdays 09h00 – 12h30. Cellar tours by appointment only.
Bonfoi Estate PO Box 9, Vlottenburg 7580. Tel: (02231) 2715. Wine maker: Johannes van der Westhuizen. Not open to the public.
Bonnievale Co-op PO Box 206, Bonnievale 6730. Tel: (02346) 2795. Fax: (02346) 2074. Wine maker: Piet Linde. Open weekdays 08h30 – 12h30, 13h30 – 17h00.
Boplaas Estate PO Box 156, Calitzdorp 6660. Tel: (04437) 33326/33397. Fax: (04437) 33750. Proprietor and wine maker: Carel Nel. Open weekdays 08h00 – 13h00, 14h00 – 17h00; Saturdays 09h00 – 12h00. Cellar tours by appointment and lunches served during December and April school holidays. Ruiterbosch is the name for Boplaas Estate's Mosselbay vineyards.
Boschendal Estate PO Groot Drakenstein 7680. Tel: (02211) 41031. Fax: (02211) 41864. Cellar master: Hilko Hegewisch. Viticulturist: Gerrie Wagener. Taphuis open weekdays 08h30 – 16h30; Saturdays 08h30 – 12h30. Daily lunches 12h30. Picnics 1 November – 30 April 12h30. Also audiovisual presentations and vineyard tours, manor house and waenhuiswinkel.
Botha Co-op PO Botha 6857. Tel: (02324) 740. Wine maker: Andre Stofberg. Open weekdays 07h30 – 12h30, 13h30 – 17h30; Saturdays 10h00 – 12h00.
Bottelary Co-op PO Box 16, Koelenhof 7605. Tel: (02231) 92204. Fax: (02231) 92205. Wine maker: Frikkie Botes. Manager: H de Preez. Open weekdays 08h30 – 12h30, 13h30 – 17h00; Saturdays 08h30 – 13h00.
Bouchard Finlayson PO Box 303, Hermanus 7200. Tel: (0283) 23515. Fax: (0283) 22726. Wine maker: Peter Finlayson. Open to the public by appointment only.
Bovlei Co-op PO Box 82, Wellington 7655. Tel: (02211) 31567/641283. Fax: (02211) 31386. Wine maker: Martinus Broodryk. Open weekdays 08h30 – 12h30, 13h30 – 17h30; Saturdays 08h30 – 12h30. Cellar tours by appointment.

Brandvlei Co-op PO Box 595, Worcester 6850. Tel: (0231) 94215. General Manager: Theuns le Roux. Wine maker: Willie Burger. Open weekdays 07h30 – 12h30, 13h30 – 17h30.

Buitenverwachting PO Box 281, Constantia 7848. Tel: (021) 7945190/1. Fax: (021) 7941351. Proprietor: Christina Mueller. Wine maker: Jean Daneel. Open for sales weekdays 09h00-17h00; Saturdays 09h00-13h00. Cellar tours weekdays 11h00 and 15h00; Saturdays (booking essential) 11h00.

Calitzdorp Co-op PO Box 193, Calitzdorp 6660. Tel: (04437) 301/328. Wine maker: James O' Kennedy. Open weekdays 08h30 – 12h15, 13h15 – 17h00; Saturdays 08h00 – 12h00. Also make Buffelskroon wines.

Cederberg Kelders Dwarsrivier, PO Cederberg 8136. Tel: (02682) 1531/ 1521. Wine maker: Flippie Nieuwoudt. Sales from premises during office hours.

Chamonix PO Box 28, Franschhoek 7690. Tel: (02212) 2494/2498. Wine made at Franschhoek Vineyards Co-op. Visitors by appointment only. Wine sales and tasting: Franschhoek Vineyards, Le Quartier Français, Die Binnehof.

Citrusdal Co-op PO Box 41, Citrusdal 7340. Tel: (02662) 94/121. Fax: (02662) 94. Wine maker: Michael de Beer. Manager: HJ Cruywagen. Open weekdays 08h00 – 12h30, 14h00 – 17h00; Saturdays 09h00 – 12h30. Cellar tours by appointment. Wines also distributed under Goue Vallei label.

Clairvaux Co-op PO Box 179, Robertson 6705. Tel: (02351) 3842. Fax: (02351) 5052. Wine maker: Kobus van der Merwe. Open weekdays 08h30 – 12h30, 13h30 – 17h30; Saturdays 08h30 – 12h00.

Clos Cabrière Estate PO Box 245, Franschhoek 7690. Tel: (02212) 2630. Fax: (02212) 3390. Wine grower and Managing Director: Achim von Arnim. Visitors by appointment only.

Clos Malverne PO Box 187, Stellenbosch 7599. Tel: (02231) 3528/72772. Fax: (02231) 98373. Proprietor: Seymour Pritchard. Wine maker up to and including 1991 vintages: Jeremy Walker. Wine maker from May 1991: Guy Webber. Open weekdays 08h30 – 17h00, Saturdays 09h00 – 13h00 and certain public holidays. 'Valley lunch' offered during December and January and cellar tours by appointment.

De Doorns Co-op PO Box 129, De Doorns 6875. Tel: (02322) 2100. Fax: (02322) 2100. Wine maker: Pieter Hamman. Open weekdays 08h30 – 12h30, 13h30 – 17h00; Saturdays 08h30 – 12h00.

De Helderberg Co-op PO Box 71, Firgrove 7110. Tel: (024) 422370. Fax: (024) 422373. Wine maker: Inus Muller. Open to the public for sales and lunches weekdays 09h00 – 17h30; Saturdays 09h00 – 13h00.

Delaire Wines PO Box 3058, Stellenbosch 7602. Tel: (02231) 91756/91213. Fax: (02231) 91270. Proprietors: Storm and Ruth Quinan. Wine maker: Christopher Keet. Open to the public weekdays, Saturdays and most public holidays 10h00 – 17h00. Tours by appointment.

Delheim Wines PO Box 10, Koelenhof 7605. Tel: (02231) 92033. Fax: (02231) 92036. Vintner: Spatz Sperling. Wine maker: Philip Costandius. Wine tasting and sales: weekdays 08h30 – 17h00; Saturdays 08h30 – 12h00. Tours weekdays 10h00 and 15h00, 1 October – 30 April only. Tour of production cellar Saturdays all year round at 10h30. Vintner's platter served from October to April and soup lunch from May to September 11h00 – 14h00.

De Leuwen Jagt PO Box 505, Suider Paarl 7624. Tel:(02211) 633495/6. Fax: (02211) 633797. Consultant wine maker: Gideon Theron. Open weekdays 08h00 – 17h00; Saturdays 09h00 – 13h00. Also light lunches served.

De Wet Co-op PO Box 16, De Wet 6853. Tel: (0231) 92710/92760. Fax: (0231) 92723. Wine makers: Kobus de Wet and Zakkie Bester. Manager: Zakkie Bester. Open weekdays 08h00 – 17h00; Saturdays 09h00 – 12h00.

De Wetshof Estate PO Box 31, Robertson 6705. Tel: (0234) 51853/7. Fax: (0234) 51915. Proprietor and wine maker: Danie de Wet. Open weekdays 09h00 – 12h30, 14h00 – 17h00; Saturdays 09h30 – 13h00. Cellar tours by appointment.

De Zoete Inval Estate PO Box 591, Suider Paarl 7624. Tel: (02211) 632375. Fax: (02211) 632817. Wine makers: Adrian and Gerard Frater. Open Monday to Saturday 09h00 – 17h00.

Die Krans Estate PO Box 28, Calitzdorp 6660. Tel: (04437) 33314. Fax: (04437) 33562. Wine makers: Boet and Stroebel Nel. Open weekdays 08h00 – 17h00; Saturdays 09h00 – 12h30. Wine tasting, cellar and vineyard tours. Lunches served December and April holidays; book for rest of year.

Diemersdal Estate PO Box 27, Durbanville 7550. Tel: (021) 963361. Fax: (021) 961810. Proprietor and wine maker: Tienie Louw. Open Wednesdays 13h30 – 18h00; Saturdays 09h00 – 17h00. Cellar tours and group functions by appointment.

Die Poort PO Box 45, Albertinia 6795. Tel: (02952) 2030. Wine maker and Proprietor: Jannie Jonker. Open to members of the public weekdays 08h00 – 18h00; Saturdays 08h00 – 13h00. Restaurant booking essential.

Dieu Donné Vineyards PO Box 94, Franschhoek 7690. Tel: (02212) 2493. Fax: (02212) 2102. Wine maker: François Malherbe. Proprietor: Robert Maingard. Open Monday to Friday 09h00 – 12h30 (December and January: Monday to Friday 09h00 – 12h30; Saturday 09h00 – 12h30.)

Domein Doornkraal PO Box 104, De Rust 6650. Tel: (04439) 6715/ 2551. Fax: (04429) 2548. Wine maker and Proprietor: Swepie le Roux. Open weekdays 09h00 – 17h00; Saturdays 08h00 – 13h00. During school holidays open weekdays 08h00 – 18h00.

Douglas Co-op PO Box 47, Douglas 8730. Tel: (053) 2981910. Fax: (053) 2982445. Wine maker and Manager: W H (Pou) le Roux. Open weekdays 08h00 – 17h00.

Douglas Green Bellingham PO Box 246, Wellington 7655. Tel: (02211) 31001. Not open to members of the public. PO Box 4617, Randburg 2125. Tel: (011) 8868290. Fax: (011) 7894503. Production: Johan Bruce. Marketing: Henry Kempen. Not open to members of the public.

Drakenstein Co-op Now known as Simondium Winery Co-op.
Drostdy Co-op PO Box 85, Tulbagh 6820. Tel: (02362) 101/ 525. Wine maker: Frans du Toit. Open weekdays 08h00 – 12h00, 13h30 – 17h00; Saturdays 08h30 – 12h00.

Du Toitskloof Co-op PO Box 55, Rawsonville 6845. Tel: (0231) 91601/91936. Fax: (0231) 91581. Wine maker: Philip Jordaan. Open weekdays 08h30 – 12h30, 13h30 – 17h30; Saturdays 08h30 – 12h00.

Eersterivier Valleise Co-op PO Box 2, Vlottenburg 7604. Tel: (02231) 93870/1. Fax: (02231) 93102. Wine maker: Manie Roussouw. Open Monday to Friday 08h30 – 17h00; open Saturdays 09h00 – 13h00.

Eikendal Vineyards PO Box 2261, Stellenbosch 7599. Tel: (024) 551422. Fax: (024) 551027. Wine maker: Josef Krammer. Open weekdays 09h30 – 17h00; Saturdays 09h00 – 12h30.

Fairview Estate PO Box 583, Suider Paarl 7624. Tel: (02211) 632450. Fax: (02211) 632591. Wine makers: Charles and Cyril Back. Open weekdays 08h30 – 18h00 (in winter, 17h30); Saturdays 08h30 – 17h00 (in winter, 13h00).

Franschhoek Vineyards Co-op PO Box 52, Franschhoek 7690. Tel: (02212) 2086. Fax: (02212) 3440. Wine makers: Deon Truter and Driaan van der Merwe. Manager: Deon Truter. Open to members of the public, weekdays and non-religious public holidays 08h30 – 13h00, 14h00 – 17h30 (May to August open 09h00 – 16h30); Saturdays 09h00 – 13h00.

Gilbeys Distillers & Vintners PO Box 137, Stellenbosch 7600. Tel: (02231) 906111. Fax: (02231) 906000. Operations Manager: Martin van der Merwe. Visitors by appointment only.

Glen Carlou PO Box 23, Klapmuts 7625. Tel: (02211) 5528. Fax: (02211) 5314. Wine maker: Walter Finlayson. Open weekdays 09h00 – 12h00, 14h00 – 16h30; Saturday 09h00 – 12h30.

Goede Hoop Estate PO Kuils River 7580. Tel: (021) 9031086. Wine maker: P J Bestbier. Not open to the public.

Goedvertrouw Bot River, Tel: (02842) 49769. Proprietor and wine maker: A H Pillmann. Not open to the public.

Goudini Co-op PO Box 132, Rawsonville 6845. Tel: (0231) 91090/91313. Fax: (0231) 6845. Wine maker and Manager: Hennie Hugo. Open weekdays 08h30 – 12h00, 13h30 – 17h00. Cellar tours by appointment.

Goudveld Wynkelder PO Box 1091, Welkom 9460. Tel: (0171) 28650. Wine maker: Merkil Alers. Open Mondays to Saturdays 08h30 – 18h00.

Grangehurst PO Box 206, Stellenbosch 7599. Tel: (024) 553625. Owner/Wine maker: Jeremy Walker.

Groot Constantia Estate Private Bag Constantia 7848. Tel: (021) 7945179/7945128. Fax: (021) 794 1999. Wine maker: Pieter du Toit. Manager: Danie Appel. Open to visitors Mondays to Sundays 10h00 – 17h00.

Groot Eiland Co-op PO Box 93, Rawsonville 6845. Tel: (0231) 91140. Fax: (0231) 91801. Manager and wine maker: Willem Loots. Open weekdays 08h00 – 12h30, 13h30 – 17h30, also for cellar tours.

Hamilton Russell Vineyards Hemel-en-Aarde Valley, PO Box 158, Hermanus 7200. Tel: (0283) 23441/23595. Fax: (0283) 21797. Chairman: Timothy Hamilton-Russell. Managing Director: Anthony Hamilton Russell. Wine maker: Storm Kreusch-Dau. Not open to members of the public.

Hartenberg Estate PO Box 69, Koelenhof 7605. Tel: (02231) 92541. Fax: (02231) 92153. Proprietor: Kenneth Mackenzie. Resident Director: JS Krige. Wine maker: Danie Truter. Open weekdays 08h30 – 17h00; Saturdays and most non-religious holidays 09h00 – 15h00. Cellar tours weekdays 10h00 and 15h00,; Saturdays 10h00. Lunches served Mondays to Saturdays 12h00 – 14h00.

Haute Provence PO Box 211, Franschhoek 7690. Tel: (02212) 3195. Fax: (02212) 3118. Proprietor: Peter Younghusband. Open Wednesdays and Fridays 14h00 – 16h00; Saturdays 09h30 – 12h00. Open daily from 1 December to 15 April.

Hazendal Estate Kuils River 7580. Tel: (021) 9035035. Wine maker: Michael Bosman. Not open to the public.

H C Collison made by The Bergkelder.

Huguenot Wines PO Box 275, Wellington 7655. Tel: (02211) 641277. Fax: (02211) 32075. Wine maker: P Matthee. Not open to the public.

Jacobsdal Estate Kuils River 7580. Tel: (021) 905360. Wine maker: Cornelius Dumus. Not open to the public.

John Platter Wines Clos du Ciel, PO Box 1750, Somerset West 7130. Tel: (0322) 58121. Wine maker: John Platter. Not open to members of the public.

Jonkheer Farmers' Winery PO Box 13, Bonnievale 6730. Tel: (02346) 2137. Fax: (02346) 3146. Wine makers: Nicholaas Jonker and Erhard Roothman. Not open to the public. Also make Bakenskop Wines.

Kaapzicht Estate PO Box 5, Sanlamhof 7532. Tel: (021) 9033870. Fax: (021) 9036272. Wine maker: Danie Steytler. Wine tastings and cellar tours by appointment only. Wine sales: weekdays 09h00 – 12h30, 13h30 – 18h00; Saturday 08h00 – 12h00

Kango Co-op PO Box 46, Oudtshoorn 6620. Tel: (0443) 226065. Wine maker: C Langenhoven. Manager: Pieter Conradie. Open weekdays 08h30 – 13h00, 14h00 – 16h45. Close 16h00 on Fridays. Also make Rijkshof wines.

Kanonkop Estate PO Box 19, Muldersvlei 7606. Tel: (02231) 94656. Fax: (02231) 94719. Proprietors: Paul, Johann and Jannie Krige. Wine maker: Beyers Truter. Open weekdays 08h30 – 17h00; Saturdays 09h00 – 12h30. Cellar tours and lunches for visitors by appointment only.

Klawer Co-op PO Box 8, Klawer 8145. Tel: Klawer (02724) 61530. Wine maker and Manager: Manfred van Heerden. Open weekdays 08h00 – 17h00; Saturday 08h45 – 12h00.

Klein Constantia Estate PO Box 375, Constantia 7848. Tel: (021) 7945188. Fax: (021) 7942464. Proprietors: Duggie and Lowell Jooste. Wine maker: Ross Gower. Open weekdays 09h00 – 17h00; Saturdays 09h00 – 13h00.

Kleine Zalze Estate c/o Gilbeys, PO Box 137, Stellenbosch 7600. Tel: (02231) 75036. Wine maker: Marius Lategan. Tours by appointment only.

Kloofzicht PO Box 101, Tulbagh 6820. Tel: (0236) 300658. Wine maker: Roger Fehlmann. Open weekdays 10h00 – 16h00 and weekends and public holidays by appointment. Estate tours and guest farm facilities available.

Koelenhof Co-op PO Box 1, Koelenhof 7605. Tel: (02231) 92020/1. Fax: (02231) 92796. Wine maker: Pieter Carstens. Manager: Helmie de Vries. Open weekdays 08h30 – 13h00, 14h00 – 17h00; Saturdays 08h30 – 12h30.

Koopmanskloof Estate PO Box 92, Koelenhof, 7605. Tel: (02231) 92225. Fax: (02231) 92355. Proprietor: Stevie Smit. Wine maker: Stefan Smit. Open Monday to Saturday 09h00 – 17h00.

KWV PO Box 528, Suider Paarl 7624. Tel: (02211) 631001. Chief of production: Charl Theron. Wine maker: W F Hacker and Johan Schreuder. Presentations Monday, Wednesday, Friday 09h30 and 14h15 Afrikaans. Monday 11h00 and 15h45 English. Tuesday and Thursday 09h30 and 14h15 English. Tuesday and Thursday 11h00 and 15h45 Afrikaans.

La Belle Provence PO Box 60, Franschhoek 7690. Tel: (02212) 2135. Proprietor: Chris Enslin. Not open to the public.

Laborie Estate (owned by KWV) PO Box 528, Suider-Paarl 7624. Tel: (02211) 632034. Fax: (02211) 633440. Wine maker: Jorrie Jordaan. Open weekdays 09h00 – 17h00; Saturdays 09h00 – 13h00.

La Bourgogne PO Box 78, Franschhoek 7690. Tel: (02212) 2115. Fax: (02212) 2689. Proprietors: Michael and Sonny Gillis. Open by appointment only.

La Bri PO Box 180, Franschhoek 7690. Tel: (02212) 2593. Fax: (02212) 3197. Proprietors: Michael and Cheryl Trull. Manager: Bill Alley. Open Monday to Friday 11h00 – 12h30; 14h00 – 16h00; Saturday by appointment only.

La Couronne PO Box 84, Franschhoek 7690. Tel: (02212) 3000/3508. Fax: (02212) 2362. Proprietor: Mike Stander and Dr Glennie van Hoogstraten. Wines made at Franschhoek Vineyards Co-op. Tasting and sales at the Co-op and at the Franschhoek Wine Tasting Centre. Wine tastings at La Couronne: Monday to Friday 10h00 – 17h00; Saturday 10h00 – 13h00; Sunday by appointment.

Ladismith Co-op PO Box 56, Ladismith 6885. Tel: (02942) 31. Wine maker: A S Simonis. Open weekdays 08h00 – 13h00, 14h00 – 17h00. Cellar tours by appointment. Also make Towerkop and Swartberg wines.

La Motte Estate PO Box 45, La Motte 7691. Tel: (02212) 3119. Fax: (02212) 3446. Proprietors: Paul and Hannelie Neethling. Wine maker: Jacques Borman. Open for wine tasting and sales: weekdays 09h00 – 16h30; Saturdays 09h00 – 12h00. Closed on public holidays.

Landskroon Estate PO Box 519, Suider Paarl 7624. Tel: (02211) 631039/631059. Fax: (02211) 632810. Wine maker: Paul de Villiers Jnr. Open weekdays 08h30 – 17h30; Saturdays 08h30 – 12h30.

Landzicht Co-op PO Box 94, Jacobsdal 8710. Tel: (053212) 132/99. Fax: (053212) 113. Wine maker: Ian Sieg. Open weekdays 08h30 – 13h00, 14h00 – 17h00; Saturdays 08h30 – 12h00.

Langverwacht Co-op PO Box 87, Bonnievale 6730. Tel: (02346) 2815. Wine maker: Johan Gerber. Open weekdays 08h00 – 12h30, 13h30 – 17h00.

La Provence PO Box 188, Franschhoek 7690. Tel: (02212) 2163. Fax: (02212) 2616. Wine maker: François Malherbe. Manager: DJ Rudd. Wine tastings and sales Monday to Sunday 09h00 – 17h00.

Lebensraum Estate PO Box 36, Rawsonville 6845. Tel: (0231) 91137. Wine maker: Kobus Deetlefs. Open Mondays to Fridays 14h00 – 18h00.

Le Bonheur Estate PO Box 56, Klapmuts 7625. Tel: (02211) 5432. Wine maker: Michael Woodhead. Not open to the public.

Le Grand Chasseur Estate PO Box 439, Robertson 6705. Tel: (02351) 2144. Wine makers: Wouter and Albertus de Wet. Not open to the public.

Lemberg Estate PO Box 108, Tulbagh 6820. Tel: (0236) 300659. Fax: (0236) 301540. Proprietor and wine maker: Janey Muller. Visitors by appointment only.

Lievland PO Box 66, Klapmuts 7625. Tel: (02211) 5226. Fax: (02211) 5213. Proprietor: Paul Benadé. Wine maker: Abraham Beukes. Open weekdays 09h00 – 17h00; Saturdays 09h00 -13h00.
Loopspruit Winery PO Box 1531, Bronkhorstspruit 1020. Tel: (01212) 24303. Wine maker: B Myburgh. Open Mondays to Fridays 08h00 – 17h00; Saturdays 09h00 – 13h00. Also make Noorderkeur wines.
L'Ormarins Estate Private Bag Suider Paarl 7624. Tel: (02211) 41024. Wine makers: Anthonij Rupert and Nico Vermeulen. Open weekdays 08h30 – 17h00; Saturdays 08h30 – 12h30 for visitors, but not for sales.
Louisvale PO Box 542 Stellenbosch 7599. Tel: (02231) 92422. Fax: (02231) 92633. Proprietors: Hans Froehling and Leon Stemmet. Wine maker: Neil Ellis. Visitors by appointment only.
Louwshoek-Voorsorg Co-op PO Box 174, Rawsonville, 6845. Tel/Fax: (0231) 91110. Wine maker and manager: Jaco Potgieter. Open weekdays 08h00 – 12h30, 13h30 – 17h00.
Lutzville Co-op PO Box 50, Lutzville 8165. Tel: (02725) 71516. Fax: (02725) 71435. Wine maker: Johan Theron, assisted by J A Rush. Open weekdays 08h00 – 12h30, 14h00 – 17h00; Saturdays 08h30 – 12h00. Cellar tours and lunches by prior arrangement.
Madeba (Graham Beck Winery) PO Box 88, Robertson 6705. Tel: 02351) 4556. Fax: (02351) 2650. Cellar master: Pieter Ferreira. OPen from 10h00.
Mamreweg Wine Cellar Co-op PO Box 114, Darling 7345. Tel: (02241) 2276/7. Fax: (02241) 2647. Wine makers: François Weich and P Rossouw. Manager: François Weich. Open Monday to Thursday 08h00 – 17h00; closes at 16h00 on Friday. Saturday 09h00 – 12h00. Available from Groenkloof Drankhandelaars.
McGregor Co-op Private Bag X619, Robertson 6705. Tel: (02353) 741. Fax: (02353) 829. Wine maker: Carel van der Merwe. Open weekdays 08h00 – 12h00, 13h00 – 17h00.
Meerendal Estate PO Box 2, Durbanville 7550. Tel: (021) 961915. Wine maker: J Starke. Not open to the public.
Meerlust Estate PO Box 15, Faure 7131. Tel: (024) 43587. Fax: (024) 43513. Wine maker: Giorgio Dalla Cia. Owner: Hannes Myburgh. Visitors by appointment only.
Meinert PO Box 7221, Stellenbosch 7600. Tel: (02231) 92120. Wine maker: Martin Meinert. Visits by appointment only.
Merwespont Co-op PO Box 68, Bonnievale 6730. Tel: (02346) 2800. Wine maker: Dirk Cornelissen. Open weekdays 08h00 – 12h30, 13h30 – 17h00.
Merwida Co-op PO Box 4, Rawsonville 6845. Tel: (0231) 91301. Fax: (0231) 91953. Wine maker: Jacobus Wolhuter. Open weekdays 07h30 – 12h00; 13h30 – 17h30.
Middelvlei Estate PO Box 66, Stellenbosch 7599. Tel: (02231) 3308. Wine maker: Jan Momberg. Not open to the public.
Mon Don Estate PO Box 360, Robertson 6705. Tel: (02351) 4183/2720. Fax: (02351) 61151. Wine maker: Pierre Marais. Open weekdays 09h00 – 12h00, 14h00 – 16h00, by appointment only.
Monis of Paarl PO Box 266, Paarl 7620. Tel: (02211) 21811.
Mons Ruber Estate Private Bag X629, Oudtshoorn 6620. Tel: (04439) 6550. Wine maker: C J Meyer. Open weekdays 08h30 – 17h00; Saturdays 08h30 – 13h00.

Montagu Co-op PO Box 29, Montagu 6720. Tel: (0234) 41125. Wine maker: Sonnie Malan. Open for visitors, weekdays 08h30 – 12h30, 13h30 – 17h00.
Mont Blois Estate PO Box 181, Robertson 6705. Tel: (02351) 3872. Proprietor: Estelle Bruwer. Wine maker: Raymond Kirby. Visitors by appointment only.
Montpellier Estate PO Box 24, Tulbagh 6820. Tel: (02362) 300723. Proprietors: Jan and Hendrik Theron. Wine maker: Jan Theron. Open weekdays 09h00 – 12h30, 13h30 – 16h30; Saturdays 09h00 – 12h00.
Mooiuitsig Wynkelders PO Box 15, Bonnievale 6730. Tel: (02346) 2143. Fax: (02364) 2675. Wine makers: Chris Versveld, Francois Claassen and Wrench Roux. Executive Director: N L (Boet) Jonker. Open weekdays 08h00 – 17h30. Cellar tours by appointment. Also make Bonwin, Monte Vista, Overberg, Overberger, Ouderust and Rusthof wines.
Môreson PO Box 114, Franschhoek 7690. Tel: (02212) 3055. Fax: (02212) 2348. Proprietors: Charles and Pauline Friedman. Wines made by and sold at Franschhoek Vineyards Co-op. Not open to members of the public.
Morgenhof PO Box 365, Stellenbosch 7600. Tel: (02231) 95510. Fax: (02231) 95266. Wine maker and General Manager: Denzel van Vuuren. Wine consultant: 'Oom' Pietie Theron. Open weekdays 08h30 – 17h00; Saturdays 09h00 – 16h00. Lunches served daily 12h00 – 14h00. Cellar tours by appointment.
Moutonne-Excelsior PO Box 290, Franschhoek 7690. Tel: (02212) 3019/2071. Fax: (02212) 2297. Wine consultants: Jan (Boland) Coetzee and Prof. Niel Matthee. Farm Manager: Dirk le Roux. Wines can be tasted at Die Binnehof, Monday to Sunday 11h00 – 20h00.
Muratie Wine Farm PO Box 133, Koelenhof 7605. Tel: (02231) 92330/6. Fax: (02231) 92790. Proprietor: Ronnie Melck. Wine maker: Christo Herrer. Manager: Hennie van der Westhuizen. Open weekdays 09h30 – 17h00; closes 16h00 on Friday. Saturday 09h00 – 13h00.
Mulderbosch PO Box 548, Stellenbosch, 7599. Tel: (02231) 92488. Fax: (02231) 92351. Proprietor: Larry Jacobs. Wine maker: Mike Dobrovic. Not open to the public.
Nederburg Wines PO Box 46, Huguenot 7645. Tel: (02211) 623104. Fax: (02211) 624887. Wine maker: Newald Marais. For daily tours, phone to book. Open weekdays 08h30 – 17h00; Saturdays (November to May only) 09h00 – 13h00.
Neethlingshof Estate PO Box 104, Stellenbosch 7599. Tel: (02231) 98988. Fax: (02231) 78171. Wine maker: Hein Hesebeck. Vintner: Günter Brözel. Open weekdays 09h00 – 17h00; Saturdays 10h00 – 16h00. Cellar tours by appointment. Reservations essential for group tastings and tours.
Neil Ellis Wines PO Box 917, Stellenbosch 7599. Tel: (02231) 92960. Fax: (02231) 92644.. Wine maker: Neil Ellis. Visitors by appointment only.
Nordale Co-op PO Box 105, Bonnievale 6730. Tel: (02346) 2050. Fax: (02231) 2192. Wine maker: Emile Schoch. Open weekdays 08h00 – 12h30, 13h30 – 17h00.
Nuy Wynkelder PO Box 5225, Worcester 6850. Tel: (0231) 70272. (0231) 74994. Wine maker and Manager: Wilhelm Linde. Open weekdays 08h30 – 16h30; Saturday 08h30 – 12h30. Cellar tours by appointment only.

Onverwacht Estate PO Box 438, Wellington 7655. Tel: (02211) 34315. Fax: (02211) 32237. Proprietor: Trevor Harris. Wine maker: Mark Ravenscraft. Manager: Fanie Louw. Open for sales, tastings and cellar tours weekdays 10h00 – 16h00.

Opstal Estate PO Box 27, Rawsonville 6845. Tel: (0231) 91066. Wine maker: Stanley Louw. Open weekdays 09h00 – 11h00, 15h00 – 17h00. Saturdays by appointment.

Oranjerivier Wynkelders PO Box 544, Upington 8800. Tel: (0541) 25651. General Manager: Noel Mouton. Open weekdays 08h00 – 12h45, 14h00 – 17h00; Saturdays 08h30 – 13h00.

Oude Nektar Estate PO Box 389, Stellenbosch 7599. Tel: (02231) 70690/7049. Fax: (02231) 70647. Proprietor: Hans-Peter Schröder. Wine maker: Pieter Smit. Open weekdays 09h30 – 17h00; Saturdays 11h00 – 16h00; non-religious public holidays 09h30 – 17h00. (Closed to the public from May to August.) Picnic lunches by appointment during December and January.

Overgaauw Estate PO Box 3, Vlottenburg 7604. Tel: (02231) 93815. Fax: (02231) 93436. Proprietor and wine maker: Braam and David van Velden. Open weekdays 09h00 – 12h30, 14h00 – 17h00; Saturdays 10h00 – 12h00. Cellar tours Wednesdays 14h30 or by appointment.

Overhex Co-op PO Box 139, Worcester 6849. Tel: (0231) 71057. Fax: (0231) 71057. Wine makers: Hennie Verster and Alkie van der Merwe. Manager: Hennie Verster. Open weekdays 08h30 – 17h00; Saturdays 09h00 – 12h00. Cellar tours by appointment.

Paddagang Vignerons Tulbagh. Tel: (0236) 300242. Fax: (0236) 300433.

Perdeberg Co-op PO Box 214, Paarl 7620. Tel: (02211) 638112. Fax: (02211) 638245. Wine maker: Joseph Huskisson. Open weekdays 08h00 – 12h30, 14h00 – 17h00.

Porterville Co-op PO Box 52, Porterville 6810. Tel: (02623) 2170. Fax: (02623) 2171. Wine maker: Klaas de Jongh. Open weekdays 08h30 – 13h00, 14h00 – 17h00; Saturdays 08h30 – 12h00.

Rhebokskloof PO Box 7141, Noorder Paarl 7620. Tel (02211) 638386. Fax: (02211) 638504. Wine maker: John Reagh. Open weekdays 08h00 – 17h00. Tours by appointment.

Riebeek Wine Farmers' Co-op PO Box 13, Riebeek-Kasteel 6801. Tel: (02244) 213/632. Fax: (02244) 281. Wine maker and Manager: Sias du Toit. Open weekdays 08h00 – 12h30, 13h30 – 17h30; Saturdays 08h30 – 12h00.

Rietrivier Co-op PO Box 144, Montagu 6720. Tel: (0234) 41705. Wine maker: Piet Frick. Open weekdays 08h00 – 13h00, 14h00 – 17h00.

Rietvallei Estate PO Box 386, Robertson 6705. Tel: (02351) 3596. Wine maker and proprietor: Johnny Burger. Open weekdays 09h00 – 17h00; Saturday 09h00 – 12h00.

Robertson Co-op PO Box 37, Robertson 6705. Tel: (02351) 3059. Wine maker: Bowen Botha. Open Mondays to Thursdays 08h00 – 12h30, 13h30 – 17h00. Friday 08h00 – 12h30, 13h30 – 16h30.

Romansrivier Co-op PO Box 108, Wolseley 6830. Tel: (0236) 311070/80. Fax: (0236) 311102. Manager and wine maker: Olla Olivier, assisted by Bartho Eksteen. Open weekdays 08h30 – 12h00, 13h30 – 17h00; Saturday 08h30 – 10h30.

Roodezandt Co-op PO Box 164, Robertson 6705. Tel: (02351) 2912/3020. Fax: (02351) 5074. Wine maker: Christie Steytler. Cellar

Master/Manager: Abe Rossouw. Open weekdays 08h00 – 13h00, 14h00 – 17h30; Saturdays 08h30 – 12h30. Cellar tours by appointment only.

Rooiberg Co-op PO Box 358, Robertson 6705. Tel: (02351) 2322/2312. Fax: (02351) 3295. Wine maker: Tommy Loftus. Cellar master: Dassie Smith. Open weekdays 08h00 – 17h30; Saturdays 08h00 – 13h00.

Rozendal Farm PO Box 160, Stellenbosch 7599. Tel: (02231) 76855. Fax: (02231) 98738. Wine maker: Kurt Ammann. Not open to the public.

Ruiterbosch Mountain Vineyards *see* Boplaas Estate.

Rustenberg PO Box 33, Stellenbosch 7599. Tel: (02231) 73153. Fax: (02213) 78466. Proprietor: Simon Barlow. Wine maker: Etienne le Riche. Open weekdays and non-religious public holidays 09h00 – 12h30, 14h00 – 16h30; Saturday 09h00 – 12h30.

Rustenburg Farm Claridge Fine Wines. PO Box 407, Wellington 7655. Tel: (02211) 641241. Fax: (02211) 643620. Wine maker: Roger Jorgensen.

Rust-en-Vrede Estate PO Box 473, Stellenbosch 7599. Tel: (02231) 93881/93757. Fax: (02231) 93000. Proprietor: Jannie Engelbrecht. Wine maker: Kevin Arnold. Open weekdays 08h30 – 12h30, 13h30 – 16h30; Saturdays 09h00 – 12h00. Cellar tours by appointment only.

Saxenburg (Saxenheim) PO Box 171, Kuilsrivier 7580. Tel: (021) 9036113. Fax: (021) 9033129. Wine maker: Nico van der Merwe. Open weekdays 09h00 – 17h00; Saturdays 09h00 – 16h00.

Simondium Winery Co-op (formerly known as Drakenstein Co-op) Box 19, Simondium 7670. Tel: (02211) 41659. Wine maker and manager: G. Wagenaar. Open weekdays 08h30 – 17h00; Saturdays 08h30 – 12h30.

Simonsig Estate PO Box 6, Koelenhof 7605. Tel: (02231) 92044. Fax: (02231) 92545. Proprietors: Malan brothers. Wine maker: Johan Malan. Wine sales weekdays and non-religious public holidays 08h30 – 17h00; Saturdays 08h30 – 12h30. Cellar tours weekdays 10h00 and 15h00; Saturdays 10h00. Light meals served during December and January. 'Simonsig Snuffelwinkel' open at above times.

Simonsvlei Co-op PO Box 584, Suider Paarl 7624. Tel: (02211) 633040. Fax: (02211) 631240. Manager and cellar master: Kobus Rossouw. Production Manager and wine maker: Philip Louw, assisted by Bennie Wannenberg. Open weekdays 08h00 – 17h00; Saturdays 08h30 – 13h00. Lunches during December holidays and cellar tours weekdays by appointment.

Slanghoek Co-op PO Box 75, Rawsonville 6845. Tel: (0231) 91130. Wine maker: Bill Pretorius. Open to members of the public, weekdays 07h30 – 12h30, 13h30 – 17h30. Closes at 16h30 on Fridays. Saturdays 10h00 – 12h00.

Soetwynboere Co-op PO Box 332, Montagu 6720. Tel: (0234) 41340. Wine maker: Jaco Smit. Open weekdays 08h00 – 12h30, 13h30 – 17h00; Saturdays 09h00 – 12h00.

Spier Estate PO Box 28, Vlottenburg 7604. Tel: (02231) 93725. Fax: (02231) 93514. Owner: Chris Joubert. Wine maker: Jan Smit. Open weekdays 08h30 – 13h00, 14h00 – 17h00; Saturdays 08h30 – 13h00. Two restaurants.

Spruitdrift Co-op PO Box 129, Vredendal 8160. Tel: (0271) 33086/7. Fax: (0271) 32937. Wine maker: Johan Roussouw. Open weekdays 08h00 – 17h30; Saturdays 08h00 – 12h00. Cellar tours and wine tasting during office hours. Wine tasting and lectures offered to large groups and snoekbraai for groups of 10–40 can be arranged by appointment.

Stellenbosch Farmer's Winery (SFW) PO Box 46, Stellenbosch 7599. Tel: (02231) 901107. Production director: Duimpie Bayly. No cellar sales. Daily tours by appointment.

Stellenzicht Vineyards PO Box 104, Stellenbosch 7600. Tel: (02231) 901103. Fax: (02231) 78171. Wine maker: Marinus Bredell. Vintner: Günter Brözel. Not open to the public, but visits can be arranged by appointment.

Stettyn Co-op Private Bag 3011, Worcester 6850. Tel: (0231) 94220. Wine maker: Tienie Crous. Not open to the public.

Swartland Co-op PO Box 95, Malmesbury 7300. Tel: (0224) 21434/21134. Fax: (0224) 21750. Wine makers: Johan de Villiers and Christo Koch. Marketing manager: Albie van Vuuren. Open weekdays 08h00 – 13h00, 14h00 – 17h00 and open Saturdays 09h00 – 12h00.

Talana Hill Chardonnay Wine Estate, Blaauwklip Rd, Stellenbosch. Enquiries: Doug Smollen. Tel: (011) 6407634. Proprietors: Doug Smollen and others. Wine maker: Jan Coetzee.

Thelema Mountain Vineyards PO Box 2234, Dennesig 7601. Tel: (02231) 91924. Fax: (02231) 91800. Wine maker: Gyles Webb. Open weekdays 09h00 – 17h00. Saturdays 09h00 – 13h30.

Theuniskraal Estate Tulbagh 6820. Tel: (02362) 2740. Wine maker: Kobus Jordaan. Not open to the public but visits can be arranged by appointment.

Trawal Wynkelders PO Box 2, Klawer 8145. Tel: (02724) 61616. Fax: (02724) 61616. Wine maker and Manager: Kobus Basson. Assistent wine maker: Frank Meaker. Not open to the public.

Tulbagh Co-op PO Box 85 Tulbagh 6820. Tel: (0236) 301001. Wine makers: Stephan Smit and Len Knoetze. Open weekdays 08h00 – 12h30; 13h30 – 17h15; Saturdays 08h30 – 12h00.

Twee Jongegezellen PO Box 16, Tulbagh 6820. Tel: (02362) 2602/4. Wine maker: Nicky Krone. Visitors by appointment.

Uiterwyk Estate PO Box 15, Vlottenburg 7604. Tel: (02231) 93711. Fax: (02231) 93776. Wine maker: Chris and Daniël de Waal. Open Monday to Saturday 09h00 – 16h30; 1 May – 31 August Saturday 10h00 – 16h30.

Uitkyk Estate PO Box 3, Elsenburg 7607. Tel: (02231)94710. Manager: Jan du Preez. Not open to the public.

Vaalharts Co-op PO Box 4, Hartswater 8570. Tel: (05332) 425111. Wine maker: Roelof Maree. Open weekdays 08h30 – 13h00 14h00 – 17h00. Also make Overvaal and Andalusia wines.

Van Loveren PO Box 19, Klaasvoogds 6707. Tel: (0234) 51505. Fax: (0234) 51336. Wine maker: Wynand Retief. Viticulturist: Nico Retief. Open weekdays 08h30 – 13h00, 14h00 - 17h00; Saturdays 09h30 – 13h00.

Vergelegen PO Box 17, Somerset West 7130. Tel: (024) 517060. Fax: (024) 515608. Owned by Anglo American Farms Ltd. Wine maker: Martin Meinert. Vineyards: Felix Faure. Not open to members of the public.

Vergenoegd Estate PO Box 1, Faure 7131. Tel: (024) 43248/43417. Proprietors: Jac and Brand Faure. Wine maker: John Faure. Open Wednesdays 14h00 – 17h00, or by appointment.

Villiera Estate PO Box 66, Koelenhof 7605. Tel: (02231) 92002/3/4. Fax: (02231) 92314. Wine maker: Jeff Grier. Viticulturist: Simon Grier. Open weekdays 08h30 – 17h00; Saturdays 08h30 – 13h00. Cellar tours by appointment only. Terrace lunches can be reserved mid- November to Easter.

Villiersdorp Co-op PO Box 14, Villiersdorp 7170. Tel: (0225) 31120. Wine maker: J P Steenekamp. Kelkiewyn wine tasting and sales centre open weekdays 08h00 – 13h00, 14h00 – 17h00; Saturdays 08h00 – 13h00.

Vlottenburg Co-op PO Box 40, Vlottenburg 7604. Tel: (02231) 93828/9. Fax: (02231) 93357. Wine maker: Kowie du Toit. Open weekdays 08h30 – 17h00; Saturdays 09h00 – 12h30.

Vredendal Co-op PO Box 75, Vredendal 8160. Tel: (0271) 31080. Fax: (0271) 33476. Wine maker: Giel Swiegers. Open weekdays 08h00 – 12h30, 14h00 – 17h30; Saturdays 08h00 – 12h00.

Vredenheim Estate Wines (Made on the farm Vredenburg.) PO Box 369, Stellenbosch 7599. Tel: (02231) 93637/93878. Proprietor: C J Bezuidenhout. Wine maker: Elzabé Bezuidenhout. Open weekdays 09h00 – 16h00. During December and January, open Saturdays 09h00 – 12h00.

Vriesenhof PO Box 155, Stellenbosch 7599. Tel: (02231) 900284/900214. Wine maker: Jan 'Boland' Coetzee. Open weekdays by appointment only.

Waboomsrivier Co-op PO Box 24, Breërivier 6858. Tel: (02324) 730. Fax: (02324) 731. Wine makers: Chris van der Merwe and Wim Viljoen. Open weekdays 08h30 – 17h00; Saturdays 08h30 – 10h00.

Wamakersvallei Co-op PO Box 509, Wellington 7657. Tel: (02211) 31582. Fax: (02211) 33194. Wine makers: Chris Roux and Pieter Rossouw. Open to visitors, Monday to Friday 08h00 – 12h30, 14h00 – 17h00.

Warwick Estate PO Box 2, Muldersvlei 7606. Tel: (02231) 94410. Fax: (02231) 94025. Proprietor and wine maker: Norma Ratcliffe. Visitors by appointment only.

Welgemeend Estate PO Box 69, Klapmuts 7625. Tel: (02211) 5210. Fax: (02211) 5239. Wine maker: Louise Hofmeyr. Open Saturdays 09h00 – 12h30.

Wellington Wynboere Co-op PO Box 520, Wellington 7657. Tel: (02211) 31163. Fax: (02211) 32423. Wine maker: Gert Boerssen. Open weekdays 08h00 – 12h30, 14h00 – 17h00.

Welmoed Co-op PO Box 23, Lyndoch 7603. Tel: (02231) 93800/1. Fax: (02231) 93434. Wine maker: Nicky Versveld. Open Monday to Saturday 08h30 – 17h00.

Weltevrede Estate PO Box 6, Bonnievale 6730. Tel: (02346) 2141/46. Fax: (02346) 2460. Proprietor and wine maker: Lourens Jonker, assisted by Kevin Grant. Open weekdays 08h30 – 13h00, 13h30 – 17h00; Saturdays 09h00 – 12h00. Cellar tours by appointment only.

Windmeul Co-op PO Box 2031, Windmeul 7630. Tel: (02211) 638043/638100. Fax: (02211) 638614. Wine makers: Bernhard Luttich and Hein Koegelenberg. Manager: Bernhard Luttich. Wine sales open weekdays 08h00 – 12h30, 13h30 – 17h00; no tasting.

Zandvliet Estate PO Box 36, Ashton 6715. Tel: (0234) 51146/51823. Fax: (0234) 51327. Wine maker: Paul de Wet Jnr. Not open to the public. Cellar tours by appointment.

Zandwijk PO Box 2674, Paarl 7620. Tel: (02211) 632368. Fax: (02211) 631884. Proprietors: Cape Gate (Chairman: Mendal Kaplan). Wine maker: Leon Mostert. Open during weekday business hours only.

Zevenwacht PO Box 387, Kuils River 7580. Tel: (021) 9035123. Fax: (021) 9033373. Wine maker: Eric Saayman. Open weekdays 08h30 – 12h30, 13h03, 17h00; Saturdays 09h00 – 12h30.

Sugar Level Laws

In 1980 regulations were introduced which strictly define any claims made on a label as to the wine's degree of dryness or sweetness.

Extra Dry
Residual sugar not more than 2,5 grams per litre.
Dry
Residual sugar not more than 4 grams per litre.
Semi-dry
Residual sugar more than 4 but not more than 12 grams per litre (if more than 9, the total acid content shall not be more than 2 grams per litre lower than the sugar content).
Semi-sweet
Residual sugar more than 4 but not more than 30 grams per litre (if the sugar is less than 12 grams per litre then the total acid content must be lower than for semi-dry per litre).
Late Harvest
Residual sugar more than 20 but less than 30 grams per litre.
Special Late Harvest
Residual sugar more than 20 but less than 50 grams per litre.
Noble Late Harvest
Residual sugar more than 50 grams per litre.

Further requirements for Late Harvest wines are stated in the *Government Gazette* of 19 December 1980:

Late Harvest

a. Shall be obtained by the complete or partial fermentation of must;
b. Shall not be fortified;
c. Shall have an alcoholic strength of at least 10% alcohol by volume;
d. Shall have a residual sugar content, expressed as invert sugar, of more than 20 grams per litre but less than 30 grams per litre, irrespective of whether such residual sugar content has been obtained through the addition of sweet must or concentrated must to the wine concerned.

Special Late Harvest

a. Shall be produced from must of which the sugar content prior to fermentation is at least 20 Balling; provided that:
- grapes of a sugar content of less than 21 Balling may not be pressed to obtain such must;
- such must may not be concentrated (dehydrated);
- no sweetening agent of any kind whatsoever may be added to such must;

b. Shall be obtained from partial alcoholic fermentation of such must;
c. Shall not be fortified;
d. Shall have an alcoholic strength of at least 10% alcohol by volume;
e. Shall have a residual sugar content of more than 20 grams per litre

but not more than 50 grams per litre, provided that such residual sugar content will be derived solely from the grapes from which such wine has been produced, and that no sweetening agent of any kind whatsoever may be added to such wine;

f. Shall have a sugar-free extract of not less than 19 grams per litre;

g. Shall possess the character which is distinctive of wine which was produced from grapes which were harvested at a full-ripe stage.

Noble Late Harvest

a. Shall be produced from grapes of which the sugar content at the time of pressing thereof is at least 28 Balling;

b. Shall be obtained from the partial alcoholic fermentation of the must of such grapes, provided that:

- such must may not be concentrated (dehydrated);
- no sweetening agent of any kind whatsoever may be added to such must;

c. Shall not be fortified;

d. Shall have a residual sugar content, expressed as invert sugar, of more than 50 grams per litre, provided that such residual sugar content shall be derived solely from the grapes from which such wine has been produced and that no sweetening agent of any kind whatsoever may be added to such wine;

e. Shall have a sugar-free extract of not less than 30 grams per litre;

f. Shall have the character which is distinctive of wine which was produced from grapes that were harvested late.

Sweet Natural

Must be more than 30 grams per litre, but need not be botrytis-infected.

Sparkling Wines

Extra dry: 15 grams per litre or less;
Dry: 15–35 grams per litre;
Semi-sweet: 35–50 grams per litre;
Sweet: more than 50 grams per litre.

Cape Vintage Guide

The following table is an attempt to indicate the range of quality between the vintages as experienced in the Cape generally. For details on different wines, consult the wine assessments.

Vintage	White Wines	Red Wines
1972	4	7-8
1973	5-6	4-5
1974	4	8-9
1975	3	4
1976	4	7-8
1977	5	4
1978	6	7-8
1979	5	4-5
1980	4	6-7
1981	7	4-5
1982	6	6-7
1983	3	4
1984	4	8-9
1985	6	4
1986	5-6	9
1987	6	8-9
1988	4-7	6-7
1989	4-6	6-8
1990	5-8	8-9
1991	6-9	8-10
1992	5-9	7-9

Key to the vintage ratings:

1-2 = Poor
3-4 = Fair
5-6 = Good
7-8 = Excellent
9-10 = Magnificent

1972 A hot, dry vintage and one of our greats – exceptional for reds and for Cabernet Sauvignon in particular.
1973 A small crop in which downy mildew gave problems and rain affected the late-ripening reds. It is generally considered that the whites of this vintage were better than the reds, although some Cabernets developed well; most should have been drunk by now.
1974 A very dry year. The consistent warmth produced high sugars and this year is considered by many as the outstanding vintage of the decade for reds. In general the whites suffered, although some Steens proved exceptional. The overall crop was down in quantity owing to poor setting conditions in the spring. Generally, the 1974 Cabernets are still showing well, although many have now reached their best. The 1974 Nederburg Auction Cabernet was judged the best Cabernet at the 1985 International Wine and Spirit competition in London.
1975 A fairly dry vintage with an exceptionally hot February which

resulted in whites of very low acid; late rains tended to spoil the late-ripening reds, especially Cabernet, although there are some outstanding exceptions. This was the largest crop since 1971.

1976 A long, cold winter with late rains and snow. The vintage took place in almost ideal conditions and all cultivars produced good quantity and quality. Some reds have proved to be outstanding.

1977 A cool winter which was followed by a wet spring and poor berry set. The harvest was troubled with rain and was plagued by extensive downy mildew damage which resulted. The Cape Riesling crop was small but produced some excellent wines. High acids benefited all whites and gave reds a very French character, although they generally lacked colour. All red varietals showed well, although most have peaked by now.

1978 Another cool wet winter followed by rains in March and April which kept sugars low. Considered overall to be a vintage of good quality and quantity.

1979 The driest and also warmest winter since 1926. February conditions were warm and wet and resulted in a high incidence of botrytis which in some areas developed into noble rot. March was dry and cool so late-ripening reds showed rather well. Some have developed well, but most are not great.

1980 Overall a good vintage with some exciting wines. Hot dry weather gave sound grapes with good sugars, but low acids. Cabernets and Cabernet-based blends are beginning to show very well.

1981 The year of the great flood at Laingsburg. This deluge did untold damage to vineyards in the Robertson, Montagu and Bonnievale areas. The cool weather from flowering to pressing resulted in relatively higher fruit acids in all wines. There was large variation of quality within wine types with some exceptionally good white wines being produced. Red grapes tended to lack sugar and colour and the wines they produced are generally lighter than usual.

1982 The biggest crop to that date with the high quality areas of Stellenbosch, Paarl, Durbanville and Constantia increasing by 20%. Almost perfect climatic conditions, however, enabled superb wines to be made. Some better reds are now showing excellent character.

1983 The crop was up some 5% on the record harvest of 1982 and it was a sound vintage, although the acid and sugar levels were generally lower than in 1982. Some exceptional wines were made, but overall 1983 did not match the great vintage of 1982. Certain cooler areas and slopes were exceptions and wines from such vineyards, as well as normal crop loads, are well-balanced and developing better than expected.

1984 The 1984 vintage was disease-free but slightly down on 1983. It was preceded by one of the wettest winters in ten years. Late bud burst meant that the harvest began some 10 days later than in 1983. A long, dry period from October to February resulted in some white varieties (such as Cape Riesling, Colombar and Steen, growing on shallow, sandy soils in the Coastal Region) ripening under stress. This gave high sugars but low acid which led to rather neutral wines. The reds, however, were magnificent, Cabernet being helped by some late rains. The late red cultivars produced excellent colour and a variety of red wine styles which are ageing well.

1985 A greater range of style and variety of wine was produced from the 1985 vintage than ever before. The total crop was almost ten per cent down on 1984 and with a few notable exceptions whites were generally better than reds. Cool conditions and frequent rains during the ripening period produced grapes with good acid/sugar ratio. The 1985 season was one of the longest ever on record. The white wines are exceptionally fragrant with an ideal sugar/acid balance. Red wines have good flavour but are lighter than those of 1984.

1986 The hottest, driest summer for a couple of decades. In most areas the vintage started four weeks earlier than usual. Overall crop was down in quantity, the late-ripening Cabernet Sauvignon being most affected. Wine makers were delighted with the quality of the grapes and some excellent wines have resulted as the fruit acids were good in spite of the heat.

1987 The overall yield was down by approximately ten per cent on the 1986 vintage, due mainly to rot attacking the grapes, but the long, cool growing season ensured optimum ripeness in healthy grapes. The outstanding characteristic of the vintage, particularly of wines from the Coastal Region, was the balanced combination of high fixed acidity, low pH and good sugar. This resulted in fruity white and red wines with good cellaring potential.

1988 The very long, cool ripening season ended very abruptly mid-vintage with four weeks of excessive heat, which brought a good deal of the crop to ripeness at much the same time. In general the cooler areas seem to have potentially good wines from the better cultivars, such as Cabernet Sauvignon, Cape Riesling, Steen and Pinotage. Some magnificent sweet dessert wines were made.

1989 A good winter chilling occurred and the vines experienced normal and natural bud burst, unlike the previous two vintages. It was a dry year with no late rains, although a cool spring lasted through to the end of December. This gave rise to slightly later ripening conditions. All these factors resulted in improved quality and a greater concentration of flavour components. A late heat wave adversely affected some Cabernets and Rieslings. This was the first 'real' Chardonnay vintage: the vines enjoyed the drought conditions and the fruit ripened superbly, with the result that good quantities were made by many producers. This vintage was marked by being the healthiest in many years; virtually no spraying for disease was required. All in all it was a sound vintage with some excellent wines, especially Cabernets and Chardonnays.

1990 This was not an easy vintage as much of the top quality crop ripened at the same time, instead of being well spaced. It seems, however, that some outstanding Cabernets, Merlots, Chardonnays and Sauvignon Blancs were made. This was the first vintage with sufficient earlier-ripening clones to have a marked effect on the picking programme. The Breede River region, including Worcester and Bonnivale, produced good Sauvignon Blancs, Colombars, Cape Rieslings and Steens. There were also some fine Gewurztraminers and the traditional Fortified Muscadels and Hanepoots were exceptionally good. The Coastal region was generally good with some excellent Cabernets. The relatively cool ripening period ended abruptly with a very hot spell from mid to late February. Sugars suddenly developed and a lot of Steen and Pinotage ripened very rapidly. This spell was followed, however, by about five centimetres of rain that caused rot in the Steen. Fortunately the Cape Doctor (south-easterly wind) blew strongly after the rain and dried the vineyards well. The early Chardonnay seems to have been good in areas ranging from Constantia, through Durbanville and Stellenbosch, to Paarl and the largest amount ever was harvested this year as the new plantings were ready. This vintage's Sauvignon Blanc is of far greater quality than last year's, while the old stalwarts, Cape Riesling and early Steen, seem to have been good even though the latter was reduced in volume by the rot that followed the rain. Quite a number of Noble Late Harvests have been made, especially in the Stellenbosch and Durbanville areas, far more than can be accommodated. The pride and joy of this year's vintage, however, was Cabernet Sauvignon. All of the cellars had excellent colours, good sugar/acid ratios and fine flavours. This, backed with the best-ever Merlot, made the first vintage of the 1990s potentially very exciting. All the reds are developing well. Sauvignon Blancs and Chardonnays are generally good.

1991 The 1991 vintage has been hailed as one of the best ever. Certainly it was one of the most favourable weather-wise. There was a lower than usual rainfall from September to December in 1990, followed by a very mild, almost cool spring and a cool, early summer. Cool evenings and good dew eased the summer strain on the vines and ensured constant moisture supply. All this resulted in some of the finest quality fruit from which some excellent wines have been made. Some of the earlier and mid-season varieties had almost perfect sugar/acid/pH balance. The late hot spell helped to increase the sugar content in some of the latest ripening varieties. Some excellent whites have appeared and early reds have good noses and lots of fruit. Amongst the better reds there are some stunners which should provide some great wines.

1992 From all accounts this is another very good vintage and early releases of whites have shown some fine Sauvignon Blancs, unwooded Chardonnays, Cape Rieslings and Steens. Early reds are good and fruity, while those in wood are, in general, excellent.

Ageing Wines

South Africans are often chided about drinking their wines too young and then concluding that they do not like red wines because they 'bite' too much. This is a gross misapprehension, resulting from drinking the right wine at the wrong time. Although vintage is not reputed to play a very important role in South African wines, knowing the vintage year is relevant to the ageing or maturing of wines in the bottle. Traditionally, South African red wines are full-bodied, needing 10 or, if you can wait that long, 20 years of maturation. Today, however, there is an increasing number of light-bodied and some distinctly fruity red wines available on the market. These are either ready for immediate drinking or need far less maturation. Buy across the spectrum and choose a light red wine to drink through the year and at least two bottles a month of select red wines to put away. In this way you will soon build up your cellar and be in that enviable position of being able to match a memorable occasion with an equally memorable wine.

Red wines

It is generally held that the older a red wine, the better.
Cabernets require about 10 years or longer to reach their peak.
Pinotages may vary from three to nine years. For a typically young Pinotage taste with a flowery flavour keep the wine for three years, but if you prefer a more full-bodied bottle with mature character, store it for five or six years or more. Research carried out in 1984 showed most people prefer Pinotage of eight years and older.
Shiraz wines are generally soft and drinkable after three years but with a further three years can mature to a very full-bodied roundness and softness.
Tinta Barocca does not require long bottle maturation, so store it for three years and then drink it.
Cinsaut reaches its peak at three years but can also be left to mature for up to 10 years. Most Cinsauts are produced for early drinking.
The ageing times related here are, however, no more than rules of thumb – the actual time will depend on how the wine was made and how it is stored. Judging the optimum time for an individual wine comes only with experience.

Nouveau wines

The concept of Nouveau wine may be fashionable but it is not new, for as long as man has made wine, much of it has been drunk before fermentation is complete. The concept of bottling young wine and marketing it as a product for early consumption is, however, relatively new.

This idea was made popular by the people of Beaujolais, and their Nouveau wines are still the most famous in the world. The first Beaujolais Primeurs were normally ready by mid-October, with the traditional date for the wine-launching festival being the Sunday nearest All Saint's Day in November. In 1935 the new *Appellation Contrôlée* laws set 15 November as the date the wines could be sold.

Only after the Second World War did this local tradition spread to Paris. In 1955 the present regulations governing the sale of Primeur came into effect, ensuring that the launch became a properly organized event. The release date is now the third Thursday in November, so that the wine can reach almost anywhere in Europe, and particularly London, by the weekend.

In 1982 Stellenbosch Farmers' Winery launched the idea in South Africa with their Nouveau Range. Walter Finlayson was quick to follow with the Blaauwklippen Nouveau and Spatz Sperling with an early Pinotage Rosé. It took the wine master, Günter Brözel, however, to produce a Gamay, the traditional grape used for this style of wine in Beaujolais. The Nederburg Gamay appeared at the Nederburg Auction on 20 April 1985, 55 days after pressing. In 1986, it was released just 30 days after harvesting. KWV and Simonsig are now both producing white variations and others who are joining the Nouveau trend are Fairview, Villiera, Woolworths, and Buitenverwachting with its colourful L'Arrivée.

Each year at the Cape Town Festival, the wine makers of the Stellenbosch Wine Route deliver their Nouveaus to the Mayor of Cape Town, while those of Paarl hold their own highly successful event on Paarl Mountain. Different means of transport are used to convey the cellars' Nouveaus to the mountain.

Production is traditionally by carbonic maceration. The wine is normally chaptalized and early fermentation occurs at fairly warm temperatures (25–30°C) to extract good colour. This fresh red wine should be enjoyed young and chilled as an ideal picnic drink or with a hot breakfast in winter.

White wines

White wines, unlike the reds, do not need long bottle maturation; in fact, most of them should be drunk immediately. One can, however, drink a white wine any time within one or two years from vintage, when the flavour is delicate, fruity and characteristically young and fresh. Some wines, especially those that are semi-sweet, benefit from storing for some two to three years from vintage.

Nederburg Edelkeur, the honey-sweet, golden-hued wine, considered the pride of the wine maker's art in South Africa, should be stored for ten years after vintage, according to Patrick Grubb, the respected British wine auctioneer. In all, very few local dry white wines will benefit with age, notable exceptions being some dry Rieslings which need two or three years to reach full development and others such as the 1974 Nederburg Auction Riesling which is ageing well more than ten years later. Some of the 'new wave' wood-aged whites will benefit with a few years of bottle age.

Sparkling wines

Most bubblies are released at the time the wine maker believes they are ready for drinking. The important part of ageing bubblies is the time spent on the lees. Once degorged, not much more dramatic development will take place other than ageing. Some *méthode champenoise* wines are at their best when degorged but will still develop in the bottle. The English (those people who live on that wet island off the coast of France) tend to enjoy very old and almost flat champagne. Most people prefer their bubblies relatively fresh. A couple of years after degorging is usually as much as one should let champagne age. Most tank-produced bubblies don't really benefit from more than a year or two in the bottle unless the wine used was exceptional, as is the case with some of the top-class German Sekts.

Glossary

Acidity All grapes contain fruit acids and these stay in the liquid when the grapes are crushed, ending up in the final wine. High fruit acid produces sharp wines, a little less produces fresh, fruity wines and very little results in soft wines.
Aftertaste *See* Farewell
Ampelography The scientific study of the description and classification of the vine and the grape.
Appearance The first step in wine appreciation which is the assessment of colour and clarity.
Aroma A term used to describe the fragrance of a wine owing to the fruit. Not to be confused with Bouquet.
Astringency The quality in a wine which makes the mouth pucker. The degree of astringency depends on the amount of tannin absorbed by the wine from the skins, pips and stalks of grapes.
Balling A measure of concentration of sugar in the grapes, expressed in degrees.
Blanc de Noir White wine made from red grapes. The skins are removed at the time of pressing and thus impart only the slightest blush to the wine.
Blending The art of 'mixing' wines of different grape varieties, vintages, areas and qualities to achieve a particular end.
Body The consistency or substance of a wine. It refers to the quantity of solid matter or extract in solution in the wine.
Botrytis cinerea (Noble rot) This is a fungoid infection that attacks ripe grapes under certain climatic conditions. In its development the fungi evaporates moisture from the grapes, causing them to shrivel and concentrate the relative sugar content. Wine makers use this process of 'noble rot' to make rich, sweet wines such as Nederburg Edelkeur and various other Noble Late Harvest wines. If the weather conditions are other than 'optimum', the fungus can rapidly turn to vulgar rot, thereby ruining the harvest.
Bottle age Mellow development observed in the bouquet of a wine and its smoothness across the palate.
Bottle sickness A loss of flavour and bouquet caused by excessive contact of the wine with air at the time of bottling.
Bouquet Fragrance in wine derived from fermentation, maturation and ageing. Not synonymous with Aroma.
Bordeaux Famous wine-producing region on the western coast of France where the main red grapes are Cabernet Sauvignon, Cabernet Franc, Merlot, Malbec, etc. and the wines are blends of those varieties. The white wines of the area are mainly Sauvignon Blanc, Sémillon and Muscadel and the wines are blends of these. Hence the term 'Bordeaux Blend' for wines using combinations of the varieties.
Brut French term for dry. Generally applied to sparkling wines and champagne with a sugar content of 1,5% or less.
Carbonic maceration Vinification without crushing grapes. Whole bunches are placed into pressure tanks and intercellular fermentation under oxygen-free conditions occurs. This process is used in Beaujolais Nouveau production.
Cask A wooden wine barrel, varying in capacity; it is usually made of oak and bound with steel hoops.

Chaptalization The addition of sugar to grape musts, either before or during fermentation, to increase the alcohol content of wine.
Charmat In short: tank-produced. *Méthode Charmat* is a patent method of producing sparkling wine where the bubbles are produced when the wine undergoes secondary fermentation in a tank. The wine is then bottled under pressure. It is a lot less expensive than doing it in individual bottles. The name Charmat is nowadays applied to most tank-produced bubblies.
Chateau Though literally meaning 'castle', it is today the name given to properties such as wine estates and vineyards in the Bordeaux region famous for their wine: Chateau Mouton-Rothschild, Chateau Loudenne, etc.
Clarity A wine must be attractive to the eye, clean and bright, not cloudy or dull.
Clean No foreign smell or taste.
Closed A descriptive term used when the potential of a young wine remains 'locked in' and does not show.
Cooper An artisan who makes and/or repairs wooden casks.
Corked
1. A wine adversely affected by an infected cork.
2. Any wine sealed with a cork.
Crisp Good acid; a clean and refreshing wine.
Crust Sediment precipitated on the inside of a bottle of wine, especially Port, after long bottle maturation.
Cultivar A term used for a grape variety used in viticulture.
Cuvée Literally, the contents of a cask, generally applied to a specially prepared blend of wine.
Decanting Process of pouring wine from the original container into a decanter, care being taken to ensure that sediment is not disturbed in the process in the case of old wines. In the case of young wines decanting serves to aerate it, thus enhancing bouquet and aroma.
Dessert wine A generic term frequently used to describe very sweet fortified wines.
Dry wine Many people confuse dryness with acidity. Legally a dry wine cannot exceed four grams of residual sugar per litre. However, a wine completely without sugar can taste very smooth and almost sweet if low in acid, whereas a wine with relatively high sugar appears drier if the acid content is high.
Elegant Harmonious and refined, with good style.
Extract The soluble solids that are non-volatile, and non-sugars.
Farewell A term used to describe the flavour and the length of time that the flavour remains in the mouth after swallowing the wine.
Feel The term used to describe the sensation that the wine gives in the mouth before swallowing.
Fortification The addition of brandy or grape spirit to wine. The process is used in making Ports, Sherries and Dessert wines.
Fresh A young, lively wine.
Fruity A wine of good acidity which gives off the aroma of fruits, not only grape; for example, Steen wines often have a guava aroma.
Full-bodied A wine high in all its individual components.
Gewürz Spicey flavour of bouquet.
Hard High tannin gives young wines a hardness which will only soften with age.
Heavy This need not be a derogatory term and is usually used to

describe a wine high in alcohol and flavours, which often needs time to mellow.

Honest No great attribute, but a good, clean, well-made wine.

Late Harvest, Special Late Harvest, Noble Late Harvest South African terms to describe a sweetish, medium- to full-bodied white wine having sugar levels from 20 g/*l* upwards. (*See* page 27.)

Lees The deposit at the bottom of the fermenting vessel. Mainly made up from the dead yeast cells. Prolonged contact of wine with lees can influence the character of the wine.

Light Low in alcohol and body, but this can be an attribute.

Maderized A term used to describe a particular aged condition of wine; a baked taste usually owing to storing conditions being too hot.

Malolactic fermentation The conversion of malic acid to lactic acid in wine, resulting in a wine which tastes less acidic.

Maturation Process whereby wines are left in wood or bottles to age, improve and mellow. The period of maturation depends on the type and character of the wine.

Mellow Softened with age.

Méthode Champenoise The method of making sparkling wine employed in Champagne in the north-east of France in which the all-important second fermentation takes place in the bottle in which the wine is ultimately sold. The method is being used more and more in the Cape.

Mousse The froth or foam produced when Perlé or Sparkling wines are poured.

Must Freshly-pressed, unfermented grape juice, with or without skins and pips.

Natural wine Unfortified table wine to which nothing extraneous has been added.

New clone This is a term used not quite correctly. New clone should imply recently developed new clones of particular cultivars. However, it is generally used to describe virus-free vines.

Noble Well bred, classy.

Nose A term for the bouquet and aroma of the wine. A wine with a good nose produces pleasant sensations when smelled.

N.V. Non-vintage; meaning no claim to the year of production.

Oak This is the preferred wood used for the casks and barrels in which wine is matured. All the finest red wines, most of the fortified wines and some white wines owe part of their quality to the flavour imparted by the oak.

Oaky An odour of oak apparent in wines aged too long in casks. It is desirable in fine red table wines but is unpleasant when excessive and especially so in white table wines.

Oenology The science of wine and wine making. The cellar as opposed to the vineyard (vineyard = viticulture).

Open A fully developed wine, showing all its characteristics.

Organoleptic Scientific term for the evaluation of wines using the senses of sight, smell and taste.

Oxidized A fault in wine owing to excessive exposure to air, and which can be detected by both the nose and palate.

Perfumed The aroma usually derived from the grape, e.g. Muscadel.

Perlé, Perlant Not quite a still wine, but not a sparkling wine either. Some bubbles of carbon dioxide have, however, been introduced, giving it a slight effervescence.

Perlé wine Slightly effervescent wine, as opposed to sparkling wine which effervesces vigorously.
Pétillant A word the French originated and is now more widely used to describe wines which, like Pérle wines, contain a little gas, being lightly sparkling.
pH This is the measure of strength of acidity and not the amount of acid. The measurement scale is such that above the value seven is alkaline and below is acid, and the lower the figure the stronger the acid. The warmer the growing climate the higher the pH of the wine made and the cooler the climate the lower the pH. This explains why many of the finest wines come from the cooler growing areas. Lower pH also helps to prevent bacterial spoilage, allows more effective sulphur dioxide use and gives wine a better colour.
Pipe A cask made of oak and tapered sharply towards the ends, it is used to mature Port. It comes in varying sizes, the most common holding 522 litres; the standard Madeira pipe is considerably smaller.
Port Name for the classic fortified wines produced in the Douro Valley of Portugal and shipped from Oporto. Port-style wines, both red and white, are produced in most wine-producing regions.
Premier Grand Crû A term used in South Africa as a name for a class of blended dry wines. This wine should be as dry as vinification techniques allow.
Red wine Made by fermenting red grapes in the presence of their skins so that the pigments in the skin can colour the wine. Red wines usually contain more tannin than whites and are often aged for a year or two in wooden barrels before being bottled.
Residual sugar (RS) All grapes contain sugar and it is the conversion of this sugar by yeast into alcohol and carbon dioxide that gives wine. If not all the sugar is converted and some remains behind in the wine, this portion is termed residual sugar.
Rosé Rosé wines are made by fermenting red grapes in contact with their skins for only a matter of hours until the wine maker judges he has obtained that degree of pink colour which gives Rosé wine its name. The juice is then separated from the skins so that no further coloration takes place and the fermentation continues as for white wine. Rosés can be semi-sweet or dry.
Rough Lacking in finesse.
Round Well-balanced and mature.
Semi-sweet A term used in South Africa to describe wines that have an excess of four grams per litre of residual sugar but not more than 30 grams. In practice wines so described normally have about 20 g/*l* and are usually white. (*See* page 27.)
Sharp A wine with high acid, which will mellow with age.
Smooth Soft texture.
Solera A system of maturing and blending Sherry to produce a consistent product year after year. The process evolved in Spain and is employed for the best sherries in South Africa. The casks are arranged in three tiers, with each supplying the one below, wine for bottling being drawn from the bottom cask.
Sound Well-made wine but without great attributes.
Sour Applied to wine spoiled by acetic acid bacteria and which is therefore vinegary. Not to be confused with Dry, Tart or Astringent.
Sparkling wine An effervescent wine owing to the presence of carbon dioxide gas.

Spicey Rich and aromatic.

Spumante Italian style of sparkling wine usually with Muscat in character and, in South Africa, usually sweet.

Stein A name used in South Africa for an extremely popular class of blended semi-sweet wines. They are characterized by a good, fruity flavour and sugar levels of 1–2% by volume. Not to be confused with 'Steen' (Chenin Blanc), which is the most widely grown grape in South Africa.

Sulphur dioxide (SO_2) The use of sulphur to sterilize wine is almost as old as wine itself. In the modern wine cellar small but effective amounts of sulphur dioxide are used as the standard sterilizing agent for casks and barrels. It is also extensively used in the vineyards to control vine disease. Compared with some European countries the sulphur level in South African wines is very low. For natural table wines the permitted maximum is 200 parts per million. This can be exceeded only in Noble Late Harvests.

Sur lie Means 'on the lees' and is usually applied when bottled directly from the casks which have not been racked. Such wines usually possess greater freshness and can have a slight 'prickle' or pétillance. More loosely applied in South Africa to wines that have spent some time on their lees prior to bottling and are not necessarily bottled direct from the cask.

Tannin A group of organic compounds occurring in the bark, wood, roots, skins, pips and stems of many plants and fruits, including the grape. It is most pronounced in red wines which pick up tannin from the skins and pips during maturation in oak barrels.

Tart Natural and agreeable fruity-acid taste in wine.

Tawny
1. Applied to wines which have turned from red to a brownish colour with maturation.
2. A type of port.

Thin Lacking alcohol, watery and feeble.

Total acidity (TA) This is the collective amount of fruit and volatile acids in a wine and is usually expressed as grams per litre.

Tough Full-bodied but needing age to soften.

Traditional Blend A phrase that I think I was possibly the first to use. I applied it to South African red blends that contained Cabernet and another cultivar or numerous other cultivars including Shiraz, Pinotage, Cinsaut and various Port varieties.

Varietal *See* Cultivar

Vermouth A fortified herbal wine, dry or sweet, flavoured with aromatic herbs. Most wine-producing countries produce vermouth-type wines.

Vin gris A pale pink wine made, as with Blanc de Noir wines, from red grapes. Not to be confused with the cultivar Pinot Gris.

Vin ordinaire An inexpensive wine often sold by the glass or carafe. Taken to mean everyday or house wine.

Vinho Verde A type of natural wine made in Portugal near to Oporto. Usually finished with a slight pétillance.

Vinosity The depth or degree to which a particular wine shows vinous qualities.

Vintage
1. Used to signify the grape-gathering season: the yield is known as the harvest.

2. The year in which a wine was made.
3. A 'vintage year' is a year in which excellent wines were made.
Virus free This is a term applied to grapes that have been cleared of virus infection and therefore perform better than those infected.
Volatile acid Fruit acids should not be confused with volatile acid which is the acid of vinegar, better known as acetic acid. It is not found in the grape and develops after the alcoholic fermentation. In minute quantities it can be quite attractive, especially in red wines, but larger amounts are unpleasant and make the wine too vinegary.
Weight A term applied to the feel of the wine in the mouth.

News

Cap Classique Local wine makers have opted for this term to be used for their *Méthode Champenoise* wines as the latter term is protected by France and can no longer be used. (Just as we cannot call such wines 'Champagne'.)
Strength/Alcohol content As of 1 June 1992, alcoholic strength must be stated on labels. This is almost common practice on better wines, but now *all* must show their alcohol content. A one degree margin is allowed.
Varietals Wine labels can now state composition of grape varieties in the blend which was not allowed previously.
Veritas New symbol of quality for South African wines. Veritas Awards have been introduced to acknowledge excellence in South African wine, now that the Wine of Origin Superior certificate has gone. Veritas Awards will consist of Double Gold, Gold, Silver and Bronze. Stickers will be applied to bottles. The wines entered for judging must be available in quantities of at least 200 cases. Judges will be drawn from the industry and results will be announced mid-September. In 1991, 854 wines were entered, of which 75 were awarded Double Gold and 133 were awarded Gold.

Best Buys of the Year

Allesverloren Tinta Barocca 1982
Avontuur Blanc de Noir 1991
Avontuur Merlot Reserve 1989
Bellingham Almeida 1986
Bellingham Brut
Bergsig Pinotage 1992
Bergsig Special Late Harvest 1991
Blaauwklippen Cabernet Sauvignon 1988
Blaauwklippen Red Landau 1984
Blaauwklippen Shiraz 1984
Blaauwklippen Zinfandel 1982, 1984, 1989
Bloemendal Bloemen Blanc 1991
Boschendal Grand Vin Blanc 1986
Chamonix Cabernet Sauvignon 1987
Chateau Libertas 1986
Delheim Cabernet Sauvignon 1989
Delheim Chenin Blanc 1987
Delheim Pinot Noir 1989, 1990
Delheim Pinotage Rosé 1987
Douglas Green Kerner 1983
Douglas Green Sauvignon Blanc 1984
Du Toitskloof Cape Riesling 1991
Du Toitskloof Chenin Blanc 1991
Eikendal Chardonnay 1991
Eikendal Special Late Harvest 1986
Goue Vallei Blanc de Blanc 1991
Groot Constantia Cabernet Sauvignon 1988
Hamilton Russell Vineyards Chardonnay 1991
Hartenberg L'Estreux 1985
HC Collison Cabernet Sauvignon 1983
Kanonkop Cabernet Sauvignon 1984
Klein Constantia Cabernet Sauvignon 1987
Lanzerac Chardonnay 1990
Lanzerac Muscat d'Alexandrie 1987
Lievland Bukettraube 1987
Lievland Rood 1988
Lievlander 1989
Nederburg Fonternel 1985
Nederburg Kap Sekt
Nederburg Noble Late Harvest 1983
Neethlingshof Rhine Riesling 1990
Overgaauw Sylvaner 1986
Robertson Bukettraube 1991
Roodezandt Hárslevelü 1986
Rooiberg Pinotage 1990
Rustenberg Gold 1989
Rustenberg Pinot Noir 1984, 1988
Simonsig Cabernet Sauvignon 1983
Simonsig Sauvignon Blanc 1986
Simonsig Shiraz 1988
Simonsig Vin Fumé 1985
Soetendal Hanepoot
Spier Fernão Pires 1990
Stellenzicht Grand Vin Blanc 1990
Swartland Blanc de Blanc 1991
The Oaks Reserve 1989
Van Loveren Cape Riesling 1987
Van Loveren Colombar 1991
Van Loveren Hárslevelü 1991
Van Loveren Muscat de Frontignan 1991
Van Loveren Red Muscadel 1990
Villiera Gavotte 1987
Villiera Sauvignon Blanc 1991
Villiera Tradition Charles de Fere 1990
Vlottenburg Gewürztraminer 1991
Welgemeend Amade 1985
Weltevrede Cape Riesling 1991
Weltevrede Colombard 1991
Weltevrede Gewürztraminer 1991
Woolworths Bianca Light 1991
Zevenwacht Gewürztraminer 1986
Zonnebloem Blanc de Blanc 1986
Zonnebloem Grand Soleil 1990
Zonnebloem Pinotage 1983
Zonnebloem Pinotage 1988
Zonnebloem Pinotage 1989

Red Wines

Bordeaux Blends

Avontuur Avon Rouge★★★★C
This is a good-value blend of predominantly Cabernet Sauvignon, 30% Merlot and about 15% Cabernet Franc. It has very good nose, deep soft flavour, and although wood is there, it doesn't dominate. It is easy to drink quite early as tannins are low, but has the ability to develop with benefit over three to five years.

Avontuur Baccarat★★★★D
From the 1989 vintage comes this excellent value for money blend of 70% Merlot and 30% Cabernet Sauvignon. Very drinkable at an early age but should develop well over another four to six years. Baccarat is pronounced without the 't', thus Baccara, and is the name of a deep red, almost black rose that has been the inspiration for Avontuur's labeling their inky, black-red wine. 1990 is along the same lines but with much deeper flavours and will certainly develop.

Backsberg Klein Babylonstoren★★★★(★)D
In keeping with the Backsberg reds, the 1984 release was surprisingly easy to drink within three years of making. Predominantly Cabernet with as much as 40% Merlot and well-wooded in new oak. The 1985 is a little more reserved but is elegant and stylish. The 1986 is 50% of each of the two varieties and is a delicious, full-flavoured wine, soft yet fruity, making delightful drinking in 1991 but will definitely develop in the bottle over three to four years. The 1987 is 40% each of Cabernet and Merlot and 20% Cabernet Franc with far more intense character. The 1988 is back to being a 50/50 blend of Merlot and Cabernet Sauvignon. A good deal of the latter is new clone, offering a very forward, fruity character which is most appealing. 1989 continues the same top quality. All have good wood and lovely flavours, and are easy to drink when released. But it will be worthwhile allowing the wine to develop in the bottle through to the end of the twentieth century.

84 ★★★★ ready, will still improve. **85** ★★★★ ready, will still improve. **86** ★★★★★ ready, will still develop. **87** ★★★★(★) ready, will still develop. **88** ★★★(★) ready, will still develop. **89** ★★★★ allow to develop.

Bertrams Robert Fuller★★★★(★)E
This blend, with its first release from the 1984 vintage, is a major departure from the traditional style of Bertrams' reds. Made under the guidance of Martin van der Merwe, the 1984 is 70% Cabernet Sauvignon and 30% Merlot. It was aged first in large wood and then spent about half a year in small new Nevers oak casks. It has the Bertrams fullness and is drinking very well in 1992. In the 1985 vintage, Merlot has been reduced to 20%, but it has more wood, giving slightly lighter but better flavoured wine. The 1986 is an excellent wine with some 70% Cabernet Sauvignon and 30% Merlot. Launched in May 1991, this is a much bigger, fuller wine and the best so far under this label. Good wood and tannin will ensure good and long ageing. This is another wine to see in the new century. 1987 has been a slow starter and is not as open as previous excellent wines, but it has the potential to develop.

84 ★★★★(★) ready, will still improve. **85** ★★★★ ready, will still improve. **86** ★★★★★ ready, will still improve. **87** ★★(★) needs time to show.

Blaauwklippen Cabriolet★★★D

First from 1983, is a delightful lightish red, comprising almost three-quarters Merlot, the balance Cabernet Sauvignon, and aged for two years in small wood. Walter Finlayson opted to sell the wine without any mention of the fact that it was rated Superior. It has aged with interest and drinks particularly well now, but has probably reached the limit of its development, although it will still hold its maturity. The 1988, sold at the Cape Independent Winemakers' Guild annual auction, is 80% Cabernet Sauvignon and 20% Merlot and is much better wine than previous vintages.

Boplaas Grand Vin Rouge★★★★D

A very limited quantity (120 cases) of the 1987 was made available in mid-1990. The 90% Cabernet and 10% Merlot give a very attractive fruity nose and good, concentrated, elegant flavours backed by fine oak. It is developing beautifully in the bottle and its 13,6% alcohol and good tannins will no doubt allow many years before it reaches its full potential. There was no 1988, but the next release is from the 1989 vintage. In this one the Cabernet Sauvignon was reduced to 50% and the balance made up of Cabernet Franc and Merlot. It is not as dramatic as the 1987, but give it time to develop. Next release will be the 1991.

Boschendal Grand Vin★★★(★)D

The first release from the 1985 vintage has proved a little disappointing. The 1986 is considerably better and easily four-star material. It apparently has less Merlot than the 1985 and is an elegant, restrained wine with good wood backing. The 1985 vintage is not developing with any excitement; it has browned considerably and should be drunk up. The 1986 is developing better.

Bovlei Co-op Grand Rouge★★(★)A

Early offerings of this non-vintaged wine were easy-drinking blends of Shiraz and Pinotage. The latest offering is a blend of Cabernet and Merlot which gives a full-flavoured, early drinking wine. Good value for money.

Buitenverwachting Buitenkeur★★★(★)D

The blend from the 1986 vintage was the cellar's entry into the Bordeaux style of wines made in the Cape. Released late in 1990 it spent 14 months in new Nevers oak before bottling. A little more than half the blend is Cabernet with a balance of 40% Merlot and a fraction Cabernet Franc. Deep in colour and character with the Cabernet showing strongly through good oak, it is developing well. The next offering is from the 1987 vintage and is almost 70% Cabernet, a little more than 15% Merlot and 15% Cabernet Franc. Also out of Nevers barrels, it has a little more body and firmer tannin. Next will be the 1988 which is about half Merlot, one third Cabernet Sauvignon and the balance Cabernet Franc. It is slightly subdued but will develop.

Buitenverwachting Grand Vin★★★★E

First release from 1988 vintage is a particularly full-flavoured, berry-type wine made from 70% Cabernet Sauvignon, 20% Merlot, and 20% Cabernet Franc, with nice toastiness from new oak. It carries a classy new label.

Cape Vintners Members Only Grand Reserve★★★★D
The 1988 is predominantly Cabernet with Merlot and Cabernet Franc, aged for a year in second fill Allier and Nevers barrels. Good character with lots of tannin. 1989 is fine wine with good berry character, from 80% Cabernet Sauvignon and 20% Merlot, backed by nice oak. Should develop well with age.
Clos Malverne Auret★★★★E
Clos Malverne only produce red wine and Auret is their flagship. Only 500 cases containing six bottles each have been produced from selected barrels of the 1988 vintage. This wine, which was released late in 1990, is a very distinct, rich, intense wine that should develop well into the late 1990s. It is all Cabernet that had been selected from 20 new 225-litre Nevers barrels where it spent 10 months. The second release was from the 1989 vintage: 1 100 cases made up of 82% Cabernet Sauvignon and 18% Merlot that has aged in new and second fill Nevers for 14 months.
Clos Malverne Auret Reserve★★★★(★)F
A limited quantity, about 120 cases, of 1990 Auret Reserve. Was the South African Champion Wood-matured Dry Red at the 1990 Young Wine Show. A blend of Cabernet and Merlot, it had 16 months in new Nevers and Allier barrels. A real mouthful of powerful flavour that will need many years to reach its potential in numbered bottles.
Delaire Barrique★★★★D
The first release, from 1988 vintage, is a well-wooded blend of equal proportions of Cabernet and the 1988 Gold Medal South African Champion Merlot. A deep, rich, full-flavoured wine with lots of fruit and good wood, it is developing well and should be at its best in eight to twelve years. The 1989 is predominantly Merlot (85%), with Cabernet Sauvignon giving a luscious, full-flavoured wine, soft in the mouth yet with lots of good oak backing. As well as it drinks now, its tannin and almost 13% alcohol will allow further development. This cellar produces deep rich reds and the 1990 of 35% Merlot and 65% Cabernet Sauvignon is again top quality with cassis, cherries and vanilla that will all develop with time.
De Leuwen Jagt Rood★★★(★)E
Still to be released from 1990 vintage is a Cabernet Sauvignon and Merlot blend. Lots of fruit, eucalyptus, and herb characters.
Delheim Grand Reserve★★★★★E
This is now firmly established as one of the Cape's great reds. Originally released from the 1981 vintage, and along with the 1982 and 1983, it was entirely Cabernet Sauvignon. Excellent small new-wood-ageing gave these wines beautiful character. From 1984 these wines have contained varying proportions of Cabernet Franc with the 1986 comprising 65% Cabernet Sauvignon, 11% Cabernet Franc and 24% Merlot (the lowest Cabernet content yet). This will rank as one of South Africa's real greats. Nowadays the blend is more or less 65–75% Cabernet Sauvignon and Merlot and usually no Cabernet Franc; 1988 and 1989 are both 75% Cabernet Sauvignon and 25% Merlot and, as always, matured in new Nevers oak for a year or more. Beautiful berry flavours, vanillas, with good tannin. The wines are surprisingly easy to drink when released, but are well worth keeping for five to six years, and are even more rewarding if you can resist the temptation a while longer. The early vintages of 1982 and 1983 are still developing in 1992 while subsequent vintages

should continue to mature. This wine has been acclaimed by critics, both locally and abroad, and has achieved excellent prices at Independent Winemakers' Guild and Nederburg Auctions. It has also been selected as a SAA Wine of the Month and awarded a gold medal at the International Wine and Spirit Competition in 1988. It remains one of the leaders in this style of Cape wine. Small quantities are bottled in magnums.

81 ★★★★★ ready. **82** ★★★★★ ready. **83** ★★★★★ ready, will still improve. **84** ★★★★★ ready, will still improve. **85** ★★★★★ ready, will still improve. **86** ★★★★★ not ready, age further. **87** ★★★★★ ready, age further. **88** ★★★★★ allow to develop. **89** ★★★★★ allow to develop.

Diemersdal Droë Rooi★★★D

The 1989 vintage is lighter in style compared with the 1988. It is made from equal quantities of Cabernet Sauvignon and Cabernet Franc with 20% Merlot. Good tannin should allow development.

Diemersdal Private Collection★★★C/D

The first public release of wines from this long-time KWV supplier came in 1991. Simply under the name Diemersdal Private Collection this is Cabernet Sauvignon and Cabernet Franc in equal proportions, and the balance some 20% Merlot. From the 1987 vintage aged in small French oak, this medium-bodied wine has good tannin and nice fruit. Age should bring better balance and smoothness.

Eikendal Classique★★★★D

From the 1987 vintage, this is a well-wooded blend of 60% Cabernet and 40% Merlot and has shown good development. The 1988 has less Merlot (30%), but is a more elegant wine. The 1989 has the same make-up but is a better wine, with good berry character, nice tannin and good oak. All vintages need four to five years to develop.

Fairview Merlot Reserve★★★★★E

Although called Merlot Reserve, this wine from the 1989 vintage contains almost one quarter Cabernet Franc. Aged in six different woods, a barrel of each has been separately bottled for interest. The balance was blended and bottled for sale. Deep rich, full berry-like character; soft in the mouth now, but will develop well over five to six years. Following the well-received 1989 is an excellent 1990 of much the same composition, but it is a much fruitier, fresher wine with good oak. It will need five to six years to mellow out.

Fairview Charles Gerard Reserve★★★★C

A deep red blend of 60% Merlot and 40% Cabernet Sauvignon from the 1987 vintage with big, bold, deep flavours. It should develop with interest over a further four to six years. The next release, from 1990, is big, full flavoured wine with 60% Cabernet Franc, 30% Merlot and 10% Cabernet Sauvignon. It has deep colour and intense flavours and will probably develop earlier than the 1987.

Fleermuisklip Robyn (Lutzville Co-op)★★(★)C

A beautiful, deep, ruby-coloured wine that takes its name from a well-known local rock feature in the area. It is made from predominantly Ruby Cabernet with small portions of Cabernet Franc and Cabernet Sauvignon.

Glen Carlou Classique★★★★★E/F

First release from 1989 vintage is gorgeous wine and will need five to eight years to show its full potential. 1990 is a great wine with lots of everything – a good blend of almost 70% Cabernet Sauvignon,

23% Merlot, 3% Cabernet Franc and 5% Petit Verdot, all giving great complexity and depth of fruit flavours, backed by good new oak. Will age beautifully.

Glen Carlou Les Trois★★★★(★)D

The first release from the 1989 vintage is a very New World red, blended from Cabernet Sauvignon (72%, almost half of which is new clone) with Merlot and Cabernet Franc. Aged in new Nevers barrels for 14 months giving deep, rich flavour. It drank very well on release and has aged beautifully over a year and will continue to do so for another four to five years. 1990 is slightly lighter but lovely wine of 50% Cabernet Sauvignon, 30% Petit Verdot and 20% Merlot.

Groot Constantia Gouveneurs Reserve★★★★E

The first release launched late in 1990 from the 1986 vintage, is a medium-bodied, wood-aged wine blended from Cabernet Sauvignon and Cabernet Franc. It is, to my mind, the best red yet to be produced by this cellar. Aged in 500-litre Nevers barrels it has subdued but definite oak backing and good fruity, berry flavours. Already very drinkable, but age for six to eight years for full reward. The 1987, a Cabernet Sauvignon and Merlot blend, is more elegant than the 1986 but has all the ability to develop. 1988 continues in good style.

Hamilton Russell Vineyards Premier Reserve★★★★E

Tim Hamilton Russell is always ready to challenge the authorities over their sometimes silly regulations, and the name of this wine is a result of one of those actions. It is a fine wine that is often overlooked because of the cellar's very fine Pinot Noir and Chardonnay. The 1988 is probably the best release to date with layers of deep flavours that will develop magnificently with five to seven years but will last well into the new century. It drinks amazingly well now, but time will be really worth the wait. 1989 is a Cabernet-Merlot blend, a little austere in 1992, but with potential to develop with benefit.

84 ★★★(★) ready, will still improve. **85** no release. **86** ★★(★) ready, will still improve. **87** no release. **88** not ready, allow to develop. **89** not ready, allow to develop.

Kanonkop Auction Reserve★★★★★F

This is made up specially each year for the Independent Winemakers' Guild Auction and is more or less a blend of the best barrels of Paul Sauer and Kanonkop Cabernet. The result is always excellent. The 1987 vintage was sold at the 1990 Auction. The 1988 and 1991 are both developing extremely well in the bottle. They are big, powerful wines with full strong nose that have lots to give. The 1989 will be at the 1992 Auction. It is decidedly New World in style and will require many years to show its full potential.

Kanonkop Paul Sauer★★★★★E

This wine was planned by Jan 'Boland' Coetzee over many years. He planted a vineyard comprising 55% Cabernet Sauvignon, 25% Cabernet Franc, 10% Malbec and Souzão, and 10% Merlot, all of which are harvested and crushed together. The 1981 was the first release and the wine is now accepted as one of the Cape's greats. Beyers Truter, who has proved himself to be a great wine maker, intends to keep Paul Sauer a great wine, and will alter the blend as the vintage determines to ensure only the very best goes into the wine. Over six to ten years, the wines develop dramatically. The 1984 is splendid and is a five-star product. The wine maker has sold 50 cases of this vintage, of which half of the bottles in each case are closed with a patent screw top and the other half with traditional corks. The intention is to obtain the opinion of collectors concerning the development of wine closed by different methods. The 1985 was the champion red at the Stellenbosch Wine Show and has a Cabernet content as high as 75%, with the balance being Cabernet Franc and Merlot. Blends nowadays are usually 70 – 75% Cabernet Sauvignon with some 15% Cabernet Franc, 10% Merlot, and sometimes fractions of Malbec and Souzão. The ageing programme can be anything from 13 months to nearly two years in Nevers small casks using 50% new barrels and the balance second fill. The 1986 is superb and the 1987 is very promising and might well be more drinkable earlier than the 1986. The 1988 vintage looks like being another great.

82 ★★★★★ ready, will improve. **83** ★★★★ ready, will improve. **84** ★★★★★ not ready, age further. **85** ★★★★★ ready, will still improve. **86** ★★★★★ not ready, age further. **87** ★★★★★ not ready, age further. **88** ★★★★★ not ready, age further.

Klein Constantia

A Bordeaux Blend is eminent. Look out for it, it will be a stunner!

Kloofzicht Alter Ego★★★★E

The Tulbagh estate with its 5 ha vineyard has produced its first wine from the 1989 vintage – mainly Merlot with some Cabernet Sauvignon. It has deep rich colour, full nose, great concentrated fruit, and deep layers of flavour backed by good French oak. As good as it tastes now, another four to six years will allow it to reach full potential. An amazing red wine for a valley known for its whites.

KWV Cathedral Cellars★★★(★) (no price available)

This unlikely name is KWV's range of improved quality wines for export. Predominantly Cabernet (60%), with equal amounts of Merlot and Cabernet Franc. The first two vintages are the 1987 and 1988, with the latter the better. Both aged less than six months in new Nevers barrels. The grapes originate as far afield as Faure and Durbanville. The 1989, which is still to be released, is much better.

La Motte Estate Cabernet Sauvignon★★★★E

Although labelled Cabernet Sauvignon, the wines from 1986 onwards contain 15% or more Merlot. The first release was from the 1985 vintage and was released in 1990 from the revitalized Rupert-owned Estate. Lightish in colour, this Cabernet has deep, concentrated, intense cultivar character, lots of nose and good backing of new wood. The 1986 is a more rounded wine but both are good and will develop well. Cellar samples show vintages to come will be stunners.

La Motte Millenium★★★★D

A blend of more than 40% Merlot and Cabernet Sauvignon with lovely character, it is soft on the palate with deep, satisfying fruity flavours backed with good oak. The first release from the 1988 vintage was followed by an equally easy-drinking 1989. Should develop well over four to six years.

Landskroon Bouquet Rouge★★★(★)B

Originally a medium-bodied blend of Shiraz and the Estate's exceptional Cinsaut, this wine has a good, fruity bouquet. The first vintage, the 1978, has developed beautifully in the bottle and now needs to be enjoyed. The 1979 was given Superior certification and has developed much like the 1978, as has the 1980, and also need drinking. The 1981 has more Shiraz, less Cinsaut and a touch of Cabernet Sauvignon, changing the character considerably. It has developed very well and is probably at its best now. The 1982 and 1983 releases are blends of 60% Shiraz and 40% Cinsaut and have softened amazingly well in the bottle yet still seem to have lots of life. The 1987 is equal proportions of Cabernet Sauvignon, Cabernet Franc and Merlot, aged for eight months in small wood, giving yet another very interesting wine under this label. The 1988 is half Cabernet and the balance equal quantities of Cabernet Franc and Merlot, and has enough tannin to develop well. It is, however, no longer available, having given way to the estate's Premier Reserve.

78 ★★★★ ready, drink up. **79** ★★★(★) ready, drink up. **80** ★★★(★) ready, drink. **81** ★★★(★) ready. **82** ★★★(★) ready. **83** ★★★(★) ready. **84** no release. **85** no release. **86** no release. **87** ★★★★ ready. **88** ★★★ ready.

Landskroon Premiere Reserve★★★(★)D

Changed from the Bouquet Rouge label with the 1988 vintage. The Bouquet Rouge from 1987 has equal quantities of Cabernet Sauvignon, Cabernet Franc and Merlot, aged for eight months in small wood to give a medium-bodied wine with light texture that has developed well over a short time. The 1988, released under the new label, has somewhat subdued character from a blend of half Cabernet Sauvignon and almost equal quantities of Cabernet Franc and Merlot for the balance. Good tannins should allow reasonable development. There have been no subsequent releases.

L'Ormarins Optima Reserve★★★★(★)F

The 1987 is a beautiful Bordeaux blend of Cabernet Sauvignon and Cabernet Franc with Merlot. Good fruit, nice spice, fine oak and lots of all. Will age beautifully.

Meerlust Red★★★★D

A second label from this famous red wine estate. Very similar to the Rubicon style, but from the 1985 vintage, which was not considered up to quality to carry the Rubicon label. Developing very well.

Meerlust Rubicon★★★★★E

A consistently excellent blend of Cabernet Sauvignon, Cabernet Franc and Merlot. The first vintage was 1980: a lovely, soft, full-flavoured wine of great complexity which developed well in the bottle and now needs to be enjoyed. The 1981 and 1982 seem to be even better than the original and will help to confirm that this is one of the best of South Africa's new-style reds. The 1983 does not contain Cabernet Franc and is showing well. The 1984 is drinking well but will be even better with time. It contains the Cabernet that was champion red at the Stellenbosch Young Wine Show and South African champion red at the Goodwood Show. Despite how good I thought cellar samples of the 1985 Rubicon were, the Estate's stringent quality parameters kept them from releasing it as they reckoned it just wasn't good enough. Instead they followed well-proven Bordeaux practice and released the wine under a second label (Meerlust Red) at a lower price. The 1986 more than makes up for the missing vintage with its magnificence. More Cabernet Sauvignon than usual, some 70%, and more Merlot at 20%, but less Cabernet Franc at about 10%. The 1987 is really super wine.

80 ★★★★ ready. **81** ★★★★★ ready. **82** ★★★★★ ready, will still improve. **83** ★★★★(★) ready. **84** ★★★★★ ready, will still improve. **85** no release. **86** ★★★★ not ready, age further. **87** ★★★★(★) not ready, age further.

Nederburg Private Bin R109★★★★E
A garnet-coloured wine with good depth of flavour from the 1985 vintage. A blend of almost 50/50 Cabernet Sauvignon and Merlot which spent time in large oak. Some 420 cases were sold for the first time at the 1989 Nederburg Auction. This is a lovely wine that will be at its best in the mid 1990s. The next release from the 1986 vintage sold at the 1991 and 1992 Nederburg Auctions. It is deep, full, soft wine that drinks very well right now but will still develop in the bottle over another four to six years.

85 ★★★★ ready to drink, will still improve. **86** ★★★★ ready to drink, will still improve.

Neil Ellis Reserve Selection★★★★D
The 1987 is the first release of this super wine. It is a delicious, full-flavoured New World wine in Bordeaux-blend style. It is 62% Cabernet Sauvignon, 30% Merlot, 8% Cabernet Franc, and is beginning to show well early in 1991. Good attractive nose with lots of oak showing together with good fruit. Keep with patience as it should develop much more.

Overgaauw D C Classic★★★★D
A deep, rich wine bottled for the Cape Independent Winemakers' Guild Auction. It usually comprises mainly Merlot and 20% Cabernet Franc with lots of wood-ageing. ('DC' are the initials of wine maker Braam van Velden's dad, Dawid Conradie.) 30 to 50 cases are sold each year. Collector's stuff!

Overgaauw Tria Corda★★★★★E
One of the Cape's first Bordeaux blends with the 1981 vintage. It was made up of Cabernet Sauvignon, with Merlot providing the balance. The Estate previously made good individual wines from these cultivars and now, in blending and good oak ageing, seems to have consistently brought out the best in both, resulting in one of the Cape's most popular Bordeaux blends. The 1981 did exceptionally well at the 1982 South African Championship Young Wine Show. The Merlot content has been increased over the years, reaching 34% in 1983. With the 1984 vintage, however, Cabernet Franc was added, resulting in a composition of 62% Cabernet Sauvignon, 22% Cabernet Franc and 16% Merlot. Since 1985 the blend has been more or less 60 – 65% Cabernet Sauvignon, 20% Cabernet Franc, and 15% Merlot, giving finer wines than before. All the vintages have developed well.

81 ★★★★ ready. **82** ★★★★★ ready. **83** ★★★★★ ready. **84** ★★★★★ ready, will improve. **85** ★★★★(★) ready, will still improve. **86** ★★★★★ not ready, age further. **87** ★★★★ not ready, age further. **88** ★★★★★ not ready, age further.

Paddamanel (Paddagang Vignerons)★★(★)C
A full-bodied, dry red with Cabernet and Merlot.

Pick 'n Pay Meritage★★★(★)D
From 1988 vintage comes a fine blend of Cabernet Sauvignon, Cabernet Franc and Merlot. Well-balanced wine with good tannin that will allow good bottle development.

Rozendal★★★★★C
From 1986 onwards this wine no longer contains Cinsaut, although that year was a blend of 50/50 Cabernet Sauvignon and Merlot and is a great wine, achieving a gold at the International Wine and Spirit Competition. It is developing well in the bottle. The 1987 is mainly

Merlot with 15% Cabernet Sauvignon and 5% Cabernet Franc. It has beautiful berry flavours, is medium-bodied, yet has good tannin. There was no 1988. 1989 remains mainly Merlot with the balance, Cabernet Sauvignon. Although concentrated now, it will develop well.

Rustenberg Gold★★★★★E

The first release, from the 1985 vintage, was 55% Merlot, 25% Cabernet Franc and 20% Cabernet Sauvignon. It is a lovely, medium-bodied wine, full of fine flavours. The 1986 is a much bigger wine, comprising 60% Cabernet and the balance, equal amounts of Merlot and Cabernet Franc. It was rated highly by visiting authorities for the New World Wine Auction and those of the Nederburg Auction. The 1987 is the same blend as the 1986 and another big wine. The 1988 is also magnificent wine.

85 ★★★★★ ready, will develop. **86** ★★★★★ not ready, age further. **87** ★★★★★ not ready, age further. **88** ★★★★★ not ready, age further.

Rust-en-Vrede★★★★★E

Simply carrying the name of the Estate, this label will be given to the Estate's finest wine of each vintage, so the product could vary dramatically. The first release, from 1986 vintage, is 75% Cabernet and 25% Merlot, with lots of good new oak. It is packed with penetrating aromas and berry flavours. There was no 1987 vintage, but this was more than made up for with a magnificent 1988 which is 75% Cabernet Sauvignon, 10% Merlot and 15% Shiraz. It has been aged in special thin Bordeaux barriques that have given a decided Bordeaux character to the wine. A beautiful wine in every way. It drinks very well now but should develop unbelievable character.

Saxonburg Novum★★★(★)E

Brash, but attractive young wine from 1990 with good berry character and hard tannins. 50% Cabernet Sauvignon, 25% Cabernet Franc and 25% Merlot. It will need time to soften.

Talana Hill Royale★★★★E

The first release from the 1988 vintage numbered only 530 cases. It is made from 50% Cabernet Sauvignon, 37% Merlot and 13% Cabernet Franc and was aged for 16 months in small French oak. It is a good firm wine with New World wine character, fine flavours and good oak backing. It would be a pity to drink it at this early age when it shows so much potential for development, so give it another five to eight years for a real treat. The 1989 is bigger and better, but will need longer to develop.

Vergenoegd★★★★D

A 1988 Bordeaux Blend of Cabernet Sauvignon, Cabernet Franc and Merlot, aged in French oak. It will be a very different wine to the Estate's traditional style.

Villiera Estate Crû Monro★★★★D

Traditionally, Monro is the middle name of the men of the Grier family who own Villiera and has been given to the red and the white flagship wines of the Estate. The first release of the red is from the 1984 vintage and is a blend of 60% Cabernet Sauvignon and 40% Merlot, which is aged in small French wood and then aged for a further 10 months in the bottle before being released. It is a very good blend which is beginning to show its full potential. A further selection of this wine is made from the best barrels and is bottled for the Independent Winemakers' Guild Auction under the label 'Private

Reserve'. An excellent wine, it needs time to show its potential. The second release from the 1985 vintage is particularly good considering the generally light vintage. The 1986, a blend of 60% Cabernet and 40% Merlot, is developing beautifully. The 1988 puts this wine firmly in the ranks of South Africa's best Bordeaux-type blends. At the time of writing, the 1990 is available and maintains the top quality. However, time should allow it to develop to its full potential.

Vriesenhof Kallista★★★★(★)C

Destined to be Jan 'Boland' Coetzee's best blend and most prestigious wine, Kallista is blended in varying proportions to take the best each vintage has to offer. The first release was from the 1984 vintage and is predominantly Cabernet Sauvignon (88%). The balance is Merlot aged in small Nevers oak, yielding a fine wine that will be accessible earlier than the Vriesenhof Cabernet. The 1985 release has 25% Merlot, making it a much softer wine, while the 1986 has greater character intensity. The 1987 Merlot content is 30%, Cabernet Franc 10% and Cabernet Sauvignon 60%. It has lovely berry flavours and is almost sweet. The 1987 has developed beautifully and is truly a five-star wine although it still needs more time. The 1988 continues the same style but is not showing its best yet; these wines all need plenty of time to develop. It is sold at the Independent Winemakers' Guild Auction and for export. The 1989 is made up of over one third Merlot blended with Cabernet Sauvignon.

84 ★★★★(★) ready. **85** ★★★★ ready. **86** ★★★★(★) ready, will still improve. **87** ★★★★★(★) not ready, age further. **88**★★★★ allow to age. **89** ★★★★★ needs time to develop.

Warwick Trilogy★★★★★E

The first release, from the 1986 vintage, is a blend of 70% Cabernet Sauvignon, 23% Merlot and 7% Cabernet Franc. This is a beautiful wine, matured for 18 months in small oak, half new and half second fill. Norma Ratcliffe tries to use natural methods wherever possible with her wine making, does no filtration and refines only with egg white. A special Trilogy Reserve – with more Merlot – was prepared for the New World Wine Auction, resulting in a wine that was ready to drink much earlier than non-NWWA wine. The 1987 is equally good and packed with developing flavours. Cellar samples of the 1988 show a fuller-flavoured yet softer wine than the previous two vintages. It contains 75% Cabernet, 15% Merlot and 10% Cabernet Franc and will drink well when released, but should be allowed time, six to eight years more, to develop full potential. The 1989 is the same blend as the 1986 but a much richer wine, soft on the palate and more accessible earlier.

86 ★★★★(★) ready, will still improve. **87** ★★★★ ready, will still improve. **88** ★★★★★ not ready, allow time. **89** ★★★★★ not ready, will develop ahead of 88.

Welgemeend★★★★★C

A multiple blend dominated by Cabernet Sauvignon, with Cabernet Franc, Merlot, Petit Verdot and Malbec playing lesser roles. From the 1986 vintage onwards Malbec was dropped from the blend. Early vintages show well, with fine wood treatment adding to the overall dimension of the wine. It will need time in the bottle to mellow, but the wait will be worthwhile. Each vintage has shown improvement: the 1982 is five-star material, as is the 1983, which is by far the softest of the wines to date. The 1984 is a rich, full, powerful wine while the 1985 is somewhat reserved. The 1986 is a magnificent wine. The 1987 is half Cabernet Sauvignon, some 24% Cabernet Franc, and Merlot making up the rest with a fraction of Petit Verdot. The result is a deep, full-flavoured wine with great character backed by good wood and is well worth ageing. The 1988 is much the same blend, although the 1987 does not have quite the same depth. The 1989 is as stylish as ever and drinks remarkably well already – but have resolve and allow it to age and develop. The same goes for the 1990.

82 ★★★★★ ready. **83** ★★★★★ ready. **84** ★★★★★ ready, will still improve. **85** ★★★★★ not ready, age further. **86** ★★★★★ not ready, age further. **87** ★★★★★ not ready, age further. **88** ★★★★(★) not ready, age further. **89** ★★★★★ not ready, age further. **90** ★★★★★ not ready, age further.

Welgemeend Douelle★★★★C

This is an intriguing blend of Cabernet Sauvignon and Malbec which develops well in the bottle. The 1987 is the best yet – deep and rich, but easy drinking. The 1988 and 1989 have a good range of flavours but are not quite up to the 1987. All are good value. No 1990.

85 ★★★ ready. **86** ★★★★ ready. **87** ★★★★ ready, will still improve. **88** ★★★(★) ready, will still improve. **89** ★★★(★) drinkable, but will improve.

Woolworths Cabernet Sauvignon-Merlot★★★★(★)D

An excellent blend of 70% Cabernet Sauvignon and 30% Merlot from the 1990 vintage. Lovely deep colour and great depth of flavour. Will benefit from a further four to six years in the bottle. Made by Neil Ellis.

Woolworths Grand Rouge★★★★C

Made in the La Motte cellars from the 1991 vintage and a blend of about 60% Cabernet Sauvignon and balance Merlot and Cabernet Franc. Good fruity nose, fine flavours and long finish. Good value.

Woolworths Le Cinquieme 895R★★★★D

Part of the Woolworths' Vintage Collection. 89 denotes the vintage; 5, the fifth in the range and R is for red. From the La Motte cellar, this wine is a blend of Merlot and Cabernet Sauvignon. Good character, nice tannin and long finish. Drinks very well now and has great development potential.

Woolworths Le Premier 881R★★★★D

Part of the Woolworths' Vintage Collection. The number 88 indicates the vintage, the 1 indicates the first release, and the R is for red. It is made up of about half Cabernet Franc and the balance Cabernet Sauvignon and Merlot from the cellars of Warwick. Fruity nose, deep flavour, good oak backing. Good to drink now, but has the potential to age over six to eight years.

Woolworths Rubato★★★(★)B

The 1987 is a blend of 60% Merlot and 40% Cabernet Sauvignon, with a good nose, full flavour and good oak. This is followed by a very good four-star 1988. Excellent value for money and decidedly good drinking at early age. It should develop well over four to five years. Has been discontinued.

Zevenwacht★★★★★E

From 1987 the vintage has decided New World character. It is full, rich wine from new clone Cabernet Sauvignon, Cabernet Franc and Merlot. It should age with interest.

Cape Traditional Blends

Aan-de-Doorns Dry Red★★B
The 1986 was a class winner at the Worcester Show. This blend of Pinotage and Cabernet develops well and is at its best after three years in the bottle. Next release is 50/50 Cinsaut and Pinotage. Deep colour, fruity, unwooded red.

Alto Rouge★★★(★)C
One of the aristocrats of South African traditional blends but one which might well move from this section to the Bordeaux blends. Until 1985 it was usually a blend of Cabernet, Shiraz and Tinta Barocca, although the proportions varied with the vintage. However, in 1985 the blend changed to include Cabernet Franc and Merlot, and had a much-reduced Shiraz content. In the future it may become a blend of Bordeaux cultivars. It would be a shame to see this great Traditional blend completely lost to the Bordeaux style. The wines of the 1970s all developed well over 12 – 15 years with the 1987 (to my mind) being the best and still very good in 1992. The wines of the 1980s have varied in character and style with a major change in blend for 1985. The 1984 is developing well and the 1985 is drinking very well now. The 1986 still needs time to develop its full potential while the 1987 drinks well now and is considered to be one of the best wines from Alto's cellar. It will be well worth ageing another five to eight years. The 1989 is a beautiful wine full of everything; rich and full with big 13,5% alcohol and will develop over the years.

75 ★★★★ drink up. **76** ★★★★★ ready. **77** ★★★ past its best, drink up. **78** ★★★★★ ready, will still improve. **79** ★★★ ready. **80** ★★★★ ready, will still improve. **81** ★★★★ ready. **82** ★★★★(★) ready, will still improve. **83** ★★★ ready. **84** ★★★★ ready, will still improve. **85** ★★★★ ready, will still develop. **86** ★★★★(★) not ready, age further. **87** ★★★★(★) not ready, age further. **88** ★★★★ not ready, age further. **89** ★★★★ not ready, age further.

Altydgedacht Dry Red★★★B
A most attractive wine from Merlot and Gamay, which makes excellent drinking wine. Must become a winner at very good value.

Backsberg Dry Red★★★B
Consistently one of the Cape's best value for money wines, if not the Cape's best wine bargain. The blend varies to cater for the vintage but always gives a lighter than medium wine with good flavours. Although ready for drinking at the time of release, it is worth keeping for a year or more. It develops well in the bottle, giving nice softness and a pleasant fruity nose. The blend always contains Cabernet Sauvignon, but has also included Shiraz, Pinotage, Pinot Noir, and even Merlot. The 1991 is as delightful as always and is an any-occasion, light, drinkable wine.

Bellingham Classic Thirteen★★★C
A light, blended dry red wine made of 13 different varieties, including Steen, but none of them commanding more than 20% (the second release does, in fact, have 20%). Six of the varieties are Port types. The first release, in 1985, was not vintage-dated and this procedure has been followed with subsequent releases. However, each release is easily recognized by the Roman numeral in the gable window on the label. The first had 'I', the second 'II', the third 'III' and so on.

They all age well over three to five years. Besides being a blend of many cultivars, the age of the wines used can vary by as much as five years, although number IV is mainly from the 1987 vintage.

Blaauwklippen Red Landau★★★C

An interesting wine, the components of which have changed over the years. Originally the blend comprised Zinfandel, Pinotage, Cinsaut and a little Cabernet Sauvignon. Since then the blend has varied with great interest and has always been good value for money. The 1988 is super with over 60% Cabernet, 30% Merlot and the balance Zinfandel. It is lovely for early drinking but will age with benefit. 1989 follows the same lines.

80 ★★★ ready. **81** no release. **82** ★★★ ready. **83** ★★★ ready. **84** ★★★(★) ready. **85** no release. **86** ★★★★ ready, will still improve. **87** ★★★(★) ready, will still improve. **88** ★★★★ ready, will still improve. **89** ★★★★ ready, will still improve.

Boplaas Dry Red★★B

This is a blend of a number of varieties which usually contains some Cabernet and Shiraz and others, all aged in small wood, giving an attractive deep red wine with a good nose and full, fruity flavours.

Bon Vino Red (Bolandse Co-op)★★★A

This is a very good attempt at keeping the price of good drinking wine at affordable levels. The cellar has three wines in 500 m*l* screw-top bottles of which this red is a blend of Cabernet, Shiraz and Cinsaut, giving a well-flavoured, easy-drinking wine.

Boschendal Lanoy★★★(★)C

The first release was the 1979 blend of Cabernet and Shiraz. The 1980 was much the same, but subsequent vintages have contained more Merlot. The 1988, 1989 and 1990 are fuller, showing more Cabernet character. The wines of the early-middle 1980s seem to have reached their best in four to five years. The 1988, 1989 and 1990, however, will age longer.

79 ★★★ past its best. **80** ★★★ drink up. **81**★★★ past its best. **82** ★★★(★) ready. **83** ★★★(★) ready. **84** ★★★★(★) ready. **85** ★★★ ready. **86** ★★★(★) ready. **87** ★★★(★) ready. **88** ★★★(★) ready, will still improve **89** ★★★(★) ready, will still improve. **90** ★★★(★) ready, will still improve.

Bottelary Co-op Adelrood★★★A

Earlier releases were easy-drinking, inexpensive blends in which Pinotage gave pleasant, refreshing fruitiness. Later bottlings have been a great improvement. It is basically a blend of various vintages of unwooded Cabernet and some Pinotage.

Cantori Vino Rosso (Gilbeys)★★★B

This is Gilbeys' Italian-style red. I'm not so sure this qualifies for the Traditional section, but it does contain some Cabernet and Cinsaut plus a good amount of mature Shiraz. On account of these three, it must qualify. The odd grape is Grenache. The combination gives a very drinkable, flavourful non-vintaged wine, and is packed in an attractive Italian-style, cork-closed bottle.

Cape Selection Grand Vin Rouge (Pick 'n Pay)★★A/B

A very typical traditional blend of Shiraz, Pinotage and Cabernet resulting in a softish, easy-drinking dry red.

Carnival Dry Red (Spar)★★A

An easy-drinking blend of Tinta Barocca and Cinsaut with a touch of Cabernet.

Chateau Libertas (SFW)★★★(★)B
The grandfather of South African blended reds, Chateau Libertas celebrated 50 years on the market in 1982 and will celebrate its 60th anniversary at the end of 1992. In 1985 it gained the Monde Selection gold award with palm leaves, the logical culmination of honours won consistently over the 50-year period, though it struggled through a comparatively indifferent patch while it was part of the Taskelder range. With the 1987 vintage, it regained all its former glory on reappearance under its own label, and recent blends are comparable to the legendary wines of the 1930s and 1940s. The 1982 was very good, but the 1983 has been much lighter, in character with the vintage. The 1984 was the best of the decade when released and at the age of four it was excellent value for money. It received Superior certification in 1988. Although modern techniques allow it to be drunk when young, it ages superbly. The 1985 is a much lighter wine which has improved dramatically since its release. The 1986 is a very good wine and has developed well. The 1987 is a very good wine but with a small amount of Merlot and Cabernet Franc being included in the blend this is another old favourite in danger of losing its identity. This should not be allowed to happen. The 1988 is a lovely wine and will develop with great benefit. It has a meaningful amount of Merlot which changes the character of this very traditional wine. Chateau Libertas often came onto the market without Superior rating, but later labelings usually gained this controversial certification which has now been done away with. A limited number of magnums are issued some two years after the 750 m*l* bottlings. The first release was from the 1978 vintage.

78 ★★★★ ready. **79** ★★★ ready. **80** ★★★ ready. **81** ★★★★ ready. **82** ★★★★ ready. **83** ★★★ ready. **84** ★★★★ ready, will still improve. **85** ★★★ ready, will still improve. **86** ★★★★ ready, will still improve. **87** ★★★★ ready, will still improve. **88** ★★★★ not ready, age further.

Claridge Red Wellington★★★(★)C
This is a big alcoholic wine (14%) made up of 50% Cabernet Sauvignon, 30% Merlot and the balance Cabernet Franc.

Delaire Cuvée Rouge★★★B
This was originally a dry blend of Cabernet Sauvignon and a touch of Pinotage, with wood-ageing showing strongly soon after it was released. Fairly light and definitely pleasant when young, it developed into a satisfying wine over 12 – 18 months. The second release was better, a combination of almost 50% Cabernet, 40% Pinotage and the balance Merlot, produced from the 1988 vintage. The 1989 has decided Pinotage character which is not surprising in that it is 85% Pinotage with only 15% Cabernet. The 1990 is a well-made wine with good oak backing. The 1991 is just as drinkable.

Delheim Dry Red★★★A
Over the years this non-vintaged blend has undergone many changes but has always been a worthwhile buy and very rewarding if kept for a year or two in the bottle. Latest blends are well-made, good-flavoured, easy-drinking wines, predominantly Pinotage but often contain 10% or so Cabernet Sauvignon or Cabernet Franc.

De Zoete Inval Grand Rouge★★A
A full-flavoured, fruity, dry red with unusual flavours, this is a blend of Cabernet Sauvignon and Cinsaut. The 1986 is still available.

Douglas Green St Augustine★★★(★)C
A fine blend of Shiraz, Pinotage, Tinta Barocca and, more recently, increasing quantities of Cabernet Sauvignon. However, no varietal dominates. It is wood-aged for almost two years in large old vats so the wood is not too apparent, although it has obviously done its work in bringing the wine together. It develops well over the years. The 1988 is a full-flavoured wine in traditional style that should develop well over the next seven to nine years.

77★★(★) ready, drink up. **78★★★** ready, drink up. **79★★★** ready, drink up. **80★★★★** ready. **81★★★(★)** ready. **82★★★★** ready. **83 ★★★(★)** ready. **84★★★★** ready. **85★★★** ready. **86★★★(★)** ready, will still improve. **87★★★(★)** ready. **88★★★(★)** not ready, age further.

Drostdy-Hof Claret Select (Oude Meester)★★A
A smooth, off-dry, wood-aged blend of many cultivars, including Cabernet, Pinotage, Shiraz and Tinta Barocca, resulting in a pleasant, easy-drinking red.

Edward Snell Special Reserve Dry Red★★★B
This is an unusual blend of Cabernet Sauvignon, Pinotage and Pinot Noir, medium-bodied, soft in the mouth with good finish. It will develop well over a year or two. It is not vintaged, so mark the label.

Goue Vallei Chianti (Citrusdal Co-op)★★B
A wine that has reappeared on the market after a break of a few years. It was originally Grenache but is now a wood-aged blend containing 60% Grenache, 30% Cinsaut and the balance Cabernet. The latest blend also contains some Tinta Barocca. This is a big, powerful wine that is surprisingly smooth and fruity.

Groot Constantia Heerenrood★★★(★)D
Heerenrood was introduced to the range of famous Constantia reds with the 1975 vintage. This first making, blended from at least four cultivars, was a well-balanced wine of fine maturing promise. It was not considered a success, however, and from 1976 onwards it has been made from more-or-less equal quantities of Cabernet Sauvignon and Shiraz, the quantities varying with the vintage. Despite the apparent potential, the earlier vintages never really lived up to expectation. The Estate invested in new wood which, along with the higher proportion of Shiraz, resulted in the 1984 being distinctly better. The 1985 developed rapidly, but the 1986 had the deepest character when released and is developing well. The 1987 is a richer, fuller wine with good wood backing and should improve with great benefit well into the late 1990s. The 1988 is 50/50 Cabernet and Shiraz and is good, full wine.

80 ★★★ ready. **81 ★★★** ready. **82 ★★★(★)** ready. **83 ★★★** ready. **84 ★★★★** ready, will still improve. **85 ★★★** ready. **86 ★★★** ready, will improve. **87★★★** ready, will improve.

Groot Constantia Rood★★★B
After I had described this non-vintage wine in the first Wine Buyer's Guide as a good braai wine, the wine maker, Pieter du Toit, responded by sending me six bottles of the product and a bag of braai wood. His driver deposited both outside my office and at the end of the day when I left for home the braai wood had been 'taken' but the wine left behind! It was a rugged blend of Cabernet Sauvignon, Shiraz and Pinotage, the good Constantia Shiraz showing through quite distinctly. A few years in the bottle makes it well worth the

wait. Not usually vintage-dated, except for the 1984 vintage. The addition of Merlot and Cabernet Franc, and 18 months in new Yugoslavian wood have resulted in a totally different wine. The bottling from the 1986 vintage is also atypical, as it is a Bordeaux-style blend aged in Nevers oak – a very different red. There was no 1987, but a very acceptable 1988 was developed from equal quantities of Cabernet Franc and Shiraz with Cabernet Sauvignon and Merlot making up the balance. It is already very good drinking, but it should still develop with benefit over four years.

Hartenberg Bin 9★★★C

A non-vintaged dry red blend sold only at the farm, and always a full-flavoured, bold wine with the original containing well-aged Cabernet, Shiraz and Tinta Barocca. Although not vintaged, there was a particularly interesting release from the 1987 vintage which was 40% each Cabernet and the unusual cultivar Pontac. The balance is Shiraz, all backed with a bit of good oak. The 1989 followed the same make-up but is a better wine. It is good value for money and well worth maturing for a couple of years.

Hartenberg Paragon★★★(★)E

This wine succeeds the estate's Premium Red Blend that was mainly an export wine with small amounts released locally. The 1986 is still available and is predominantly Cabernet (60%), with Shiraz (30%) and the balance of 10% Pontac from the Estate's more than 40-year-old Pontac vines. This is a most unusual blend that had two years in oak to bring it all together. The previous release was 1984. Good, strong flavours are evident. The blend may not be repeated for a while as the old Pontac vineyard is being replanted.

Helderberg Co-op Vin Rouge★★★A

This wine replaced the Co-op's Dry Red and Special Red. The blend has varied with the years, the latest being a strange mixture of Cabernet, Cinsaut, Merlot and Pinot Noir. This gives a pleasant-flavoured, medium-bodied wine that drinks well but will also develop with a year or two in the bottle.

Kanonkop Kadette Rooiwyn★★B

Described by the wine maker as 'informal' wine which should be served chilled, this is a well-flavoured, good-value-for-money blend that varies from vintage to vintage, and has included Pinotage, Cabernet Sauvignon and Cinsaut, aged for three months in new oak. The 1989 is 20% Cabernet and the balance equal quantities of Pinotage and Pinot Noir. It has developed well in the bottle over the past two years. Regrettably the 1989 is the last vintage.

Kleindal Cuvée Rouge★★B

A good, well-flavoured wine that makes for enjoyable early drinking, yet has potential to improve after a year or more in the bottle. This blend varies with the vintage, although the wine is non-vintaged, but is predominantly Pinotage with Cabernet and Shiraz.

Kleindal Roodewyn★★★(★)C

From the 1989 vintage comes a good character Cabernet-based blend with Pinotage.

Koelenberg (Koelenhof Co-op)★★★A

This is a fruity, dry blend containing Cabernet Sauvignon. It is most suitable for casual occasions and good value for money.

Laborie (KWV)★★★C

The first vintage of this wine was the 1979. It was deep in colour with considerable Cabernet character, and, although blended with Pinotage, Shiraz and Tinta Barocca, the individual cultivars were not discernible. Originally somewhat severe, it has softened with age, yet it still has to reach its best. The 1980 is a much softer wine and the 1981 showed a disturbing browning within six years of age. The 1983 has developed a rich but curious character, attractive to some people but not to others. The next release will be the 1987.

Laborie Taillefert (KWV)★★★D

A wine from the same cellar as Laborie and of much the same blend – Cabernet Sauvignon, Shiraz, Pinotage and Cabernet Franc – but with a very different result. Medium-bodied, it lacks fruit but has good wood and is reasonably smooth on the palate. The 1984 has been a bit disappointing as it has aged, but the 1983 shows fresher wood and has developed well. It featured at the 1990 Nederburg Auction. The 1985 is a better wine showing good oaking; a fuller wine with cleaner Cabernet character. Next release is the 1987.

Lievland Lievlander★★★B

Originally a delightfully bright, easy-drinking wine made from Cinsaut with some Cabernet. The blend varies with the vintage but is a *vin ordinaire* with 'class' and excellent value for money.

Nederburg Baronne★★★(★)C

The first four vintages of Baronne – 1973, 1974, 1975 and 1976 – varied considerably but were all excellent wines and have matured magnificently. A very definite style of wine has now emerged, not far removed from the Nederburg Selected Cabernets of old, which were reputed to be blends containing predominantly Cabernet and lesser quantities of Shiraz, Pinotage and Cinsaut. Whatever the composition, the result is a fine, full-flavoured, deep-red wine which is acceptable when young but has every potential for fine ageing. This wine has very good berry-like aroma and flavour, and will bring true delight if aged for five years or more. The 1976 vintage was very good, as was the 1979. The 1980 and 1981 have proved their early potential and are excellent now. The 1984 is a fuller wine and is tremendous in 1991. The 1985 is more austere and needs drinking. The 1986 is bigger, fuller and better than previous vintages and will develop well. The 1987 drinks very well at this early age and may peak earlier than previous vintages. The 1988 is fine, full wine.

73 ★★★★★ drink up. **74** ★★★★★ ready. **75** ★★★ drink up. **76** ★★★★ ready. **77** ★★★ drink up. **78** ★★★★ ready. **79** ★★★(★) ready. **80** ★★★★ ready. **81** ★★★ ready. **82** ★★★★ ready. **83** ★★★ ready. **84** ★★★★ ready. **85** ★★★(★) ready. **86** ★★★★ ready. **87**★★★(★) ready, will still develop. **88** ★★★★ ready, will still develop.

Nederburg Edelrood★★★★C

Edelrood is a top-quality, dry red in which no particular variety shows, but as a harmonious whole it is hard to beat. Originally launched as an uncomplicated, pleasant dry table wine of light body and acid with moderate tannin, recent vintages have taken on a more definite and demanding style: it is now a wine to be reckoned with and one that needs time to show its best. The 1979, 1980, 1981, 1982, 1983, 1984, 1985 and 1986 vintages carry Superior certification and have been major award winners in many overseas competitions. Edelrood ages extremely well and is destined to be the best of Nederburg's regular range. The 1988 is very good.

78 ★★★★★ drink. 79 ★★★★★ drink. 80 ★★★★★ ready. 81 ★★★★ ready. 82 ★★★★ ready. 83 ★★★★ ready. 84 ★★★★ ready. 85 ★★★★ ready. 86 ★★★★ ready, will still improve. 87 ★★★★ ready, will improve. 88 ★★★★ ready, will improve.

Nederburg Private Bin R115★★★★(★)E

Originally a light, elegant blend of almost equal quantities of Shiraz and Cabernet Sauvignon and although a traditional Cape blend, it was done in a style new to the Cape. The first release, from the 1980 vintage, was launched at the 1986 Nederburg Auction and the 1981 and the 1982 were sold at the 1987 and 1988 Auctions respectively. The Cabernet Sauvignon, not the Shiraz, has been wood-aged, giving a light, red wine, full of flavour and beautiful bouquet. The 1982 is a bigger wine and requires more time to soften than the earlier vintages. The dark-purple 1983 needs time to develop and will probably reach its best in the mid-1990s. The 1984, sold at the 1991 Auction, is very fruity and although very drinkable now, still has the ability to develop. The 1985 at the 1992 Auction is fine wine; good to drink now, but will still develop for a few years.

80 ★★★★ ready. 81 ★★★★ ready. 82 ★★★★★ ready. 83 ★★★★ ready. 84 ★★★★(★) ready, will still improve. 85 ★★★(★) ready, will still improve.

Nederburg Private Bin R103★★★★★E

One of the classic South African red wines and a worthy successor to the much-vaunted Nederburg Selected Cabernets of pre-Wine of Origin days. Exceptionally smooth, it is bold and dry with good Cabernet character touched off with Shiraz and Cinsaut – the traditional South African blend. This is a rich, glowing wine which needs plenty of ageing (10 or more years) to bring it to its best. The 1976 vintage is magnificent yet still has considerable life to come. It is sold only at the Nederburg Auction. The vintages released to date have been 1975, 1976, 1978, 1979, 1980, 1981 and 1982. The last three vintages are magnificent wines and will probably develop longer than any of the previous vintages. The 1982 is particularly good and demanded higher average prices at the 1991 Auction than previous vintages. The 1983 sold at 1992 Auction is excellent to drink now, and over the next two to three years.

75 ★★★★★ drink. 76 ★★★★★ drink. 77 no release. 78 ★★★★★ ready. 79 ★★★★★ ready. 80 ★★★★★ ready. 81 ★★★★★ ready. 82 ★★★★★ ready, will still develop. 83 ready, will still develop.

Neethlingshof Lord Neethling Rouge★★★(★)D

The 1983 is an interesting blend of equal proportions of Tinta Barocca and Cabernet Sauvignon, aged in new small oak. It should age with benefit. The 1984 is disappointing (just three stars) and has not shown the class of the 1983 vintage. The 1986 is a major improvement with lots of flavour. The 1987 is the best to date and four-star, and with the good quality developments at this cellar, this should be a wine to watch in the future.

Oude Nektar Grand Vin★★★(★)C

The 1989 is a good value for money wine with good character and potential. It is made from Cabernet Sauvignon and Shiraz.

Paddarotti (Paddagang Vignerons)★★C

More fun from Paddagang. A good, full-bodied red in which Pinotage features along with some Cabernet.

Pick 'n Pay Dry Red★★★B
A good-flavoured, good-drinking wine from 1990 made by Lievland. It is a blend of Cinsaut, Cabernet and Shiraz, with good oak backing. Soft and good to drink now and over the next few years.
Rooderust★★★B
A medium-bodied, oak-aged wine blended from a number of varieties including Cabernet Sauvignon and Shiraz. The 1979 carries Superior certification. The 1981 has probably reached its limit.
Roodeberg (KWV)★★★(no price available)
A wine with a remarkable reputation as it is available only to wine farmers and for export. Recent vintages show considerable change away from the old-fashioned 'Dikvoet' style (this applies especially to the 1984. The blend contains at least four varieties – Cabernet, Shiraz, Pinotage, Tinta Barocca – but seldom does any one exceed 25%. Regrettably, the 1985 does not have the quality of the 1984. More recent vintages are better with the 1987 and 1988 being a softer, more drinkable wine.
Roodendal Reserve★★★★C
From 1982 vintage comes a blend of Cabernet, Merlot and Shiraz aged in seven different oaks. A very different wine.
Roodezandt Roode Huiswyn★★(★)B
Originally a full, earthy blend of Cabernet Sauvignon and Tinta Barocca which needed ageing, the 1983 and 1984 are 100% Cabernet. The 1983 was light and made easy drinking, but now needs to be drunk up. The 1984 is very good in 1992. The 1986 reverted to the original blend of equal proportions of Cabernet Sauvignon and Tinta Barocca, and has developed well. The 1989 is a blend of Cinsaut and Tinta Barocca, which is light and fruity, making for easy drinking. The 1990 is a little more full in the mouth and should develop well in the bottle.
Rooiberg Co-op Roodewyn★★★A
An early-drinking, smooth blend originally of Cabernet Sauvignon, Pinotage and Tinta Barocca which has a good touch of wood. The 1983 was a very pleasant, elegant blend, the 1984 fuller and the 1985 light and definitely for early, but easy drinking. Since then, the 1986 and 1987 have been fuller, more concentrated wines with the 1988 a very good drinking wine. More recent wines are heading for Bordeaux blends. The 1990 contains both Cabernets, Merlot, Pinotage and good oak. When the Pinotage goes it will move category. Meanwhile it's a lovely wine.
Rustenberg Dry Red★★★★(★)C
Previously known as Rustenberg. A classic among South African wines, Rustenberg is always interesting and, given time in the bottle, rewards the taster with elegantly fine flavours. Traditionally, it comprises two-thirds Cabernet Sauvignon and one-third Cinsaut, blended at the crusher so that the combined cultivars ferment together. Softer and fruitier than many local reds, its excellence has brought it to many Nederburg Auctions. (A case of 1974 sold at the 1990 Auction for R7 100!) The 'odd' year vintages of the 1970s seem better than the 'even' years, but all are good. In the 1980s, quality continued to improve with each year, the 1980 to 1983 vintages seeming more elegant than their predecessors. The 1982 vintage is more full-bodied than the others and will need longer than the usual five to seven years to peak. The 1983 is a fine wine and the 1984 is

full of character with everything that rewards many years of patient ageing. The 1985 has full Cabernet character with lots of fruit and good wood-backing and is probably the last of the really 'old' style. With the ageing of the Cinsaut vineyards, lesser quantities of Cinsaut are being used and a typical blend would be 60% Cabernet Sauvignon, 20% Cinsaut and then 10% each of Cabernet Franc and Merlot. The 1987 is a slightly sterner wine; the 1988 a lovely soft, flavourful wine; the 1989 looking to be a decidedly Claret style.

78 ★★★★★ ready. **79** ★★★★ ready. **80** ★★★★★ ready. **81** ★★★★ ready. **82** ★★★★★ ready. **83** ★★★★ ready, will still improve. **84** ★★★★★ ready, will still improve. **85** ★★★★ ready, will still improve. **86** ★★★★★ ready, will still improve. **87** ★★★★ will need time to develop. **88** ★★★★ already drinking well, will still improve. **89** ★★★★ already drinking well, will still improve.

Rozendal★★★★C

The 1983 vintage is a blend of Cinsaut and Cabernet Sauvignon which has improved with time beyond all recognition. The 1984 contains more Cabernet and is showing better character at an earlier stage than the 1983, though it will need longer to develop its full potential. These two vintages have unusual character and show great promise. In subsequent vintages Merlot replaced Cinsaut. There was no release of a 1985. The 1986 is the first with Merlot.

Rusthof Dry Red (Mooiuitsig Wynkelders)★A

A medium-bodied, dry red blended from Cabernet and Pinotage.

Saxenburg Connoisseurs Blend★★★C

A wood-aged blend of Cabernet, Cinsaut and Tinta Barocca from the 1990 vintage. It needs some time to smooth out.

Simonsig Adelberg★★★(★)B

This good blend is usually made from Cabernet Sauvignon and Shiraz, and ages with reward. The 1983 vintage shows good potential while the purple-coloured 1984 is less woody. The 1985 is the most complex release, yet it is light and elegant. The 1986 was a little disappointing but the 1987 is a much fuller, fine-flavoured wine, while the 1988 is a fruitier, finer wine with good oak backing, as is the 1989. The 1990 and 1991 are fine wines and definitely four-star quality. They develop well over three to five years and are exceptional value for money.

Simonsvlei Co-op Simonsrood★★(★)A

This wine was formerly labelled Claret, and was a good example of a medium-bodied Cinsaut. It then became a Cinsaut-Pinotage blend with a short term in wood, giving better depth; then Cinsaut and Shiraz with some 10% Cabernet. The latest release contains a proportion of Zinfandel. A short period in large wood gives good drinking wine. It is available in either corked-closed bottles or in even less expensive screw-top bottles.

Springlands Classique Rouge (Vriesenhof)★★★B

A wine produced for Drop Inn by Vriesenhof and blended from Cabernet, Shiraz and some Merlot, giving a robust, full-flavoured dry red that is good value for money. Will develop well with time.

Swartland Co-op Dry Red★★★B

A good dry blend originally of Cinsaut, Tinta Barocca and Pinotage, with a touch of Cabernet. Nowadays the Cabernet content is up to 20%. Light, easy-drinking wine.

Tassenberg Reserve★★★C
Very good value blend of Cabernet Sauvignon, Merlot and Cinsaut with lots of flavour which should develop well over three to four years.
Valley Smooth Red (Gilbeys)★★A
A light-bodied, easy-drinking, off-dry red with a hint of Cabernet coming through the Cinsaut base.
Vaughan Johnson's House Red★★★★C
A typical, well-made traditional blend of reducing amounts of Cinsaut, Shiraz and Cabernet Sauvignon. It has full flavour, good nose, is easy drinking and good value for money.
Vredenheim 200★★B
A 1989 vintage released to commemorate the 200-year anniversary of the farm's homestead. A complex blend of Cabernet, Carignon, Shiraz and Tinta Barocca; a light, aromatic wine.
Waboomsrivier Co-op Roode Wagen★★A
Originally a Cabernet Sauvignon and Cinsaut blend of medium body with good depth of character, but now a mellow, early-drinking, wood-aged blend of equal proportions of, usually, Cabernet Sauvignon and Pinotage.
Warwick Femme Bleue★★★★E
A non-vintaged wine produced before Warwick certified their wines. It has developed very well and is now very much a collector's item.
Welmoed Co-op Rouge Sec★★★A
Originally an unusual blend of 75% Shiraz and 25% Pinotage, giving a pleasant dry red. It then became a blend of Shiraz and Pinotage, and nowadays is usually a blend of some 50% Cabernet and 25% each of Shiraz and Pinotage and aged more than a year in large oak. A good, easy-drinking wine with the ability to develop in the bottle. Good value for money. A regular medal winner at Stellenbosch and Cape shows.
Woolworths Selected Cape Red★★★A
This is a most agreeable, dry red blend based on Cinsaut and Shiraz with small amounts of Cabernet and Merlot, with good nose and flavour. A bargain at the price, and as easy-drinking as it is at the time of purchase, it is well worth ageing, although you will have to keep your own records as it is not vintage-dated.
Zevenwacht★★★(★)C
The 1983 was a little light, while the 1984 is a luscious, four-star wine with good fruit supported by good wood. The earlier vintage was matured in big wood, while the latter spent a year in small oak and large oak successively. It is a very good example of the traditional South African blend of Cabernet Sauvignon and Shiraz. The 1985 needs time to develop, while the 1986 and the 1988 are well-made wines with Cabernet showing nicely.

Dry Red Blends

Aan-de-Doorns Vin Rouge★★A
A flavourful, dry red blended from Pinotage and Tinta Barocca. Although it makes easy drinking on release, it improves in the bottle, and is best after four to five years.

Allesverloren Swartland Rood★★★B
This was a well-balanced blend of Shiraz, Pinotage and Port varieties producing a dry red of interesting character that improved with time. It is no longer produced and most needs to have been drunk.

Altydgedacht Tintoretto★★★★C
The 1981 was a most unusual deep-flavoured wine, the good fruit and meaty flavours of which are due to its equal quantities of Barbera and Shiraz grapes. This is a wine that, as attractive as it is when young, has definitely benefited with time in the bottle and is currently drinking very well. This wine was originally launched under the name Barbiraz, but the Wine and Spirit Board rejected the name as it too closely resembled the cultivars from which it was made. (I thought it a fine name.) The next release from the 1986 vintage is a blend of 75% Shiraz and 25% Barbera. Don't be fooled by the wine's lightish colour or pass it off as an insignificant wine – it isn't. Its alcohol exceeds 13,5% and it needs time to develop. The 1987 is a quieter wine while the 1988 is probably the 'biggest' so far, having 70% Shiraz and 30% Barbera with lots of good wood. Next release will be from the 1989 vintage some time in 1993.

81 ★★★★ ready. **86** ★★★★ ready, will still develop. **87** ★★★(★) ready, will still develop. **88** ★★★★ ready, will still improve.

Ashton Co-op Dry Red★★(★)A
A good value wine available in convenient screw-top bottles. Latest is a blend of Pinotage and Tinta Barocca. It is a fresh, fruity wine that drinks easily when young.

Autumn Harvest Country Claret (SFW)★★A
This is a smooth, easy-drinking red blend in which no particular varietal is obvious. It is only available as a so-called box wine and is not intended for ageing.

Beaufort Claret (Solly Kramer)★★A
Remarkable value for a dry red, this wine has plenty of good nose and deep, soft flavours.

Beaufort Dry Red (Solly Kramer)★★(★)A
A fruity dry red blend of Cinsaut and Tinta Barocca.

Bergenrood★★★C
Good-drinking, well-flavoured, medium-bodied dry red blend.

Bloemdal Dry Red (Jacobsdal Co-op)★★A
Basically a Pinotage with bright colour, fruity nose and fairly sharp on the palate.

Botha Co-op Droë Rooiwyn★★A
An attractive, easy-drinking wine made from equal proportions of unwooded Cinsaut and Pinotage, with the latter showing quite strongly. Neither 1988, the first vintage, nor 1989 are certified.

Casal da Serra Vinho Tinto Seco★★★B
A respectable dry red with good nose and soft, generous flavour. It drinks easily on its own while also making an ideal accompaniment to a meal.

Cedar Rouge (Cederberg Kelders)★★★B
A Pinotage aged in new oak; easy-drinking, non-vintaged red.
Cellar Cask Premier Claret★★(★)B
A dry red of the Cellar Cask brand, but presented in a 750 m*l* bottle and closed with a cork. Despite the advertisement claiming that the wine is 'corked', I found it to be a very pleasant, dry red blend that is good value for money.
Cellar Reserve Dry Red (Hyperama)★★A
A good blend of half Cinsaut and equal quantities of Tinta Barocca and Pinotage. A soft, easy-drinking red.
De Doorns Co-op Grand Rouge★★A
A robust, full-bodied Pinotage without finesse.
De Doorns Co-op Roodehof★★A
Quite similar to the Rouge (above), but showing some bottle age.
De Wet Co-op Dry Red★★★A
The Co-op's first attempt at a red is a blend of equal proportions of Cabernet Franc and Cinsaut. A nice combination that is a bit tannic to start with, but should smooth out after a year or so in the bottle.
Domein Doornkraal Kannaland★★B
A blend of Pinotage and Merlot with a full, soft, almost sweet taste. An unusual wine.
Douglas Green St Raphael★★B
A popular non-vintaged wine. Recent blends have shown an improvement. It is Pinotage-based with some Cinsaut giving a light-bodied, pleasant wine.
Drostdy-Hof Waveren Vin Noir★★★B
This is a well-aged wine which has lost its original fresh and fruity character and now has a hint of bottle age. It has been given more than a year in small oak. A well-made wine in the past, from Cabernet, Pinotage and Shiraz, but nowadays more likely to be Cabernet-Pinotage. It usually has a bit of age and oak at the time of release. Good value, well-flavoured wine.
Eersterivier Vin Rouge★★A
Pleasant-flavoured quaffer from mainly Pinotage and 25% Cinsaut.
Le Foyer Dry Red (Eersterivier Valleise Co-op)★★A
In an effort to keep the price down, the range of Le Foyer wines are packed in 500 m*l* screw-top bottles and are available only at the cellar. The dry red is a Pinotage-based braai wine.
Eikendal Vineyards Duc De Berry Rouge★★★B
A dry blend, with early releases, which have developed well, of predominantly wood-aged Shiraz. From the 1986 vintage onwards, the blend contains 70% Cinsaut, 20% Shiraz and small quantities of Cabernet and Merlot, resulting in easy drinking sooner than usual.
Fairview Paarl Red★★(★)B
Originally a non-vintaged blend containing aged Pinotage and Shiraz; then a light Pinot Noir which progressed to a Cabernet-based full wine; now an ageing light Pinot Noir.
Goede Hoop Vintage Rouge★★★(★)B
Originally an interesting blend of Shiraz, Tinta Barocca and Cinsaut. The 1974, 1975 and 1976 vintages were all very good and developed well in the bottle. There were no releases in 1977 and 1979, but a very different wine was released with the 1978 vintage. Said to be a blend of equal parts of Cabernet Sauvignon, Shiraz and Pinotage, it carried Superior certification, but it will probably need considerably

longer to achieve the smoothness of the earlier blends. The 1980 is excellent and differs again in its make-up with Shiraz, Tinta Barocca and Carignan being used. The 1981 is a full, firm wine, but has not developed well. The 1982 is a lovely wine, being a true blend in which no cultivar predominates and is touched off with new oak. The 1983 is similar but shows more wood. The 1988 is Shiraz and Pinotage with a fraction of Cabernet.

74 ★★★★ drink up. **75** ★★★ drink up. **76** ★★★★ ready. **77** no release. **78** ★★★★ ready. **79** no release. **80** ★★★★ ready. **81** ★★ ready. **82** ★★★★ ready. **83** ★★★(★) ready. **86** ★★★(★) ready. **87** ★★★★ ready. **88** ★★★★ ready.

Goudveld Estate Soewenier★B
A medium-bodied, dry red made from Pinotage on the Orange Free State's only wine estate.

Hemel-en-Aarde Valley Vin Rouge★★★★C
A delightful, easy-drinking, medium-bodied wine, with a good range of flavours in the mouth. The lightness in colour comes from the 75% Pinot Noir that has been aged in oak for a short period. The balance is well-flavoured Shiraz. The wine is non-vintaged but usually released about a year after vintage. It will develop with two to three years in the bottle.

Kellerrood (Marcows)★★★B
A well-made Pinotage-based wine that develops well over a year.

KWV Bonne Esperance Red★★(no price available)
A light, easy-drinking, unremarkable dry red available to KWV members and for export in one-litre, screw-top bottles.

Louwshoek-Voorsorg Co-op Dry Red★A
A light, dry red, made from Cinsaut.

Mamreweg Claret (previously called Dry Red)★★A
This wood-aged, dry red blend varies with the vintage, but usually contains Cinsaut, Pinotage and Tinta Barocca. Always a good-value, quaffing wine. It is not vintage-dated.

Mons Ruber Estate Conari★★A
An unusual, early drinking, dry red in which Cabernet dominates. It has an almost marzipan aftertaste.

Mont D'Or Noble Rouge (Drop Inn)★A
A good, honest, easy-drinking, dry red.

Monterey Rouge (Western Province Cellars)★★A
Current releases are an improvement on earlier wines. Good value for money.

Mooiuitsig Overberg Dry Red★A
An honest blend of various cultivars giving a light-bodied, easy-drinking, fruity wine which should be consumed when young.

Onverwacht Rouge de Noir★★B
A fruity-nosed, simple wine with a definite Cinsaut base and some Tinta Barocca.

Oranjerivier Wynkelders Droë Rooi★A
Originally a light-bodied Pinotage but now made from Grenache.

Overgaauw Overtinto★★★★B
A very good blend of Port varieties, including Tinta Barocca, Comifesto, Francisca, Malvasia Rey and Souzão. This is one of the more unusual South African red wines tasting, not surprisingly, like a dry Port. It is full-bodied and ages well. It is no longer being produced and it is a pity to see such an interesting wine disappear. Most

vintages are still developing but earlier ones will soon need to be consumed – I'm sure with satisfaction.

Overmeer Selected Red★★B
Good, easy drinking wine in which Cinsaut dominates.

Overvaal Dry Red (Vaalharts Co-op)★★B
Light, easy-drinking dry red from Pinotage.

Party Pack Dry Red (Drop Inn)★★(★)A
Obviously Pinotage-based from the clean, distinctive nose. Young, bright and easy on the palate. Good value.

Paddajolais (Paddagang Vignerons)★★★B
When chilled, this bright-red blend, originally of Cabernet Sauvignon, Shiraz and Merlot – later of Pinotage and Tinta Barocca – drinks incredibly well as young wine.

Paradyskloof Claret (Vriesenhof)★★B
This and the Roodewyn are young wines at popular prices produced by Jan 'Boland' Coetzee. The Claret contains Cabernet Sauvignon and the Roodewyn, Shiraz. They are both full-flavoured wines with good character.

Paradyskloof Rouge★★★(★)C
This non-vintaged blend of Merlot with Cabernet and Shiraz has replaced the Roodewyn and Claret labels. Good character with fine oak backing, and good value for money. Drinks easy on release yet has the potential to develop over three to five years.

Pascali Rosso ★★★B
For its price this is a particularly enjoyable, dry red wine which goes well with Mediterranean food. It is blended from Merlot, Pinotage and Shiraz with some oak age. It has good nose and full, deep flavour which shows a rare complexity for a wine of this price.

Porterville Co-op Dry Red★★A
Mainly Pinotage with some Cinsaut from 1991 vintage.

Ravenswood Dry Red (Pick 'n Pay)★★A
Sold only in the 5 *l* box, this wine is shy on the nose, but pleasant enough on the palate. A simple blend of Cinsaut and Pinotage.

Rebel Dry Red★A
The best of the Rebel range: a dry red braai wine.

Rheboksloof Dry Red★★★C
A good, clean-flavoured, easy-drinking dry red. The non-vintaged bottles need to be marked with the purchase date to give you an indication of the age. Two to three years will give gratifying development.

Rijckshof Claret (Kango Co-op)★★(★)A
The first release was an exceptional wine, although it did not meet the normal quality criteria, being blended from 70% Cabernet with an unusually high alcohol content of 16,5%, with 30% (less alcoholic) Tinta Barocca. Aged in 500-*l* Nevers puncheons for 18 months and developing well over the year, this is a full-bodied, bold wine with vague porty tones. The fresh, fruity, unwooded 1989 release is a very different wine, comprising predominantly Tinta Barocca with 10% Cinsaut and 10% 'other reds'. The 1991 offers small quantity and light quality.

Romansrivier Co-op Vino Rood★★★A
This replaces the former Rood which was a surprisingly full blend of Cabernet Sauvignon and Pinotage. The replacement is a light-blend Cinsaut and Tinta Barocca which is ready for early drinking, but develops over a year in the bottle. It is good value for money.

Rooiberg Co-op Selected Red★★(★)A
This is a wine that varies in composition year by year. Recent years have been Pinot Noir, Shiraz and Merlot with the latest, Pinot Noir, Shiraz and Cinsaut.
Rozendal Val de Lyn★★★(★)C
Mostly Merlot with some Cinsaut from the 1989 vintage; a very nice drinking wine at this early stage.
Simondium Claret★★A
A dry red from Cinsaut.
Stellenbosch Wine Route Vin Rouge★★★B
A label available on 1,5 *l*, returnable plastic flasks and produced by Delheim. Pinotage-based, it is good, easy drinking.
Tassenberg (SFW)★★★B
Our most popular red, quaffed by some but drunk with respect by those who know and understand wine.
Taverna (Distillers Group)★★B
A somewhat light dry red.
Tulbagh Co-op Claret★★A
An unwooded blend of Cinsaut, Pinotage and Tinta Barocca giving a medium-bodied dry red.
Twee Rivieren Grand Vin Rouge (WP Cellars)★(★)A
A medium-bodied, dry red wine which has good, clean flavour.
Valley Dry Red (Gilbeys)★★A
A good, no-nonsense, dry red, of predominantly Cinsaut.
Villa Rossini Rosso (Union Wines)★★(★)B
This is Union Wines' venture into Italian-style wines; made from Cinsaut and Shiraz, giving a full-flavoured, relatively light red that makes easy drinking and is sold in screw-top, one-litre bottles.
Vino Roma Rosso (SFW)★★★B
SFW's red entry into the current 'Italian' fashion. Surprisingly good, it is made from unwooded Shiraz (two thirds) with the balance, Pinotage. It is easy, early-drinking wine, but develops well over a year.
Vino Uno Rosso Secco (Du Toitskloof)★★★A
This cellar's effort to keep the cost of drinking down. Inexpensive 500 m*l* screw-top bottles of good-drinking Cinsaut-based wine.
Vinovat Dry Red (Marcows)(★)A
A very ordinary dry red.
Vintner's Choice Grand Vin Rouge (Drop Inn)★★A
A good, honest, medium-bodied red wine with a pleasing taste. Made from Cinsaut, Tinta Barocca and Pinotage, it has every potential to develop with a few years in the bottle.
Vredenheim Léger★★A
A light-bodied, ordinary dry red.
Welgemeend Amadé★★★(★)B
This wine was first produced in 1979 from equal quantities of Grenache, Pinotage and Shiraz, crushed and fermented together. In 1983 the blend changed considerably, becoming 50% Grenache, 44% Shiraz and 6% Pinotage, which produced a much better, fruitier wine. The 1983 has developed in the bottle and is drinking well in 1990. The 1985 was the Alphen Wine of the Month for non-Cabernet blends during 1988. Matured in good wood, the 1986 has as little as 12% Pinotage with Grenache and Shiraz making up almost equal parts of the balance. The 1987 is very good with a blend of some 50% Grenache, 40% Shiraz, and the balance Pinotage. It drinks very

well in 1992. The 1988 is a lighter wine but has very pleasant flavours. The 1989 and 1990 are back to being mainly Shiraz and Grenache and as little as 10% Pinotage. A lovely, fruity wine with a very pleasing palate, even at an early stage. With a few years, this smooth, medium-bodied wine full of lovely flavour develops with great benefit.

85 ★★★ ready. **86** ★★★ ready. **87** ★★★★ ready, will still improve. **88** ★★★(★) ready, will still develop. **89** ★★★★ ready, will still develop. **90** ★★★(★) ready, will still develop.

Woolworths Blue Label Rouge★★(★)C

A nouveau-style wine from Gamay without added sulphur dioxide. For cool, early drinking.

Woolworths Petit Vin Dry Red★★★B

A good-drinking dry red in 250 m*l* Tetrapak.

Yellow Label Red (Checkers)★★A

An easy-drinking red with Pinotage character and Cinsaut sweetness.

Zevenrood (Zevenwacht)★★B

A non-vintaged bold, full-flavoured, wood-aged wine which has good character and is based on Shiraz with small amounts of Pinotage and Pinot Noir.

Cabernet Franc

Landskroon Cabernet Franc★★★(★)C

The first of these wines on the market was the 1979 vintage. In general, it is a medium-bodied, well-flavoured wine which ages with distinction. The 1989 is the best yet. It has good, full nose, lots of fine flavours with some wood backing. It will develop well over four or more years. The 1990 is not quite as full and will probably peak slightly earlier.

79 ★★★★ past its best. **80** ★★★ ready. **81** ★★★ past its best, still enjoyable. **82** ★★★★ ready. **83** ★★★ ready. **88** ★★★ ready, will still develop. **89** ★★★★ already tasty, will still develop. **90** ★★★★ ready.

Warwick Cabernet Franc★★★★D

Initially bottled only for export to the UK. The 1988 made an appearance here in limited quantities. A special selection of 1989 will be available at the 1992 Cape Independent Winemakers' Guild Auction. A clean, lively wine with lots of attractive fruit.

Cabernet Sauvignon

Aan de Doorns Cabernet Sauvignon★★B
A dry red which has shown continual success in local competitions. In general, it ages over three to four years to become a smooth wine with distinct Cabernet character. The 1987 is a softish, dry wine suitable for relatively early drinking and not for ageing like those of the early 1980s. The 1988 is much the same and 1990 is definitely early drinking wine.

Allesverloren Cabernet Sauvignon★★★★C
Until the 1982 vintage, this was usually full-bodied Cabernet made in the traditional style. Thereafter there was a difference in style with the prominence of new oak. The 1982 has a deep, full flavour, developed beautifully, but now needs to be enjoyed. Of the earlier vintages, the 1978 was good and the 1979 one of the better wines of a poor vintage. The 1980 needs drinking. The 1981 is a superb, full, rich wine from a vintage which has been discounted by many, but is now ready for drinking. The 1982 is as good as the 1984 and developing just as well. The 1983 is lighter, like so many others of that vintage, and is now at its best. The 1984 has made good use of new oak, which adds extra dimension to the wine – probably one of the best of the decade. The 1985 was a gold medal winner at the Cape Young Wine Show. Its appearance in the bottle, however, has shown it to be a little reserved compared with the 1982 and 1984. The 1986 is a fine, big, complex wine with good oak. The 1987 is a big, full wine that will need plenty of time to develop. The same applies to the 1988 which is a massive wine, full of character and lots of tannin and 13,5% alcohol. It will need lots of time to tame.

74 ★★★★★ ready. **75** no release. **76** ★★★★★ ready. **77** ★★★ past its best. **78** ★★★★ ready. **79** ★★★ ready. **80** ★★★★ ready. **81** ★★★★ ready. **82** ★★★★★ ready. **83** ★★★★ ready. **84** ★★★★(★) ready. **85** ★★★★ ready. **86** ★★★★(★) not ready, age further. **87** ★★★★ not ready, age further. **88** ★★★★ not ready, leave to age.

Alphen Cabernet Sauvignon★★★★C
Alphen upgraded their wines in 1980 and have revised their style and operation, again making the wines at Kleine Zalze, a South African champion cellar, drawing grapes from a wide area around Stellenbosch, Helderberg and Somerset West. The 1980 is rich, smooth and not entirely dry, and has improved in the bottle. The 1982 is a four-star wine and should not be underrated. The 1983 is drinking well and the 1984 was ready for consumption on release. The 1985 is a lighter wine and should be drunk now. The 1986 is good and needs time to show. The 1987 is the first from the new style with 1988 being a very good drinking wine at an early age. Most of the early to mid-1980s need to be enjoyed now.

80 ★★★★ ready. **81** no release. **82** ★★★★ ready. **84** ★★★(★) ready. **83** ★★★ ready. **85** ★★★ ready. **86** ★★★(★) ready, will still improve. **87** ★★★★ ready, will still develop. **88** ★★★★ age further.

Alto Cabernet Sauvignon★★★★E
A big, specially matured, full-bodied, deep-coloured Cabernet. The 1970 had a lot of tannin and took years to round out and to realize its potential. This wine was not bottled between 1972 and 1975, but

supplies were resumed in 1976 with a fine, less powerful wine. The 1977 vintage is a light wine of which very little appeared on the South African market. The 1978 was also a lighter-styled wine than usual for Alto. The 1979 was definitely a more medium-bodied wine which, although appealing, was not as fruity as other vintages, yet developed beautifully over ten years. The 1980 was only released in 1986 and shows Alto's true style. The 1982 is a big, alcoholic wine that needs time to smooth out; it was selected by SAA as a Wine of the Month during 1990 and has done well on auction. The 1984 is a big, powerful, full-flavoured wine that will be at its best in the early '90s. There was no 1985, but the 1986 followed in outstanding style and should develop very well.

🍷 **76** ★★★★★ ready. **77** ★★★ ready. **78** ★★★★ ready, will still improve. **79** ★★★ ready. **80** ★★★★ ready, will still improve. **82** ★★★ ready, will still improve. **84** ★★★★ ready, will still improve. **85** no release. **86** ★★★★ allow time to develop.

Altydgedacht Cabernet Sauvignon★★★(★)D

Altydgedacht is an interesting Estate where, many years ago, Mrs Jean Parker made outstanding Cabernets until she decided to send her grapes to Nederburg. Today her sons are in business, John looking after the vineyards and Oliver making the wine. Oliver's first release of Cabernet is from the 1982 vintage: a light, stylish wine which has developed beautifully. The 1985 was the next release and is surprisingly full for the vintage – a most attractive wine which is developing well. The 1986 is a big wine that still needs time to smooth out. The 1987 is a big strong wine with plenty of potential, as is the 1988, which will be at its best at the end of the century.

🍷 **82** ★★★ ready. **85** ★★★★ ready, will still improve. **86** ★★★★ ready, will still develop. **87** ★★★★ not ready, age further. **88** ★★★★ not ready, age further.

Ashton Co-op Cabernet Sauvignon★★B

The heavily-wooded 1984 was followed by a 1987 wine which is pleasant, light and fruity. It is developing well but is not designed to last long, and is at its best now. The 1988 has good wood backing; nice, fruity wine. The 1989 is an improvement with good wood.

Avontuur Cabernet Reserve★★★(★)D

The 1987 is a firm, full wine and cellar samples of the 1989 seem curiously light.

Avontuur Cabernet Sauvignon★★★(★)D

The 1987 is a well-made, dry wine with good cultivar character backed by fine wood. This old and established farm has returned to making its own wine in a well-equipped winery on the farm. The 1988 is a lovely rich, full-flavoured wine that will develop well.

Backsberg Cabernet Sauvignon★★★★(★)C

This was the first wine to be awarded Superior status under the Wine of Origin legislation and is a regular prizewinner. Most vintages have Superior status, are undoubtedly excellent, and all have considerable varietal character. Backsberg is one of the few cellars that can offer older vintages of their Cabernets and usually have three or four vintages available. They are surprisingly consistent wines. All are ageing well, and it is hard to choose between the years. The 1981 was lighter than previous vintages, the 1982 much fuller, with a good oakiness not previously noticeable. The 1983 and 1984 are the last of the Estate's earlier-style wines. The 1985 shows a very different, fuller wine which should age with great benefit over eight to 10 years. The 1986 was the best Cabernet to date from this Estate, but the 1987 is even better with great Cabernet character backed by good wood, and will definitely age with benefit. The 1988 is a little shy and will drink earlier than the 1987. The 1989 is showing new clone Cabernet character and is a delicious wine that will develop with great benefit.

72 ★★★★ drink. **73** ★★★ past its best. **74** ★★★★ drink. **75** ★★★★★ past its best. **76** ★★★★★ drink. **77** ★★★ past its best. **78** ★★★★ ready. **79** ★★★ drink. **80** ★★★★ ready. **81** ★★★ ready. **82** ★★(★) ready. **83** ★★★ ready. **84** ★★★★ ready. **85** ★★★★ ready. **86** ★★★★(★) ready, will still improve. **87** ★★★★(★) ready, will improve. **88** ★★★(★) ready, will still improve. **89** ★★★★ not ready, age further. **90** ★★★★ allow to develop.

Bellingham Cabernet Sauvignon★★★★(★)C

The first release of this wine was the 1980 vintage and heralded a dramatic change in the quality of Bellingham products. The 1980 has very good Cabernet nose and just a hint of fresh oak, giving subtle complexity which has developed well with time. It has probably reached its best, but has the ability to hold. The 1981 is just as good. The 1982 is a good, full wine which is developing well. The 1983 is a little lighter and needs to be drunk. The 1984 and 1985 are similar in that they are much more forward wines. The 1986 is the best so far; it is a fine, deep wine and will probably peak in the mid-1990s.

80 ★★★★ ready. **81** ★★★ ready. **82** ★★★★ ready. **83** ★★★(★) ready. **84** ★★★★ ready. **85** ★★★(★) ready. **86** ready, will still improve.

Bergsig Cabernet Sauvignon★★★E

The early wines were very soft, yet full-flavoured and nicely wooded. The wines of the 1980s had better fruit. All develop well and drink easily at four to five years. The 1988, 1989 and 1990 have more oak and a soft finish, and are ready for drinking when released – although they will develop over two to three years.

Bertrams Cabernet Sauvignon★★★★C

In the middle to the late 1970s, this was one of the finest Cabernets of the Stellenbosch district and was judged champion red wine at the South African Championship Wine Show at Goodwood in 1975, 1978 and 1979. It had its own distinct, full-bodied character with deep aroma and moderately high tannin. Usually a powerful wine with an excellent ageing potential of 10 years plus. The 1982 and 1983 were still of the old Bertrams style and are showing well now, and the 1984 is very different, with a slightly subdued nose, but with every potential to develop over many years. The 1985 is of a more modern style and is a finer, more elegant wine. The 1986 shows a developing style that is very pleasing and the 1987 continues to show improving style. The cellar is to be congratulated on releasing their wines when they are a full five years old and have developed good bottle age. The Bertrams Cabernets now make regular appearances at the Nederburg Auction.

79★★★ ready. **80** ★★★★ ready. **81** ★★★★ ready. **82** ★★★★ ready. **83**★★★★(★) ready. **84** ★★★★ ready, will still improve. **85** ★★★★ ready, will still improve. **86** ★★★★ ready, will improve. **87** ready, with lots of development potential.

Beyerskloof Cabernet Sauvignon★★★★★F
The first production from this small cellar on the lower slopes of the Koelenhof hills comes from the 1989 vintage. The wine has full Cabernet character and lots of berry, backed by wood. It is well-packed in traditional Bordeaux-tapered bottles with a most attractive label. The pack received a 1991 Loerie award and the wine was selected as the Alphen Wine of the Month for the best 1989 Cabernet Sauvignon. The 1990 is another beauty, while cellar samples indicate that the 1991 is going to be a stunner. Expensive, but worth the search; will all age majestically.

Blaauwklippen Cabernet Sauvignon★★★★(★)E
A light style of Cabernet with a decidedly Bordeaux character. The well-rounded 1980 vintage won the then wine maker, Walter Finlayson, the Diners Club Award in 1982 for the second year running. It is definitely a five-star wine, which is still developing extremely well in the bottle. The 1981 was a lighter wine, in keeping with the vintage, but has developed well in the bottle. The 1982 is a fine wine, but the 1983 is slightly out of character. The 1984 is magnificent, however, and the 1986 and 1987 are even better. The 1985 has not lived up to my original expectations. As good as it is, it is not developing as well as the 1984, 1986 and the potentially stunning 1987. Wine making now rests in the hands of Jacques Kruger who was the assistant for many years. He has a particular touch for red wine as witnessed in the 1987 and 1988 wines. 1990 cellar samples look very good. These wines need six to eight years to develop to their full potential. Also available in 375 m*l* (half) bottles.

🍷 **78** ★★★★ drink. **79** ★★★★ drink. **80** ★★★★★ ready. **81** ★★★ ready. **82** ★★★★★ ready. **83** ★★★ ready. **84** ★★★★★ ready, will still develop. **85** ★★★★ ready, will still improve. **86** ★★★★★ ready. **87** ★★★★ ready, will still develop. **88** ★★★★★ not ready, age further. **89** not ready, age further.

Blaauwklippen Reserve Cabernet Sauvignon★★★★★D
This wine is produced for the Cape Independent Winemakers' Guild Auction. Small quantities are selected and bottled with the Guild's Auction label. They are always deep, magnificent wines packed with Cabernet character, shown off with excellent oak. The 1985 was chosen by SAA as a Wine of the Month. The 1986 is a big, powerful wine with lots of berry flavours, as is the 1987. The great complexity of the wine ensures superb development in the bottle over many years to come.

🍷 **82** ★★★★★ ready. **83** ★★★★★ ready. **84** ★★★★★ ready, will still improve. **85** ★★★★★ ready, will still improve. **86** ★★★★★ not ready, age further. **87** ★★★★★ not ready, age further.

Bloemendal Estate Cabernet Sauvignon★★★★D
The first release was from the 1987 vintage which was launched in 1990. It is an elegant, fruity wine, full of berry character, good tannin and nice oak background. The 1988 is a delicious, elegant wine with layers of fruit and berry flavours backed by good wood. Next up, the 1989, is a little lighter and more elegant wine, but with the same good fruit and wood.

Bolandse Co-op Cabernet Sauvignon★★★(★)B
Many of the earlier vintages were indifferent but, during the late 1970s and '80s, they have shown great promise – the 1977 having

aged with elegance over the years. The 1982 vintage has performed surprisingly well and is regularly rated higher in tastings than many of the more fancied wines. The 1983 is as full-bodied as the others and, in 1989, was selected for sale at the Nederburg Auction. The 1984 shows more wood and will develop greater complexity than earlier vintages. The 1985 has benefited from maturing for a year in wood. The 1986 is showing very well and has good development potential. Some of the 1985, 1986 and 1987 vintages have been bottled in magnums. A portion of the 1987 has been aged in American oak with a decidedly woody effect. The 1988, 1989 and 1990 vintages are in keeping with the cellars quality and are excellent value for money.

82 ★★★ ready. **83** ★★★ ready. **84** ★★★★ ready, will still improve. **85** ★★★★ ready. **86** ★★★★(★) ready, will still improve. **87** ★★★★ not ready, age further. **88** ★★★★ not ready, age further. **89** ★★★(★) not ready, age further. **90** ★★★★ age further.

Boplaas Cabernet★★★(★)D

A surprisingly good Cabernet from this inland area. The 1985 has good cultivar character touched with good new wood, and has developed well over the years. The 1986 is a fruity, lean wine, with the 1987 showing more character. The 1988 and 1989 show improved style and will develop better than earlier vintages. These satisfying wines are probably at their best in five to seven years. The 1990 is fuller bodied but continues the improvement in style.

Botha Co-op Cabernet Sauvignon★★★B

This is a consistently good wine which is usually released within one year of production. Most develop well over six to eight years. There was no release of the 1984 vintage, and the full-wooded 1985 was released before it was a year old; the 1986 at about six months. The 1986 tastes almost sweet, is amazingly soft, and was a wine for early consumption. The 1987 was released before the year was out and needed more ageing before drinking. The 1988 is medium-bodied, has good flavours, and is fairly forward. Good value wine.

85 ★★★ ready. **86** ★★★ ready. **87** ★★(★) ready, will still improve. **88** ★★★ ready, will still improve.

Bottelary Co-op Cabernet Sauvignon★★★B

Early vintages like the 1976 were full-bodied and fairly robust Cabernets that aged with great benefit over six to eight years. Recent vintages are much lighter and more medium-bodied. Those of the 1980s are all on the light side but have developed quite well over a year or so.

82 ★★★ drink. **83** ★★★ drink. **84** ★★ drink. **85** ★★ drink. **86** ★★★(★) ready. **87** ★★★ ready. **88** ready, will still improve.

Bovlei Co-op Cabernet Sauvignon★★★B

A regular medal winner, this full-bodied wine needs time to show its best. The 1987 is a light, elegant fruity wine which drinks easily when young and will be followed by a big, heavier 1988.

Buffelskroon Cabernet (Calitzdorp Co-op)★★B

The 1989 is a fairly ordinary, light-bodied wine followed by a similar style wine in 1991.

Cape Vintners Members Only Cabernet Sauvignon★★★★D

From the 1988 and 1989 vintages comes a berry-flavoured wine with good deep tones.

Cederberg Kelders Cabernet Sauvignon★★★B
This unusual cellar has improved its Cabernet vintage by vintage. The 1978 was a dramatic Grand Champion Red at the Olifants River Young Wine Show and winner of a gold medal at the Goodwood show. The wines of the early 1980s were for early consumption. The 1986 vintage heralded a total change of style and quality, and deserves three stars. A portion of the wine is aged for a year in large old vats, with the balance aged in new American and French oak, producing a lovely flavoured wine. The 1987 is a much bigger, fuller-flavoured wine that should develop with great interest. I have not tasted the 1988, but the 1989 is a very acceptable wine.

Chamonix Cabernet Sauvignon★★★C
The 1986 vintage was specially made to celebrate the Huguenot tercentenary and is a nice, light-style wine which has good cultivar character balanced with new wood. The 1987 is a fuller, better-flavoured wine.

Clairvaux Co-op Cabernet Sauvignon★★A
The initial offerings were medium-bodied and rather ordinary. The 1984 was a clean wine with good character, albeit on the lightish side. The next release carries no vintage date as it is a blend of 1985 and 1986. It is a fuller wine that is ready for drinking now. The 1988 is medium-bodied, easy-drinking wine that is now showing its age, with the 1989 appearing much the same.

Clos Malverne Cabernet Sauvignon★★★★E
The first release from this Devon Valley cellar came from the 1988 vintage and numbered 450 cases. The cellar will specialize in Cabernet and Cabernet blends, with total production not exceeding 4 500 cases. Small quantities have been produced from the 1986 and 1987 vintages, and show great character. The 1989 has good complexity and is a rich, full-flavoured wine which will develop well. The 1990 follows the same dense style with deep colour and lots of berry flavours. It should also develop well.

De Leuwen Jagt Cabernet★★★D
The 1989 is a medium-bodied, well-wooded wine, and the 1990 is a more elegant, deeper flavoured wine.

Delheim Cabernet Sauvignon★★★★C
One of the Cape's top-quality wine bargains. Although this used to be a fairly light-bodied wine, it had most attractive qualities which made pleasant drinking at four to five years. The 1982 vintage showed considerable change in quality, and was full of good cultivar character. This vintage has been particularly well wood-treated: the cultivar still dominates, but the wood has added complexity and softened the wine. The 1983 reflects the vintage with a lighter but well-flavoured wine. The 1984 is a deep, beautiful wine packed with character and has tremendous potential to develop very well in the bottle. The 1985 was launched in May 1987 and made easy drinking sooner than the 1984. The 1986 contains 25% Merlot that gives it a greater depth of character and made it very drinkable now, although it has every potential to develop in the bottle over five to eight years. It won Alphen Wine of the Month in August 1988. The 1987 is a good successor with 18% Cabernet Franc and 4% Merlot, backed with very good wood. The 1988 is a very good, complex wine and the 1989 has a most attractive nose and flavour. Cellar samples of 1990 are looking very good.

82 ★★★★ ready. 83 ★★★★ ready. 84 ★★★★ ready, will still improve. 85 ★★★★ ready, will still improve. 86 ★★★★(★) ready, will still improve. 87 ★★★★(★) ready, will still improve. 88 ★★★★(★) not ready, age further. 89★★★★(★) not ready, age further.

De Zoete Inval Cabernet Sauvignon★★C

A wine with a very distinctive character. It has its devotees, although I didn't like it when I drank it young; it probably needs time to develop. The 1980 carries Superior certification and is showing positive development in the bottle. Three vintages are available, the youngest being the 1981. The cellar believes in selling well-aged, old-style wines.

Die Krans Cabernet★★★B

A well-wooded, full-flavoured wine, still to be released from the 1991 vintage.

Diemersdal Cabernet Sauvignon★★★D

The first release from the 1988 vintage is a robust wine with good fruit and fair tannin that should enable it to age well. The 1989 is full of berry and vanilla flavours, and has good wood backing.

Dieu Donne Cabernet★★★(★)C

One of the cellar's best wines. The first release from the 1991 vintage is a medium-bodied wine with a good fruity nose and oaky background. It will develop with time.

Douglas Green Cabernet Sauvignon★★★(★)D

Many South African Cabernets have improved a great deal over recent vintages and this wine is no exception. Originally a Cabernet and Cinsaut blend of fairly full body and high tannin, the 1979 saw a change in style from an early-drinking wine to one requiring some bottle-ageing, and was certainly by far the best seen under this label up to that time. The 1980, 1981 and 1982 carry Superior certification. The 1981 is past its best and the 1980 and 1982 need to be consumed. There was very little of the 1983 vintage. The 1984 is a very light wine, rather like a Rosé, and has little cultivar character. Drink up. The 1985 is very pleasant, with attractive fruit and pleasant palate, and is a good example of the traditional-style Cape Cabernet. It was selected for the 1989 SAA Wine List. The 1986 has more character and is more attractive. The 1987 was somewhat reserved. The 1988 release is a better wine made in the traditional style, having spent 18 months in large vats. It should develop well in the bottle over six to eight years. The 1989 was released in a new pack.

78 ★★★ drink. 79 ★★★★ drink. 80 ★★★ ready. 81 ★★★ past its best. 82 ★★★★ ready. 83 ★★★ ready. 84 ★★★ ready. 85 ★★★★ ready. 86 ★★★★ ready, will still improve. 87 ★★★ ready. 88 ★★★★ ready, will still improve. 89 ★★★(★) ready, will still improve.

Du Toitskloof Cabernet★★★C

This attractively labelled 1988 vintage is a rich, full wine with good wood backing. It is the best wine from this cellar, and should develop with interest. The 1989 is slightly lighter, medium-bodied and fruity with fine wood.

Eersterivier Valleise Co-op Cabernet Sauvignon★★★C

The early vintages of 1977 and 1979 were light, easy-drinking wines that did not develop well. There were no further releases until 1982, when a fuller-bodied, deeper-style wine came onto the market, followed by a similar wine in 1983. Both developed well in the bottle and were at their best in 1989. The 1984 was surprisingly light and should have been drunk by now. The 1985 was also fairly ordinary but the 1987 is an attractive, wood-aged, medium-bodied wine for early drinking. The 1988 is also a medium-bodied, but better flavoured, wine from new, early ripening clones. No 1989 was bottled. The 1990 continues the improvement shown in the 1988. This is good wine for drinking four to five years from the vintage.

Eikendal Vineyards Cabernet Reserve du Patron★★★(★)E

This is a more extensively wood-aged wine than the cellar's regular Cabernet, and sales are reserved to just two bottles per person. The first release from the 1984 vintage has developed beautifully. The next release, from 1987, is a super four-star wine. Powerful flavours and good tannin should allow it to age with benefit.

Eikendal Vineyards Cabernet Sauvignon★★★D

This cellar made a fine début with the blending of a small amount of Shiraz, giving its Cabernets greater complexity and the potential to develop well. The 1984 contains some softening Cinsaut, having spent 10 months in small wood. It is a good, rich, deep-coloured wine, drinking very well in 1992. The 1985 was lighter, but the 1986 is an excellent deep, full-flavoured wine with good fruit and wood. The 1987 needs time to settle, while the 1988 is already drinking well. The 1989 has 30% Merlot which makes it very drinkable.

Fairview Cabernet Sauvignon★★★★B

This is a regular award-winner. Early vintages were powerful, robust wines needing seven to ten years to smooth out, but in the late 1970s and early 1980s the style changed. These wines are now medium-bodied, far more elegant, and drink well much earlier than previous vintages. The 1983 is fairly full for the vintage and shows fine Cabernet character without wood influence. There is a small amount of the extremely fine, wood-aged 1983, which was only available from the Estate. The 1984 shows some of the old style of robustness tempered with a bit of wood. The 1985 is a lighter wine, while the 1986 and 1987 are considerably richer, finer wines. 1988 was skipped, but the 1989 is firm wine with good cultivar character.

Fairview Reserve Cabernet★★★★D

From both the 1986 and 1987 vintages come very good deep, full-flavoured, small-wood-aged wines. As good as they taste now, they will benefit from six to eight years of development.

Fleur Du Cap Cabernet Sauvignon (Bergkelder)★★★★(★)D

These are always good, medium-bodied, elegant Cabernets with good varietal nose. They are well-balanced, with clean, full Cabernet character which makes pleasant drinking when relatively young, yet they always have the potential to age well. The 1976 vintage was excellent at six years. The 1978 is probably the best of the 1970s' vintages, with the 1979 not far behind. Those of the early 1980s are outstanding: full of fruit and delightful cultivar character. The 1982 and 1984 are excellent; they drink very well now and are beautiful examples of fine wine-making. They usually carry Superior certification. It appears that the 1983 was not launched. The Superior 1985 is good, but is not as full as the 1984. The 1986 and 1987 are both very good wines with lovely depth of flavour and excellent oak backing. Although they drink well on release, they have enough tannin to age with distinction.

82 ★★★★(★) ready. 83 no release. 84 ★★★★(★) ready, will still improve. 85 ★★★(★) ready, will still improve. 86 ★★★★ ready, will still improve. 87 ★★★★ ready, will still improve.

Fleur du Cap Oak Collection (Bergkelder)★★★★D

A collection of six 750 m*l* bottles of Cabernet. Five of these are aged in different kinds of oak; three French (Nevers, Allier and Limousin), and the other two in Spanish and American oak. The sixth Cabernet is a fine blend with a deep purple/red colour, packed with varietal fruit and a good underlay of oak. A lovely wine with Superior certification. All six wines are from the 1986 vintage.

Glen Carlou Cabernet Sauvignon★★★★(★)E

First release from 1990 vintage is a super wine from new clone Cabernet, richly packed with all the best Cabernet can give and potential to develop into one of the Cape's best.

Goede Hoop Cabernet Sauvignon ★★★D

This first release from the 1987 vintage is beginning to show well after a quiet start.

Goedvertrou Cabernet Sauvignon★★★★E

Still to be released but will come from the 1991 vintage which has good berry character and nice wood. Something to look forward to from this cellar.

Goue Vallei Cabernet Sauvignon (Citrusdal Co-op)★★★C

The 1984 was a pleasant, light-bodied wine with a slight woody character. The 1986 is a better wine and will need a year to smooth out. The 1988 has lots of wood and high tannin, and needs time to smooth out. The 1989 is an improvement on previous releases. Good value for money.

Groot Constantia Cabernet Sauvignon★★★★C

The Cabernets of Groot Constantia have an enviable reputation of elegance and refinement. Consistently good during the 1970s. The vintages of the early 1980s are pleasant enough but do not seem to be improving as dramatically as Cabernets shown by other Cape cellars. The later 1980s are very different, with better fruit and fine oak character. The 1985 was good for a generally poor year. The 1986 is an improvement in all respects, while the 1987 and 1988 are both very good wines.

78 ★★★★ ready. **79** ★★★ past its best. **80** ★★★★ ready. **81** ★★★ ready. **82** ★★★★ ready. **83** ★★★ ready. **84** ★★★★ ready. **85** ★★★★ ready. **86** ★★★★(★) ready, will still improve. **87** ★★★★ not ready, age further. **88** ★★★★ not ready, age further.

Hartenberg Cabernet Sauvignon★★★(★)F

The 1979 was the first vintage of this wine since the classification of the farm as an Estate. A good, soft Cabernet which developed well over 10 years and still has the potential for further ageing. The 1980 is a more substantial wine with better complexity and will probably live even longer than the 1979. The 1981 is much lighter; 1982 and 1983 are in keeping with the cellar's full-flavoured style, but they drink well earlier than the 1979 and 1980. The 1983 is medium-bodied and more forward than earlier vintages. The 1984 is a big, full wine that will develop well in time. The 1985 is not the usual full Hartenberg style, but a fine wine all the same. The 1986 is much better in all respects – a full-bodied wine that drinks well now but has lots of development potential.

79 ★★★ ready. **80** ★★★★ ready, will still improve. **81** ★★★ ready. **82** ★★★★ ready, will still improve. **83** ★★★★ ready, will still improve. **84** ★★★★(★) ready, will still improve. **85** ★★★ ready, will still improve. **86** ★★★★ not ready, will develop with time.

H C Collison Cabernet Sauvignon (Bergkelder)★★★(★)C

The first release was a 1981 Cabernet which has fine features and carries Superior certification. The next release, from the 1982 vintage, is far better wine and excellent value for money: the kind of wine one should buy to age in the cellar. Considering the vintage, the 1983 is very good and has developed well. The 1984 is an excellent example of good Cabernet. The 1985 is a surprisingly good wine for the vintage and carries Superior certification. All have developed well. There has been no release since 1985.

81 ★★★ ready. **82** ★★★★ ready, will improve. **83** ★★★ ready. **84** ★★★★ ready, will improve. **85** ★★★(★) ready, will improve.

Helderberg Co-op Cabernet Sauvignon★★★B

Wines from this Co-op have changed for the better over the past few years and the Cabernet probably best illustrates this change in style. From the mid-1980s, the Cabernets are full in style. The 1986 was full of tannin and is only now softening out. The 1987 is also big and deep with lots of flavours, and makes an unusual change to this kind of wine as it is without any wood influence. The 1988 is a young, tannic wine that should develop well. There is no 1990 and very little 1989. The next release is from 1991. Excellent value for money.

85 ★★(★) ready. **86** ★★ ready, will improve. **87** ★★★ ready, will improve. **88** ★★★ ready, will improve. **89** ★★★ ready. **90** no release. **91** ★★★(★) will need time to develop.

Huguenot Cabernet Sauvignon★★★B

Soft old-style, but not unattractive wine.

Kanonkop Cabernet Sauvignon★★★★★E

A deep, rich, elegant wine of powerful character. The Cabernets vary with the vintage but are always very good and feature regularly at the Nederburg Auction. The 1973 wine, the first to be bottled at Kanonkop under its own label, was a full-bodied and rather robust Cabernet carrying plenty of wood. It took a gold medal at the 1975 Stellenbosch Young Wine Show. The early 1970s all developed well into the early 1990s. The wines of the later 1970s are all good, and needed a full 10 years to reach their best. The 1979 vintage is probably the best of the 1970s, but the 1980 set the new decade off to a grand start. The 1980s are all good and will show their best 12 – 15 years from vintage. The 1987 is everything a Cabernet should be, with lovely fruit flavours and excellent wood, without the intensity of the 1986. The 1988 tastes very good already and might be one vintage that will develop more quickly – it could be great in eight to ten years and not the regular 15 years! The 1990s have all been intense, deep wines and their release is eagerly awaited.

73 ★★★★★ drink. **74** ★★★ drink. **75** ★★★★ drink. **76** ★★★★ ready. **77** ★★★ drink. **78** ★★★★★ ready. **79** ★★★★ ready. **80** ★★★★ ready, will still improve. **81** ★★★★★ ready. **82** ★★★★★ ready, will still improve. **83** ★★★★ ready. **84** ★★★★★ ready, will still improve. **85** ★★★★ ready, will still improve. **86** ★★★★★ ready, will still improve. **87** ★★★★(★) not ready, age further. **88** ★★★★★ not ready, age further.

Klein Constantia Cabernet Sauvignon★★★★★E
Ros Gower has produced magnificent wines at the revamped Constantia Estate and the Cabernets have accumulated all kinds of awards including South African Championship for cultivar and overall champion, as well as much acclaim from overseas critics. The first release from the 1986 vintage is a stunner and as good as it tastes now, will develop over many years to come. The 1987, released mid-1991, is a big, beautiful wine with a very high alcohol content of 13,7%, layers of flavour and good firm tannins that will carry the wine well into the next century. The 1988 is still to be released and is superb wine.
86 ★★★★★ good now, but will age with distinction. **87** ★★★★★ good now, but will age with distinction.
Kleindal Cabernet Sauvignon★★★B
Good, non-vintage wine, without complexity, that has developed well in the bottle.
Kleindal Director's Reserve★★★(★)C
A very good Cabernet from the 1987 vintage: it has nice fruit, good wood backing, and has developed very well in the bottle.
Koelenhof Co-op Cabernet Sauvignon★★(★)B
A dry, oaky wine (the 1985 somewhat too oaky) with insufficient cultivar character. The 1986 is better balanced and deserves three stars. It drank well in 1990, when it was probably at its best. The 1987 is better still. The 1988 is on the light side although it is a good improvement on previous releases.
KWV Cabernet★★★(no price available)
Clean, sound wines without much vintage variation which are supplied to members and also for export. These wines are not of the same quality as the Cape's commercial Cabernets, but have old-style appeal and make pleasant drinking.
La Cotte Cabernet Sauvignon (Franschhoek Vineyards)★★B
This wine is produced in limited quantities, with the 1988 rather better than usual.
Landskroon Cabernet Sauvignon★★★★C
This Cabernet has good varietal character with a rather unusual minty nose and good wood. A fair amount of bottle age is needed before it settles down. The 1978 has Superior certification and was sold at the 1983 Nederburg Auction. The 1979, 1980 and 1981 are more medium-bodied and made good drinking by the end of the 1980s. The 1982 is a big, bold wine which is now reaching its full potential. The 1983 is lighter and past its best. There were no releases from the 1985 and 1986 vintages. The 1987 shows a change in style, with new wood very evident. The 1988 is the best ever but will need time to develop. The 1989 follows the trend and 1990 is altogether better in depth of character and layers of flavour.
78 ★★★★ ready. **79** ★★★★ ready. **80** ★★★★ ready. **81** ★★★ ready. **82** ★★★★ ready. **83** ★★★ past its best, still enjoyable. **84** ★★★★ ready, will still improve. **85** no release. **86** no release. **87** ★★★(★) ready, will still improve. **88** ★★★★ not ready, age further. **89** ★★★★ not ready, needs time.
La Provence Rougeance★★★C
An attractive young Cabernet with distinct oak backing.
Le Bonheur Cabernet Sauvignon★★★★(★)E
It seems that whenever Michael Woodhead sets out to make a wine,

he does so with distinction. The 100% Cabernet from the 1982 vintage has been well aged in small wood, giving a beautiful, full-flavoured wine which has every potential to develop in the bottle to become one of the Cape's great Cabernets. At ten years of age the wine is beautiful and has loads of life to go. Keep an eye on the corks, however, as they are rather inferior, which is a pity. The 1983 is a lighter wine, in keeping with the vintage, but it still has fine character and is probably at its best now. The 1984 and 1986 are the best so far, deep and full-flavoured wines with lots of fruit and fine wood giving great complexity. The 1987 continues the trend and is full of fruit with good oak and fine tannin. It will develop with distinction.

82 ★★★★ ready, will still develop. **83** ★★★★ ready. **84** ★★★★★ ready, will still improve. **86** ★★★★★ not ready, age further. **87** ★★★★★ not ready, age further.

Le Moutonné Cabernet Sauvignon★★★C

This Franschhoek cellar has bottled a very good, full-flavoured 1984 Cabernet from grapes harvested in the Stellenbosch district. This dry, deep-flavoured wine is about at its best now. The next release was an older 1982 wine which now needs to be enjoyed. The 1987 is a good wine with every ability to develop well in the bottle.

82 ★★★ ready. **84** ★★★ ready. **87** ★★★(★) ready, will still improve with time.

Lievland Cabernet Sauvignon★★★★D

The 1984 vintage is the first release and is drinking particularly well in 1992. The 1985 is a lightish wine, but, from 1986 onwards, this Cabernet, along with all of the reds from this cellar, has developed into a very good wine. The 1986 is a really super wine with a deep satisfying richness. The 1987 is a little leaner but elegant all the same. The 1988 is bigger and better and really brings Lievland into the top quality category. This wine was awarded the Alphen Wine of the Month selection plus a gold medal at the Stellenbosch Bottled Wine Show. The 1989 follows with the same quality and is enriched with over 20% Merlot.

84 ★★★ ready. **85** ★★(★) ready. **86** ★★★(★) ready, will still improve. **87** ★★★(★) ready, will still improve. **88** ★★★★ age further. **89** ★★★★ age further.

L'Ormarins Cabernet Sauvignon★★★★E

(These wines are sold under the name 'Maison du Roi' in honour of the first owner.) The release of the 1983 L'Ormarins Cabernet was made only in 1988. It is a deep, rich wine with a lot of good wood, which will benefit with age. The 1984 is a fuller wine, deep, rich and full of tannin, and should develop well with time. The 1986 is a magnificent, full-flavoured, beautiful wine and the 1987 is equally grand (not yet released).

83 ★★★★ ready, will still improve. **84** ★★★★(★) ready, will still improve. **85** ★★★★ not ready, age further. **86** ★★★★★ not ready, age further.

McGregor Co-op Cabernet Sauvignon★★★B

The 1975 was the first McGregor Cabernet to be offered to the public, and only a few hundred bottles were produced. The 1977 vintage was a better product and showed promise of improvement in the bottle. A period of 10 years preceded the next release, which is a light-bodied, dry, fruity red for early drinking. The 1990 has a fair amount of wood backing the clean Cabernet character.

Meerlust Cabernet Sauvignon★★★★★E
The Meerlust Cabernet has a superb reputation, and justifiably so. A fine wine, this one is usually lighter-bodied and stylish. All releases have been certified Superior. The 1977, 1979 and 1985 vintages were not marketed, but the 1978 leaves no doubt about its outstanding quality and should be enjoyed now. All the 1980s are excellent, with 1980 and 1984 being perhaps the best so far. The 1986 is a beautiful, big wine that will need many years to show its full potential. Cellar samples of the 1987 and 1988 seem to be even better. A feature of the Meerlust Cabernets is their complex nose and excellent flavour, set off by the judicious use of new wood. It is not surprising, then, that they have been consistent winners at young wine shows, and judged more than once as South African champion.

75 ★★★★ drink. **76** ★★★★★ drink. **77** no release. **78** ★★★★ ready. **79** no release. **80** ★★★★★ ready. **81** ★★★★ ready. **82** ★★★★★ ready. **83** ★★★★ ready. **84** ★★★★★ ready, will improve. **85** no release. **86** ★★★★★ not ready, age further.

Middelvlei Cabernet Sauvignon★★★★(★)D
The 1981 vintage was the first release of a Cabernet from this Estate, and it won gold medals at the Stellenbosch and the South African Championship shows. It has an admirable cultivar character which has obviously had good ageing in new small wood before bottling, producing a complex wine which is drinking very well right now. The 1982 is a bigger, fuller wine with good depth of character and will age longer than the 1981. The 1983 has a very different nose, but the 1984 is a big, powerful wine that will develop over many years. There was no release from the 1985 vintage, but the 1986 more than makes up for it with a lovely full-flavoured wine that will age with distinction, as will the well-made 1987, which is very fine wine.

81 ★★★★ ready. **82** ★★★★ ready. **83** ★★★★ ready. **84** ★★★★ ready, will still improve. **85** no release **86** ★★★★(★) not ready, age further. **87** ★★★★(★) needs time to develop.

Mons Ruber Estate Cabernet Sauvignon★★C
The 1986 is the first attempt I've seen from this pocket-size Klein Karoo Estate. It has a strange but not unattractive nose and pleasant flavour, and developed well up to 1990. The 1990 is the next release – an unwooded, clean, light wine.

Morgenhof Cabernet Sauvignon★★★(★)D
Morgenhof, on the foothills of the Simonsberg, has been revitalized and their 1984 Cabernet was their first release. They couldn't have picked a better vintage with which to begin. A deep-coloured, well-balanced wine with fine character backed with good wood, it has enough tannin to develop well with time and was sold at the 1991 Nederburg Auction. There was no release of the 1985 vintage, but the 1986 is available – a lighter wine which tastes good now and probably won't age as long as the 1984 vintage. The 1988 shows better and bigger, with good fruit and oak, and should develop well.

84 ★★★★ ready, will still improve. **85** no release. **86** ★★★ ready. **87** no release. **88** ★★★(★) needs time to develop.

Muratie Cabernet Sauvignon ★★★(★)(no price available)
First samples of the 1990 and 1991 look far better than anything from this cellar before. Devotees of the old-style wines insist it needs long bottle-ageing, an opinion which is supported by recent tastings of the 1971 and 1976. Hopefully they will appreciate the new style.

Nederburg Auction Cabernet Sauvignon★★★★★E
The 1974 vintage is much the same as the 1972, and is regarded as one of the world's great Cabernets – its many honours include best Cabernet on show at the Club Oenologique International Wine and Spirit Competition, winning against worthy entrants from France, Italy, Spain, California and Australia. These special Cabernets from the cellar are released only after 10 or more years and sold exclusively at the annual Nederburg Auction. This very elegant wine with fine features was ready for drinking when released at the Auction yet still has the ability to develop further.

74 ★★★★★ ready. **75** ★★★★★ past its best, still enjoyable. **76** ★★★★★ ready. **77** ★★★★(★) ready. **78** ★★★★★ ready, will still improve. **79** ★★★★★ ready, will still improve. **80** ★★★★★ ready, will still improve. **81** ★★★★★ ready, will still improve.

Nederburg Paarl Cabernet★★★★(★)E
The Cabernets of Nederburg are internationally renowned for their own distinct style of deep, red richness in which cultivar character is heavily prominent. Delicious and full, they require good bottle-ageing before they reach their full potential (they peak between 10 and 15 years). Attractive as they are when young, they should not really be opened before they are at least five years old and beginning to show some of their promise. Patience and self-denial will be amply rewarded. Nederburg elevated Cabernet to the status of the most sought-after cultivar in South Africa. For many years, though, it could not be certified Superior because it contained less than the stipulated 75% of the cultivar required by law. Some magnificent vintages were produced during this time, however, the most outstanding being 1972, 1974, 1975 and 1976. Those of the 1980s were consistently good and always very accessible, yet all aging between 12 and 15 years.

72 ★★★★ drink. **73** ★★★★ drink. **74** ★★★ ready. **75** ★★★★ ready. **76** ★★★★★ ready. **77** ★★★★ ready. **79** ★★★(★) ready. **80** ★★★★ ready. **81** ★★★ past its best, still enjoyable. **82** ★★★★ ready. **83** ★★★ past its best, still enjoyable. **84** ★★★★ ready. **85** ★★★★ ready, will still improve. **86** ★★★★(★) not ready, age further. **87** ★★★★ not ready, age further. **88** ★★★★ not ready, age further.

Neethlingshof Cabernet Sauvignon★★★(★)E
The 1975 vintage was beautiful: deep and rich with complex flavour. The 1976, lighter in style, has also developed very well and should be drunk now. The wines of the early 1980s tend to be much lighter and finer than their predecessors and this, together with the use of new oak, allows much earlier drinking. The 1982 has good character, while the 1983 has developed into an excellent wine – 13 cases being selected for sale at the 1989 Nederburg Auction. After a disappointing start the 1984 is developing well. Now that Günter Brözel is in charge, things have changed. He couldn't have made the wine, as he wasn't there yet, but the 1986 is a giant step forward: a beautiful wine with a fine oak backing. It will need time to reach its full potential. The 1987 and 1988 are beautiful well-made wines packed with character, lots of fruit and good oak, and will develop well.

86 ★★★★ not ready, age further. **87** ★★★★(★) not ready, age further. **88** ★★★★★ not ready, age further.

Neil Ellis Vineyard Selection Cabernet Sauvignon★★★★C
The 1984 Cabernet was a creditable start to a new venture. Made from grapes selected from a vineyard in the Stellenbosch area, it is a fine wine with good cultivar character and good use of wood from an excellent vintage. It is drinking very well in 1991 and is now worth four stars. The 1985 is very good, considering the vintage and it might even age longer than the 1984. The 1986 is by far the best vintage and, as it develops, is heading for five-star status: big, deep-coloured wine filled with fruit flavour and backed by good wood. It will require lots of bottle development. There have been no releases since.

84 ★★★★ ready, will still improve. **85** ★★★(★) ready, will still improve. **86** ★★★★(★) not ready, age further.

Oude Libertas Cabernet Sauvignon (SFW)★★★★B
Although this range has now been discontinued there are a number of good vintages still available. This underestimated wine never really became popular, but aged with great benefit. The 1976 and 1978 vintages were outstanding and while the 1979 was not highly regarded when released, it has now aged into a delightful wine. The 1980 (the last) is probably the best and deserves four stars. It has matured into a beautiful wine. The middle 1970s need to be drunk. The 1979 and 1980 are excellent in 1992.

Oude Nektar Cabernet Sauvignon★★★(★)D
The 1988 and 1989 releases are complex wines with good oak and firm tannin.

Oude Rust Cabernet Sauvignon (Mooiuitsig)★★B
A very light, dry red with clean Cabernet character.

Overgaauw Cabernet Sauvignon★★★★(★)D
One of South Africa's consistently good Cabernets with no less than seven vintages of the 1970s receiving Superior certification. The wine has an unmistakable cellar characteristic on the nose and good wood treatment which complements the Cabernet without overwhelming it. An excellent wine made from some of South Africa's best Cabernet grapes, it is known to mature with rare distinction over 10 years or more. The wines of the early 1980s have taken on a fine style. The 1982 has developed very well to date, while the 1983 is surprisingly slow in developing. The lightish-coloured 1984 makes up for in character what it lacks in colour and should be ready in the early 1990s. It appears regularly at the Nederburg Auction. The 1985 is light and firm with fine character. The 1986 is very Bordeauxish, an elegant fine wine that will develop with distinction. The 1987 is much the same and will develop equally well.

75 ★★★ ready. **76** ★★★★ ready. **77** ★★★ past its best. **78** ★★★★ ready. **79** ★★★ ready. **80** ★★★★ ready, will still improve. **81** ★★★★ ready. **82** ★★★★ ready, will still improve. **83** ★★★★★ ready, will still improve. **84** ★★★★ ready, will still improve. **85** ★★★★(★) not ready, age further. **86** ★★★★(★) not ready, age further. **87** ★★★★(★) not ready, age further.

Pick 'n Pay Cabernet Sauvignon★★★(★)C
Part of the 'added-value' range and made by Simonsig. The 1987 is deep in colour, and has very good Cabernet character backed with clean oak. This is a good, dry Cabernet that drinks well now, and has the potential to develop well over six to eight years.

John Platter's Reserve Cabernet Sauvignon★★★(★)
This lovely, light Cabernet Sauvignon from the 1986 vintage is full of cultivar flavour and was well-matured in oak. Half the blend was aged in new Nevers oak and half in new Limousin barrels for 17 months. It received very little cellar handling and was treated in much the same manner as practised in Bordeaux. Now that John has sold Delaire, this must be a collector's item.
Rheboksklоof Cabernet Sauvignon★★★★D
A first release from the 1989 vintage was taken almost entirely by the Alphen Wine Club. A very good début that bodes well for the future. It has good cultivar character, backed by French oak, and will develop well in the bottle over the next four to six years. The 1990 is full of character; good fruit, fine flavours, good oak and firm tannin. It will develop well.
Riebeek Wine Farmers' Co-op Cabernet Sauvignon★★B
A full-bodied, fiery, dry red wine. More recent vintages have been toned down by some wood maturation. There was a big gap between vintages, from 1985 to 1988.
Robertson Co-op Cabernet Sauvignon★★★B
The first vintage was 1983, which takes the place of Robroi. It showed well, with good cultivar character and reasonable wood. The 1986 and 1987 vintages were light-bodied while the 1988 vintage is a somewhat fuller wine. The 1989 sports a handsome new label and is a bold, strong wine, and an improvement on other vintages. The 1990 has its own definite character – rather nice.
Romansrivier Co-op Cabernet Sauvignon★★★B
This is light Cabernet that has improved with each vintage and since 1987 has been given a little wood age. They drink quite well when two or three years old.
Roodendal Cabernet (SFW)★★★B
The first appearance of Roodendal was the 1979 vintage, one that proved a remarkable bargain for such good quality wine. Unfortunately, the next vintage, the 1981, appeared not to be in the same class when it was released, but it developed surprisingly well. The 1983 vintage which carries Superior certification was very shy to show, but has developed. The 1985 is an improvement on 1981 and 1983, while the 1987 is the best to date – a lighter-style Cabernet.
Roodezandt Co-op Cabernet Sauvignon★★★B
The earliest release was a very good 1978 vintage which has aged well. The 1979 was a little coarse and has not developed well. The 1980 was good, but the floods of 1981 prevented a release from that year. The 1982 and 1983 vintages are good value for money. The 1984 is full of cultivar character and drinks well now but could develop as promisingly as the 1978. I have not seen a 1985 but the 1986 is a good, firm, medium-bodied wine that will develop well. There is a gap of a number of years as vineyards were replanted. The 1990 is now available and has been blended with some Ruby Cabernet, resulting in a very attractive, fresh wine.

78 ★★★★ ready. **79** ★★★ past its best, still enjoyable. **80** ★★★ ready. **81** no release. **82** ★★★ ready. **83** ★★★ ready. **84** ★★★(★) ready. **85** no release. **86** ★★★ ready, will still improve. **87, 88, 89** no releases. **90** ★★★(★) not ready, age more.

Rooiberg Co-op Cabernet Sauvignon★★★B
A Wine of Origin Robertson with good balance of cultivar and wood,

this usually light red wine ages well in the bottle. It regularly wins honours at the young wine shows (including a gold medal at Goodwood in 1982). The 1983 was a good wine, but is probably past its best now. The 1984 is fuller in body and will have longer life, peaking in the early 1990s. The 1985 is much lighter in all respects and should be enjoyed now while the 1984 develops. The 1986, 1987 and 1988 are all good wines that can be enjoyed reasonably young.

83 ★★★ ready. **84** ★★★(★) ready, will still improve. **85** ★★★ ready. **86** ★★★ ready. **87** ★★★ ready, will still improve. **88** ★★★ ready, will still improve. **89** ★★★ ready.

Rozendal Colour Label Magnums★★★★D

In 1983 Kurt Amman produced a 100% Cabernet and aged it in Nevers oak for 18 months, resulting in a full, richly-flavoured wine that is developing very well in the magnums in which it was bottled. There is a range of 15 different colourful labels, 12 of these by the Stellenbosch artist, Larry Scully, from his series, 'Views of Stellenbosch', one by Kurt's wife, Lyn, and two by his daughter, Natalie (one depicting the wine-making process, the other a bridal couple). Another Colour Label issue will be a 1989 Magnum series with the same blend as Rozendal: 80% Merlot and 20% Cabernet.

Rustenberg Cabernet Sauvignon★★★★(★)E

The full-bodied Rustenberg Cabernet has not been available for as long as the dry red. Nevertheless, it has established its place as one of the Cape's best wines of this cultivar. It is difficult to place one vintage above another, but certainly the later years have greater varietal character and are more complex than the earlier ones. Of the 1975 vintage, the Estate released a special issue of 625 numbered bottles, which were distributed during the Stellenbosch tercentenary celebrations. The 1982 is a magnificent wine, although it does not carry Superior certification. It is developing beautifully in the bottle and will continue to do so well into the 1990s. In keeping with the vintage, the 1983 is lighter and a little disappointing. The 1984 more than compensates for the 1983: it is a beautiful wine and should develop well. The 1985 should be consumed while the 1984 develops. The 1986 is a magnificent wine, big, bold and full of cultivar character, while the 1987 is elegant with good flavour. The 1988 is a refined, elegant wine as is the 1989.

71 ★★★★ past its best, still enjoyable. **72** ★★★★★ ready. **73** ★★★★ ready. **74** ★★★★ ready. **75** ★★★★ ready. **76** ★★★★ ready, will still improve. **78** ★★★★★ ready. **79** ★★★★ ready. **80** ★★★★★ ready, will still improve. **81** ★★★ ready. **82** ★★★★★ ready, will still improve. **83** ★★★★ ready. **84** ★★★★★ ready, will still improve. **85** ★★★★ ready, will still improve. **86** ★★★★★ not ready, age further. **87** ★★★★ not ready, age further. **88** not ready, age further. **89** ★★★★★ not ready, age further.

Rustenberg Cabernet Sauvignon Reserve★★★★F

This is big and powerful wine out of the 1984, 1986 and 1987 vintages and is kept for special occasions. To be followed by 1989. It is deep, rich, attention-grabbing wine for sipping and savouring.

Rust-en-Vrede Cabernet Sauvignon★★★★E

The Estate's maiden vintage Cabernet (1979) was good, but succeeding ones were disappointing, and the critics were quick to claim beginner's luck. The 1982 is, however, an exceptionally good wine.

It drank well on release, and has continued to develop to date. The 1983 was judged South Africa's champion young red wine but developed more quickly than the 1984 and is probably past its best now. The 1980s all showed well with 1985 perhaps the weakest of a very fine line-up. All develop very well in the bottle.

🍷 **79** ★★★★(★) ready. **80** ★★★★ ready. **81** ★★★ ready. **82** ★★★★(★) ready, will still improve. **83** ★★★ ready. **84** ★★★★(★) ready, will still improve. **85** ★★★★ ready, will still improve. **86** ★★★★(★) not ready, age further. **87** ★★★★(★) not ready, age further.

Saxenburg Private Collection Cabernet★★★D

From the 1990 vintage comes a good, clean, deep-flavoured Cabernet with fine oak backing.

Simonsig Cabernet Sauvignon★★★★C

South Africa produces some superb Cabernets and Simonsig is known for being consistently amongst the best. From SA Young Wine Championship in 1977 to the 1984 which won a gold medal at the International Wine and Spirit Competition in London and, I am proud to say, is the first winner of my Trophy for the best South African Red on show. Seeming to improve with each vintage the 1986 and 1987 are great wines, while the 1988 is generally more elegant and refined.

🍷 **77** ★★★★(★) past its best. **78** ★★★ ready. **79** ★★★★ ready. **80** ★★★ ready. **81** ★★ past its best. **82** ★★★ ready. **83** ★★★ ready. **84** ★★★★(★) ready, will still improve. **85** ★★★★ ready, will still improve. **86** ★★★★★ not ready, age further. **87** ★★★★(★) will develop. **88** ★★★★ needs time.

Simonsvlei Cabernet Sauvignon★★★C

A medium- to full-bodied Cabernet with good cultivar character. Usually very full in the mouth with enough tannin to age well, it has appeared at a number of Nederburg Auctions and has regularly won gold medals at local shows. It has been somewhat erratic over the vintages, with 1982 the best of the 1980s. Latest vintages are a little disappointing, but sales show otherwise.

🍷 **81** ★★★ past its best. **82** ★★★(★) drink. **83** ★★★ drink. **84** ★★(★) drink. **85** ★★★(★) ready. **86** ★★ ready. **88** ★★★(★) ready. **89** ★★★ ready.

Spier Cabernet Sauvignon★★★C

This is a sound wine showing definite Cabernet character; usually on the light side with 1985 being even lighter than usual. The 1984 is the best to date, and the 1986 is much the same. The 1987 is lighter in style. The 1988 will follow.

🍷 **84** ★★★(★) ready. **85** ★★★ ready. **86** ★★★ ready, will still improve. **87** ★★★ ready, will still improve.

Springlands Cabernet (Drop Inn)★★A

A non-vintage, easy-drinking, soft wine with Cabernet character and some wood.

Stellenryck Cellarmaster's Choice (Bergkelder)★★★★★E

A special release from the 1987 vintage. The best casks available were selected and blended by Dr Laszlo to produce remarkable wine. It was aged in new French oak and shows great style and character, and will develop well over time.

Stellenryck Collection Cabernet Sauvignon ★★★★★E

The 1980 and 1982 products under this label are magnificent, full, deep wines which will reward after more years of ageing. Both are five-star wines and are developing beautifully. There is no 1983, but the 1984 is a magnificent wine and carries Superior certification. The 1986 is a beautiful, big, deep-flavoured wine that will need years to show its true potential. The 1987 continues the fine quality.

80 ★★★★★ ready. **81** ★★★★ ready. **82** ★★★★★ ready, will still improve. **83** no release. **84** ★★★★★ not ready, age further. **85** no release. **86** ★★★★★ not ready, age further. **87** ★★★★★ not ready, age further.

Stellenryck Historic Wine Museum Cabernet Sauvignon 1975 (Bergkelder)★★★★(★)E

This wine, which is 100% Cabernet, was bottled especially for Stellenbosch's tercentenary in 1979. All those fortunate enough to have some in their private cellars and have resisted drinking it should thoroughly enjoy their wine now.

Stellenzicht Cabernet Sauvignon★★★★D

The first release from this spectacular new cellar is from the 1987 vintage. It is well made wine with lots of character that will need time to show its full potential.

Swartland Co-op Cabernet Sauvignon★★B

Over the years this has gone from somewhat coarse and bold to good, harmonious wine. It is usually medium-bodied and develops well over two to three years, so it's good for fairly early drinking.

85 ★★ ready. **86** ★★★(★) ready. **87** ★★(★) ready. **89** ★★★ not ready, age further. **90** ★★★ not ready, age further.

Thelema Cabernet Sauvignon★★★★★E

The release from the 1988 vintage is a good first effort with lots of exciting character. The 1989 is a bench-mark wine; a beautiful wine packed with layers of fruit flavours, entirely from new clone Cabernet, and backed with fine new French oak. It tastes good now, but patience will be well rewarded as it will develop magnificently. The 1990 takes this cellar well on its way to being consistently one of the Cape's best.

Uiterwyk Cabernet Sauvignon★★★(★)D

This is a very consistent wine which has regularly received Superior certification. Deep purple when young, it ages elegantly, reaching a depth of complexity not to be found in many other Cabernets. With its fine balance between cultivar and wood, the 1974 was the most outstanding of the 1970s' vintages. The 1982 is outstanding: blended with a little Merlot, and spending almost two years in wood, it has developed well into the 1990s. The 1987 and the 1988 are rich, full wines – also with a touch of Merlot.

76 ★★★★ past its best. **77** ★★★ past its best. **78** ★★★★ ready. **79** ★★★★ ready. **80** ★★★★(★) ready. **81** ★★★ ready. **82** ★★★★ ready. **83** ★★★(★) ready. **84** ★★★★ ready. **86** ★★★ ready, will still improve. **87** ready, will still improve. **88** not ready, will improve.

Uitkyk Carlonet★★★★(★)E

Today's Uitkyk Carlonets taste seductively ready at an early age, but deceptively so, for they need time to fulfil their true potential. Through the late 1970s and mid-1980s, this wine developed dramatically in style and quality. There were no releases of the poorer vintages of 1979, 1981 and 1985. The 1986 is a soft, pleasant wine with good cultivar flavours and nice oak. The 1987 is a more intense wine and although drinkable, already has the structure to age with benefit through to the late 1990s. The 1988 will need time.

74 ★★★★★ past its best, still enjoyable. **75** ★★★★ ready. **76** ★★★★★ ready. **77** no release. **78** ★★★★ ready. **79** no release. **80** ★★★ ready. **81** no release. **82** ★★★★★ ready. **83** ★★★★ ready. **84** ★★★★★ ready, will still improve. **85** no release. **86** ★★★★ ready, will still improve. **87** ★★★★ not ready, age further. **88** ★★★★ not ready, age further.

Vergenoegd Cabernet Sauvignon★★★★(★)C

The wines of the 1970s and 1980s were of a style very distinctive to the Estate, and no doubt influenced by its close proximity to the sea. This is medium-bodied wine with great depth of character giving a very long-lasting finish and an interesting complexity. Wood-aged in old vats, it was consistently certified Superior. It developed well over five to ten years, and sold regularly at the Nederburg Auction and, in earlier days, was a consistent grand champion at the SA Championship Wine Show. The vintages of the early 1980s are richer, fuller and have beautiful depth of character which will reward good bottle ageing. The wines of the late 1980s show a difference in style and reflect the use of new French oak. The 1987 begins to show some new life, whereas the 1988 should show a change in style.

72 ★★★★ drink. **73** ★★★★ past its best. **74** ★★★★★ drink. **75** ★★★ past its best. **76** ★★★★★ ready. **77** ★★★ ready. **78** ★★★★ ready. **79** ★★★ ready. **80** ★★★★★ ready. **81** ★★★★ ready. **82** ★★★★★ ready. **83** ★★★★ ready. **84** ★★★★ ready, will still improve. **85** ★★★(★) ready. **86** ★★★(★) ready, will still improve. **87** ★★★(★) not ready, age further. **88** ★★★★ not ready, age further.

Villiera Cabernet Sauvignon★★★(★)C/D

This wine was launched with the 1983 vintage. Medium-bodied, undoubtedly Cabernet but rather too heavily wooded, the overall style nevertheless augured well for the future. The 1984 and 1986 are fuller and, to my taste, better wines in every respect, fully deserving four stars. They have good wood character coming from both French and American oak. From 1988 on, the wines are leaders in their field. The 1988 is a superb wine, full of intense character and a depth of flavour not found in any previous vintage. The 1989 is a little quieter to start, but is developing beautifully.

83 ★★★(★) ready. **84** ★★★★ ready, will still improve. **85** no release. **86** ★★★★ ready, will still improve. **87** ★★★★ ready, will still improve. **88** ★★★★★ not ready, age further. **89** ★★★★ not ready, age further.

Vlottenburg Co-op Cabernet Sauvignon★★★B

Good value for money, this dry, honest and uncomplicated wine was originally unwooded. Nowadays it receives good wood, adding an extra dimension to the wine as demonstrated with the 1986 and 1987. These last two vintages should develop with interest. The 1988 is not quite up to the past two vintages standard but this is a factor of the year. The 1989 is possibly the best so far.

Vredenheim Cabernet Sauvignon★★★D

The first release, from the 1987 vintage, is a little light in all respects. There is no 1988; the next release will be from the 1989 vintage.

Vriesenhof Cabernet★★★★★D

The name was changed from simply Vriesenhof to Vriesenhof

Cabernet with the 1984 vintage. The 1984 is a beautiful wine, with lots of Cabernet character backed with good young wood. As attractive as the wine is now, your patience will be rewarded if you can wait until 1994 before sampling. The 1985 is lighter but has good cultivar character. The 1986 is a big, beautiful wine and five-star material. The 1987 is much the same but still needs lots of time to smooth out. The 1988 appeared somewhat subdued and soft on release, but is already developing and won't disappoint. The 1989 is 50/50 new clone and old clone giving lovely floral-berry character wine with lots of elegance.

84 ★★★★(★) ready, will still improve. **85** ★★★ ready, will still improve. **86** ★★★★★ not ready, age further. **87** ★★★★★ not ready, age further. **88** ★★★★★ not ready, age further. **89** ★★★★★ not ready, age further.

Warwick Cabernet Sauvignon★★★★(★)D/E

Warwick farm has produced good quality grapes for many years, but Norma Ratcliffe crushed them for the first time in 1984. The resulting wine is only for tasting at the farm. Norma's experience in Bordeaux has taught her to handle the wine as little as possible and not to use artificial agents nor cold stabilization. The first release, of some 1 500 cases is from the 1985 vintage. It has good, clean cultivar character with fine oak backing after 16 months in small, new Nevers oak and it will develop over the next five to eight years. The 1986 is a much more complex and impressive wine that will need many years to show its full potential. The 1987 vintage contains a portion of Warwick's gold medal winning Merlot and the result is beautiful. The 1988 and 1989 have the potential to be tremendous.

85★★★★(★) ready, will still improve. **86**★★★★★ not ready, age further. **87** ★★★★(★) not ready, needs time. **88** ★★★★★ not ready, needs time. **89** ★★★★★ not ready, needs time.

Welgemeend Cabernet Sauvignon★★★★C

The 1986 was the last vintage as all the Estate's Cabernet was required for its blends. However, from 1990 some Cabernet will again be available. Hooray!

Wellington Wynboere Co-op Cabernet★B

The first Cabernet released from this Co-op was the 1984 vintage, a wood-aged wine that has improved in the bottle. The 1983 is much lighter and should be enjoyed now. The 1984 is a very good dry wine that will definitely age with benefit. The 1985, 1986 and 1987 are good medium-bodied wines that are excellent value for money.

Welmoed Co-op Cabernet Sauvignon★★★B

These are well-made wines with good cultivar flavour and nice wood backing, and have a good record of Young Wine Show successes. The 1988 shows lovely style and flavour and should develop well in the bottle. The 1989 is good, four-star wine, and very good value.

Woolworths Cabernet★★★C

Two unwooded, ready-for-drinking, pleasant wines without much character from the 1984 vintage. The labels are the same, but I prefer the red capsuled wine to the gold capsuled. The 1986, from Fairview, has fair cultivar character and no wood. It has developed well and is very satisfying in 1992.

Woolworths Vintage Cabernet Sauvignon★★★★C

The excellent 1986 from Vriesenhof has lots of fruit flavour backed with good wood. It should be very good in the mid-1990s. The 1987 is excellent wine at that price, and well worth trying plenty of as it will age with great distinction; lots of flavour, good oak.

Zandvliet Cabernet Sauvignon★★★(★)E

The 1984 vintage is a surprisingly good wine and drinks very well. The 1987 is a good follow-up.

Zandwijk Cabernet Sauvignon★★★D

Made according to Jewish religious requirements. The 1988 was released in 1991, and is a big bold wine, full of tannin, which needs time to soften.

Zevenwacht Cabernet Sauvignon★★★★D

The 1983 is a firm, elegant wine, which was matured in small French and large Yugoslavian oak, while the 1984 is much bigger, full of fruit and good wood. The latter is showing very well in 1990, and should continue to age with benefit over a number of years. The 1985 is surprisingly good for a weak vintage. The 1986 follows the same lines as the 1984 but made with more complexity with the addition of some 15% Merlot. The 1987 is by far the best, made from new clone Cabernet blended with Merlot and Cabernet Franc. The 1988 is also a fine wine.

84 ★★★★ ready, will still improve. **85** ★★★(★) ready, will still improve. **86** ★★★★ not ready, age further. **87** ★★★★(★) not ready, age further. **88** ★★★★(★) not ready, age further.

Zonnebloem Cabernet Sauvignon (SFW)★★★★(★)C

Traditionally a full-flavoured, stout wine which ages with great benefit, it has been a consistent feature of the South African market since the early 1920s and, considering the enormous volume produced over the decades, it has sustained a remarkably high standard. More recent vintages have seen a move to a more modern style and better use of new small oak is playing a noticeable role. Up until the Coastal region was proclaimed, a wine like Zonnebloem Cabernet could not claim Superior certification. With the formation of the Coastal region, the wine received its first Superior and did so for the subsequent eleven vintages to 1986. By the time the 1987 was released in early 1991, the Superior certification system had been dropped. Zonnebloem Magnums are released some three to four years after the 750 m*l* bottles. To date, the Magnum releases are from the 1978, 1979, 1980, 1981, 1982, 1983 vintages with the 1984 due in 1992. The more recent vintages are quite outstanding, with the exception, perhaps, of the 1981, which, although Superior, showed less well when launched; it is nevertheless developing well in the bottle. The 1986 is a pleasing development in style, showing much better fruit and good wood. The 1987 has signs of the more modern style with the 1988 being the best release of the 1980s.

76 ★★★★ drink. **77** ★★★ past its best. **78** ★★★★ ready. **79** ★★★★ past its best. **80** ★★★★ ready. **81** ★★★(★) ready. **82** ★★★★ ready. **83** ★★★(★) ready. **84** ★★★★(★) ready, will still improve. **85** ★★★★(★) ready, will still improve. **86** ★★★★(★) ready, will still improve. **87** ★★★★(★) not ready, age further. **88** ★★★★★ not ready, age further.

Ruby Cabernet

McGregor Co-op Ruby Cabernet★★★B
This is an interesting introduction from 1990 vintage. It has good berry flavour, no wood, and is fresh and clean. Easy drinking at an early age.

Waboomsrivier Co-operative★★B
The 1987 was released very young and has developed pleasantly over the years. The 1988 has more body, is lively, fruity and ready for drinking. The 1990 and 1991 were ready for drinking on release.

Cinsaut

Du Toitskloof Co-op Cinsaut★★★A
A good, deep, full, well-made wine which develops splendidly after a year or two in the bottle. This is a good example of what can be done with Cinsaut. Throughout the 1980s this Co-op produced very acceptable wines from Cinsaut. The 1990 and 1991 are delightful, medium-bodied, ruby-coloured, fruity-fresh, flavoured wines that drink very well now and have enough tannin to allow development over a few years. Good value for money.
Kaapzicht Cinsaut★★★B
Launched from 1990 vintage as a wine to drink young. It is drinking very well mid-1992 and shows no negative signs of ageing. Light-coloured, fruity wine made for easy, uncomplicated drinking.
Landskroon Cinsaut★★★(★)B
This is a fairly fruity wine with medium body and the finesse which lacks in many lesser Cinsauts. It provides enjoyable drinking, proving that this cultivar, when correctly handled, can produce good dry reds. The 1974 aged very well and peaked at six years; the 1976 was even better, and the early 1980s' vintages maintained the attractive quality of the previous vintages, as do the more recent vintages of 1986 and 1987. The 1988, 1989 and 1990 are a little lighter in character and have the slightest touch of oak.
Mamreweg Cinsaut★★★A
This is undoubtedly the cellar's best wine. The 1977 vintage developed nicely in the bottle and made easy drinking after two years. From then the cellar produced South Africa's champion Cinsaut for three years in succession (1978, 1979 and 1980). All have looked good in the bottle, the 1979 developing particularly well. The vintages of the early 1980s have become fuller bodied, with 1986 and 1987 being particularly good for early, easy drinking. The 1989 was soft and fruity and needed to be drunk young. Releases from the 1990s' vintages are a little fresher and not to be taken lightly, with a high 13% alcohol content.
Perdeberg Co-op Cinsaut★★(★)A
At first this Cinsaut was not produced regularly, but this trend has changed over the past few vintages. It is a good, honest, medium-bodied, dry red. The 1987 had an arresting character which is missing in the lighter-bodied 1988.
Roodezandt Co-op Cinsaut★★A
Roodezandt is producing Cinsaut while their Cabernet is being replanted. The label says 'light', but the releases to date have had respectable alcohol content of between 12,5 and 14,0%! The 1990 and 1991 are good-flavoured wines.
Swartland Cinsaut★★A
The heavy, full-flavoured 1973 vintage was sold at the 1979 Nederburg Auction and was definitely a four-star wine. Its age has given it a soft bouquet, and its heaviness, virtually unique in a Cinsaut, has rounded it out into a fine wine which goes down admirably – an astonishing achievement after all these years. Although on the full side, more recent wines do not seem to have the same depth. They drink well when young. The 1988 is a deep, full-flavoured wine but the 1989 is not quite up to the old standard, although pleasant enough. The 1990 continues with its popular style and growing demand.

Vergenoegd Cinsaut★★★(★)B
A really good Cinsaut which is easy to drink at two years and develops really well in the bottle. The 1978 vintage was the first Cinsaut to be certified Superior. The vintages of the early 1980s are all good, which proves just how much can be done with this much-maligned cultivar. Mother Nature did not provide good Cinsaut in 1983, 1984 and 1985, and none was bottled at Vergenoegd. The 1986 was released in 1988 and is delightful, light-bodied, well-flavoured wine that drinks very easily. The 1989 is very good drinking and has good wood.
Waboomsrivier Co-op Cinsaut★★B
A typical, light, dry red. The 1990 is very pleasant.
Wamakersvallei Co-op Cinsaut★★A
A good, light Cinsaut.

Gamay

(*See also* Nouveau wines, page 225)
Vlottenburg Co-op Gamay Noir★★A
First produced from the 1985 vintage, this release was not particularly good, having none of the fruit associated with the cultivar. The 1986 and 1987 vintages were an improvement, with the 1988 very good. The 1989 has a nice oak background. The 1990 is a pleasant, soft wine with a dry finish. This light, dryish wine needs to be drunk young and chilled.

Grenache

A number of cellars use Grenache in various blends. Citrusdal seems to be the only cellar to have labelled a wine 'Grenache' but does not seem to have done so since 1982. The Droë Rooi from Oranjerivier Wynkelders is made from Grenache and the Citrusdal Chianti is 60% Grenache. Lutzville make a Blanc de Noir from this variety as well.

Merlot

Avontuur Merlot★★★(★)D
Very good Merlot character backed with good wood. So far it has been produced in minute quantities. I look forward to future, more plentiful releases.

Backsberg Merlot★★★(★)C
The first release from the 1989 vintage has a most enticing nose and is full of soft, yielding flavours and mouth-filling qualities. The 1990 is along the same lines – lovely when young, but probably best within three to four years of vintage. Excellent value for money.

Boplaas Merlot★★★(★)C
This has been a good wine throughout the 1980s. The 1986 is very good and probably at its best in 1992. The 1987 vintage is attractive and the 1988, although a well-made wine, seems to lack the life of the earlier vintages. The 1989 is well-made elegant wine that should develop as well as the 1986.

Boschendal Jean de Long Merlot Auction Reserve★★★★E
This is a super wine from the 1991 vintage with only 30 cases being sold on the 1992 Cape Independent Winemakers' Guild Auction. It is fine, elegant wine, full of berry nose, soft fruit in the mouth and good oak background.

Buitenverwachting Auction Reserve★★★★E
The 1989 vintage provided 100, six-bottle cases for the 1991 Cape Independent Winemakers' Guild Auction. It is big wine with lots of flavour and good oak.

Cape Vintners Members Only Merlot★★★★D
Very well-made wine with deep, soft flavours and full fruity nose. Aged in Nevers oak giving good, but not obtrusive, oak backing. From 1990 vintage. Youthful zest needs two to four more years for it to reach its best. Good value, good wine from Overgaauw.

De Leuwen Jagt Merlot★★★D
First release from 1990 vintage. Good nose, pleasant fruity flavour, with fairly tannic finish. Should soften out over another year or two.

Delheim Merlot★★★★(not for sale)
A small quantity of the 1986 was bottled under the Delheim Collectors label. It is a splendid wine full of fine flavours, and is ageing with great benefit. The Collectors Label wines are not for sale, but are given away to friends of Delheim. The Merlot is also used to soften their Pinotage. An amount of the 1990 was bottled for sale.

Domein Doornkraal Merlot★★★B
The first release from the 1990 vintage is a medium-bodied, soft-charactered wine that makes good, early drinking. Good value for money. No 1991 has been released.

Fairview Merlot Reserve ★★★★D
The first release from 1989 is excellent well-balanced wine with fine fruit and good wood. It is developing well. The 1990 is fuller, fruitier wine with good oak.

Fleur du Cap Merlot★★★★C
From the 1990 vintage comes this very drinkable fruity wine, which is very soft in the mouth. This signifies a break in the Fleur du Cap tradition of not releasing their reds until they are five years old, because they believe this wine is good at two years and will probably peak by five years.

Glen Carlou Merlot★★★★E
The first vintage, the 1988, is deep in colour and has good nose and lots of fruit backed by good wood. The 1989 is a most attractive, big, full wine which should develop well with age. The 1990 has a whole percent more alcohol at 13,4%, and a lot more potential. It is lovely, full-flavoured wine. The cellar sample of 1991 promises even better wine, full of berry-cherry character.
Le Moutonne Merlot★★★(★)D
The first release from 1990 is soft, easy wine. The 1991 is considerably better with 20% Cabernet Franc. Nice fruit, good oak.
Meerlust Merlot★★★★D
The 1984, backed with good wood and touched with a small fraction of Cabernet, was a most attractive wine to drink when released and super in 1992. There was no release from the 1985 vintage. The 1986 is bigger and better while the 1987 (yet to be released) is a five-star stunner.
Overgaauw Merlot★★★★C
The Cape's first Merlot came from the 1982 vintage. A deep wine, full of flavour and interest, it has developed beautifully in the bottle. The 1983 is lighter and will probably not reach the height of the 1982, although the 1984 and 1986 are very good. The 1987 is a beautiful wine. It drinks very well now and is probably best enjoyed by the mid-1990s. The 1988 is a magnificent wine full of fruity flavours and backed with good wood, and is likely to become five-star material.
Uiterwyk Merlot★★★D
The 1984 was a big wine with deep colour and rich flavour, it has no evident wood flavour in its make-up, in spite of maturing for a year in big, old vats. But it's still very good. The 1987 vintage is darker in colour but light in flavour, and the 1988 is somewhat reserved and, with the evident tannin, probably needs a few years to develop.
Villiera Merlot★★★★(★)D
The 1989 and 1990 are both excellent wines and it's no wonder this cellar's Merlot was judged South Africa's best. It is deep dark wine packed with fruit and spice, and will develop with benefit.
Vlottenberg Co-op Merlot★★★B
The first release from the 1989 vintage, which was a little shy on release, is now beginning to show more fruity flavours against a good oak backing. The 1990 is an improvement.
Warwick Merlot★★★★E
As one would expect from Warwick, a fine Merlot with deep, wonderful flavours and most attractive nose. The 1989 is the first commercial release. As good as it is now, control yourself and allow another four to five years' development, when it should be great.
Warwick Special Reserve 1987★★★★(No price – auctioned)
A beautiful, deep-coloured wine with plenty of fruit and flavour and lots of tannin that will enable it to develop over many years. Only 20 cases were made for the New World Wine Auction in 1990. The 1990 vintage appeared at the 1992 Cape Independent Winemakers' Guild Auction. These are fine wines that are worth seeking out.
Woolworths Le Deuxieme 902R★★★★E
Part of the Woolworths' Vintage Collection. The number 90 indicates the vintage; 2, the second in the range; and the R stands for red. Excellent straight Merlot from Rustenburg and needing two to four years to develop.

Pinotage

Aan-de-Doorns Co-op Pinotage★★B
A fruity, dry wine with typical Pinotage nose, and most suitable for early drinking.

Altydgedacht Pinotage★★★C
The 1983 was a soft, well-flavoured wine with good cultivar character and nice wood. The 1986 is a very different Pinotage, having aged 10 months in new Spanish oak, and is developing well in the bottle. The 1987 is also very oaky but from American oak. There was no release from the 1988 vintage and the 1989 had some American oak, giving good, full, masculine wine.

Avontuur Pinotage★★★B
An easy-drinking Pinotage. The 1987 vintage has good cultivar nose without the distinctive Pinotage ester which will appeal to many. The flavour is good with a nice soft feel in the mouth. The 1988 is a soft, early-drinking wine.

Backsberg Pinotage★★★B
This is always a delightful wine that can be consumed young, when the fruity Pinotage bouquet can be fully appreciated. It can also be aged with benefit. It develops a wide, full flavour which, together with its deep colour, gives the impression of a seemingly much heavier wine. The 1984 and 1985 vintages offer a change in style, yielding deeper, bigger wines. Recent vintages were more like the old style, but the 1988 is a much bigger wine. The 1989 is a full-flavoured delicious wine and probably the best ever. The 1990s are following a similar style.

88★★★ ready. **89★★★(★)** ready but will still develop. **90 ★★★(★)** ready, but will still develop.

Beaufort Pinotage (Solly Kramer)★★★A
This is a good example of a Pinotage: good cultivar nose and fine flavour; the latest being a full-bodied, easy-drinking wine.

Bellingham Pinotage★★★B
This wine has shown improvement with each year and now has typical Pinotage fruitiness; it is delightful when young and slightly chilled. Current bottlings will, no doubt, age better than the earlier ones. From the 1986 vintage, however, the wine is vintage-dated. From 1988 the wines are big, bold, and forceful.

Bergsig Pinotage★★★B
A pleasant, light wine, without the typical Pinotage nose. The 1982 was wood-aged, and by 1988 it had developed into a fine wine and deserved an extra star. The 1985 and the 1987 are good but lighter in style; the 1988 and 1989 is less fruity but drink easily. The 1990 is bigger and fuller flavoured, yet still easy, early drinking.

Bertrams Pinotage★★★C
Throughout the 1980s this was a very reliable, easy-drinking fruity wines with good cultivar character. It improved as the decade progressed and by 1987 was excellent wine. The 1988 is a lighter and more elegant wine and the 1989 follows this style. It is now one of the Cape's best Pinotage wines.

81 ★★★ past its best, still enjoyable. **82 ★★★** ready. **83 ★★★** ready. **84 ★★★★** ready. **85 ★★★** ready. **86 ★★★★** ready, will still improve. **87 ★★★★** ready, will still improve. **88 ★★★★** ready, but will still improve. **89 ★★★★** allow more ageing.

Bolandse Co-op Pinotage★★★(★)A
This is a cellar noted for its good reds, and the Pinotage is no exception. The 1976, 1977 and the 1978 developed well over about 10 years. The Pinotages of the early 1980s are all full-bodied and need to be consumed within four to six years, when they are at their best. The 1986 is particularly good. The 1988 is lighter-bodied for early drinking. The 1989 is a little fuller but again for early drinking. The 1990 is a big full wine with nearly 14% alcohol. They are all very good value for money.
Bonnievale Co-op Pinotage★★A
A typical medium-bodied Pinotage. The 1990s are brightly coloured and Nouveau in style.
Botha Co-op Pinotage★★★A
A consistently good Pinotage with a long record of show successes. Its good balance and full flavour allow it to age well over five to seven years. The wines of the early 1980s seem to be slightly fuller-bodied with the 1983 and 1984 already showing well – the latter having the potential to develop well into the early 1990s. From the 1985 vintage onwards, each vintage has had some ageing in wood. The 1987 is the best release to date with the 1988 good, but not as outstanding. There was no release from the 1989 or 1990, but this might be resumed from the 1991 vintage.
87 ★★★★ ready, will still improve. **88** ★★★(★) ready, will still improve.
Bovlei Co-op Pinotage★★★A
A frequent prize-winner at shows. The 1986 is a very full wine, while the 1987 and 1988 are lighter in body but have good flavours. The 1989 is fuller and better.
Buffelskroon Pinotage (Calitzdorp Co-op)★A
Very much a *vin ordinaire*, without much cultivar character. This wine is not bottled with each vintage.
Cape Vintners Members Only Pinotage★★★(★)C
One of the new-style Pinotage wines. Attractive, fruity nose, with the eight months of small oak ageing showing on the nose and softening the Pinotage character. From 1989 vintage and very drinkable, but will benefit from another four to six years in the bottle.
Cederberg Kelders Pinotage★★B
Never a typical Pinotage, the Cederberg Kelders Pinotage always seems to have more cellar character than cultivar character – lots of wood and little Pinotage character. Nevertheless this is an attractive wine. The 1987 has developed with interest. I missed the 1988, but the 1989 is similar to before with the 1990 (not yet released) having unusual nose but good flavour. It has enough tannin to age well.
Clairvaux Co-op Pinotage★★A
A tough, dry wine from the 1988 vintage; not for ageing, and has not been seen since.
Clos Malverne Pinotage★★★(★)D
This cellar is making a speciality out of Pinotage. The initial release from the 1989 vintage is a full-flavoured, well-wooded wine with lots of fruit. It is developing well in the bottle. The 1990 is a classy wine, and 1991 continues in bold, generous style. They will all age with benefit over eight to ten years.
Culemborg Pinotage★★★B
An inexpensive, pleasant cultivar wine which is excellent value for

money and has very good Pinotage character. It is vintage-dated. The 1986 has developed well in the bottle over four years. All vintages since are along the same lines.

De Doorns Co-op Pinotage★★A

One of the heavy-bodied, powerful Pinotages.

Delheim Pinotage★★★(★)B

Up to 1986 this has been a medium-bodied, dry red with good cultivar character. Aged about a year in large Limousin vats before bottling, this gives the wine more class than most Pinotages. The 1983 vintage is particularly fruity and pleasant while the 1985 is a fine elegant wine. With 1986, Philip Costandius blended some 20% Merlot with the Pinotage, producing a serious wine of most unusual dimension. It drinks particularly well now but should age with interest. The 1987 has 25% Merlot and is a big, beautiful wine with soft plummy flavour that makes it most attractive – as is the 1988. The 1989 and 1990 follow the same attractive style, and all develop well in the bottle.

Die Krans Pinotage★★(★)B

This is one of the better natural wines from this cellar, which benefits from some wood-ageing.

Diemersdal Pinotage★★★C

Wine that is big in character, soft in style, with lots of fruit, and a clean finish. It has enough tannin to age in the medium term. First release came from the 1989 vintage.

Douglas Co-op Pinotage★A

From the 1990 vintage comes the first release under this label (previously sold as Dry Red). It is recognizable as Pinotage, medium-bodied, yet a little awkward in the mouth. The 1991 is fuller, better, with a touch of Tinta Barocca.

Douglas Green Pinotage★★★(★)C

A fairly full-bodied Pinotage of good quality and probably slightly underrated by the wine-drinking public. Although earlier vintages were blended with Cinsaut, it is unmistakably Pinotage when young. Its slightly overbearing quality tones down with a year or two in the bottle and it becomes very acceptable. It carries a vintage date. The 1978 has developed very well; the 1979 is even better but is reaching the stage where it needs to be consumed. The vintages of the 1980s are far smoother than earlier vintages at the time of bottling, which adds to the wine's acceptability. The 1986 is a full, rounded wine that drinks well in 1992. The 1987 was a more dominant wine, while the 1988 is a well-made wine that might need time to develop. These wines usually carried Superior certification (when it existed) which is fairly unusual for Pinotage. The 1989 is in new packaging.

79 ★★★ past its best, drink. **80** ★★★★ ready. **81** ★★★★ ready. **82** ★★★★ ready. **83** ★★★ ready. **84** ★★★★ ready. **86** ★★★(★★★★) ready. **87** ★★★ ready. **88** ready. **89** ★★★ ready, will still develop.

Du Toitskloof Co-op Pinotage★★★B

First release from 1990 is a little subdued showing as much wood as cultivar. Early-drinking wine which might develop in the bottle.

Eersterivier Valleise Co-op Pinotage★★★B

Consistently reliable, fruity wine of the fuller-bodied style with a good record of show successes. At the time of release, earlier vintages were ready for early drinking. The late 1980s and early

1990s are distinctly Pinotage and best when young and fresh; medium bodied, fresh and fruity. Good value for money.

Fairview Pinotage★★★B

This is usually a full, powerful, dark-coloured wine which is distinctly different from most other Pinotages. The 1979 is the best of the 1970s' vintages and is perhaps rather less powerful. The 1980 is very good, the 1982 even better and the 1984 has good, full body and lovely fruit. Although the 1985 is light, it is a fine wine. The 1986 has more character. The 1987 is a good, sound wine, while the 1988 is one of the best to date. The 1989, 1990 and 1991 continue the style.

79 ★★★★ drink. **80** ★★★ drink. **82** ★★★★ ready. **84** ★★★ ready. **85** ★★★ ready. **86** ★★★ ready. **87** ★★★ ready. **88** ★★★ ready, will still improve. **89** ★★★ ready, will improve. **90** ★★★ ready, will improve.

Fairview Pinotage Reserve★★★★C

The 1989 is excellent value for money and one of the Cape's great Pinotage wines; wood aged, good fruit, fine tannins, and developing beautifully in the bottle.

Fleur Du Cap Pinotage (Bergkelder)★★★★C

When the Fleur du Cap wines were introduced, this was one of the poorest of the range, but it has since developed into a really fine Pinotage. Well-balanced and medium-bodied, with good fruit and fine cultivar character, it ages very well. The 1978 vintage was outstanding, rating a good four stars. The 1979, which also showed great promise, is quite robust, but elegant and complex. The 1980 vintage is as good and has developed well. The 1984, released in 1989, spent 16 months in small French oak. It is a lovely wine and carries Superior. The 1985 is a firmer, harder wine. The 1987 is big, fruity and tannic. The 1988 is a lovely wine although it does not show too much cultivar character; it will develop well. These wines need some four to five years to show their pace, but develop well up to 10 years, and some will last much longer.

80 ★★★★ ready. **82** ★★★★ ready. **83** ★★★ ready. **84** ★★★★(★) ready. **85** ★★★ ready. **86** no release **87** ★★★(★) ready, will still improve. **88** ★★★★ ready, will still develop.

Goudini Co-op Pinotage★★A

A typical, young Pinotage.

Goue Vallei Pinotage (Citrusdal Co-op)★★★B

A wine with a good, fruity nose, suggesting lightness, yet remaining full of flavour and not short of body. It is now receiving a little wood-ageing to add further dimension. It is best consumed within three to four years.

Groot Constantia Pinotage★★★B

A rather robust-flavoured Pinotage, which develops into a soft, full-bodied red. The 1978 was outstanding wine and still beautiful in 1991; the 1981, 1982 and 1983 vintages show good promise. The 1984 is very attractive in its youth and should age with benefit, while the 1985 is a little lighter. The 1986 is a full-flavoured, fruity wine with lots of cultivar character and will be well worth ageing. The later 1980s are all good powerful wines with potential.

Helderberg Co-op Pinotage★★(★)A

A moderate wine which has changed quite considerably from vintage to vintage, although more recent ones, with their typical cultivar character, have been very light yet markedly better. Released within the year of the vintage, the 1991 is a fuller wine. Also available in sensible 500 m*l* bottles.

Kaapzicht Pinotage★★★C

The 1990 is a smooth, full-bodied wood-aged wine.

Kanonkop CIWG Pinotage★★★★★E

The 1990 is magnificent wine, full of deep rich flavours. The 1991 is a massive, magnificent effort! Both will need a long time in the bottle to develop.

Kanonkop Pinotage★★★★C

This has long been one of South Africa's bench-mark wines: big and bold with a lot of complex cultivar character mingling well with good wood. The 1976 vintage was one of the best Pinotages of that year. The 1978 was also extremely good, but the 1979 lacked some of the complexity of previous and subsequent vintages. The 1980 set a standard against which Pinotage wines generally could be judged. The 1981 is a little more discreet, but the 1982 and 1983 are back to full character. Both the 1984 and 1985 spent 10 months in large French oak vats. The 1984 is very like the 1982, and is showing well in 1992. The 1985 is a lighter wine and will peak earlier than the 1984. It was judged winner of the Diners Club Award in 1987. The 1986 is a full-flavoured, high-alcohol wine which is magnificent now but still has lots of life to go to reach its potential. It should be magnificent. The 1987 is also a high alcohol wine (13,8%) and has been aged for 12 months, partly in big vats and partly in small casks. It is great right now but will still develop a lot more over another three to four years. The 1988, 1989, and 1990 continue in character and prove that this cellar continually makes one of the greatest Pinotage wines. They are also excellent value for money.

80 ★★★★(★) ready. **81** ★★★ ready. **82** ★★★★ ready. **83** ★★★★ ready. **84** ★★★★ ready, will still improve. **85** ★★★★ ready. **86** ★★★★(★) ready, will still improve. **87** ★★★★ ready, will still improve. **88** ★★★★ ready, will still improve. **89** ★★★★ ready, will still improve. **90** allow to develop.

Klawer Co-op Pinotage★B

The 1985 is the first vintage of this wine to come my way. Medium-bodied and fruity, this dry red is ready for early consumption. The 1988 has Pinotage esters covered by oak. The 1991 will be the next vintage to be released.

Kleindal Pinotage★★★B

Like all the wines under this label, this is a good example of the cultivar and reasonable value.

Koelenhof Co-op Pinotage★★B

This used to be a full-flavoured wine with real young Pinotage punch. The 1986 vintage received some wood-ageing which softened the fruit to make for pleasant, early drinking. The 1988 was a somewhat weak effort but the unwooded 1989 is much like the old style, full of Pinotage ester. The 1990 makes early, easy drinking.

KWV Pinotage★★(No price available)

For members and for export only. Usually somewhat subdued style. In spite of being certified Superior, the 1984 is decidedly quiet and now very tired. The 1986 is full traditional style. Late 1980s all follow a traditional style, with good flavour and ageing potential.

Landskroon Pinotage★★★B

Over the years, this cellar has produced a deep Pinotage without the initial full fruit associated with this cultivar. The vintages since 1977 have been very good and the 1979 is the best of the 1970s. The 1983 and 1984 are especially appealing. The 1982 is developing nicely while the 1983 and 1988 are in keeping with the cellar's regular quality. The 1987 was selected as the 1988 Alphen Pinotage Wine of the Month. The 1988 and 1989 show good class, with the 1990 following the same style. These wines age very well into good, dry reds with very little hint of their cultivar.

Landzicht Estate Pinotage★★★(★)C

This Pinotage has good, full depth of Estate varietal character, one with a long history of consistently good wine. Since 1980 all releases receive wood-ageing. The 1986 is one of the best, being full-flavoured and well-wooded. Next release: 1989.

82 ★★★★ ready. **83** ★★★ ready. **84** ★★★★ ready. **86** ★★★★ ready. **89** ★★★(★) ready, will still improve.

Lanzerac Pinotage★★★★(no price available)

Although this wine has long been off the market, old stocks are traditionally used as the first and last lots at the Nederburg Auction where they reach incredible prices. I have come across numerous bottles in private cellars and I have recently enjoyed the 1978 and 1979 vintages, both of which were very impressive. I have also had the pleasure of serving these wines on numerous occasions to overseas wine connoisseurs, who are always impressed.

Mamreweg Co-op Pinotage★★(★)A

Originally this was a very light Pinotage. Recent releases have been fuller and have some wood character, which tones down the very typical nose. Best enjoyed in their youth.

Meerendal Pinotage★★★★C

This is one of the big Pinotage wines, wood-matured with a good balance between wood and cultivar. It ages well in the bottle, showing great improvement over a few years. The 1978 vintage gained a gold medal at the 1982 International Wine and Spirit Competition in Britain. The wines have subsequently won other international awards. The 1983 is one of the best ever, which is a remarkable feat considering the poor vintage. The 1984 and 1985 are big, attractive wines. The 1987 is one of the best of the 1980s, more refined than usual with good, deep flavours and lovely clean aftertaste. The 1988 is fine wine with 1989 lighter and more elegant, but it will age with benefit. The wine is only released after five years.

Middelvlei Pinotage★★★(★)D

This is always an interesting, and reliable, good red wine and although it is medium-bodied, it has rich character. As with most good Pinotages it tends to lose cultivar as it ages, but becomes most satisfying with time. The 1976 vintage was still exceptionally good in 1992. More recent vintages have been lighter in style, the 1978 being the best of the 1970s and about at its best now. The vintages of the early 1980s sustain the quality with the 1980 lacking the usual Pinotage ester, while the 1981 is a big wine which has needed time to tone down. The 1982 is a big, almost old-style wine, certified Superior, while the 1983 is a lovely four-star wine which has benefited from good oak. There was no 1984, and the 1985 is not as attractive as previous releases. The 1986 is a fine, rich wine with full flavours and enough alcohol (13,7%) and tannin to develop well with time. The 1987 is so far the best from the the 1980s.

72 ★★★★ drink. **73** ★★★ past its best, drink. **74** ★★★ ready. **75** ★★★ past its best. **76** ★★★★ ready. **77** ★★★ ready. **78** ★★★★ ready. **79** no release. **80** ★★★★ ready. **81** ★★★ ready. **82** ★★★ ready. **83** ★★★★ ready. **84** no release. **85** ★★★ ready. **86** ★★★★ ready. **89** ★★★★ ready, will still develop.

Nederburg Pinotage★★★D

Nederburg Pinotage is usually only available on the export market, except for one local release in the early 1970s. There are occasional releases of Nederburg Pinotage at their annual Auction.

Nederburg Auction Pinotage★★★★E

A specially selected wine sold only at the Nederburg Auction. The 1978 vintage has rich character and lingering smoothness, and became more voluptuous as it aged. The 1976 still has the grace of a fine wine. The 1981 is a beautiful wine, showing that this cultivar can hold its own among the classic varieties and proving that Pinotage, when well made, is a wine to be taken seriously. The 1981 vintage was sold at the 1992 Nederburg Auction.

Neethlingshof Pinotage★★★D

This is one of the most interesting wines to emerge from the Neethlingshof cellar. The early vintages had overwhelming Pinotage ester and were bottled without any wood-ageing. Initially, the new owners removed Pinotage from their list, but it returned with the 1984 vintage released in 1988, which was somewhat over-wooded and lacked any real Pinotage character. The 1986 is considerably better and 1988 is fine wine that is developing well.

Oranjerivier Wynkelder Pinotage★A

Light wine with some cultivar character and wood backing.

Oude Libertas Pinotage (SFW)★★★★F

This was the successor to Lanzerac Pinotage, the world's first marketed Pinotage. It had a robust style, yet tended to remain soft in the mouth, with strong, fruity varietal character which was very marked when young. It matured in the bottle, however, undergoing remarkable character change to produce a rich-flavoured, mellow wine with surprising depth which still does justice to the finest tables. It is a great pity that the 1981 vintage was the last of these historic wines: the regular Oude Libertas range has ceased to exist. The 1973 release is still remarkably good. The 1978 in magnums, released to commemorate 25 years of Pinotage as a commercial wine, is magnificent. Twenty cases were sold at the 1991 Nederburg Auction where old vintages are used to open and close the bidding.

Oude Nektar Pinotage★★(★)C

The first vintage sampled was the 1983, a fairly subdued wine of medium body but deep colour. There was no 1984, but the 1985 was a light, smooth wood-aged wine. Next was a 1986: a beautiful, full, cultivar wine that fully deserves four stars. The 1987 was not as good when released but is developing well. The 1989 is bold, full wine and will also benefit from more time in the bottle.

Oude Rust Pinotage (Mooiuitsig)★★A

A fruity, light, dry red.

Overgaauw Pinotage★★★(★)A

This was always a good wine, well-wooded and medium-bodied with good fruit. Unfortunately, it is no longer being produced, although a few bottles may still be found. They are worth searching for, as they have developed beautifully.

Paradyskloof Pinotage (Vriesenhof)★★★B
This is a good example of pure Pinotage cultivar character, which drinks well when young but is worth keeping to allow it to develop.
Perdeberg Paarl Pinotage★★★A
Usually a consistently good wine that develops quite a complex nose after a short while. It is, however, more enjoyable when on the younger side. The 1988 is a good, medium-bodied, drinking wine. The 1989 has a less typical Pinotage nose, yet is still attractive wine that drinks easily. The 1991 has the old-fashioned Pinotage ester.
Pick 'n Pay Pinotage★★★(★)C
The 1990 is typical, full, rich Pinotage with good fruit and wood in the modern style of Kanonkop. Good to drink now, but with plenty of ageing potential.
Porterville Co-op Pinotage★★A
A light, typical Pinotage which drinks very easily when young. The 1989 has decided Pinotage nose. The next release will be from the 1992 vintage.
Rheboksskloof Pinotage★★★★D
A very different Pinotage aged in American oak and showing unusual character. It is deep purple, almost opaque, has deep flavour, is soft on palate yet fairly tannic. It should develop with great interest.
Riebeek Wine Farmers' Co-op Pinotage★★A
This used to be a simple, medium-bodied Pinotage. Six months in wood, however, has made the 1984 more complex and it has developed well. The next release was from the 1988 vintage and there's another wait for the release of the 1991.
Romansrivier Co-op Pinotage★★(★)A
A good cultivar wine. Recent vintages are delicate but well-bodied.
Rooiberg Co-op Pinotage★★★B
This is a wine which has improved over the years. The 1980s were all of interest and needed four to six years to show their best. The late 1980s and early 1990s seem to be for earlier drinking.
Rouge de Nuy★★★A
The Nuy Co-operative is situated in the foothills of the Langeberg range between Worcester and Robertson. The area is better known for its white wines, but the micro-climates here produce some very interesting reds, of which this Pinotage is one. It is medium-bodied, dry and with good, fruity Pinotage nose. Though slightly sharp when young, it settles down very quickly into a pleasant drinking wine. The 1983 vintage was a medal winner at the South African Championship Wine Show. The 1985, which has an unmistakable, but not overpowering, Pinotage nose, made very good early drinking, as did the 1987. The 1988 is fuller, bigger wine that has developed well over two years. The 1989 and 1990 are both good wines.
Saxenburg Private Collection★★★(★)C
Released from the 1989 vintage, this is a most appealing wine of which 70% was aged in French oak and 30% in American oak for 10 months; a very good wine. Nothing has been released from 1990, though there should be a release from 1991.
Saxenburg Pinotage★★(★)C
The 1985 vintage was the first of the new Saxenburg wines from the revamped Saxenburg property, now owned by the Swiss families Bührer and Harrer. It was a most unusual presentation of this cultivar. Good late 1980s but no 1990 – hopefully still to be released.

Simonsig Pinotage★★★C
This is a wine with a long, successful history, with some vintages ageing with incredible benefit. It frequently features as a young wine champion, but is always good and worth ageing. The 1989 and 1990 continue the quality.
Simonsig Pinotage Reserve★★★★(★)E
A spectacular wine from 1989. It is well oak-aged, has lots of fruit, with good tannin; it will age with considerable benefit.
Simonsvlei Co-op Pinotage★★★★C
This used to be a full- rather than medium-bodied wine. It is not heavy, yet it has powerful Pinotage character. Most of the grapes originate from the hot north-western slopes of the Simonsberg and so develop high sugar and alcohol content – more than 13,5% by volume. The wine is wood-aged for 18 months before bottling, thereafter developing well to give, at some five or six years of age, a fully rounded and smooth wine. It is a regular award winner at regional and national shows. The 1975 and 1976 vintages were offered at the 1977 and 1978 Nederburg Auctions respectively. The 1979 was probably at its best in 1987. Since 1988, it has been made lighter in style. Recent vintages are fine, firm wines with good fruit and reasonable ageing potential.
Slanghoek Co-op Pinotage★★★A
From 1990 comes a wooded and an unwooded Pinotage, both with good fruit.
Spier Pinotage★★★C
The earlier wines had full Pinotage taste and a somewhat earthy background. They needed a good two years to smooth out to reflect the cultivar. Vintages varied slightly in character but after a year or two settled into their distinctive style. The 1974 was an outstanding wine and the 1976 developed in a similar fashion. The wines of the 1980s are fuller and more forceful than those of the mid-1970s, but are not as stylish. The 1983 is probably the best of the decade. The 1984 is a good successor but is not quite up to the same standard. The 1986 was big and powerful, but the 1987 was a lesser wine. The 1988 is a much better wine. The Estate has available various older vintages of their Pinotage.
Spruitdrift Co-op Pinotage★★(★)A
This is a wine that is improving vintage by vintage, gaining gold medals at the South African Championship Wine Show. It has good, typical cultivar character. An excellent example of the Pinotage cultivar, the 1983 had deep colour, good nose and full flavour, giving a wine which has aged well over the years. Since 1986 the wine is aged for nine months in puncheons and this tames the Pinotage ester, making it a very easy-drinking wine. The 1990 and 1991 are both very acceptable drinking wines.
Swartland Pinotage★★★(★)A
This wine, with its full and rich Pinotage nose, was the first to evoke interest in this Co-op. The 1975 vintage needed taming at the time of release, but smoothed out and developed well over 10 years. The 1973, sold at the 1978 Nederburg Auction, had deep colour and soft flavour. Later vintages have been far less robust but nevertheless have very good Pinotage character and are regular class winners at regional and national shows. Since 1986 the wines have been considerably lighter than usual and will not have the long life of the

wines of the 1970s. The 1989 was a slight lapse in character but the 1990 is back to the regular style.

Uiterwyk Pinotage★★C

A Pinotage of usually medium body, Uiterwyk has cultivar character toned down with wood. The 1978 vintage has aged very well, and vintages of the early 1980s all show good potential, although the 1983 needs drinking now. The 1984 and 1985 are both better wines than the 1983 and are developing with benefit. The 1987 is developing well and the 1988 is a wine in fine traditional style. The 1986 is the best release to date; a three-star wine. No 1989 was released.

Villiersdorp Co-op Pinotage★★B

A wine with big, soft body and typical cultivar nose. Recent vintages have received some wood, making them easy, early-drinking wines.

Vlottenburg Co-op Pinotage★★B

A good-flavoured Pinotage with interesting fruitiness.

Waboomsrivier Co-op Pinotage★★A

This Co-op wins an impressive number of regional show medals each year. The wine is wood-aged for a year, giving unusual nose to a medium-bodied wine. Good value for money.

Wamakersvallei Co-op Pinotage★★A

A typical, light-style young Pinotage wine. It is a regular class winner at local shows.

Welmoed Co-op Pinotage★★(★)B

This is usually a medium-bodied wine of good cultivar character which is best for early drinking. The 1984, however, has had some wood-ageing, which has given it better balance. Since 1985, the cellar has produced nice, easy-drinking wines.

Woolworths Pinotage★★★A

A Wine of Origin Paarl, this is unmistakably a young Pinotage, which is dry and full of cultivar character. It is not vintage-dated but is definitely for youthful drinking.

Zevenwacht Pinotage★★B

To date this has been an unusual Pinotage in which the typical cultivar fruit has been substituted with wood. The 1987, however, is a very pleasant, lighter-bodied dry red. The 1988 is simple wine, while the 1989 is a better wine and developing well.

Zonnebloem Pinotage (SFW)★★★★B

It was to be expected when Zonnebloem introduced a Pinotage to its range that it would be an outstanding addition, matching the traditional excellence of its Cabernet. This it has done with a full-bodied wine of impressive colour and depth, and of distinguished character. The wine should be given every opportunity to age to realize its full potential. Outstanding vintages of the 1970s were 1974, 1976 and 1979, while the 1975 had developed surprisingly well by the late 1980s, despite its poor reception when released. The 1979 might have been the best of the 1970s. The 1982 also promises to develop with great benefit, as will the 1983 which is a four-star wine. Although the 1983 is very good, of the 1980s the 1984, 1985, 1986, 1987, 1988 and 1989 are big, bold, beautiful wines.

74 ★★★★★ drink. **75** ★★★ drink. **76** ★★★★★ drink. **79** ★★★★★ drink. **82** ★★★★ ready. **83** ★★★★ ready. **84** ★★★★★ ready. **85** ★★★★(★) ready. **86** ★★★★ ready, will still improve. **87** ★★★★ ready, will still improve. **88** ★★★★ not ready, needs ageing **89** ★★★★ not ready, needs ageing.

Pinot Noir

Backsberg Pinot Noir★★★C
The 1985 was the first release of this wine. The 1990 is light bodied with distinct cultivar character, fruity and very drinkable.

Blaauwklippen Pinot Noir★★★★C
This rather fickle variety has baffled most wine makers beyond the borders of Burgundy. Walter Finlayson persevered with the cultivar when at Blaauwklippen and has been particularly successful with it. He has established himself as the pioneer and is now the expert in the Cape with this cultivar. The first vintage, the 1979, was well received. Beginner's luck, some might say, but the vintage variation since then has been remarkable. Practice makes perfect, however, and the 1984 was really very good and deserved its five stars. The 1985 is still one of the best Pinot Noirs produced in the Cape and was selected as a SAA Wine of the Month. The 1986 is developing well in the bottle while the 1987 shows great promise. With Walter's departure, Jacques Kruger has continued the good work. The 1987 and 1988 are both fine, medium-bodied fruity wines.

🍷 **79** ★★★★ ready. **80** ★★★★ ready. **81** ★★★ past its best, still enjoyable. **82** ★★★★★ ready. **83** ★★★★★ ready. **84** ★★★★★ ready. **85** ★★★★★ ready. **86** ★★★★ ready, will still improve. **87** ★★★★ ready, will still improve. **88** ready, will develop.

Boplaas Pinot Noir★★★C
From the 1989 vintage comes a good, fresh fruity-styled wine that drinks very well.

Bouchard Finlayson Pinot Noir★★★★E
From the 1991 vintage with grapes from Elgin, this wine has good cultivar character with fine oak backing. Well worth waiting for.

Buitenverwachting Pinot Noir★★★C
The first release was from the 1986 vintage. It is a full, strong Pinot Noir with a decidedly French farmyard character which developed well. There was no release from 1987 but the 1988 is a very good wine – flavourful, light, soft and elegant – as is the 1989.

Delheim Pinot Noir★★★C
Early attempts were fun, but in 1980 this Pinot Noir suddenly became a serious wine, its very subtle oak blending well with cultivar character. The 1981 was more complex, but has not developed as well as the 1980 and should, I believe, be drunk now. The 1982 and 1983 vintages are good wines, but the 1984 had the best combination of wood and cultivar flavours for that time. It drinks very well now. The 1985 is a deep-coloured but much lighter-bodied wine with fine cultivar character. The 1986 is a super wine, fully deserving four stars. The 1987 may not be as good as the 1986, but it's better than any of the previous vintages and was an Alphen Wine of the Month Club choice. The 1988 has the makings of a very good wine. It will develop well, as should the 1989. The 1990 is even better.

🍷 **85** ★★★ ready, will still improve. **86** ★★★★(★) ready, will still improve. **87** ★★★(★) ready, will still develop. **88** ★★★★ ready, will still develop. **89** ★★★(★) ready, will still develop. **90** ★★★★ allow to age.

Eikendal Vineyards Pinot Noir★★★C
The first release from the 1988 vintage is a medium-bodied, complex

wine with good fruit and wood – an interesting first attempt that promises to develop in the bottle. The 1989 is a bigger, fuller wine but to date has not developed much cultivar character. No 1990 vintage was released.

Fairview Pinot Noir★★★B

Pinot Noir is a relatively recent addition to the Fairview range, as it is with the other Cape cellars producing from this cultivar. It first appeared in 1982 and won a gold medal at the SA Championship Wine Show. It has not developed as well as anticipated; nevertheless, it made fair drinking in 1988. The 1983 vintage did not show as well, but the 1984 has more promise and is developing with benefit. The 1985 and 1986 are both developing well. The 1987 has good fruit flavour, backed with good wood, and the 1988 looks very promising.

82 ★★★ ready. **83** ★★★ ready. **84** ★★★ ready. **85** ★★★(★) ready, will still improve. **86** ★★★ ready, will still develop. **87** ★★★ ready, will still develop. **88** ★★★ leave to develop.

Fairview Pinot Noir Reserve★★★(★)C

From the 1987 vintage comes a big wine with lots of flavour and distinct wood. It is developing well in 1992.

Glen Carlou Pinot Noir★★★★E

Made by Walter Finlayson, one of the Cape's pioneers of quality Pinot Noir. The 1990 is very good in every respect and should develop well in five to seven years. The 1991 is slightly lighter, but with good character. This is a wine to watch for future releases.

Hamilton Russell Vineyards Pinot Noir★★★★★E

This wine used to be labelled 'Grand Vin Noir' and did not carry Wine of Origin certification, so dating the vintage is a little difficult if one is unfamiliar with the labels. For a guide to the vintages, look for the large, light red print on the neck label; for example, the P3 is the 1983 Pinot Noir, P4 the 1984 Pinot Noir. Each release seems to be better than the last, the pleasing results of a combination of cultivar, good wood and excellent cellar technique. The 1982, 1983 and 1984 are all very good, as is the 1985, which is showing very well now. It is vintage-dated, but still carries the name Grand Vin Noir. From 1985 the vintage is printed on the label. The 1986 is labelled Pinot Noir and is vintage-dated. I once wrote, 'To my mind this is the best Pinot Noir yet produced in the Cape and compares well with any anywhere', and this was proved later in 1989 when it was judged by Diners Club to be the best in South Africa. The 1987 also looks great. It seems the Finlayson brothers discovered the secret of making Pinot Noir in South Africa. Wine making is now in the capable hands of Gail Kreusch-Dau. Both the 1988 and 1989 maintain the high standard.

82 ★★★★★ ready. **83** ★★★★★ ready. **84** ★★★★★ ready. **85** ★★★★★ ready, will still improve. **86** ★★★★★ ready, will still improve. **87** ★★★★★ ready, will still improve. **88** ★★★★★ ready, will still improve. **89** ★★★★★ ready, will still develop.

Hamilton Russell Vineyards Pinot Noir Reserve★★★★★F

A wine specially selected from the 1989 vintage. Beautiful.

Landskroon Pinot Noir★★(★)C

While others have struggled, Landskroon seemed to have mastered this cultivar quite quickly with their early releases. Each vintage since 1978 has been good. The 1980 appeared at the 1985 Nederburg

Auction. The 1981 and 1982 vintages were both encouraging, but do not keep up with some of the other Cape Pinot Noirs of more recent vintages. The 1984, however, is decidedly disappointing and was the last release until the 1989. Good fruit flavours are evident that will require time to develop.

Meerlust Pinot Noir★★★(★)D/E

The first release, in 1980, showed signs of class. The 1981 was even better; the 1982 fuller and more complex, yet delightfully light in body and very drinkable four years later. The cellar master, Giorgio Dalla Cia, predicted a life of 10 years or more for this wine and he was not wrong. The 1984 is one of the better wines from this cultivar produced in the Cape. The 1985 is better still, with good flavours, medium body and 13% alcohol. The 1986 is developing well. The 1987 is one of the best in the Cape, with concentrated character full of live fruit; delicious wine. The 1988 is lovely wine but will have to go some way to match the 1987.

81 ★★★★ ready, will still improve. **82** ★★★(★) ready. **83** ★★★(★) ready. **84** ★★★★ ready. **85** ★★★★(★) ready. **86** ★★★★(★) ready. **87** ★★★★★ ready, will still improve. **89** ★★★★ ready, will still improve.

Muratie Pinot Noir★★C

This is one of the oldest wines with a Pinot Noir label and it is very different to the modern style. The 1976, 1977, 1978 and 1979 vintages were sold at the Nederburg Auction. Vintages have varied, and although they do not compare favourably with modern efforts, they have a loyal following. Now under Melck ownership, the wine has taken a dramatic change in style. The 1991 is light, soft and full of flavour, and should develop with benefit.

90 ★★★ ready to drink, will still improve. **91** ★★★ ready to drink, will still improve.

Nederburg Pinot Noir★★★★C

The first release of this limited edition was from the 1982 vintage. A fine firm wine with clear cultivar character and reserved use of new oak, it is of high quality and certainly good value for money. The 1983 is an even better wine and has confounded quite a number of British connoisseurs as to its origin. The 1984 is a firm, full wine that is developing well. The 1986 is a good wine that, on release, had a strange bitterness in the finish. With time this has gone and the wine is developing with great interest. The 1987 is a good example of clean wine making with the cultivar.

82 ★★★★ ready. **83** ★★★★(★) ready. **84** ★★★(★) ready, will still develop. **86** ★★★(★) ready, will still develop. **87** ★★★★(★) ready, will still develop.

Rooiberg Co-op Pinot Noir★★(★)B

The 1987 vintage is a creditable Pinot Noir, which has good colour, a fruity bouquet, a soft palate and a little wood. It developed in the bottle. The 1988 is young and robust with some interesting flavours, while the 1989 is an improvement and deserves three stars. The 1990 is a light, easy-drinking, fruity wine along Nouveau lines.

Ruiterbosch Mountain Vineyards Pinot Noir★★★B

This cultivar, grown in the cool mountain vineyards on the slopes of the Outeniqua Mountains overlooking Mossel Bay, gives a wine with a definite Burgundian character. I look forward to its appearance on the market.

Rustenberg Pinot Noir★★★★C

A relative newcomer to this well-established cellar, this Pinot Noir has a distinctive, rich aroma and medium body, combining well to give an attractive wine. First released in 1978, it has since improved and can be considered to have come of age with the 1982 vintage, an assessment confirmed by the 1983, while the 1984 and the 1986 were better still. The 1984 has been very successful at many tastings and has been most acceptable to many visiting British connoisseurs. These are very rich, full-flavoured wines which will certainly age with benefit over five to eight years, although they drink well on release. The 1985 is a little disappointing when compared with the 1984 and 1986; nevertheless, it is very good. The 1987 has some Burgundy farmyard character and will develop. The 1988 is a powerful, full-flavoured, very fruity wine, which is soft in the mouth and very drinkable ahead of the 1987. The 1989 shows well.

78 ★★★ past its best, still enjoyable. **80** ★★★ ready. **82** ★★★(★) ready. **83** ★★★(★) ready. **84** ★★★★ ready, will still improve. **85** ★★★(★) ready. **86** ★★★★ ready. **87** ★★★★ ready, will still improve. **88** ★★★★ ready, will still improve. **89** ★★★★ ready, will still develop.

Simonsig Pinot Noir★★★(★)C

This cellar's Pinot Noir has a character all of its own. It might not appeal to all, but it is well worth trying. The 1982 has shown well in recent tastings. The 1983 and 1984 are better wines and are developing well. Although light in character, the 1984 has superb flavour, drinks very well, and is probably at its best now. There were no bottlings of 1985 and 1986. The 1987 is good but had a strange, bitter aftertaste when released. This has now disappeared. The 1988 has a delicious berry flavour and is probably the most elegant release.

82 ★★★★ ready, will still improve. **83** ★★★ ready, will still improve. **84** ★★★★ ready, will still improve. **85** no release. **86** no release. **87** ★★★(★) ready, will still improve. **88** ★★★(★) ready, will still improve.

Woolworths Pinot Noir★★★★C

This is a very good example of the cultivar, which showed well at two different tastings. Showing good Burgundian characteristics and produced by Rustenberg Estate, it is excellent value for money and one of the best Woolworths' wines. This applies particularly to the 1987 and 1988.

Shiraz

Allesverloren Shiraz★★★★C
The first release, from the 1982 vintage, is a super wine more in the style of an Australian than a South African Shiraz. It is a big wine in every way (nose, flavour, body and alcohol – exceeding 13%), so treat it with due respect. It is ageing well. There were no releases of the 1983, 1984, and 1985, but the 1986 is a big fruity wine with lots of tannin that will allow long ageing. The 1987 is another full wine with more berry nose, deep layers of flavour, and good oak backing. The 1988 is excellent big wine with lots of alcohol and flavour.

82 ★★★★ ready. **83** no release. **84** no release. **85** no release. **86** ★★★(★) ready, will still develop. **87** ★★★★ ready, will still develop. **88** ★★★★ ready, will still develop.

Altydgedacht Shiraz★★★C
The first release is from the 1987 vintage and has the smokey-type Shiraz character. It is light in style, and beginning to loosen out and develop more flavour. Next release will be from 1989.

Backsberg Shiraz★★★★C
An extremely well-made wine with deep, distinctive Shiraz character, this has been a firm favourite over the years. The 1974, 1975 and 1976 vintages were magnificent in 1986, while those of the later 1970s developed well. All the vintages of the 1980s show great promise; the 1983 is a five-star product and the 1984 is a big, full wine in all respects, while the 1985 and 1986 are superb wines which are developing well. Ageing for 10 years seems to be the optimum for these wines. The 1987 and 1988 are just as full of flavour, but are softer and appear to be developing more quickly. The 1989 is another lovely, full wine that will develop over a longer period of time than the 1988. The 1990 has more tannin and will take longer to develop. They are lovely wines that are excellent value for money.

74 ★★★★ drink. **75** ★★★★ drink. **76** ★★★★ drink. **83** ★★★★★ ready, will still improve. **84** ★★★★(★) ready. **85** ★★★★ ready. **86** ★★★★ ready, will still improve. **87** ★★★★ ready, will still develop. **88** ★★★★ ready, will still develop. **89** ★★★★ ready, will still develop. **90** ready, will still develop.

Bellingham Shiraz★★★★D
A far cry from the original no-star, non-vintage Bellingham product, today's wines are rich, deep and complex with plenty of Shiraz character. The four-star 1980, which led Bellingham's first appearance at the 1986 Nederburg Auction, drinks beautifully in 1992 and still has plenty of life ahead. The 1981 is developing slowly, but the 1983 is not in keeping with Bellingham's usually high quality, and probably due to the vintage. The 1984 is a very good wine, full of cultivar character and backed with good wood. The 1985 has the smokey character so often referred to in a Shiraz, yet seldom experienced. The 1986 continues the quality and style; it was ready for drinking on release but will still develop with time. The 1987 makes a dramatic change with 25% Cabernet in the blend giving greater complexity. Fine wine. It regularly carried Superior certification.

80 ★★★★(★) ready. **81** ★★★★ ready. **82** ★★★★ ready. **83** ★★★ ready. **84** ★★★★(★) ready, will still improve. **85** ★★★★(★) ready, will still improve. **86** ★★★★ ready, will improve. **87** ★★★★ ready, will develop.

Bertrams Shiraz★★★★E

A very impressive dry red, with unusually good body for a South African Shiraz. It has been well-aged in good wood and is a most complex wine, appreciably fuller than most other Shiraz labels. The 1979 vintage is outstanding, and probably at its best now. Each vintage of the 1980s seems to be better than its predecessor. The 1980 is excellent and will develop with great benefit. The 1982 is an exception, not living up to the reputation of its predecessors, but the 1983 is a very good wine. The 1984 is a big beautiful wine that is one of the best of the 1980s. The 1985 is a little slow in developing. The 1986 is truly a great wine and certainly one of the Cape's best-ever Shiraz wines. It will develop magnificently with time. This Shiraz usually carries Superior certification and regularly appears at the annual Nederburg Auction.

75 ★★★★ past its best, still enjoyable. **76** ★★★★ ready. **78** ★★★★ ready. **79** ★★★★★ ready. **80** ★★★★★ ready. **81** ★★★ ready. **82** ★★★★ ready. **83** ★★★★ ready. **84** ★★★★★ ready, will still improve. **85** ★★★(★) ready, will still develop. **86** ★★★★(★) ready, will still develop.

Blaauwklippen Shiraz★★★(★)D

This is a rich, well-coloured Shiraz with a good touch of wood. The 1981 vintage was full-bodied and the 1982 even fuller, proving to be one of the best and developing into a definite four-star wine. The 1984 is a full-bodied wine with very typical cultivar character. The 1982 and 1984 vintages have developed well to date and must be about at their best now. The 1987 is one of the best, fully deserving four stars. The 1988 is a rich, full wine with farmyard nose and good flavour. The 1989 needs time to develop. The later vintages are ready for drinking on release but benefit from time in the bottle.

80 ★★★ ready. **81** ★★★ ready. **82** ★★★★ ready. **83** ★★★ ready. **84** ★★★★ ready. **85** ★★★(★) ready. **86** ★★★ ready, will still improve. **87** ★★★★ ready, will still improve. **88** ★★★(★) ready, will still improve. **89** needs time to develop.

Bon Courage Shiraz★★(★)B

A plain wine with big alcohol from the 1989 vintage, that could develop with time.

Bottelary Shiraz★★★(★)B

This wine has developed into a very attractive, well-balanced product with definite Shiraz character. It ages well over four to five years. Bottlelary Shiraz is one of the Cape's better Shiraz wines – proved by the 1987. It has good character that develops well over four to five years and is excellent value for money. The 1988 is a little paler in character, but the 1989 is back to normal.

Bovlei Co-op Shiraz★★B

The first release was from the 1987 vintage, which was a medium-bodied wine with good cultivar character unaffected by any wood maturation. Later productions augur well.

Cape Vintners Members Only Shiraz★★★D

An unusual Shiraz from the Van Loveren cellar – oak-matured giving attractive softness and flavour from 1987 vintage. Easy to drink now, but will age well for another two to four years.

Delheim Shiraz★★★★B

A light South African Shiraz which rounds off beautifully after a year or more in the bottle. The 1974 and 1976 vintages were excellent and continued to develop well a decade later. The 1979 and 1980 vintages are full of interest and are delivering their potential, while the 1983 is powerful in every respect and at its best now. The 1984 has equally good character but does not have 1983's astonishing alcohol content of almost 14%. It is showing very well now but will still develop. The 1985 was a tamer, more elegant wine that is probably at its best now. Both 1986 and 1987 have excellent cultivar noses, nice flavour and a soft feel in the mouth. Overall, the 1987 is a better wine that should age well. The 1988 is a clearer character wine, soft in the mouth and has developed well into 1992. The 1989 contains some Merlot, making it very easy drinking, but with its 14% alcohol will no doubt last well. The 1990 looks equally good and will develop over another three to four years.

74 ★★★★ past its best, still enjoyable. **76** ★★★★★ ready. **80** ★★★★ ready. **82** ★★★ ready. **83** ★★★★ ready. **84** ★★★★ ready. **85** ★★★ ready. **86** ★★★(★) ready, will still improve. **87** ★★★★ ready, still improve. **88** ★★★(★) ready, will still develop. **89** ★★★(★) ready, will still develop. **90** ★★★(★) ready, will still develop.

Diemersdal Shiraz★★★B

Available in 500 m*l* screw-top bottles and first released from the 1989 vintage. Well wooded wine with good potential.

Die Krans Estate Shiraz★★★B

The first release, from the 1989 vintage, has a wide range of pleasant aromas and full flavour – a very good first attempt. The 1990 is full of youthful zest and backed by good oak, with potential to develop. As the vines age, the resulting wines will probably be even better.

Douglas Green Shiraz★★★C

The 1981 vintage was the first release of this wine and carried Superior certification. It had full flavour, was soft on the palate, but lacked in finish. Those in the 750 m*l* bottles are now past their best. The 1981 magnums carry Superior certification and are very drinkable now. After a long period of time a very good 1984 was released, also with Superior certification, followed by a good, old-style 1986. The 1987 has more defined nose and is considered a finer wine. The 1988 is in the new bottle and label and has fair cultivar character.

Fairview Reserve Shiraz★★★★C

The first release from the 1987 vintage is a super, full-flavoured and fruity wine that will develop with considerable interest. There was no 1988. The 1989 is a decidedly easy wine to drink, yet is packed with deep, rich flavours. It certainly is under-priced. The 1990 is particularly fine wine.

87 ★★★★ ready, will improve. **88** no release. **89** ★★★★ ready, will still develop. **90** ★★★★ ready, will still develop.

Fairview Shiraz★★★(★)B

The early wines were full of flavour and heavy in character, and used to be consistent carriers of Superior certification. This cellar now produces regular class winners at the Paarl Wine Show, but latest bottlings lack the big fullness of the earlier wines. The 1982 is an excellent wine and deserves four stars. The 1983 is less attractive but has developed in the bottle. The 1984, 1985 and 1986 are good wines but lack the richness of earlier vintages. The 1987 is soft, full-flavoured, and one of the best of recent releases. The 1988 is medium-bodied wine.

74 ★★★★ drink. **75** ★★★ drink. **76** ★★★★ drink. **77** ★★★ drink. **78** ★★★★ ready. **79** ★★★ past its best. **80** ★★★★ ready. **81** ★★★ ready. **82** ★★★★ ready. **83** ★★★ ready. **84** ★★★★ ready. **85** ★★★ ready. **86** ★★★ ready, will improve. **87** ★★★ ready, will improve. **88** ready, will develop.

Fleur Du Cap Shiraz (Bergkelder)★★★(★)C

A good, rich, red wine with a noticeably Shiraz aroma and taste. In the older Fleur Du Cap wines these characteristics tended to dissipate with time, leaving a fairly robust wine with a spicy aftertaste of great interest. More recent vintages, particularly the 1978, are better balanced and have clearer cultivar character. They all improve with a few years in the bottle. The 1980 vintage is excellent and carries Superior certification. The 1981 was a lighter wine and needs to be consumed now. The 1985 was not released. By far the best is the 1986 which is a big, full-flavoured, mouth-filling wine that drinks very well now. The 1987 is clean in style, backed with good wood as is the 1988.

80 ★★★★ ready. **81** ★★★ past its best, still enjoyable. **85** no release. **86** ★★★★ ready. **87** ★★★★ ready, will still develop. **88** ★★★(★) ready, will still develop.

Groot Constantia Shiraz★★★★C

In the 1970s and early 1980s the Shiraz was usually Groot Constantia's best wine and consistently one of South Africa's better Shirazes – evidence that many of the country's finest reds come from the cooler growing areas. From the later 1980s the Shiraz is still very good, but the Estate is producing other excellent reds. The wines usually age well; the 1974 is truly excellent, showing the use of new wood, and should develop with great benefit in the bottle. The 1983 is a big, full, rather coarse wine but one which will undoubtedly soften in the bottle. The 1986 is a deep, full wine which is developing very well in the bottle and was the best of the 1980s until the 1987, which is a very good wine with lots of depth and good mouth-filling qualities. The 1988 continues the style.

73 ★★★★ ready. **74** ★★★★ ready. **82** ★★★★ ready. **83** ★★★(★) ready. **84** ★★★★(★) ready. **85** ★★★★ ready, will develop. **86** ★★★★(★) ready, will improve. **87** ★★★★(★) ready, will develop. **88** ★★★★ give time to develop.

Hartenberg Shiraz★★★★E

The first release was a very good wine from the 1979 vintage. It was full of cultivar character and is still developing. The 1980 is even better. The 1981 reflects the characteristics normally associated with Shiraz and is a fine wine which drank well when released, but has developed beautifully and is super now. The 1982 maintains this cellar's ability to produce very good quality Shiraz. The 1983 and 1984 maintain the cellar's good reputation. The 1985 does not have quite the class of previous vintages but is very good nonetheless. It is aged in large wood for a year and only released after six years in the bottle, making very acceptable drinking then, but with enough to go for a few more years. They all carry Superior certification. The 1986 has massive 14% alcohol but lots of fine character.

79 ★★★★ ready. **80** ★★★★ ready. **81** ★★★★ ready. **82** ★★★★ ready. **83** ★★★★ ready. **84** ★★★★ ready, will still improve. **85** ★★★(★) ready, will still develop. **86** ★★★★ needs time to develop.

Helderberg Co-op Shiraz★★(★)B
This is usually a fairly robust wine which softens in the bottle. It has good Shiraz character as demonstrated by the 1985, which had a smokey nose and drank well in 1988. The release from 1990 is medium bodied and very drinkable.

Klawer Co-op Shiraz★★A
This is the best red wine from this cellar and one which develops surprisingly well over some four years. It is a regular class winner at local shows, with the 1982 receiving gold at the SA Wine Show. The 1984 developed splendidly but is probably past its best now. The 1985 was the last vintage bottled – the next will be from the 1991 vintage and is still to be released.

Klein Constantia Shiraz★★★★D
The first release of a Shiraz from this Estate was from the 1986 vintage. It is a big, complex wine that will age with benefit. The 1987 is a beautiful, deep-flavoured wine with great elegance. The 1988 is lighter and more elegant in style; very much Cape-modern. Sensational now, they will be tremendous in the mid-1990s.

KWV Shiraz★★★(no price available)
One of the KWV's best natural wines, this Shiraz usually carries Superior certification and is made in the traditional style. It is at its best after about five to six years.

La Motte Estate Shiraz★★★★D
The 1985 vintage provided the first release from this cellar. A lovely wine full of individual character, it has lots of aroma and full, distinctive flavour. The 1986 is a beautiful, deep, intense wine of the modern-style Cape Shirazes, and will age with great benefit. The 1987 continues the good quality and clean style.

Landskroon Shiraz★★★★C
This is an award-winning wine with more character than most Cape Shiraz wines, and although easy to drink when young, it will develop and soften considerably in the bottle. The 1978 vintage was outstanding and all those since have been very good. However, I believe everything up to and including 1981 has passed its best. The 1982 is drinking very well in 1992. The 1983 is more advanced. The next vintage bottled was the 1987, which is a super wine and developing well. The 1988 is full of flavour and, as drinkable as it is now, will probably peak in the mid-1990s. The 1989 is a little subdued and will probably develop with a few more years; it is remarkable value for money. The 1990 is fine wine with good berry flavours.

78 ★★★ drink. **79** ★★★ drink. **81** ★★★ drink. **82** ★★★★ ready. **83** ★★★(★) ready. **87** ★★★★ ready. **88** ★★★★ ready, will still develop. **89** ★★★(★) ready, will still develop. **90** ★★★★ needs time to develop.

Lievland Shiraz★★★★D
The Estate's first attempt was the 1983 vintage, and the result was a very good, light-bodied wine with fine Shiraz character, developing good complexity in the bottle. The 1985 is a good, wood-aged, easy-drinking wine which has developed very well. The 1986 is bigger and fuller, while the 1987 is full of flavour but is a more elegant wine of medium body. The 1988 is softer and almost sweetish, but is equally full of flavour. It was chosen by the Alphen Wine of the Month Club as the most recommended wine in the Shiraz category. The 1989 continues in the exciting style developed over

the years. Lievland is making dramatic moves with their recent well-oaked wines, and these are now accepted as amongst the great Shirazes of the Cape.

85 ★★★ ready. **86** ★★★(★) ready. **87** ★★★(★) ready, will still improve. **88** ★★★★ ready, will still improve. **89** ★★★★ ready, will still improve.

L'Ormarins Shiraz★★★★E

The 1983, the first release, is a medium-bodied, lighter-type, yet full-flavoured Shiraz. It was launched late in 1988 in very small quantities and is retailing at a very high price. The 1984 is bold, yet elegant, and full of flavour; it is developing very well. The 1986 is an elegant, well-oaked wine with good depth of flavour and a soft feel in the mouth. The 1987 is softer than usual but good.

83 ★★★★ ready. **84** ★★★★ ready, will develop. **86** ★★★★ ready, will develop. **87** ★★★★ ready, will develop.

Meerendal Shiraz★★★(★)C

This medium-bodied, dry wine develops remarkable smoothness with ageing. It has performed consistently well over the years, its own cellar character blending well with that of the varietal character. The Meerendal Shiraz (and the Pinotage) won gold medals at the 1982 International Wine and Spirit Competition in the UK. The 1980 vintage was out of character, but the 1981 is as good as ever, and later releases carry Superior certification. The 1982 was a little dull at first, but developed well with time. There is a large gap in the vintage, with the next release being the 1987: a big, full-flavoured wine that has a very different character. It has a strange, uncharacteristic nose but a nice flavour. Hopefully, it will develop with time.

81 ★★★★ ready. **82** ★★★ ready. **87** ★★★ age further.

Middelvlei Shiraz★★★C

The first release from the 1988 vintage is a very good, well-made wine full of cultivar character.

Muratie Shiraz★★★B

Released from the 1990 vintage comes a youthful, full, broody wine which should develop with a few years. The 1991 is similar.

Nederburg Shiraz★★★★(★)C

The Nederburg Shiraz wines are expansive, with deep flavours which develop exceedingly well over eight or more years. To date, only the 1974, 1975, 1976, 1977, 1978, 1982 and 1984 vintages have been released, and then, only at annual Nederburg Auctions.

74 ★★★★(★) ready. **75** ★★★★ past its best, still enjoyable. **76** ★★★★(★) ready. **77** ★★★★ ready. **78** ★★★★(★) ready. **82** ★★★★(★) ready. **83** no release. **84** ★★★★(★) ready.

Oude Nektar Shiraz★★★C

The 1983 was a full-bodied wine with good Shiraz character. The 1984 has good wood backing the cultivar character and is developing well. The fullish 1985 has good wood and attractive flavour, while the 1986 is lighter and the cultivar smokiness is nearly lost in the woodiness. The 1987 is an improvement.

Paradyskloof Roodewyn (Vriesenhof)★★★★A

Good value Shiraz with fine cultivar flavour.

Pick 'n Pay Shiraz★★★★C

The 1987 comes from Simonsig out of this good red wine vintage and a year in oak, giving intense flavour concentration. This wine has good ageing potential.

Riebeek Wine Farmers' Co-op Shiraz★★(★)A
A full-flavoured Shiraz. The 1982, 1986 and 1988 vintages have been released, and the last two are developing with benefit. Next release will be from the 1989 vintage.
Rooiberg Co-op Shiraz★★★B
The first release was from the 1985 vintage which is a well-wooded wine with a small amount of Souzão, giving added complexity and a greater depth of colour. It has bottle-aged with interest. The 1986 is better still, with more flavour, and has developed well. The 1987 is a big wine, but without the attractiveness of the two earlier vintages. It will probably develop with time. The 1988 is young and robust with interesting flavours, as is the 1989.
85 ★★★ ready. **86** ★★★(★) ready, will still improve. **87** ★★(★) ready, will still develop. **88** ★★★ ready, will still develop. **89** ★★★ will still develop.
Rust-en-Vrede Shiraz★★★★E
The 1979 vintage was an outstanding wine with full flavour which has developed well in the bottle. The 1982 is a great wine which, as it ages, deserves a full five stars. Ironically, the Wine and Spirit Board initially would not award it a Superior rating. The 1983 is a lighter wine and it developed beautifully over five years. The 1984 is good but not as flavourful. The 1985 is a beautiful wine, full of fine flavour and is ageing with great benefit. The 1986 is a lovely, big, tasty wine and the 1987 and 1988 are big, bold and full-flavoured.
79 ★★★★ ready. **80** ★★★★ ready. **81** ★★★★ ready. **82** ★★★★★ ready, will still improve. **83** ★★★★ ready. **84** ★★★★ ready. **85** ★★★★(★) ready, will still improve. **86** ★★★★ ready, will still improve. **87** ★★★(★) not ready, age further. **88** ★★★(★) not ready, age further.
Saxenberg Private Collection Shiraz★★★C
From the 1990 vintage, comes a rich, fruity, pleasing wine.
Simonsig Shiraz★★★★D
The vintages of the later 1970s were all full-bodied, deep, red wines with fine aroma, and they aged very well. The early wines of the 1980s are better and lighter with greater finesse, the 1982 being fuller in all respects and deserving four stars. It has developed well and is probably at its best now. The 1984 is very good and is backed by good wood. It was selected by SAA as one of its Wines of the Month. The 1985 is a little out of character, but the 1986 is similar to the 1984. Drink the 1985 before the 1984 and 1986. The 1984, 1986 and the 1987 make this wine one of the best of the modern Cape Shirazes. The 1987 is a deep, intense wine with good soft oak in the background. The 1988 and 1989 show fine quality with lots of character, and are easy early drinking wines.
80 ★★★ ready. **81** ★★★ ready. **82** ★★★★ ready. **83** ★★★ ready. **84** ★★★★ ready, will still improve. **85** ★★★ ready. **86** ★★★★ ready, will still improve. **87** ★★★★ ready, will still improve. **88** ★★★★ ready, will still develop. **89** ★★★★ ready, will still develop.
Simonsvlei Co-op Shiraz★★★(★)C
These are good value, good quality wines which have gained a respectable number of gold medals at regional and national shows. The vintages of the 1980s are worth keeping for five to eight years. The 1987, 1988, and 1989 are very satisfying wines.

Spier Shiraz★★★D
Although the cellar does not produce a Shiraz with every vintage, the maiden vintage of 1976 was a good one. The 1981 vintage has developed well, while the medium-bodied 1984 has good cultivar nose and flavour backed by good wood. It drinks well now. The 1986 is a fuller wine that needs a few more years in the bottle. The 1987 is a lighter-styled, fruity wine. No 1988 was released, but the 1989 is fuller-bodied wine.

Springlands Shiraz (Drop Inn)★★★B
A pleasant, well-made, dry wine with smokey Shiraz character, which will benefit from a few years in the bottle.

Swartland Shiraz★★B
This is not produced every vintage but, when available, it is a full-bodied, dry wine with the kind of nose described by some as 'smokey'. The 1989 is developing well in the bottle.

Uitkyk Shiraz★★★(★)D
The wines of Uitkyk are marketed by Bergkelder and their decision to discontinue this label in 1973 was a sad one. The 1973 Uitkyk Shiraz, in 375 *ml* bottles, was memorable: smooth, luscious, full-flavoured and, at eight and nine years of age, a superb wine. Consider yourself fortunate if you manage to track down a bottle or two. Fortunately, Uitkyk Shiraz was reintroduced with a fine wine from the 1981 vintage that has developed well. The next release is from the 1985 vintage which is a very 'correct' sort of wine. It has distinct cultivar character and is ready for drinking. The 1986 is a four-star wine in the newer Cape style with berry rather than smokey flavours and good wood backing. This is fine wine with enough tannin to develop with benefit.

Van Loveren Dry Red★★★B
This wine is labelled Dry Red but is 100% Shiraz with a smokey character and a bit of wood. It is a robust wine that needs a few years to soften.

Vergenoegd Shiraz★★★★C
First released on the open market in 1978, this attractive, deep red wine had the character to develop well with time, peaking in about 1985/7. Subsequent vintages have been very good. The 1982 has developed beautifully. The 1983 is lighter, in keeping with the vintage, and very different to the usual Vergenoegd Shiraz. It is a superb wine all the same. The 1984 is developing a unique nose as it ages. The 1985 has the kind of cultivar character that tends towards 'leather' rather than 'smokey', which is also a characteristic of the 1986. The 1987 is a Shiraz in the old style: full leathery character, and a soft, pleasing drink, yet with enough tannin to develop. The 1988 shows good fruit and is soft in the mouth.

85 ★★★(★) ready, will still improve. **86** ★★★(★) ready, will still improve. **87** ★★★(★) ready, will still develop. **88** ★★★(★) needs time.

Welmoed Shiraz★★★B
This is the best of the cellar's reds: big and bold, with every potential to age well over the years, which it needs in order to soften. The 1984 and 1985 have not been wood-aged and show good bottle development. The 1987 is well aged in large old wood, and on release makes enjoyable drinking. The 1989 is the best release to date and good value for money.

Woolworths Shiraz★★★B

Produced by Fairview. The 1983 and 1984 are good examples of the cultivar and are both developing well in the bottle. The 1986 is a big, alcoholic wine that should age well. The 1987 and 1989 are super wines with deep full flavours, and lots of alcohol. They will develop well with age and are well worth laying down.

86 ★★★ ready, will still develop. **87** ★★★★ ready, will still develop. **89** will develop well.

Zandvliet Shiraz★★★(★)C

The 1975 was apparently released only for export, but occasionally a few bottles found their way to local tastings and were considered very good. The 1976 vintage was released with a fanfare of publicity. It had excellent cultivar character, was light and fruity, soft to taste and so palatable that I wondered how well it would keep. In fact, it aged very well and at six years was beautifully soft and mellow. Floods prevented the release of a 1981 vintage, but the 1982 was acclaimed as the best ever and carried Superior certification. But I believe the 1985 was better. The 1983 and 1984 are very light and are at their best now. The 1986 is even better, with the 1987 better still – a lighter, more elegant wine.

75 ★★★ past its best, still enjoyable. **76** ★★★★ past its best, still enjoyable. **77** ★★★ past its best. **78** ★★★★ past its best. **79** ★★★ past its best, still enjoyable. **80** ★★★ ready. **81** no release. **82** ★★★ ready. **83** ★★★★ ready. **84** ★★★ ready. **85** ★★★★ ready. **86** ★★★★ ready, will still improve. **87** ★★★★ ready, will still develop.

Zevenwacht Shiraz★★★C

The Shiraz from this cellar is usually a big, bold, Porty-type wine that develops well. The 1988 is a departure in style: a super, well-flavoured wine with all the traditional descriptions of leather, pepper and smokey, and worthy of four stars.

Zonnebloem Shiraz (SFW)★★★★C

The 1974 vintage was an elegant, soft Shiraz with a very interesting character: one which developed beautifully in the bottle and is magnificent in 1992. The full-bodied 1975 is soft, smooth, and voluptuous. It has developed with age into a really lovely wine. The 1976 vintage is also an excellent wine which is evolving a complexity seldom found in South African products. The 1978 and 1980 are both beautiful to drink now. The 1979 is excellent and lighter bodied than usual, but now at its peak. The 1981 is also very good now, and although the 1982 was a slow starter, it is developing great character in 1992. The 1983 is a textbook example of how a Shiraz should be made; light and full of character, this is a beautiful wine which is at its best now. The 1984 is a bigger, bolder wine. The 1978, 1979 and 1980 vintages, which are available in magnums, are all drinking well in 1992. The 1985 is typical of the vintage and is a great wine. The 1986 is another lovely wine, while the 1987 is a little disappointing, but should develop well. The 1988 is back on track.

74 ★★★★★ ready. **75** ★★★★ past its best, still enjoyable. **76** ★★★★★ ready. **78** ★★★★ ready. **79** ★★★ ready. 80 ★★★★ ready. **81** ★★★★★ ready. **82** ★★★★ ready. **83** ★★★★★ ready. **84** ★★★★ ready, will improve. **85** ★★★★(★) ready, will age further. **86** ★★★★ ready, will improve. **87** ★★★ ready, will improve. **88** ★★★★ not ready, will improve.

Tinta Barocca

Allesverloren Tinta Barocca★★★(★)C
Like most of the wines from this Estate, the Tinta Barocca is usually full-bodied and powerful, needing time to mellow. The 1972 vintage was exceptional and in 1988 was amazing to drink, which just goes to show that these wines can age well over 10 to 15 years. The 1978 was not certified Superior, yet 10 years later, it developed into a super wine. The 1980 is big and bold, like the 1978, but the 1981 is much lighter. The 1982 is very different, aged in new wood, giving an unusually fine wine under the label. The 1983 is somewhat subdued and not up to the cellar's usual standard. There is a gap in vintages with the next being the 1986 which is big and full like the 1980, 1987 and 1988.

🍷 **80** ★★★★ ready. **81** ★★★(★) ready. **82** ★★★★ ready. **83** ★★★ ready. **84** no release. **85** no release. **86** ★★★★ ready, will still improve. **87** ★★★(★) ready, age further. **88** ★★★(★) not ready, age further.

Die Krans Tinta Barocca★★(★)B
This was the cellar's best offering but it was discontinued for a while after the 1979 vintage, which has developed with interest. The next release was the 1986, which is a bit disappointing. The 1987 is a pleasant wine and 1988 shows good wood. The 1989 and the 1990 are both much better wines and will develop well. Both have spent five months in oak.

Goue Vallei Tinta Barocca (Citrusdal Co-op)★★A
This is a full-bodied wine with the 1984 having a colossal 15% alcohol! The 1986 has good wood to back the full fruit. The 1987 has a flowery, fruity, attractive character, nice wood, and will develop into the mid-1990s. No release from 1988. The 1989 is developing well and 1990 is tamed by some new oak ageing.

Mamreweg Co-op Tinta Barocca★★A
The first release, the 1986, showed good character, but the 1987 is very light and for early consumption. The 1988 and 1989 were pleasant, easy-drinking wines, and the 1991 continues in this style.

Onverwacht Estate Tinta Barocca★★★B
As other producers drop the use of this cultivar for dry red wine, this cellar is making their best effort with it. The first release from 1989 was tough and tannic but it is developing well. The 1990 had good berry flavours and new French oak backing that added extra dimension. The 1991 is the best yet, with good layers of fruit flavours, plums, cherries and vanilla. It will drink well, earlier than some of the previous vintages.

Oude Libertas Tinta Barocca (SFW)★★★(★)B
This was the first South African label to carry the name Tinta Barocca. Though discontinued, it was popular, and odd bottles are still to be found in many cellars. It was a blend and therefore better balanced than most other Tinta Baroccas. A fairly hefty wine, well-wooded, rich and mellow, it aged with benefit for eight or more years. It is a great pity that it is no longer made.

Riebeeck Co-op Tinta Barocca★★(★)B
Despite earlier comments, the 1988 is developing well by 1992, and the 1987, which was a lesser wine, drinks well now. The next release will come from the 1991 vintage.

Roodezandt Co-op Tinta Barocca★★B
A medium-bodied wine that has varied considerably and should be consumed while in its youth. There is a gap from the 1986 vintage until the release of the unwooded 1990, which has 5% Cabernet. It is a fairly full-bodied, somewhat plain wine. The next release, from 1991, is 100% Tinta Barocca.

Rust-en-Vrede Tinta Barocca★★★(★)C
This is a wine of great appeal and with an excellent record in its short show history. It has good cultivar character which blossoms at an early age to make easy, rewarding drinking. It has improved with each vintage. The 1982 is delightful now and shows a finesse not found in other Tinta Baroccas. The 1983 is lighter and was a gold medal winner at the Stellenbosch show. As the 1984 has been well wood-aged, much of the cultivar character has been lost; nevertheless it is an attractive wine. The 1985 is a thinnish wine but rated Superior. The 1986 is a lot like the 1982, deep, rich and full, and could be confused with Cabernet. (It had 25% Merlot blended into it.) The 1988 is a big, earthy wine, also with over 20% Merlot, making a most attractive, good-flavoured, winter wine. This was the first Tinta Barocca selected by SAA. The 1989 continues the good drinking style. The 1986 drunk in early 1992 is in peak condition.

Swartland Co-op Tinta Barocca★★C
The 1986 and the 1988 vintages were big, full wines, but the 1987 was very light and a bit disappointing. The 1989 and 1990 are back to the regular style.

Vergenoegd Tinta Barocca★★★B
An excellent example of this variety: an easy, early-drinking wine. The 1983 has strong nose and flavour, while the 1984 has delightful character. The 1985 is lighter wine, while the 1986 is more in the traditional style of this Estate. The 1987 has strong varietal character and should age well. The 1988 is in line with the Estate's good, consistent style, as is the 1989.

Zinfandel

Bertrams Zinfandel★★★(★)E
An interesting speciality from Bertrams: usually medium-bodied and well-wooded with reasonable acid, it drinks well within three to four years. The 1984 was by far the best in the old style. The 1985 is a bit weak in character but the 1986 is a lovely wine, full of berry fruit and has developed well. The 1987 is a complete departure, having had some time in new French oak, as has the 1988. A delightful wine.
Blaauwklippen Zinfandel★★★(★)D
This Estate is famous for its Zinfandel: the 1980 vintage won the first Diners Club Award in 1981. There was no 1981, but the 1982 and 1984 have been very good. They are high-acid, medium-bodied, fruity wines, ageing well. These wines were made by Walter Finlayson, who is considered to be the father of Zinfandel in the Cape. The 1983 is lighter, in keeping with the vintage, yet has very good berry character. The 1985 and 1987 both have good fruit, backed by good wood. The 1988 is a lovely, berry-flavoured wine with spicy side tones and worth four stars. The 1989 is magnificent, masculine wine with an alcohol content exceeding 14% – and all the fruit and flavour to go with it. This is well-balanced, well-wooded wine that will develop with great benefit.
Hartenberg Zinfandel★★★C
A light-bodied, full, fruity wine. The first vintage was the 1981, from vines originally planted by Walter Finlayson, who introduced the variety to Blaauwklippen. The 1982 is full and fruity and developing well. The 1983 was not up to standard but the 1984 is a good, easy-drinking wine. The 1985 and the 1988 vintages are delightful, lively wines, while the 1989 is slightly wooded, which adds extra dimension to the wine.
Welmoed Co-op Zinfandel★★B
The first release, from the 1986 vintage, was lacking in cultivar character, but the 1988 and 1989 are much better wines with good cultivar character and a soft taste for early drinking.

Sweet Red Wines

Calitzdorp Co-op Semi-sweet Red★★A
Not as sweet as the label suggests, this Pinotage-Tinta Barocca blend is a surprise to the palate all the same. It is light-bodied yet rather filling to drink.
De Zoete Roodt (Helderberg Co-op)★★★B
A semi-sweet red from unusual cultivars.

White Wines

Blended/Non-varietal Dry White Wines

Altydgedacht Tygerberg Wood-aged White★★★B
If you want a dry white with character, this is it. The first release was a blend of a 1985 Steen with 40% 1982 Steen which had been in large oak vats, previously used for ageing red wines for more than two years. This produced a full-flavoured dry wine of considerable body and good character which, by 1992, has developed most unusual flavours. The next release was a blend of 40% of this wine with the balance Steen from the 1986 vintage. This wine did not quite have the wood of the first release, but it was still a most attractive wine. This sort of solera process produces wines which are full of character and a welcome variation to the rather stereotype dry whites. Both wines have developed well in the bottle. The third release is predominantly 1986 Steen, which has been aged for more than a year, blended with unwooded Sauvignon Blanc and Bukettraube from the 1987 vintage. The result is a very different wine which, in 1992, has deep flavour and probably needs to be drunk. The next release is about 50% Chenin Blanc, 30% Sauvignon Blanc (that shows well) and the balance Bukettraube. This is good, full-flavoured wine.

Avontuur Blanc de Blanc★★A
A fresh, dry white, of predominantly Chenin Blanc. The 1991 is a very different wine.

Avontuur Grand Vin Blanc★★★(★)B
The first two vintages, 1987 and 1988, differed dramatically. Both are good bone-dry wines blended from Sauvignon Blanc, Chenin Blanc and Sémillon, showing lots of pleasing character. The 1987 has developed very well in the bottle and is by far the more dominant wine. The 1989 wine is a pleasing product; it is lighter and more neutral for early consumption. It is now a blend of 50/50 Sauvignon Blanc, which had four months wooding, and Sémillon. It is a coarser wine than previous vintages and will need time to develop.

Badsberg Co-op Tafelwyn★★(★)A
Previously off-dry but finished dry from the 1990 vintage. Made from 20% Chenin Blanc and 80% Servan Blanc, it is light, pleasant, and easy drinking.

Beaufort Blanc de Blanc★★A
A refreshing, crisp, dry white which is very good value for money, blended from Cape Riesling, Sauvignon Blanc and Sémillon.

Belladonna Blanc de Blanc (Oude Nektar)★★★A
A pleasant dry white from Olasz Riesling. The label features the Belladonna lily which I find an odd choice as the name is connected with deadly poison!

Bergendal Bergenblanc★★★B
A Sauvignon Blanc-based blend with Chenin Blanc and Rhine Riesling, this is a well-made, dry, fruity wine with fresh flavours. Easy drinking.

Bon Vino (Boland Co-op)★★★A
Very inexpensive, very quaffable, fruity dry white from Steen. It is sold in 500 m*l* screw-top, returnable bottles which helps to keep the price down.

Boschendal Blanc de Blanc★★★(★)C
This is a well established, reliable label from the cellar; mainly Chenin Blanc and Rhine Riesling with 15% Sauvignon Blanc that gives good flavour and brisk finish.
Botha Co-op Vin Blanc★★A
A light dry white blend of Clairette Blanche and Riesling.
Bouchard Finlayson Blanc de Mer★★★D
A blend of mainly Rhine Riesling with Pinot Gris and Gewürztraminer that underwent malolactic fermentation, giving it a softness that makes it appear not as dry as it actually is. It is lightly flavoured, with slight muscat tones, and fruity finish.
Buitenverwachting Buiten Blanc★★★(★)B
A most refreshing dry wine with attractive nose and full flavour which drinks very easily. The blend has varied over the vintages but seems to have settled on mainly Sauvignon Blanc with lesser quantities of Rhine Riesling and Pinot Gris. It is not wooded.
Cape Selection Blanc de Blanc (Pick 'n Pay)★★(★)B
Easy drinking, fruity dry wine.
Cape Vintners Members Only Blanc de Blanc★★★(★)B
A delicious, light, fruity dry white blended from Sauvignon Blanc, Colombar and a touch of Muscat de Frontignan which gives enticing nose. Dry, clean finish. Easy drinking.
Casal da Serra Vinho Branca Seco★★★B
A good, crisp, dry white with appealing nose and fruity character. It drinks easily as an appetizer but also goes well with seafood.
Chant de Nuit (Nuy Co-op)★★★★A
This is a very good blend of Colombar and Steen, with a touch of something that produces a finely flavoured, bone-dry, white wine with a most appealing pineapple nose, coming from a grape called Ferdinand de Lesseps. This variety is not acceptable by the authorities and their fine wine is uncertified, hence the change of name from Nuy (a place) to Nuit, a fantasy name. Despite its dryness, it is soft across the palate, with a good clean finish. Recent vintages are four-star quality with good, all-round character. They are best enjoyed when young and fruity.
Culemborg Blanc de Blanc (Union Wine)★★A
A pleasant, dry, fruity blend.
Danie de Wet Blanc de Blancs★★★B
A good value, non-wooded, easy-drinking, fresh blend of Sauvignon Blanc, Chardonnay and Cape Riesling.
De Leuwen Jagt Leuwen Blanc★★★B
A good value, dry white mainly from Steen; well-balanced with good fresh finish.
Delheim Heerenwijn★★★A
This is an easy-drinking, well-made wine of varying blends that is always attractive, fresh and lively. It should be enjoyed when young and is excellent value for money. If stars were issued for always being satisfying, this wine would certainly be a four-star product!
De Zoete Inval Blanc de Blanc★B
An odd, non-vintaged dry white that is showing lots of bottle age. Needs to be drunk immediately.
De Zoete Inval Capri★★B
A bottle-aged dry white with a strange but not unpleasant herby-type character.

Die Krans Grand Vin Blanc★★★A
An intriguing blend of 20% Colombar, 30% Fernão Pires, 40% Hárslevelü and 10% Muscat d'Alexandrie. It has a fascinating fruit salad nose and is pleasant, easy drinking as a fresh young wine.
Dieu Donne Blanc de Blanc★★★B
First release from 1992 is a Rhine Riesling and Chenin Blanc blend. This is attractive, easy-drinking wine that is not bone-dry, yet not really off-dry.
Domein Doornkraal Serenade Droog★★(★)A
A multiple blend in which Sauvignon Blanc shows plus lots of Muscat and other fruity flavours. Best enjoyed young.
Douglas Green Blanc de Blanc★★B
A pleasant, clean, fresh, non-vintaged wine, from Steen. Pretty pack.
Douglas Green St Vincent★★B
A non-vintaged, dry, white *vin ordinaire* of the 'Saint' series. Also part of the new range.
Du Toitskloof Blanc de Blanc★★★B
The blend has varied over the vintages but the latest is all Steen. Good nose, lots of fruit, nice flavours, clean finish.
Edward Snell Blanc de Blanc★★★B
A non-vintaged, dry white wine. The blend may vary, but the quality is constant.
Eersterivier Valleise Co-op Vin Blanc★★★A
The blend varies but is always reliable and fruity with no variety dominating. It has a crisp dry finish and is best enjoyed young.
Eikendal Vineyards Blanc de Blanc★★★B
This Blanc de Blanc has developed vintage by vintage into a most attractive, fresh, fruity wine that is best enjoyed in its youth. It comprises mainly of Steen, with a touch of Sauvignon Blanc. The latest release has extra dimension, with a fraction of wooded Riesling.
Fairview Charles Gerard★★★B
The 1991 and 1992 are unwooded Sauvignon Blanc-Chenin Blanc blends. Good easy drinking wine.
Fairview Charles Gerard Reserve★★★★(★)C
The 1991 is excellent oak-fermented wine. It is a blend of Sauvignon Blanc and Semillon; big, full-flavoured wine with lots of character and good oak. It should develop as well as the 1990.
Golden Alibama (SFW)★★A
An inexpensive dry wine, coloured 'brandy brown' with caramel. It has surprisingly good flavour when chilled and served as an aperitif.
Goue Vallei Blanc de Blanc (Citrusdal Co-op)★★★A
This cellar has improved its quality and image over the past few years with labels depicting the flowers of Namaqualand. Latest vintages are unwooded 50/50 blend of Chenin Blanc and Sauvignon Blanc. Lovely fresh fruity nose, crisp acidity on the palate, clean finish.
Gouvino (Goudini Co-op)★★A
A dry fruity blend in 500 m*l* returnable bottles.
Groot Constantia Blanc de Blanc★★★C
Another dry white blend. It was originally a blend of Steen, Weisser Riesling and Fernão Pires, giving a good, fruity nose and clean, crisp palate which developed well in the bottle over a year or so. Recent releases are Steen and Sauvignon Blanc blends, with the 1988 and 1990 containing some 15% Pinot Gris, offering full-flavoured wine that drinks well when young.

Grünberger Blanc de Blanc (Bergkelder)★★★(★)B
A lovely, dry, refreshing, white wine with a broad flavour spectrum in which various varieties, including Sauvignon Blanc and Steen, are so harmoniously blended that no one predominates, but together they produce a wine of individual character. Now in a tall slender Rhine bottle rather than the old flask shape.
Hamilton Russell Vineyards Grand Vin Blanc★★★(★)C/D
The blend of this interesting wine has changed almost from vintage to vintage, as has the name. The latest is mainly Chardonnay, with 30% Sauvignon Blanc and an interesting touch of 10% Gewürztraminer. It is most attractive, very satisfying drinking wine that has potential to develop in the bottle.
Hartenberg Bin 3★★★C
An attractive dry white wine with a good, zesty character, available only at the farm. Although the blend varies, the latest contains Sauvignon Blanc, Sémillon and interesting Auxerrois.
Hartenberg Chatillon★★(★)C
Hartenberg launched its new image as an Estate in 1985 with a range of seven wines. One of these, Chatillon, was a blend of Riesling, Steen and Sémillon of which the last-named is the main component. The blend has varied with the vintage but is always full of interest and lots of flavour. Latest are Sauvignon Blanc and Auxerrois.
Haute Provence Blanc Royale★★★B
The original release from the 1989 vintage was 60% Sémillon and the balance Sauvignon Blanc, resulting in a good dry white. A similar blend with attractive oak backing has been continued.
Haute Provence Grand Vin★★(★)B
A product of the Franschhoek Vineyards Co-op scheme. The name changes with the vintage but it is pleasant, if unexciting, dry wine.
Helderberg Co-op Vin Blanc★★A
This is a medium-bodied blend of Steen, Colombar and Sauvignon Blanc, giving a very popular pleasant dry wine.
Hemel-en-Aarde Vin Blanc★★★(★)B/C
Previously only available in Hermanus, but now released for national distribution through public demand. The blend varies but usually contains Sauvignon Blanc, Chenin Blanc, Kerner and Rhine Riesling. It is matured on the lees, giving pleasing complexity. Enjoy its youthful freshness or age to allow richness to develop.
Inglewood Blanc de Blanc (Neil Ellis Wines)★★★(★)B
A good value, attractive drinking wine with nice flavours from Steen, Sauvignon Blanc and Sémillon, with brisk finish.
Jonkheer Edelweiss Dry White★★A
A dry wine which, year after year, offers pleasant, easy drinking.
Kango Co-op Premier Blanc★(★)A
A variable blend, usually of Sauvignon Blanc, various Rieslings and a touch of Muscat.
Klein Constantia Blanc de Blanc★★★★C
A big, beautiful wine at 13% alcohol, produced because the Estate believed its Sauvignon Blanc from the 1987 vintage was not up to their style and standard. It was blended with Chenin Blanc to produce South Africa's best combination of these two varieties. As good as it tasted when released, it has developed into one of South Africa's greatest dry whites. I have regularly served it to many overseas fundis and they have all rated it as one of South Africa's best wines.

Regrettably this was a one-off. Some 200 cases (6 x 750 m*l*) were sold at the 1992 Nederburg Auction at R126 per case.

Koelenhof Co-op Koelenhoffer★★★A

A surprisingly good, light, dry blend that has varied with the vintage and now contains Sauvignon Blanc amongst others. It makes easy drinking when young and fresh.

KWV Bonne Esperance Dry White★★(no price available)

A technically well-made dry wine, without character, presented in litre bottles.

KWV Cape Floret★★(no price available)

An awkward, oak-aged Steen.

La Bri Blanc de La Bri★★★B

A product of the Franschhoek Vineyards Co-op scheme, this is a very fashionable wine blended from Sauvignon Blanc and Sémillon. The latter is given a little wood-age, which adds extra dimension to the blend. Although this wine is usually best enjoyed when young, a tasting of every vintage produced indicates that this wine definitely ages with interest.

La Couronne Richesse★★★B

The first release is a 50/50 blend of Sauvignon Blanc and wooded Sémillon, resulting in a full-flavoured, high-acid wine. Although a little aggressive when young, it has smoothed out over a period of time. Later releases are known to contain more Sauvignon Blanc and are better wines.

Ladismith Co-op Swartberg Aristaat★★(★)A

An unusual dry Steen which is very good value for money.

La Gratitude (SFW)★★★(★)B

One of South Africa's famous old-timers, it was brought up to date with the 1985 vintage with a touch of subtle new small French oak. It has improved each vintage since, with the 1991 lovely, with good wood showing yet without masking the attractive fruitiness. La Gratitude has been around for too long to be fashionable, but is still far better than many 'new' wines. Very good value for money.

La Provence Cuvée Blanche★★B

The 1990 is 60% Sémillon, 34% Sauvignon Blanc and 6% Chardonnay. It has been well-wooded in French and American oak, is a big wine with lots of alcohol and needs time to develop.

Langverwacht Co-op Blanc de Blanc★★(★)A

Good value Sauvignon Blanc/Colombar blend.

Le Foyer Dry White (Eersterivier Co-op)★★(★)A

A good-tasting blend of Steen and Sauvignon Blanc in 500 m*l* screw-top bottles.

Lord Neethling Blanc (Neethlingshof)★★★C

A light, dry, slightly wooded Chardonnay-Sauvignon blend.

Mamreweg Co-op Blanc de Blanc★★A

A fruity, fresh dry white from Steen and Clairette Blanche, it is best enjoyed when very young.

McGregor Co-op Blanc de Blanc★★(★)A

The 1991, as per the 1990, is 40% each of Riesling and Colombar and 20% Sauvignon Blanc. Fresh and fruity, these wines are best enjoyed when young.

Mon Don Blanc de Blanc★★A

Nice, easy-drinking, good-value wine from Sauvignon Blanc, Colombar and Steen.

Mon Don Mystère★★(★)B
The 1988 developed good bottle age over two years. The 1991 is light, dry and pleasant, and good value.
Monfort Blanc de Blanc (Solly Kramer)★A
A very ordinary, dry white.
Montpellier Blanc de Blanc★★★B
A dry light blend from Sémillon and Sauvignon Blanc making pleasant, easy-drinking wine.
Mooiuitsig Dry White★A
An ordinary, dry, white wine.
Morgenhof Blanc de Blanc★★(★)B
No longer vintaged. A pleasant, easy-drinking Steen-Sauvignon Blanc blend.
Muratie Dry White★★(★)B
Blended from Steen, Sémillon, Riesling and Palomino, this is a pleasant, easy-drinking dry white.
Nederburg Prelude★★★★C
The first release from the 1988 vintage appeared early in 1990, the launch coinciding with the 16th Nederburg Auction. It is a very good blend of Sauvignon Blanc and Chardonnay, that has been just sufficiently wood-aged to tone the components, but not to be obviously woody. Each vintage since has been progressively better.
Nederburg Private Bin D207★★★★B
Produced for the first time in 1983, and then perfected in 1984, now the 1985, 1986, 1987 and 1988 have followed with fruity noses and dry, refreshing flavour coming from predominantly Fernão Pires. It is excellent while young and fresh, yet has the ability to age well. It has so far only been released at the Nederburg Auction. The latest vintage, the 1988, was released at the 1989 Nederburg Auction.
Nederburg Private Bin D212★★★(★)C
A seldom-produced, absolutely dry wine packed with flavour. It ages exceptionally well. Nederburg Bin wines are prefixed 'S' for the Sweet Wines, 'D' for Dry Whites and 'R' for the Reds. The Bin Series is only released at the annual Nederburg Auction.
Nederburg Private Bin D218★★★D
The first release of this wine was from the 1987 vintage at the 1989 Nederburg Auction. It was blended from 80% Sauvignon Blanc and 20% Pinot Blanc, and then aged for six months in small oak, giving a full, complex nose packed with fruit flavours and backed with good acidity. Releases of vintages 1988, 1989 and 1990, vary in quantity from 360 to 950 cases. High alcohol and good acid allow these wines to develop with distinction over four to five years.
Oom Tas (SFW)★★(★)A
South Africa's original Blanc de Noir, although in those days the Blanc de Noir colour was not fashionable, so it was tinted with caramel. Its strong-looking hue belies the lightness of Oom Tas. This is a blend of Blanc de Noir, Cinsaut and dry Hanepoot which gives the attractive fruity nose. It is a well-balanced, well-made wine that makes a very good aperitif when chilled.
Oude Bos Droë Wit (Drop Inn)★★★B
A particularly good dry white made from Steen.
Paddadundee (Paddagang Vignerons)★★(★)B
A blend of Sauvignon Blanc, Chenin Blanc and Rhine Riesling giving a full-flavoured dry white.

Paddasang (Paddagang Vignerons)★★(★)C
This is a dry wine produced by the Paddagang Vignerons from grapes grown on their small vineyards and vinified at the local Co-op. The main varieties included in the blend are Sauvignon Blanc, Chenin Blanc and Colombar.
Paradyskloof White★★★B
Excellent value for a wooded dry white from mainly Pinot Blanc and Sauvignon Blanc. A good complex wine with fine, long finish.
Pascali Bianco★★★B
A very palatable partner to the red Pascali. An easy-drinking dry wine with good flavour.
Pick 'n Pay Grand Vin Blanc★★★(★)B
A very well-made, oak-matured white of predominantly Sauvignon Blanc. The 1990 is complex, with good notty character that will develop well over a year or two.
Rhebokskloof Grand Vin Blanc★★★C
A pleasant blend in which no single variety dominates; it is fermented and matured in French oak. It is a blend of various varieties including Sauvignon Blanc. It is crisp, clean, pleasantly fruity, and delightful when young, but ages well over two to three years. It drinks easily and well, especially in the ambience of the Estate's restaurant.
Rietrivier Co-op Blanc de Blanc★★A
An unusual blend of Colombar, Steen and Hárslevelü, giving a dry white with lots of flavour.
Romansrivier Co-op Blanc de Blanc★★★B
A dry wine with good Sauvignon Blanc character. Brisk clean finish.
Roodezandt Blanc de Blanc★★★A
A dry blend that varies vintage by vintage, but usually a good, full-flavoured, easy-drinking wine.
Rooiberg Co-op Selected Dry White★★★A
A very pleasant, clean, dry white, usually blended from Steen, Colombar and Ugni Blanc or Clairette Blanche. It is available with a screw-top.
Rovino Dry White★★A
An inexpensive dry white blended from Colombar, Clairette Blanche and Ferdinand de Lesseps. Attractive nose and good flavour in 500 *ml* screw-top bottles.
Saxenburg Blanc de Blanc★★★B
A fresh, clean dry wine containing Sauvignon Blanc and Chenin Blanc, touched out with Gewürztraminer. It is best enjoyed young.
Simondium Co-op Vin Blanc★(★)A
A rather plain and neutral dry white.
Simonsig Vin Fumé★★★(★)B
Originally a wood-aged blend based on Steen with some Sauvignon Blanc and Kerner added, it is nowadays predominantly Sauvignon Blanc. The 1981 vintage was called Blanc Fumé, and was the subject of some debate between Frans Malan and the authorities, who ruled that the name could only be used for wines made entirely from Sauvignon Blanc. Hence the change to Vin Fumé. Nowadays the cultivar 'Sauvignon Blanc' appears on the label. The quality continues through all the recent vintages. This wine drinks exceptionally well when very young, but also has the ability to age with appeal over three to four years. It is good value for money.

Simonsvlei Co-op Blanc de Blanc★★A
An interesting blend with good, fruity nose and pleasant taste. Steen comes through but is tempered by other varieties, including Riesling, resulting in a well-balanced blend that varies with the vintage. It was previously labelled Selected Dry White.
Stellenbosch Wine Route Vin Blanc★★★B
A dry white blend based on Cape Riesling produced by Delheim in 1,5 *l* returnable plastic flasks.
Stellenzicht Grand Vin Blanc★★★★C
This wine has developed over the vintages into a really super wine, with almost enough Sauvignon Blanc to qualify for cultivar certification. The next biggest portion is Auxerrois, with touches of Chardonnay and Pinot Gris. It is very French in style with lots of fine oak; delicious full flavour, great when young but with ageing potential.
Stellenzicht Heerenblanc★★★★C
A very well-made wine from Sauvignon Blanc and some Rhine Riesling. Fine for drinking on release, with potential to develop well in the bottle.
Swartland Co-op Blanc de Blanc★★★B
A dry white where the blend varies with the vintage and can include Steen, Riesling, Sauvignon Blanc, Sémillon or Hárslevelü.
Twee Jongegezellen 39 Grand Prix★★★B
A wine with a pleasing, attractive, fruity bouquet and refreshing palate – a blend of the Estate's best cultivars in which the Muscat shows on the nose and Rieslings give good body. Almost dry, it makes easy drinking. The 1991 is particularly good.
Valley Dry White (Gilbeys)★★A
A pleasant, light, dry white.
Van Loveren Blanc de Blanc★★★B
The blend differs with the vintage. Nowadays Sauvignon Blanc makes up the biggest percentage of the blend (40–50%) with the balance made up of Colombar with Hárslevelü and Muscat de Frontignan. Very dry, good, fruity, full-flavoured wine to be enjoyed when young. Good value for money.
Vaughan Johnson's Good Everyday Dry White ★★★ B
A multiple blend giving easy-drinking, fresh-flavoured wine, and now available in stores other than Vaughan Johnson's. Good value for money.
Villa Rossini Bianco★★A
One of the spate of Italian-style wines to enter the market during 1989. A not quite dry, flavoursome wine sold in returnable one-litre, screw-top bottles.
Villiera Blue Ridge Blanc ★★★ B
A bright, dry blend including Chenin Blanc, Sauvignon Blanc and Rhine Riesling offering good flavour and brisk finish.
Vino Roma Bianco★★A
A dry white, Steen-based blend for easy drinking. Previously called Roma White, but geared up and replaced to cater for the current Italian fashion.
Vino Uno Secco (Du Toitskloof)★★(★)A
A dry white from Steen in 500 m*l* screw-top bottles. Easy-drinking.
Vredendal Co-op Classic Dry White★★A
This wine replaces the cellar's Premier Grand Crû and is a dry blend of Chenin Blanc, Colombar and Sauvignon Blanc.

Weltevrede Blanc de Blanc★★★B
The blend varies, with the latest releases of Steen and Colombar, in which both give of their best to produce an attractive, flavourful, fruity, dry white.
Weltevrede Privé de Bois★★★C
The first release was the 1979 Privé, with a touch of wood giving it added dimension. Since then it has developed into a well-made, dry, wooded white, usually from Colombar and Steen. Good value.
Woolworths Blanc de Blanc★★★B
From Villiera. A very good Sauvignon Blanc-Chenin Blanc blend with lots of flavour and fruit.
Woolworths Le Troisieme 913W★★★★
Part of the Woolworths' Vintage Collection. The number 91 indicates the vintage; 3, the third in the range and the W stands for white. This is one of the finest Sauvignon Blanc and Chardonnay blends, with nearly 70% of the former. Big alcohol, cask-fermented, gives fruity nose and lots of toasty flavours. Good to drink now, but after a year or two in the bottle it will be a stunner.
Woolworths Petit Vin Dry White★★B
A dry white in 250 m*l* Tetrapak.
Zandwijk Klein Draken ★(★)
A Steen-based, dry white blend.
Zevenwacht Blanc de Blanc★★★C
A blend of Riesling, Sauvignon Blanc and Steen, giving a fresh, dry, fruity wine that drinks well when young but has the potential to develop in the bottle. Good value.
Zevenwacht Vin Blanc★★B
A well-made, dry blend of Steen and Riesling. Budget-priced.
Zonnebloem Blanc de Blanc (SFW)★★★(★)B
A very good, Steen-based blend with a pitch of nose and flavour seldom found in such a dry Cape wine. It is vintage-dated and best enjoyed when young. Good value for money.
Zonnebloem Grand Soleil (SFW)★★★★C
Soleil, pronounced 'sollay', means sun, and this definitely is a warm-hearted wine, produced from Sauvignon Blanc, Chenin Blanc and Chardonnay. The first release was from the 1988 vintage and has a tinge of gold colour and attractive grassy nose, with a touch of new oak. Nice rich, buttery vanilla in the mouth, and satisfying to swallow. Sauvignon Blanc from the Helderberg, Chenin Blanc from Stellenbosch Kloof and Chardonnay from Durbanville have combined well to give an elegant wine that is developing beautifully in the bottle. The 1991 is a very good blend that drinks well.

Blended/Non-varietal Off-dry/Semi-sweet White Wines

Arthur Freedberg Beau Blanc (Rebel)★★(★)B
A Steen-Sauvignon Blanc-based, semi-sweet light wine.
Autumn Harvest Ausberger(SFW)★★(★)A
A light, off-dry, consistent white wine with fruity nose and good, clean palate.
Autumn Harvest Stein(SFW)★★(★)A
A good, semi-sweet white wine with consistently pleasing character.
Avontuur Nuit St Pierre Vin Blanc★★(★)B
A very pleasant off-dry wine that drinks very easily. It is made from Chenin Blanc and is best enjoyed when young and fresh.
Avontuur Insensata★★(★)B
A semi-sweet wine from mainly Steen with 10% Weisser Riesling.
Backsberg Bouquet Blanc★★★B
Chenin Blanc-based blend with 20% each Muscat Ottonel and Rhine Riesling. The Muscat gives a most attractive nose. Clean, full-flavoured wine with enough fruit acid, and very easy drinking.
Badsberg Co-op Badlese★★A
A very light, slightly fruity, semi-sweet white wine based on Steen.
Beaufort Stein★★A
A pleasant, easy-drinking, semi-sweet white.
Bellingham Blancenberger★★★B
A Sauvignon Blanc-based blend with Steen, finished off-dry.
Bellingham Johannisberger★★★(★)B
This is a particularly pleasant wine with attractive Muscat nose followed by a full-flavoured, semi-sweet taste. A lovely wine, and long-time market leader in its category.
Blaauwklippen White Landau★★★(★)B
An off-dry, delicate and consistently good blend of varieties which has improved with time and the introduction of more interesting cultivars. It is lovely when young and fresh but also ages with interest, developing an elusive complexity. Good value for money.
Bloemendal Estate Bloemen Blanc★★★(★)A
The first release from this new Estate was from the 1987 vintage – an off-dry wine with good Steen character. Since then it has become a much more attractive wine: an off-dry blend of Cape and Rhine Rieslings. It is presented with a most attractive label showing a brightly-coloured waterblommetjie. Recent vintages continue to be similar blends and are just as attractive. Judging by its rapid improvement of quality over the last three vintages, this is a cellar to watch.
Bolandse Co-op Bon Vino Semi-sweet★★A
This is Bolandse Co-op's attempt to keep the cost of wine down. It is a semi-sweet Steen in 500 m*l* screw-top, returnable bottles.
Bolandse Co-op Stein★★A
A full-flavoured, semi-sweet Steen that is best when young and fresh but can age and develop very well.
Bon Courage Bouquet Blanc★★★(★)B
A dryish blend (although nearly 11 g/*l* sugar), of Colombar and Gewürztraminer which shows well on the nose. Best enjoyed young.
Bonfoi Estate Ouverture★★★B
A semi-sweet white based on Steen, with good acidic finish, which replaces Chenin Blanc.

Bonistein (Mooiuitsig Wynkelders)★A
A fruity Steen which makes pleasant drinking.
Bonnievale Co-op Blanc de Blanc★★(★)A
This is an off-dry white blended from Sauvignon Blanc and Colombar, making pleasant drinking when young.
Boplaas Vin Blanc★★A
A nice, easy-drinking, wine made from Chenin Blanc and Colombar.
Boschendal Grand Vin Blanc★★★(★)D
This was launched in the same year as the farm's 300th anniversary, in October 1985, with splendidly festive French flair. It was basically Sauvignon Blanc fermented and aged in French oak, a delicate wine with enticing nose and pleasant palate, which drank well at an early stage. Nowadays it has settled on a 75% Sauvignon Blanc and 25% Rhine Riesling blend, giving much more complex wine which improves with age. It has really become one of the Cape's consistently better white wines. With Boschendal's pedigree it is a pity the presentation is so similar to that of the really noble Baron d'L, the classic French wine from the Loire.
Boschendal Le Bouquet★★★(★)C
Although technically semi-sweet, the high fruit-acid counteracts the sweetness, giving a refreshing, attractively flavoured wine with delightful nose. It shows good Gewürztraminer, layered with fine Muscat. Recent vintages are very attractive wines.
Bovlei Co-op Stein★★A
Made from Steen and finished semi-sweet, this is a gold medal winner at regional shows.
Brandvlei Co-op Stein★★A
A Steen-based blend which offers a full-bodied, semi-sweet white with powerful bouquet.
Breughel Stein (Aroma Group)★★A
A semi-sweet white based on Steen.
Cantori Bianco★★★B
A very pleasant, easy-drinking wine from Cape Riesling, Sauvignon Blanc and Sémillon, finished off-dry.
Cape Vintners Members Only Bouquet Blanc★★★B
A very drinkable semi-sweet wine with a subtle touch of Muscat from the 1992 vintage.
Carnival Stein (Spar)★★A
A semi-sweet white blend based on Steen and Colombar.
Cederberg Kelders Dwarsrivier Weissberger★★★A
A much-improved, semi-sweet, white wine with good fruity nose and pleasant flavour providing easy drinking.
Cellar Cask Premier Semi-sweet★★A
An easy-drinking, semi-sweet wine, available in cork-closed bottles.
Cellar Cask Select Johannisberger★★★B
A Steen-based semi-sweet with fruity nose and brisk finish.
Cellar Reserve Stein (Hyperama)★(★)A
A Steen-based semi-sweet wine.
Chamonix Bouquet Blanc★★★B/C
This label has replaced the Vin Blanc. An off-dry wine with a most attractive guava nose, it develops well over a year or two in the bottle.
Culemborg Blanc de Blanc (Union Wine)★★(★)B
A good, vintaged, value-for-money wine with pleasant flavour from a Riesling-Steen blend, finished off-dry.

Culemborg Stein (Union Wine)★★A
A good example of a clean, fruity, semi-sweet wine made from Steen. It is vintage-dated and very good value for money.
De Doorns Co-op Stein★★A
A strong-flavoured, semi-sweet white.
Delheim Goldspatz Stein★★★B
This tasty, happy, semi-sweet white, which has good vinous character, is a smooth, finely flavoured wine. In a whole range of very ordinary Steins, this is in a class of its own. Latest vintages have clean botrytis touch. Good acid balances the sweetness. Consistently of a surprisingly high standard.
De Wet Co-op Huiswyn Stein★A
A light-bodied, semi-sweet Steen, previously labelled 'Huiswyn Semi-sweet'.
De Zoete Inval Demi Sec★★D
Like all the wines from this cellar, it is very individual, with a somewhat aged character, but intriguing nevertheless. Definitely different in a range of very similar semi-sweets.
Die Krans Bouquet Blanc★★(★)A
A blend of 60% Colombar and 40% Hanepoot, crushed and fermented together to give a fresh, fruity, pleasant, off-dry wine. Best enjoyed in its youth.
Die Poort Fröhlich Stein★★A
A non-vintage, semi-sweet Steen, touched off with some Muscat from this 'remote' and unusual winery on the Gourits River.
Domein Doornkraal Kuierwyn★★(★)A
Originally a multiple blend of 40% each of Steen and Hanepoot and 10% each of Colombar and White French. Nowadays the Effesoet is 80% Steen and 10% each of Hanepoot and Sémillon. It comes in two versions: an off-dry (described above) and a decidedly semi-sweet that is mainly Steen with 35% Colombar and 15% White Muscadel.
Domein Doornkraal Serenade★★A
The first releases from this Klein Karoo cellar at De Rust were three wines which appear under the same name, 'Serenade': a dry in a hock bottle, an off-dry in a Bordeaux bottle, and a semi-sweet in a Burgundy bottle. They were all from the 1987 vintage and were pleasant, acceptable products made from Steen, Colombar, Hanepoot and Muscat Ottonel, pressed and fermented together. From the 1988 vintage they have produced a plain, dry version as well as a better semi-sweet, fruity, Muscaty product. The 1990 version of Effedroog is mainly Steen and the Semi-soet is almost equal quantities of Colombar and Steen and 15% Muscats.
Douglas Co-op Stein★B
A semi-sweet blend of Steen and Colombar.
Douglas Green St Anna Schloss★★B
A non-vintaged, semi-sweet, fruity white in the range's new attractive packaging – the picture on the label showing a decidedly Rhine river scene.
Douglas Green Stein★★★D
A consistent, clean-flavoured semi-sweet that was selected for SAA in 1989. Now in the range's attractive new packaging.
Douglas Green St Morand★★★B
The blend of some six white cultivars, all capable of producing good fruity noses, creates this wine's most attractive aroma. Although

classed as off-dry, it tastes sweeter due to lack of good fruit acid. This non-vintaged wine should be consumed while still fresh and young. It also appears in the range's new attractive packaging.

Drostdy-Hof Stein Select(Oude Meester)★★A
A good, semi-sweet Steen with clean finish.

Edward Snell Johannisberger★★★B
Delightful fresh nose coming from the blend of Rhine Riesling, Gewürztraminer and Steen, finished semi-sweet. Best when young and fresh.

Eikendal Vineyards Duc de Berry Stein★★B
Produced by Eikendal Vineyards, this is an easy-drinking, semi-sweet wine.

Fairview Bouquet Fair★★★★B
Charles Back produced a delightful off-dry fruity wine from the 1990 vintage using Steen and Gewürztraminer. A winner. This is followed by a bright, muscaty-flavoured 1991. Good value, nice drinking.

Fleur Du Cap Emerald Stein (Bergkelder)★★★B
Many rather indifferent wines are offered under the name of Stein, but this one has class and quality: a semi-sweet, almost Late Harvest wine, full of flavour. It is vintage-dated and always very reliable.

Franschhoek Vallei Stein★A
Usually a *vin ordinaire*, this is a semi-sweet Steen which must be consumed while young.

Golden Mustang★A
Semi-sweet, golden wine sold in screw-top bottles.

Graça (SFW)★★★(★)B
This is a wine which has developed both in character and quality since its first release and is now a market leader in its category. Slight pétillance sets off the good flavours of the Sémillon and Sauvignon Blanc blend. This is a well-made wine which allows easy drinking. Rapidly recognized as a good drinking wine, it is now one of South Africa's firm favourites. It is extremely versatile as proven in recent research tastings where it came first in a Rhine Riesling tasting, second as a Sauvignon Blanc, rated by far the best Sémillon and among the best Cape Rieslings! It contains no Riesling whatsoever! With recent changes in crayfish regulations the bottle can no longer be used as a reliable measure in the Cape.

Groot Constantia Bouquet Blanc★★★A
A good-value, Muscat-based, off-dry wine.

Groot Constantia Stein★★★A
Recent vintages are lively semi-sweet wines, and are very pleasant when young and well-chilled. Good value for money.

Grünberger Stein (Bergkelder)★★★C
The original of the range and still its principal wine. It is blended from a Steen base in a constant and definite semi-sweet style to suit the vintage, and is one of South Africa's most popular wines.

Hartenberg Bin 6★★★C
A semi-sweet white, available only at the farm. A slight hint of botrytis makes this a very pleasant, easy-drinking wine.

Haute Provence Larmes des Anges★★(★)B
A semi-sweet blend of Steen and Muscat d'Alexandrie giving a very light flavoured but pleasantly scented wine. The name means 'Angels Tears' and comes from the legend in which the angels wept tears of joy on tasting the fruits of a fine vintage!

Helderberg Co-op Vin Sucre★★A
A pleasant, light, semi-sweet wine, also available in 500 m*l* bottles.
Honey Blossom (SFW)★★B
A well made, semi-sweet white.
Honigtraube (Groot Eiland Co-op)★★A
Mainly Bukettraube with a touch of Ferdinand de Lesseps. Extra-attractive nose and sweet finish.
Huguenot Stein★★A
Pleasant semi-sweet wine with fresh finish.
Jonkerskloof Selected Stein (OK/Hyperama)★★A
Semi-sweet fruity wine in 5 *l* bottles.
Kango Co-op Herfsgoud★★B
A semi-sweet showing fair fruit from the Colombar and White Muscadel blend.
Kango Co-op Bouquet Petit★★B
A new release based on Morio Muscat, with Steen and Colombar. Not too sweet.
Kango Co-op Xandré★★B
An off-dry wine made originally from Muscat d'Alexandrie, hence the name, but now a blend of Colombar and Muscadel. It is sold in inexpensive, screw-top bottles.
Kellerprinz Selected Stein(SFW)★★A
A semi-sweet, fresh and fruity Stein with good, clean flavour.
Klawer Co-op Blanc de Blanc★★A
An off-dry blend of two thirds Colombar and one third Muscat Ottonel. It is light-bodied and pleasantly refreshing when chilled.
Koelenhof Co-op Koelenheimer★★(★)A
(Previously known as Koelenhof Co-op Stein.) Recent releases have been very good. Koelenheimer was Steen-based and touched off with Hanepoot; now Sauvignon Blanc, Riesling, Colombar and a touch of Hanepoot.
KWV Bonne Esperance Stein★★(no price available)
A semi-sweet white in litre bottles.
Laborie(KWV)★★★B
An off-dry blend of several varieties, with the terpene character of Rhine Riesling evident in later releases. It develops well in the bottle over two to three years.
Laborie Taillefert White (KWV)★★★(★)C
This is one of a range of wines launched in 1988 by the KWV as a tribute to the French Huguenot, Jean Taillefert, the original owner of Laborie. It is an off-dry blend based on Rhine Riesling with lots of bottle age.
La Bri La Briette★★★B
Introduced to celebrate La Bri's 10th anniversary. A blend of 'Rhine Riesling for fruitiness, Sémillon for smoothness and Sauvignon Blanc for richness' – or so the advert and back label say. At any rate, it is a very pleasant, easy-drinking wine.
Landskroon Bouquet Blanc★★★B
Steen-based wine with Morio Muscat giving most attractive nose. Finished off-dry and delightful as a young wine.
Landzicht Stein★A
A semi-sweet blend of Chenel, Hanepoot and Colombar.
Le Foyer Semi-sweet (Eersterivier Co-op)★★(★)A
A slightly muscaty semi-sweet white in 500 m*l* screw-top bottles.

Le Pavillon Blanc (Boschendal)★★★ (★)B
Good value, just off-dry, but so well balanced that it appears almost dry. Good blend of Chenin Blanc, Riesling and Chardonnay. Attractive fruity bouquet, good flavour and crisp, clean finish.
Les Chênes C'est La Vie★★B
This wine was previously labelled 'La Fleur'. One of the major merchants challenged the use of the name, however, so Sarel van Vuuren, used the French version of his exclamation 'Well, that's life', as the new name for the wine. This off-dry white is a blend of predominantly Sémillon and the balance Sauvignon Blanc.
L'Etoile Legere (Bergkelder)★★★B
An off-dry, well-made, Steen-based wine.
Lieberstein (SFW)★★A
This is the semi-sweet white wine which led the natural wine revolution of the mid-1960s, and still has a considerable following. When young and fresh, it is delightfully flavoured and pleasing.
Lievland Cheandrie★★★A
A lovely wine, with good scented nose, it is not as sweet as most Steins. It has relatively low alcohol, but makes pleasant, easy drinking and is excellent value.
Mamreweg Co-op Stein★★A
An inexpensive, semi-sweet Stein.
Matin Soleil Vin Bouquet (Môreson)★★B
A pleasant Chenin Blanc with nice fruity nose and is easy drinking.
Merwespont Co-op Blanc de Blanc★★★A
Off-dry Steen-Colombar blend with fruity nose and fresh finish.
Mont D'Or Stein (Drop Inn)★A
A semi-sweet, white *vin ordinaire*.
Monfort Stein (Solly Kramer)★A
A semi-sweet white with easy-drinking qualities.
Monterey Stein (Western Province Cellars)★A
A vintage-dated, sound, semi-sweet blend.
Montpellier Huiswyn ★★A
A fruity, pleasant, good drinking wine from Colombar, Sauvignon Blanc, Sémillon, Steen and Pinot Blanc.
Montpellier Suzanne Gardé★★(★)B
An off-dry wine with intriguing flavour and a slight hint of Sauvignon Blanc. From 1990 it is vintage dated.
Nederburg Elegance★★★(★)C
The first release, from the 1987 vintage, was wine with a delightful fruity nose and off-dry taste, full of gentle Muscat flavours. It has improved over the vintages and now has good Rhine Riesling content which gives greater complexity. The slight fresh finish gives the impression of being drier than it really is. Easy-drinking wine.
Nederburg Fonternel★★★B
Its production has now ceased, but, as Fonternel ages with interest, it is worth keeping the later vintages to enjoy the bottle-developed flavours. It was a pioneer of the off-dry, fruity type wine and many similar wines are now being produced by other cellars.
Nederburg Pinot Blanc★★★C
The first release from 1989 is a soft, off-dry, pleasant wine without much cultivar character. The 1990 and 1991 are better and drier.
Nederburg Private Bin S311★★★B
Wine made for sale at the Nederburg Auction; lovely Late Harvest

style that have aged well. Lots of tropical fruit and spices – a lovely drink and usually at good value for money.

Nederburg Private Bin S312★★★★C

In keeping with the 'S' series, this wine is sweet but not cloying. It has a most beautiful tropical-fruit nose and a flavour of great complexity. With a few years of bottle-ageing it evolves magnificently. It is sold only at the Nederburg Auction.

Nederburg Private Bin S333★★★★C

Apparently the sweetest of the three 'S' Bins (they are all, in fact, of much the same sweetness), this wine has a special appeal which is due to the gentle touch of the Muscat. It ages with great distinction. It is sold only at the Nederburg Auction and is an absolute delight.

Nederburg Private Bin S354★★★★(★)D

The first release, of the 1982 vintage, was sold at the 1985 Nederburg Auction. Since then there have been vintages 1982, 1984, 1985, 1986, 1987 and 1988. It is a lovely, fruity blend of Weisser Riesling and Gewürztraminer, offering a wealth of sweet flavour balanced by good acid. The 1988 has been hailed as the best ever, and was the last one to be released.

Nederburg Stein★★★(★)B

A remarkably consistent wine which has been a favourite for many years. Its good, clean flavour and sprightly zest account for its attractiveness. Occasionally, releases have been certified Superior. It has enjoyed increased popularity over the last year.

Neethlingshof Neethlingshoffer★★★C

The first release from the 1988 vintage was an off-dry blend of some five cultivars, none of which shows on its own. It is now based on Rhine Riesling with some Cape Riesling and Sauvignon Blanc. A well made easy-drinking wine.

Onverwacht Bouquet Blanc★★★B

An attractive Steen-Colombar blend introduced from the 1991 vintage, with good fruity nose and clean finish.

Oude Nektar Le Bouquet Blanc★★★B

An interesting off-dry blend of Chenin Blanc, Muscat d'Alexandrie and Olasz Riesling with soft fragrant nose and full, complex flavour.

Oranjerivier Wynkelders Stein★A

This is a well-made, well-balanced, semi-sweet Steen, which drinks well when young. Served chilled, it makes a good aperitif.

Oude Rust Stein (Mooiuitsig Wynkelders)★A

A fruity Steen.

Overmeer Stein★★A

A well-balanced, easy-drinking, semi-sweet white.

Overvaal Stein (Vaalharts Co-op)★★A

Semi-sweet and soft – the best wine from this cellar.

Platanna (Paddagang Vignerons)★★C

Produced from the small, unique vineyards surrounding the Paddagang Wine House, this is one of the range from the Paddagang Vignerons. The wines are as much fun as their labels. Platanna is a light, fruity, semi-sweet wine made from Steen.

Platteklip Off-dry White★★A

A Rebel housebrand with a pleasant Muscat character making for very easy drinking.

Platteklip Semi-sweet White★★A

A fairly ordinary, semi-sweet Steen in the Rebel housebrand range.

Porterville Co-op Blanc de Blanc★A
An off-dry Steen.
Ravenswood Selected Stein (Pick 'n Pay)★(★)A
A Steen-based semi-sweet white.
Rebel Stein★A
A fresh, semi-sweet, white wine.
Rheboksklоof Bouquet Blanc★★★B
An unwooded blend of Chenin Blanc and Colombar, resulting in a soft easy-drinking, undemanding wine. Best drunk within two years to enjoy its youthful fresh fruitiness.
Romansrivier Co-op Vin Blanc Special Reserve★★★A
A most unusual semi-sweet Cape wine, best enjoyed when young and slightly chilled.
Rooiberg Co-op Selected Stein★★★A
A consistently good, fruity, semi-sweet Steen with clean finish. Good value for money.
Rovino Semi-sweet White (Romansrivier Co-op)★★A
The blend is Colombar and Chenel, finished semi-sweet.
Royal King (SFW) B
A semi-sweet white which is coloured brown with caramel to meet market requirements.
Rusthof Stein (Mooiuitsig Wynkelders)★★A
A pleasant, semi-sweet wine blended from Steen, Colombar and Muscat, giving a much fruitier nose than most Steins.
Simondium Co-op Vin Blanc★★A
An off-dry version of a similar label.
Simonsig Mustique★★★B
An attractive, off-dry blend of various Muscat cultivars with a hint of botrytis. It does consistently well in wine club selections and was selected by the SAA panel. Good drinking.
Simonsig Sonstein★★★B
A slightly sweet, Stein-style of wine which has some interesting vintage variations, which is always good, well made, and well balanced. It appears under various private labels, and deserves its popularity. Enjoy this wine in its youth and well-chilled.
Simonsvlei Co-op Stein★★A
This is usually a well-balanced, semi-sweet wine; recent vintages are medium-bodied and pleasant.
Swartland Co-op Stein★★A
A semi-sweet white with good fruit.
Tasheimer Goldtröpfchen (SFW)★★★B
One of the first post-Second World War wines to appear in a semi-sweet style, it quickly became one of South Africa's most popular semi-sweet whites, and remains so today (although it did disappear for a while into Stellenbosch Farmers' Winery's Taskelder range). Once again marketed as an individual brand, the wine is fruity, well-balanced and surprisingly full-flavoured. Its smooth texture makes it a pleasure to drink and, when young, it has a delicate freshness and a good, clean, crisp finish. The 1987 was the first vintage-dated Tasheimer to appear.
Towerkop Stein (Ladismith Co-op)★A
A pleasant, semi-sweet blend from Steen and Colombar.
Twee Jongegezellen Schanderl★★★★C
This is an outstanding example of the art of blending. The inviting,

flowery bouquet promises a sweetish wine, but instead it is crisp to taste, just off-dry, and makes excellent drinking within three years of the vintage. Made mainly from a unique red clone of Muscat de Frontignan and blended with Gewürztraminer and Weisser Riesling, it is especially delightful when young and fresh.

Twee Rivieren Selected Stein (Western Province Cellars)★★A
A semi-sweet wine with fresh nose and clean finish.

Uiterwyk Kromhout★★★(★)B
Recent vintages have been very characterful, well-flavoured semi-sweet wines with brisk finish. Despite the name, it is not wooded.

Villa Rossini Bianco (Union Wines)★★B
This is part of Union Wines' venture into Italian-style wines. Although finished off-dry it appears to be drier, and is best when young. It is sold in screw-top, litre bottles.

Valley Kaapse Keur (Gilbeys)★★A
A popular, off-dry, easy-drinking wine.

Valley Stein (Gilbeys)★★A
A good, clean, honest, semi-sweet white, based on Steen, which drinks very easily.

Villiera Sonnet★★★B
A delightful, off-dry wine based mainly on Steen with catching, fruity nose from small amounts of spicy cultivars.

Vintner's Choice Premier Vin Blanc (Drop Inn)★★A
An off-dry white in the Vintner's Choice range described as 'House Wines'. It is based on Colombar.

Vintner's Choice Stein (Drop Inn)★★A
A semi-sweet wine from Steen. Nice flavour, little nose.

Virginia (SFW)★★A
South Africa's largest-selling wine, this is a Steen-based, semi-sweet blend which, when young, is considerably better than many of the more expensive products on the market.

Vredenheim Debuut Wit Tafelwyn★★A
An off-dry blend of Rhine Riesling and Colombar, with fruity nose and clean finish.

Wamakers Vallei Co-op Stein★A
A well-flavoured, off-dry Steen.

Wellington Wynboere Co-op Stein★★A
A good-value, semi-sweet white.

Witzenberg Stein Select (Oude Meester)★A
A very pleasant, fruity, semi-sweet wine with good grapey nose.

Woolworths Bouquet Blanc★★★B
Produced by Zevenwacht, this is an elegant, off-dry, white wine with a hint of Muscat nose.

Woolworths Selected Cape White★★(★)A
From Rooiberg. A fruity, off-dry, white wine which drinks well when chilled.

Woolworths Stein★★★A
This wine has an attractive nose and a pleasant, semi-sweet flavour with enough acidity to give nice freshness. It is excellent value for money. Also in 5 *l*.

Yellow Label Stein (Checkers)★★A
Semi-sweet white wine with pleasant nose.

Zevenwacht Bouquet Blanc★★★B
A lovely off-dry blend with lots of attractive tropical flavours. It

usually has very good Muscat nose. It is good, off-dry, pleasant, well-made wine that develops well with time in the bottle.

Zevenwacht Stein★★(★)B

A good, light, fruity wine with Steen character. Very good drinking and good value.

Light Wines

Bellingham Premier Light★★(★)B
This is a dry wine, the latest release blended from Riesling and Bukettraube. It has nice fruity nose, is off-dry and alcohol content is about 9%.

Bernini Sparkling Grape Beverage (Distiller's Co-op)★★★B
A delightfully 'grapey', very fizzy, sweet wine with a low alcohol content (5%).

Bergsig Le Bouquet Light★★(★)A
A lovely light wine, with good Muscat nose, made from Hanepoot and with a slight bubble. It is semi-sweet and alcohol is usually only about 7%.

Bon Courage Bouquet Light★★★A
It has attractive nose and more flavour than most 'light' wines. The alcohol is around 9%, and the mere fraction of sugar still qualifies this wine as dry although it is not sold as such.

Cellar Cask Premier Light★★(★)A
A pleasant, fruity, dryish white with low alcohol.

De Wet Co-op Pétillant Fronté★★★A
A pretty, light wine with delicate Muscat aromas from Muscat de Frontignan. Good pétillance and a low alcohol content of 9%.

Drostdy Hof Extra Light★★★B
About 9,5% alcohol. An attractive, easy-drinking dry white. The other Drostdy Hof Lights have been culled. Good value for money.

Fleur du Cap Natural Light (Bergkelder)★★★B
This is probably the most consistent of the Light wines. It has good nose, nice flavour and still has an alcohol content of only 9%.

Twee Jongegezellen Light★★★B
A naturally produced product. TJ Light has nice fruitiness from Gewürztraminer, Muscat and other varieties, as well as good flavour, combining to promote easy drinking. The alcohol content is usually about 8%. Consistently one of the best light wines.

Vredendal Co-op Meisie★★(★)A
A light, pleasant-tasting wine with crisp finish.

Woolworths Bianca Light★★★B
From Delheim. This wine is blended from Clairette Blanche, Muscadẹl and Steen, giving very acceptable, easy-drinking wine. The alcohol content is under 10% and the sugar is 9,5 g/*l*.

Woolworths Musque Light★★★B
From Simonsig. Less than 10% alcohol and just off-dry. Lovely fresh Muscat scents and fresh flavour. A delightful light wine.

Woolworths Rosso Light★★B
From Villiera. Rosso Light has an alcohol content of less than 10%, and is made from Cinsaut, Carignan and Cabernet.

Bukettraube

Altydgedacht Bukettraube★★★B
Attractive, just off-dry wine, with good cultivar character. Easy drinking with a fresh finish.
Ashton Co-op Bukettraube★★★A
A very good semi-sweet wine with fine nose and flavour that finishes far drier than one would expect.
Backsberg Bukettraube★★★B
A consistently good wine which has good cultivar nose and lovely, full, semi-sweet flavour. Drink and enjoy in its youth.
Bolandse Co-op Bukettraube★★★A
An easy-drinking, young wine with good cultivar nose, finished off-dry. All releases are best when young.
Bottelary Co-op Bukettraube★★★B
A very pleasant, semi-sweet, young wine with attractive nose and good cultivar character. Good, easy-drinking wine.
Bovlei Co-op Bukettraube★★A
This wine was introduced in 1986 and has since kept the same style: a semi-sweet white with fruity nose and flavour.
Cederberg Kelders Bukettraube★★(★)B
An attractive, semi-sweet, soft fruity wine with good cultivar character when launched, it is best enjoyed while young.
Du Toitskloof Co-op Bukettraube★★★(★)B
This Co-op has a reputation for producing particularly good Bukettraube, which is usually semi-sweet and full of flavour, with good fresh finish.
Fairview Bukettraube★★★B
Lots of tropical fruit flavours mingling with distinct Muscat make this semi-sweet wine nice, easy drinking.
Goue Vallei Bukettraube (Citrusdal Co-op)★★B
Nowadays a good cultivar wine that is semi-sweet, tasty, Muscaty and easy drinking.
Huguenot Bukettraube★★★B
Pleasant, easy-drinking, semi-sweet wine with soft Muscat flavour.
Koelenhof Co-op Bukettraube★★(★)B
A pleasing, semi-sweet wine with a nose which has more Muscat than Bukettraube.
Lievland Bukettraube★★★B
The 1989 is a lovely, fruity wine and could well be the last. It has aged with benefit.
Lutzville Co-op Bukettraube★A
Off-dry wine which makes pleasant drinking.
Neethlingshof Bukettraube★★★C
A fine, highly-scented, semi-sweet wine that drinks very easily.
Nuy Co-op Bukettraube★★★A
This is a gold medal winner at regional and national shows, and one of the better examples of this cultivar. It is just off-dry, lovely when young and fresh, yet has the ability to age over two to three years. Very pleasant and good value for money.
Robertson Co-op Bukettraube★★★(★)A
Consistently one of the better examples of this cultivar. There may be slight variations in vintage but it is usually off-dry and full of fruit-salad scents and flavours. Best enjoyed when fresh and young.

It is consistently the best natural white from this cellar and good value for money.

Rooiberg Co-op Vinkrivier Bukettraube★★A

This wine has varied since its first release in 1983. Recent vintages are off-dry and have attractive Muscat nose and sound flavour. For the best enjoyment, drink when young.

Simonsvlei Co-op Bukettraube★★B

A regular medal winner at regional shows, this wine is finished semi-sweet for bottling. Recent vintages are finished semi-sweet and have good, satisfying scents and flavours. Soft, easy drinking.

Spier Bukettraube★★B

A wine with sweet, honeyed nose, and full almondy flavour; a very different style.

Swartland Co-op Bukettraube★★B

A semi-sweet wine with good fruit and a Muscat nose which makes for easy drinking.

Vredendal Co-op Bukettraube★★(★)A

A semi-sweet wine with Muscat nose and a soft taste.

Chardonnay

Aan de Doorns Chardonnay★★B
First release from 1991 is an unwooded dry white. Easy-drinking wine with little varietal character.
Aan de Wagenweg Chardonnay (Bergkelder)★★★★E
Only two releases – one from 1988 and the other from 1989, both in small quantities. Made from grapes grown in the Durbanville district, the wine is fermented in the barrel and then aged on the lees for a year. It was bottle-aged for another 12 months. It has lots of fruit and a lovely pear-drop nose that is backed with good oak. It is developing very slowly. The 1989 vintage is a more attractive wine and has already developed buttery, tasty flavours. There have been no subsequent releases.
Alphen Chardonnay★★★C
A good, clean, undemanding Chardonnay with nice citrus tones and subtle oak backing.
Altydgedacht Estate Chardonnay★★★D
A 1991 Chardonnay follows the previously non-certified Chardonnay called Charade which has developed well in the bottle. The 1991 has enticing nose and layers of complex flavours with good oak backing. It drinks well now and has the potential to develop.
Ashton Co-op Chardonnay★★B
First release from 1991 vintage has slight citrus nose and lots of wood. In early 1992 it drinks well and flavours have married better.
Avontuur Le Chardon★★★E
The 1990 and 1991 are a change in style and without the buttery fullness of the 1989. A harder, more acidic wine is now being made that will need time to soften and develop.
Backsberg Chardonnay★★★★(★)D
This cellar produces one of the Cape's best. The 1985 won the Diners Club award in 1986 for the best wooded white wine. The 1986 was a gold medal winner at the International Wine and Spirit Competition in London in 1988. The 1990 is a lovely elegant wine with lots of citrus tones on subtle oak. The 1991 shows more vanilla. Delightful wines. The 1989 seems to have settled into a fine, fruity style that is fairly distinctive of Backsberg.

🍷 **81** ★★★ drink. **84** ★★★(★) drink. **85** ★★★★★ drink. **86** ★★★★★ ready. **87** ★★★★ ready. **88** ★★★★ ready. **89** ★★★★(★) ready, will still develop. **90** ★★★★ ready, will still develop. **91** ★★★★ needs more time to develop.

Bellingham Chardonnay★★★C
A light, fruity wine with clean acidic finish, which needs some time to develop.
Bellingham Reserve Chardonnay ★★★★ E
An altogether different product, this is barrel-fermented, big wine with lots of citrus and toasty flavours from 1991 vintage that need to marry. It should prove to be very good.
Blaauwklippen Chardonnay★★★E
The 1981 vintage was the first release. The style has varied over the years but has always been good quality; the 1983 was perhaps better balanced, and the 1984, admirable cultivar character backed with considerable wood. It showed very well in 1988, having developed greater complexity than any of the earlier vintages. No 1985 was

bottled. The 1986 has developed into a lovely wine, but the 1988 could be the best of the 1980s. There was no 1989, but the 1990 is fine wine with buttery flavour, good oak and tones of lime, and is developing well. The 1991 is another big wine that will need time to settle. Also available in 375 m*l* bottles.

83 ★★★ ready. **84** ★★★(★) ready. **85** no release. **86** ★★★★ ready. **87** ★★★★ ready. **88** ★★★(★) ready, will still improve. **89** no release. **90** ★★★★(★) ready, will still improve. **91** ★★★(★) needs time to develop.

Bloemendal Estate Chardonnay★★★E
The Bloemendal Chardonnay was yet another first from the 1989 vintage. It has good cultivar character, nice woody/vanilla backing, and has developed well. The 1990 has good citrus flavour backed by good toast from American oak. It will age well with 13,6% alcohol. The 1991 has good character, even at a very early stage.

Bon Courage Chardonnay★★★C
The first attempt from the 1988 vintage was a good dry white, but it still has to show good varietal character. The 1989 is a great improvement – a soft, full-flavoured wine, with nice butter/toasty, woody background. The 1990 is a great improvement, having lovely vanilla, fruity flavour. The 1991 is barrel-fermented and has greater complexity than any of the earlier releases.

Boplaas Chardonnay★★★B
This is one of the least expensive Chardonnays, but it has pleasing character, good oak backing and is easy to drink.

Boschendal Chardonnay★★★★E
Released in July 1989, the first wine was from the 1986 vintage. It was disappointing, and has not developed well. However, subsequent vintages have been a great improvement. The 1987 began to show improvement and has developed well in the bottle; the 1988 is a lovely soft, full-flavoured wine that is delicious now. The 1989 started well but hasn't developed. The 1990 continues with the high quality, elegant style, and the 1991 is a super wine.

87 ★★★ ready. **88** ★★★(★) ready **89** ★★★ ready, will still develop **90** ★★★★ will still develop **91** ★★★★ will still develop.

Bottelary Co-op Chardonnay★★B
This wine has little recognizable character but is a pleasant drink. The 1989 vintage was bottled as Blanc de Blanc, and the 1990 certified as Chardonnay.

Bouchard Finlayson Chardonnay★★★★E
A good first from 1991 vintage from grapes grown at Elgin. It has good fruity nose, nice toasty wood, fine clean finish, and should develop well.

Buitenverwachting Chardonnay★★★★E
With a couple of vintages bottled, the cellar has now settled into a well-flavoured, good quality wine, full of cultivar flavour. It has lots of fruit, with some lemon backed by nice woody toast that will develop well over three to five years.

Cape Vintners Members Only Chardonnay★★★(★)D
Very good, well-oaked wine with citrus nose and vanilla flavours from 1991 vintage. Delicious drinking now and over the next two to three years. Made by Vlottenburg.

Cathedral Cellars Chardonnay★★★(★) (no price)
Produced only for export. The 1990 is well-made wine with good

early showing yet appears not to be developing in the bottle. Given the best fruit from Durbanville, finest cellar conditions and best wood, one looks forward to exciting wine in the future.

Claridge Chardonnay★★★

Barrel-fermented, long lees contact and malolatic fermentation, make this first effort from the 1991 vintage very creditable. It is big rich wine, with buttery and citrus tones, backed by good oak. Released mid-1992.

Danie de Wet Chardonnay★★★★D

Aromas bursting out of the tasting glass means high volatility from lots of alcohol: not a problem. Big wine with layers of deep flavours of all kinds of citrus and vanilla, with fine oak backing, which will develop well. The 1989 was the first release followed by an equally good 1990.

Danie de Wet Chardonnay Bateleur★★★★E

The most expensive of the four Danie de Wet Chardonnays, and of the 1990 vintage it is the smoothest if not the most flavourful. It will need time to develop its full potential.

Danie de Wet Chardonnay Bon Vallon★★★★C

An unwooded, well-priced wine with lots of good citrus and clean cultivar character. The first release from 1990 was followed by a similar 1991. It will develop well over a few years.

Danie de Wet Chardonnay Clos de Roche★★★★C

Wood fermented and then spending only a short time in wood afterwards, from grapes grown inside the rock-walled Bon Vallon 'Clos' dedicated to the late Hungarian viticulturalist Desiderius Pongracz who gave Danie lots of aid in his early days. A very fruity wine with deep citrus flavours backed by vanilla. First release from the 1990 vintage.

Delaire Chardonnay★★★★E

The first release from 1987 showed that this cellar was going to be good for Chardonnay. The 1988 had good cultivar character with lemon taste and fine wood. The 1989 is a fresher style with the fuller, toffee-type taste, hints of citrus and good wood. It was easy to drink when released but has developed with benefit in the bottle. The 1990 is a lovely, full, luscious wine. With 13,5% alcohol, it will develop with benefit. The 1991 is the most stylish to date: lovely fresh nose with good citrus flavours where lime shows the most. It will develop well over three to five years.

De Leuwen Jagt★★★C

The cellar sells two wines from the 1991 vintage – one slightly wooded and the other totally unwooded. Both have good character but are a little light on fruit.

Delheim Chardonnay★★★★D

The first release, from the 1988 vintage, had high fruit that is now developing well in the bottle. The 1989 vintage is a great improvement with full voluptuous character, good citrus flavours and buttery woody backing. It is one of the leading Chardonnays of 1989. The 1990 is far fruitier and more graceful; it will develop with benefit. The 1991 is a big wine with nice fruit and will also develop well.

De Wetshof Chardonnay★★★(★)D

The first release came from the 1981 vintage, though it contained a legal quantity from the 1980 harvest. It was launched with fanfare and received acclaim as a full, dry wine with very good wood tones.

It certainly was excellent, but a year later seemed to have lost its majesty. The 1982 vintage is a much better wine, with a complexity of flavour derived from cultivar, cellar style and good wood. The 1983 began to show better use of wood, and the 1984 was an excellent wine with good fruit and fine wood. There has been very little of the 1985 available as it was judged the overall winner for the best wine at the Vinexpo Wine and Wine Machinery Exhibition at Bordeaux in 1987. I have missed the 1986, and the 1987 is a little lacking in flavours, but those that are there are very good. The 1988, 1989 and 1991 are considerably better wines than anything before, being far more complex.

81 ★★★ drink. **82** ★★★ drink. **83** ★★★(★) drink. **84** ★★★(★) drink. **85** ★★★(★) ready. **87** ★★★(★) ready. **88** ★★★★ ready. **89** ★★★★ ready, will still develop. **90** ready, will still develop.

De Wetshof Estate Finesse★★★★D

This is an unwooded Chardonnay from the Cape's earliest producer of the cultivar. Lovely fresh, fruity wine from the 1990 vintage, followed by an even better 1991.

Diemersdal Chardonnay★★★C

First release from 1990 vintage is fruity, fine wine with a touch of light oak backing.

Dieu Donne Chardonnay★★★B

Big dry wine with lots of buttery/lemon flavour and woody background which will need time to settle. First release from 1991. The 1992 will be available late 1992.

Dieu Donne Chardonnay (unwooded)★★★B

First release from 1992 is fresh, fruity, with attractive citrus nose.

Drostdy-Hof Chardonnay★★★B

A very acceptable product in this everyday range of wines with good cultivar character. Good value for money and much better than many of the 'fancy' cellars. Very pleasant drinking wine.

Du Toitskloof Co-op Chardonnay★★★B

First release from the 1991 vintage; forceful, butterscotch wine with lots of wood, that will need time to marry and smooth.

Eerste Rivier Valleise Co-op Chardonnay★★★C

First release from 1989 had tropical fruit with reasonable oak backing. For early drinking. The 1990 and 1991 are improvements and more elegant wines.

Eersterivier Valleise Co-op Chardonnay Bin 7★★★C

Yet to be released from the 1990 vintage. It is showing good bottle development, decided citrus character and good oak.

Eikendal Chardonnay★★★★D

The 1991 is a fine wine, full of satisfying fruity flavours and nice butterscotch character. It will develop over three to five years.

Fairview Chardonnay★★★D

The first release from the 1990 vintage has lots of fruity flavour with butterscotch overtones. The 1991 is a great improvement – full of flavour, and an elegant wine in fine style.

Fleermuisklip Chardonnay (Lutzville Co-op)★★C

Koekenaap is an unlikely name of origin but that's where the grapes for this wine come from, with an incredible yield of 16 tons per hectare! Recognizable citrus-type Chardonnay character with reasonable wood backing.

Fleur Du Cap Chardonnay (Bergkelder)★★★(★)D
The first Chardonnay to be listed on a regular wine list was the Fleur du Cap 1988, made from grapes from eight- to ten-year-old vines grown in the Durbanville area. With almost 13% alcohol content, this wine has distinct cultivar character but is not really developing in the bottle. The 1989 is softer and better flavoured with nice citrusy layers. The 1990 is altogether better wine with very good flavour and a most attractive nose. Wood is subdued but good, and it has nice fresh finish. It should develop well.
Glen Carlou Chardonnay★★★★(★)E
A beautiful wine full of nose and flavour, made from the 1988 vintage, was a first for this new 'cellar'. The 1989 is fuller, bigger wine in all respects and will certainly develop with great benefit in the bottle. The 1990 is big, full-flavoured wine with citrus, fruit and vanilla flavours, and good oak. This is a delicious wine that is developing with great benefit. The 1991 is great and one of the Cape's best: lots of citrus and buttery flavours with good wood which will develop well. The Reserve Chardonnays from this cellar are superb.
Goedvertrouw Chardonnay★★★(★)F
The 1991 is an improvement on the very creditable first release from 1990. Good toast, nice citrus, hints of lemon. Very small production, hence the high price.
Graham Beck Wine of Madeba Chardonnay★★★★C
The first release from 1991 vintage is beautiful wine with enticing nose and delicious full flavour; lots of citrus backed by good oak. Relatively large quantity for such good quality.
Groot Constantia Chardonnay★★★(★)E
The first vintage was the 1988 and heralded a promising start with good cultivar character marrying well with new wood. It will need time to develop. The 1989 is big, better-flavoured wine with nuances of lemon, backed with good wood. The 1990 brings this cellar into the top line of Cape Chardonnays; good clean flavours and good wood make this a fine wine that will develop with benefit. The 1991 shows even more improvement. It is well made with good depth of flavour and greater complexity. It should develop well.
Hamilton Russell Vineyards Chardonnay★★★★(★)E
This wine used to be called Premier Vin Blanc, but since 1985 has been certified as Chardonnay. The first vintage was the 1983, which developed beautifully. The 1984 is a softer wine and despite my original doubts, this has developed beautifully. The 1985 vintage was the best to date when launched. It has the style of a well-wooded Chardonnay and was released as such; it is still developing with great benefit and is showing extremely well. The 1986 is a little lighter, yet in 1992 has developed into a superb wine. The 1987 is showing very well. It has very good cultivar character, backed by good wood. It is developing with great benefit and, like the 1985, become a five-star wine. The 1988 is definitely a five-star wine and was the best release at that time. It has developed beautifully in the bottle. The 1989 is great and will develop with benefit over six to eight years, although it was good when released. The high alcohol of 13% and total acidity of 6,5% will ensure safe ageing. The 1990 is less woody. The 1991, made by new wine-maker Storm Kreusch-Dau, could well be the best ever. While 1992 is still very young, it has style. Since 1989, half bottles have been available.

🍷 **83** ★★★ drink. **84** ★★★ drink. **85** ★★★★ ready. **86** ★★★★ ready. **87** ★★★★(★) ready, will still improve. **88** ★★★★★ ready, will still improve. **89** ★★★★★ ready, will still improve. **90** ★★★★(★) (new style) ready, will still improve. **91** ★★★★(★) ready, will still improve.

Hamilton Russell Vineyards Chardonnay Reserve★★★★★F

From the 1989 vintage came the first Hamilton Russell Vineyards Chardonnay label. Only selected bunches were used to produce this wine, as will be the case from now on for the Reserve. Wine making is in the traditional style of the Cote d'Or and aged in small French oak for nine months. It is then held for at least another nine months in the bottle before being released. The bottle is easily recognized by its darker background and white shield on the neck label. The 1989 is a delicious wine with everything one could ever expect from this grape. The 1990 is absolutely stunning. Both wines make tremendous drinking now but will develop over eight to twelve years.

Hartenberg Chardonnay★★★E

From the 1991 vintage comes a barrel-fermented, big wine that will need time to settle down.

Haute Provence Chardonnay★★(★)C

The 1990 and 1991 are acceptable dry white wines without much cultivar character.

John Platter Chardonnay★★★★D

The first release was from the 1987 vintage and it seems to be improving each time I taste it. It is developing a lemon character, and a slight hint of good wood is showing.

Klein Constantia Chardonnay★★★★★F

I tasted it first with the Australian Chardonnay master, Len Evans, and he fully agreed that the first Chardonnay wine from the 1988 vintage was one of the best in the Cape. A total of 130 dozen bottles were sold at the New World Wine Auction in 1990, at prices in excess of R30,00 per bottle. It has plenty of lovely complex flavours but the nose still has to develop. European, American and Australian fundis out here for the NWWA and the Nederburg Auction reckoned this wine's flavour, blended with Meerlust's nose, would be amongst the world's best. It has just got better and better with each vintage. The 1989 has all kinds of citrus flavours and good vanilla. The 1990 is top-class with fine nose, and deep layers of flavour. It is full of fruit, with good oak and fresh finish, and will develop with great benefit. It is big, but beautifully elegant.

Kleindal Chardonnay★★★D

This is an unwooded Chardonnay with good cultivar character and nice clean finish. It is good to drink now but will develop.

Koelenhof Co-op Chardonnay★★(★)C

The 1991 is easy-drinking wine with pleasant flavour from fruit and wood. It is not for ageing, so drink early.

La Couronne Chardonnay★★★D

This is a rather subdued but pleasantly drinkable wine with lots of different nuances and flavours, but not in much volume except for the woodiness. Given time, the first release from 1991 could develop.

Lanzerac Chardonnay★★★(★)C

Unwooded wine with fine varietal character; lots of mouth-filling flavour. Excellent value for money. A considerably better drink than many of the fancied names.

Le Bonheur Chardonnay★★★C
Early expectations that this could be one of South Africa's best Chardonnays have not been fulfilled. They are good wines, for sure, but not up to the standard usually associated with this cellar. They are fruity, soft and tasty and developing age rather than character.
Le Moutonne Chardonnay★★★D
The first release from the 1991 vintage was a good attempt, with buttery, citrus flavours and background wood, but all a bit reserved. I look forward to future vintages.
Lievland Chardonnay★★★(★)
Not commonly available at time of writing, but cellar samples show well-made wine, of fine style with citrus flavours and good wood.
Louisvale Chardonnay★★★★E
This is a beautiful wine from the 1989 vintage, especially for a first attempt. It has big, full flavour, yet is soft in the mouth, with nice toasty butteryness and layers of citrus. It drinks well now but has everything to develop with benefit in the bottle. The 1990 is a similar wine with deeper toasty, and clean citrus-peach flavours. The 1991 continues the fine style. Lovely wines.
Louisvale Chavant★★★(★)D
Released early, after four months in oak, this is a blend of tank-fermented and cask-fermented wine. It has full varietal flavour with good buttery and lemon tones, and light oak complexity.
L'Ormarins Chardonnay★★★★D
The first release from the 1987 vintage gave a hint of what was to come, although it didn't show so well to start. It is now developing real substance in the bottle and subsequent vintages are on-going improvements. The 1988 has fruitier nose, fuller palate and is developing well. The 1989 is a wine to be respected; a big, full wine with stylish character, with an intensity of lemon/lime character backed by oaky vanilla and firm tannin. It is not for drinking immediately and should be allowed to age to the mid-1990s to get full benefit of potential. The 1990 shows that this cellar has established itself as consistently one of the Cape's better Chardonnay producers. The 1991 is bright, fruity wine with all the best that Chardonnay can give. Another big attraction is its good price.

87 ★★★(★) ready/drink. **88** ★★★★ ready, will still develop. **89** ★★★★(★) ready, will still develop. **90** ★★★★ ready, will still develop.

Lutzville Chardonnay★★C
The first release from 1989 has developed its own individual character over three years. The 1990 has better cultivar character and makes a pleasant drink.
Meerlust Chardonnay (no price or star rating available)
Only experimental amounts have been produced to date, but are everything one would expect from Meerlust. Overseas fundis reckon that the 1988 and 1989 cellar samples of this wine, along with those of Klein Constantia, could be blended to produce the world's best. I hope that this will eventually be released for general consumption.
Mondial Chardonnay (Gilbeys)★★★★E
The first release from the 1990 vintage comes from grapes grown between Paarl and Durbanville, and the Stellenbosch side of Bottelary hills. This is a good clean product with a most attractive nose and flavour. The 1991 release will be more complex, with compo-

nents from throughout the winelands giving the most wide-ranging character of any Cape Chardonnay. Because the country's Wine of Origin laws will not allow vintage dating on wines made from grapes coming from different areas or origin, and made in a central cellar, this lovely wine cannot be vintage dated. You will have to learn how to differentiate the unique pack each year. The crazy thing is that when exported the wine *is* allowed to carry a vintage date. Where's the logic?

Mont Blois Chardonnay★★★C

A fairly light and austere wine with some toasty, citrus flavour that could develop with time. The 1990 is much better, with good fruit and clean finish.

Neethlingshof Chardonnay★★★★E

Neethlingshof delayed their entry into the fashionable field of Chardonnay to ensure they launched one of the best – an 'elegant, good varietal fruit, with a whisper of wood' (Brözel's words) – from five and six year-old vineyards. It is a blend of wooded and unwooded wine, the unwooded component a class winner in the 1990 SA Young Wine Show. It is delicious wine in fine style that will develop well.

Nederburg Auction Chardonnay★★★★D

Very little of this fine wine is available. Only 2 400 x 750 m*l* bottles of the 1984 vintage were sold at the 1987 Nederburg Auction and, according to Patrick Grubb, the auctioneer, it had superb palate, perfect balance and the potential to develop well over two to three years, which it has done. In 1988, the *Decanter's* panel rated it second only to the Mondavi Reserve 1985, against some of the world's greatest. Some of the 1985 vintage was chosen as the Wine of the Month on SAA's overseas flights during December 1987. The 1985 Special Auction Wine, of which there are only 3 300 bottles, is excellent but very expensive. The 1986 will need time to develop, but is now showing very well. The 1987 was criticized on release but is now beginning to show well; its faint flavours have developed more strongly and good nuances of citrus mingle with vanilla. The 1988 is altogether better with flowery nose and good depth of flavour. It is clean and stylish, and is developing beautifully in the bottle. The 1989 is positively exciting and 450 were sold at the 1992 Auction. It is now well established as an Auction feature and a much admired wine.

84 ★★★★ needs drinking. **85** ★★★(★) needs drinking. **86** ★★★(★) ready. **87** ★★★ ready. **88** ★★★★ ready, but still developing. **89** ★★★★ ready, but still developing.

Nederburg Chardonnay★★★★D

Very different to the Auction wine, the first general release of this wine from the 1989 vintage was made at the 1991 Auction lunch. It is now a regular part of the Nederburg range. A portion is wood-fermented; the balance in stainless steel. The result is a complex, refreshing, limey wine with a buttery background, good fruit acid and the slightest touch of oak. It makes delicious drinking at the time of release and develops well over two to four years. It is good to have a classy Chardonnay at a reasonable price.

Neil Ellis Chardonnay★★★★D

This is lovely, elegant wine from the 1990 vintage with lots of citrus and vanilla flavours in deep layers backed by fine oak. Lots of lees contact and malolactic fermentation give great complexity. As good as it is to drink now, it will reward ageing over four to six years. The 1991 follows in similar good style.

Overgaauw Chardonnay★★★★(★)D

The 1986 was rich, full-flavoured wine and the 1987 is even better, having a very good combination of cultivar and wood. It was the highest-priced white wine at the 1989 Nederburg Auction. The 1988 is five-star material, a big, full, fruit-flavoured, well-wooded wine in the New World style that is developing well with time in the bottle. The elegant 1989, which has toffee and butterscotch flavours, is still developing well. The 1990 is the best balanced, drinking very well now, but it will probably be at its best earlier than the 1988 and 1989. Lovely wine, and a very satisfying drink.

Pick 'n Pay Chardonnay★★★★C

Made by Backsberg from 1990 vintage. Lightly wooded, medium-bodied, delicate citrus flavours and crisp, dry finish. Drinks well now and will develop over another two to three years.

Rheboksklоof Chardonnay★★★E

This is the first release from the 1991 vintage and comes from very young wines. It is light, elegant wine with fine citrus tones backed by good wood, and a most encouraging start.

Rietvallei Estate Chardonnay★★★D

The first release from the 1987 vintage was a somewhat stern and formal wine. It had very little nose and flavour, but what there was, was good cultivar. The 1988 is a far better wine with good cultivar character, and the 1989 better still – big wine that will develop well.

Robertson Co-op Chardonnay★★(★)C

This prolific producer has two first-release Chardonnays out of the 1990 vintage. One is an unwooded, medium-bodied firm wine with good citrus character, the other, a barrel-fermented wine that spent four months on its lees and is labelled 'Sur Lie'. It is a more complex wine that would benefit with more age. The 1991s are better.

Rooiberg Chardonnay★★★B

Pleasant-flavoured, easy-drinking, unwooded, well-made wine.

Rooiberg Chardonnay Sur Lie★★(★)C

An oak-fermented Chardonnay with more wood flavour than cultivar, but soft and buttery.

Ruiterbosch Mountain Cuvée Chardonnay★★★(★)D

This is elegant, fine-flavoured wine from the cool mountain vineyards overlooking Mossel Bay. Cask-fermented oak is gentle and allows fresh fruit flavours to lead. The first release comes from the 1991 vintage.

Rustenberg Chardonnay★★★

The Estate's new wine is considered the regular release, while the existing wine becomes Chardonnay Reserve. The first release from 1990 follows the trend to less wooded Chardonnay at a lower price. It has good fruit, is fresh on the palate and has good finish. It should develop well in the bottle.

Rustenberg Chardonnay Reserve★★★★E

The first limited release of this wine was in 1986: a good combination of fruit and wood giving a softish wine which has developed elegance over four years. The 1987 was a great improvement, with good cultivar and nice wood. The 1988 is great, showing very good cultivar character with fine wood mingling into the flavour, giving a spicey tang to the taste. It drinks very well now but will develop over three to four years. The 1988 Chardonnay is now sold under the Rustenberg name, previously reserved for the Estate's red wines. (The whites of Rustenberg were previously sold under the name of its sister farm, Schoongezicht.) The 1989 is full rich wine that is developing well. The 1990 is labelled 'Reserve' and deservedly so; it is full, complex, well-made wine, with good balance backed by fine wood. It will develop well.

86 ★★★ ready. **87** ★★★(★) ready. **88** ★★★★ ready, will still improve. **89** ★★★★ ready, will still develop. **90** ★★★★ ready, will age further.

Simonsig Chardonnay★★★★(★)C

After an indifferent start in 1980 and 1981, the 1982 vintage obtained Superior certification. With its very good nose and fair flavour, this wine gained acclaim at a tasting in Spain arranged by the world authority, Miguel Torres, competing very successfully with good Chardonnays from around the world. It was also a gold medal winner at the 1985 International Wine and Spirit Competition in Britain. The 1983 is a bigger, bolder wine which showed well in the bottle in 1987. The 1985 was certified Superior and is developing well. The 1986 and 1987 are a totally different style of wine, having the big full character of the New World approach. The 1988 is five-star material with the toasty, buttery character associated with the world's greatest Chardonnays. The 1988 Reserve won a gold medal and the Cape Wine Academy Trophy for the best South African White Wine at the International Wine and Spirit Competition in Britain in 1990. The 1989 follows well with good fruity nose and fine caramel and toffee flavours. The 1990 is a splendid wine which will develop well over five to seven years. Together with the cellar's Reserve these wines are now well established amongst the Cape's constant best.

82 ★★★★ drink. **83** ★★★★ drink. **84** no release. **85** ★★★★ drink. **86** ★★★★(★) ready, will still improve. **87** ★★★★ ready, will still improve. **88** ★★★★★ ready, will still improve. **89** ★★★★★ ready, will still improve. **90** ★★★★★ ready, will still develop.

Simonsvlei Co-op Chardonnay★★★D

The first release from the 1988 vintage was disappointing, but the 1989 was better with some wood and lemony character. With the 1990 vintage came great improvement, good citrus and nice fruit along the Chablis style. The 1991 is much bigger wine and will develop better than the 1990, which needs to be drunk up.

Springlands Chardonnay (Drop Inn)★★★C

Well made, light wine with buttery character and quite woody.

Talana Hill Chardonnay★★★★★F

Seventy cases of the 1988 vintage were sold at the 1990 New World Wine Auction. Made by Jan 'Boland' Coetzee from grapes grown on a small Stellenbosch property, this is wine that will need time to develop. It is well-made, medium-bodied and finely-flavoured. The 1989 is a stylish wine and is developing well. The 1990 is elegant, with good citrusy flavours, is soft in the mouth and has fine oak backing. These wines are well worth seeking out.

Thelema Chardonnay★★★★★D

The first release from the 1988 vintage is an elegant wine with a fine, fruity, pear-like nose and full, soft flavour backed by the fine use of good wood. It tasted good on release but is now beginning to develop its potential. The 1989 is one of the Cape's best and is full of the intense flavours of citrus, lime, peach and toasty wood. The 1990 confirms Thelema as among the best. It is a beautiful, elegant wine, full of fine complex flavours that will develop with great benefit. The 1991 is a stunner and keeps Thelema right up with the very best, if not leading the way. It is very well-priced for such super wine.

Tradouw Chardonnay (Barrydale Co-op)★★★C

A surprise from the 1989 vintage was Barrydale Co-op's first release of a wood-aged Chardonnay. Along with the 1990, this was a good early attempt. The 1991 has good citrus character backed by lots of oak, and is a rich wine with clean finish, that needs time to round out. Tradouw is the grapes' Wine of Origin Ward. Bottles are labelled with the words 'Sur Lie', without mention of the Co-op.

Uitkyk Chardonnay★★★(★)D

The first release in the Estate's new livery comes from the 1991 vintage. It is fairly hard wine that will need time to show, but has the elements to develop with time.

Van Loveren Chardonnay★★★★E

The first release, the 1987 vintage, is very creditable for a first attempt. It has shown well at a number of tastings. The 1988 is a big wine with 14% alcohol. It was originally almost alcoholically bound, not yielding much nose or flavour, then bloomed, showing all kinds of citrus fruits, butterscotch and good wood characteristics. The 1989 is equally alcoholic but shows its form much earlier. It is consistently well rated in blind tastings and makes big, soft, easy drinking. The 1990 follows the same lines. The 1991 is full of good cultivar flavour and tastes very good now, but will develop very well.

Villiersdorp Co-op Kroonland Chardonnay★★★(★)C

Big, full, yet soft in the mouth, this is one of the best Co-op Chardonnays. Excellent value for money.

Vlottenburg Co-op Chardonnay★★★(★)D

A dramatic first release from the 1990 vintage attracted great attention. Elegant, complex wine with good citrus flavours backed by fine oaky toastiness, it was the 1990 South African Young Wine Show Champion wooded white. Regrettably, there was very limited production. The 1991 is not as showy, but is very drinkable, and there's more of it.

Vredendal Co-op Koekenaap Chardonnay★★★B

First made from only 10 tons, picked on 13 February 1989, on the second last block of the Olifants Rivier irrigation scheme with the Atlantic Ocean less than a kilometre away. The cellar manager, Giel Swiegers, received advice from Imanuel Béné of Cave Cooperative de Vine. The result was very pleasing for a first attempt and won a silver medal at the International Wine and Spirit Competition in the UK in 1991. The 1990 is another good effort, though perhaps not quite the quality of 1989, but very pleasant all the same. The 1991 is very pleasant, easy-drinking wine, best in its youth.

Vriesenhof Chardonnay★★★★(★)D

To date, very little of this wine has been available. The 1986 suggested that this was a cellar to keep an eye on. The 1987 was not exciting, but with the 1988, the wine has really come into its own. Showing good flavours in the New World style, this is a wine that will develop with benefit in the bottle. The 1989 has the complexity one would expect from Jan 'Boland' Coetzee. It is a big, rich, full-flavoured wine with layers of fruit including lemon and lime, butterscotch and toasty wood. The 1990 is a delicious wine full of flavoury lime, lemon, vanilla, butteriness, and with good oak backing. The 1991 is going to be stunning. These wines develop with great benefit.

🍷 **86** ★★★(★) ready. **87** ★★★ ready. **88** ★★★★ ready, will improve. **89** ★★★★(★) ready, will still improve. **90** ★★★★★ ready, will still improve. **91** ★★★★★ good now, will develop.

Weltevrede Estate Chardonnay★★★★D

The first release, from the 1989 vintage, has a decidedly citrus character. This was a good effort for a first release and it is developing surprisingly well in the bottle. The 1990 is lovely wine and developed beautiful nose and flavour over two years. The 1991 is even better and the best from this cellar.

Woolworths Chardonnay★★★★C

The 1991 from Vriesenhof cellars is an excellent follow-up on the fine 1990. Well wood-aged without wood dominating; attractive citrus nose with good buttery flavours. Good for drinking now, yet has lots of ageing potential.

Woolworths Chardonnay (unwooded)★★★★C

The 1991 from Neil Ellis is a blend of old South African clone with that from Davis (California) clone. Good fruity flavours and developing well in the bottle.

Woolworths Chardonnay Magnum★★★(★)D

With Danie de Wet of De Wetshof move away from Bergkelder and doing his own labels, he has produced a series only in magnums from 1991. Good citrus flavours; excellent for dinner parties.

Zandwijk Chardonnay★★★E

This first release from this kosher wine farm is one of its better products. From the 1989 vintage, it was released in March 1990 and is immediately drinkable and much better tasting than most imported kosher wines. The 1991 is, so far, the best from this cellar.

Zevenwacht Chardonnay★★★C

First release from 1990. Good citrus nose, nice buttery flavour, with good oak backing. This wine is developing well.

Zonnebloem Chardonnay (SFW)★★★(★)D

The first release from the 1989 vintage was very shy in character when released. It has, however, developed very well in the bottle, and is medium-bodied with citrus-type flavours and a hint of oak in the background. It is ageing well. The 1990 is a lovely, very friendly wine, with good nose and flavour. It drinks well now, but will develop. In a very short time it has established itself as one of the better 'drinking Chardonnays'. Very affordable.

Chenel

Andalusia Chenel (Vaalharts Co-op)★B

A clean, semi-sweet wine, and the only Chenel to survive!

Chenin Blanc/Steen – Dry

Aan-de-Doorns Chenin Blanc★★★A
A consistently good dry wine, a regular award winner at regional shows and good value for money. Good cultivar character.
Backsberg Chenin Blanc★★★B
The 1991 and 1992 are lovely, fruity bright wines, full of varietal flavours. Enjoy in their youth.
Boland Co-op Chenin Blanc★★★A
The 1991 is a dry wine with good varietal character. It has good fruity finish when young.
Bottelary Co-op Chenin Blanc★★(★)A
This cellar has a reputation of producing good dry white wine from this cultivar. It is delicate, fruity and clean, with fresh finish.
Douglas Green Chenin Blanc★★★B
This is a pleasant, dry wine with good cultivar nose and smooth palate. It develops well in the bottle over a year or two. In the revamped range, the 1991 is exactly described on the new label.
Fairview Chenin Blanc★★★(★)B
Originally a big, bold wine, but nowadays a more elegant and very attractive, fruity wine with fresh finish. It is best enjoyed young.
Helderberg Co-op Chenin Blanc★★(★)A
A delightful, light, easy-drinking dry wine with Steen character.
Koelenhof Co-op Chenin Blanc★★B
A good, fresh, dry wine with cultivar character which shows well when young.
Ladismith Co-op Chenin Blanc★★A
A light, dry wine with good cultivar character when young.
Landskroon Chenin Blanc★★★A
This mainly red-wine Estate has also produced fairly ordinary Chenin Blancs. However, with the 1990 and 1991 vintage, the quality has improved.
Louwshoek-Voorsorg Co-op Chenin Blanc★★A
This is dry Chenin Blanc, with good fruit flavours and rare guava nose when young.
Mamreweg Co-op Dry Steen★★A
The 1989 is a great improvement on earlier vintages and the 1990 and 1991 continue the quality improvement. It has good cultivar nose and flavour, and is finished dry.
Onverwacht Chenin Blanc Dry★★B
This is an easy-drinking dry white, with the latest release having good cultivar character.
Opstal Steen★★(★)A
This Steen has very good cultivar nose and high acid. It is very dry.
Perdeberg Co-op Chenin Blanc Dry★★★A
This cellar produces a bright, semi-sweet wine, and a more serious, dry version which has been a consistent award winner. The 1988 was South Africa's Champion dry white but very little ever appeared in the bottle. Recent vintages are bigger and fuller.
Roodezandt Chenin Blanc★★★A
Always consistent, this dry wine has good cultivar character and is best when young.
Romansrivier Co-op Chenin Blanc★★★A
This is a delightful, fresh, fruity wine with lots of cultivar character.

Saxenberg Chenin Blanc★★B
One of the nice fruity dry wines with full flavour.
Simonsig Chenin Blanc★★★B
This is a very well-balanced, dry wine with excellent varietal character. Recent vintages should be enjoyed in the bloom of their youth.
Simonsvlei Co-op Dry Steen★★★A
A gold medal winner at the South African Championship Wine Show, this is a well-made, dry wine with fine character.
Swartland Co-op Steen★★★A
A big, dry white with lots of cultivar character and a wine well worth ageing for a year or so. This is one of the better Co-op Steens.
Vlottenburg Co-op Steen★★★A
This is a pleasing, fresh, dry Steen of good drinking quality which has shown considerable improvement over the years.
Welmoed Co-op Dry Steen★★★A
A regular medal winner at regional and national shows. This Steen is always soft and dry with good cultivar flavour. It is easy-drinking.
Woolworths Chenin Blanc★★★A
From Rooiberg, comes a pleasant, dry Steen with nice, fruity finish, for easy drinking.

Chenin Blanc/Steen – Off-dry/Semi-sweet

Agterkliphoogte Co-op Chenin Blanc★★A
An off-dry, lowish alcohol, easy-drinking wine from 1991 vintage.
Boschendal Chenin Blanc★★★B
Clean and fruity, this soft, tasty, off-dry wine ages particularly well, yet also drinks very nicely when fresh and young. Vintages of the 1990s are delightful wines with super cultivar character that is set off well by being finished off-dry.
Botha Co-op Chenin Blanc★★A
Recent vintages are pleasant when fresh and young. They are fractionally off-dry, have attractive fruity nose, and are easy drinking.
Cederberg Kelders Chenin Blanc★★A
An unusual, semi-sweet Steen. Since 1988 these have been full, soft, easy-drinking wines. The 1991 has a particularly good guava nose.
Du Toitskloof Co-op Chenin Blanc★★★(★)A
This off-dry wine with its fruity nose and good palate has improved over the vintages and is a regular winner at local shows. The 1988 has a beautiful, fruity nose and was delightful when young. It also developed in the bottle. The 1989 was not up to standard, but the vintages of the 1990s are delightful wines with good cultivar character.
Eersterivier Valleise Co-op Chenin Blanc★★(★)A
This is usually a consistently good dry wine that is frequently an award winner at regional and national shows. It has good cultivar nose and often the elusive guava character which is much sought after in Chenin Blanc. The 1988 was off-dry and out of character. The 1989 was back to the usual good drinking quality, and the 1990 was particularly good. The 1991 is decidedly semi-sweet but still a good drink and value for money.
Franschhoek Co-op Chenin Blanc★★(★)A
A just off-dry, full flavour but light on nose wine.
Goudini Co-op Chenin Blanc★★A
A fruity, off-dry wine.
Goue Vallei Chenin Blanc★★A
A semi-sweet wine with good cultivar nose. Latest releases make very pleasant, easy-drinking wines.
Huguenot Chenin Blanc★★A
A fairly ordinary wine with sweet, full taste.
Kleindal Chenin Blanc★★★B
This wine has a very nice fruit salad nose, is soft across the palate yet has nice fresh finish – just off-dry.
KWV Chenin Blanc★★★(no price available)
An off-dry wine with attractive nose and pleasing flavour. It is one of the KWV's best products and one of our better exports.
La Cotte Chenin Blanc (Franschhoek Vineyards)★★(★)B
A pleasant, fruity, semi-sweet wine with a popular following.
Landskroon Chenin Blanc★★★A
The best Chenin Blanc ever from this Estate came from the 1990 vintage; semi-sweet, fresh, fruity, clean character wine. The 1991 is lighter but drinks well, and is most enjoyable when young.
Les Chênes Chenin Blanc★★★A
This is one of a number of grape growers who have their wines made at the Co-op and then marketed under their own label. The wines are best when young.

Lutzville Co-op Chenin Blanc★★A
This is an off-dry, fruity white that is at its best when young.
Mamreweg Co-op Chenin Blanc★★A
A pleasant, easy-drinking, off-dry wine. The latest releases are an improvement on those released in the past.
Matin Soleil★★B
The 1991 is drier than previous releases; fuller wine.
Merwida Co-op Chenin Blanc★★A
A semi-sweet wine with Late Harvest Steen character.
Mon Don Chenin Blanc★★★A
This is a full, fruity, off-dry wine with 1990 showing improved flavour and fresh finish.
Montagu Muskadel Boere Chenin Blanc★★A
The 1990 has good guava nose and is almost dryish.
Morgenhof Chenin Blanc★★(★)B
This is a gentle, soft wine with fruity, off-dry finish. The 1990 has more character than previous releases.
Nuy Co-op Effesoet Steen★★★A
Slightly sweet and with a good cultivar character, this most agreeable, medium-bodied wine has been a champion at the South African Championship Wine Show and has also carried Superior certification.
Opstal Chenin Blanc★★★A
This Estate produces two wines from the same cultivar. A much more delicate wine than the Steen, the off-dry Chenin Blanc makes light, easy drinking. The 1990 was particularly good.
Perdeberg Co-op Chenin Blanc Semi-sweet★★★(★)A
A delightful, fruity wine that has its flavours enhanced by being finished semi-sweet.
Riebeek Wine Farmers' Co-op Chenin Blanc★★★A
This particularly good, semi-sweet wine is a consistent medal winner. It has subtle cultivar nose and soft palate, and must be enjoyed when young.
Rietrivier Co-op Chenin Blanc★A
A semi-sweet wine.
Roodezandt Co-op Chenin Blanc Semi-sweet★★★A
The 1990 is most attractive with lots of flavour, and a remarkable 13,7% alcohol. The 1991 tops 14% alcohol!
Rooiberg Chenin Blanc★★(★)A
This is a soft, off-dry wine which won a gold medal at the South African Championship Wine Show.
Rooiberg Vinkrivier Chenin Blanc★★★(★)A
This delightful Chenin Blanc was made from grapes grown along the Vink River (hence Wine of Origin Vinkrivier). It has strong varietal nose, light acid and good, rounded taste, finished off-dry.
Simonsvlei Co-op Chenin Blanc★★★A
This is one of the cellar's better products. A pleasant, off-dry wine with slight spicey aroma and delicate but fresh flavour, it is charming when young, and this is when it should be enjoyed for it does not usually age with benefit. An exception is the Superior 1977, which had developed beautifully when sold at the 1979 Nederburg Auction. Recent vintages are fruity, pleasant young wines.
Slanghoek Chenin Blanc★★★A
This is a very good and attractive Chenin Blanc. Recent vintages

have been fuller, not entirely dry, and very attractive. It received Superior in 1979 and 1980. Recent vintages are fresh and fruity.

Spruitdrift Co-op Chenin Blanc★★★A

The cellar is now making particularly good dry and off-dry wines from this cultivar.

Swartland Co-op Chenin Blanc★★A

A well-balanced, clean-tasting, semi-sweet wine.

Tulbagh Co-op Chenin Blanc★★A

An off-dry, medium-bodied wine with light flavour.

Villiersdorp Co-op Chenin Blanc★★★A

A semi-sweet wine with good cultivar character. Easy drinking.

Vino Uno Amabile (Du Toitskloof)★★(★)A

Pleasant, semi-sweet blend of mostly Muscat d'Alexandrie and some 20% Steen. Easy drinking in 500 m*l* screw-top bottles.

Vlottenburg Co-op Chenin Blanc★★★A

A well-balanced, off-dry wine with good cultivar character and a popular following.

Vredendal Co-op Chenin Blanc★A

A very pale Steen in all respects, finished off-dry.

Waboomsrivier Co-op Chenin Blanc★★A

A well-made, easy-drinking wine finished semi-sweet.

Welmoed Co-op Chenin Blanc★★★A

A very pleasant, off-dry wine with good fruit and nice flavour.

Clairette Blanche

Aan-de-Doorns Clairette Blanche★(★)A

Light in character, this wine is brisk and refreshing when young.

De Wet Co-op Clairette Blanche★★A

A fruity, dry white wine with subtle nose and pleasant flavour.

Goudini Co-op Clairette Blanche★★A

A pleasant, dry, easy-drinking wine and a regular award winner at local and national shows. The 1990 is very pleasant, with tropical fruit nose.

Overhex Co-op Clairette Blanche★★A

Pleasant, light, easy-drinking wine.

Colombar(d)

Aan-de-Doorns Colombar★★A
This is an occasionally semi-sweet and sometimes off-dry wine with good cultivar character. It is a regular award winner at regional and national shows. There was no 1989 release but 1990 and 1991 are semi-sweet with little cultivar character.
Agterkliphoogte Co-op Colombar★★★A
A pleasant, light wine with usual cultivar nose. The 1990 is much improved. There is also a 1991.
Andalusia Colombar (Vaalharts Co-op)★★A
A dry wine with some cultivar character. Ordinary, quaffing wine.
Ashton Co-op Colombar★★A
Light-styled, fruity, dry wine.
Bakenskop Colombar (Jonkheer)★★★B
A good cultivar wine finished off-dry, making pleasant drinking.
Barrydale Co-op Colombar★★A
This Co-op used to produce both a dry and an off-dry Colombar. It now produces only a semi-sweet, low-alcohol wine.
Bonnievale Co-op Colombard★★A
This cellar offers two Colombars, one dry and the other off-dry. Both have good, fruity nose and full, cultivar flavour.
Brandvlei Co-op Colombar★★A
A good, fresh, fruity, semi-sweet wine.
Calitzdorp Co-op Colombar ★★A
First release from 1991 is dry and pleasant.
De Doorns Co-op Colombar★A
An off-dry, pleasant Colombar.
Douglas Co-op Colombar★★A
Dry white from 1990 showing bottle age.
Du Toitskloof Co-op Colombard★★★A
A full-flavoured, off-dry wine that does well at young wine shows; consistently one of the better Colombars.
Kango Co-op Colombar★★B
An off-dry, light-style wine with little nose but pleasant taste.
Klawer Co-op Colombar ★★★A
This is usually a light, off-dry wine, but a semi-sweet version won a gold medal at the International Wine and Spirit Competition held in Britain in 1986. The 1991 is an easy-drinking, off-dry wine.
Langverwacht Co-op Colombar★★A
This cellar produces a pleasant, dry Colombar.
Louwshoek-Voorsorg Co-op Colombard★★A
An off-dry, pleasant, fruity wine.
Mamreweg Co-op Colombar★★A
A nice, fresh, off-dry wine for early drinking.
McGregor Co-op Colombar★★A
An off-dry, easy-drinking wine, best enjoyed while young.
Merwida Co-op Colombar★★★A
A delightful, off-dry wine with a full, fruity nose. Some of the 1978 vintage was certified Superior and was sold at the 1979 Nederburg Auction. After a long absence this wine was re-introduced with the 1989. The 1991 is light and off-dry – not up to Auction standard!
Montagu Muskadelboere Co-operative Colombar★★A
An off-dry wine with typical cultivar character.

Neethlingshof Colombard★★★B
An appealing, dry wine with good aromatic nose. This wine has been discontinued but the 1988 is still available.
Nordale Co-op Colombard★★A
A good wine with nice Colombar character. Until 1988 it was finished off-dry; since then it has been dry.
Nuy Co-op Colombard★★★★A
Nuy produces two Colombars: one dry and the other semi-sweet. The dry is fairly tart with full cultivar nose and good full flavour. The semi-sweet is fuller in the mouth and usually the finer wine: it develops well in the bottle and is consistently one of the better Colombars. Both wines rank about the best in the Cape and the best you can get.
Opstal Colombar★★★A
This is an off-dry white with clean nose and light flavour. The 1991 is better than usual.
Oranjerivier Wynkelders Colombar★★A
Originally a full-flavoured, dry, white wine, but now finished off-dry. This is one of the better wines from the cellar.
Oude Rust Colombard★★(★)B
A good off-dry wine, with plenty of Colombar character, for early, easy drinking.
Overhex Co-op Effesoet Colombard★★(★)A
This full-bodied, semi-sweet wine is pleasant on the palate and has good fruit. The wine is best enjoyed when young.
Perdeberg Co-op Colombar★★(★)A
Not always available; finished dry and with soft cultivar character.
Riebeek Wine Farmers' Co-op Colombard★★★A
This is a light wine which has won regional and national awards. Latest releases are only just off-dry.
Rietrivier Co-op Colombar★★A
An off-dry wine and a regular regional champion.
Robertson Co-op Colombard★★★A
The Robertson Co-operative is a consistent producer of top quality wines and is justifiably regarded as the 'home' of Colombar. Latest releases are a little on the quiet side.
Romansrivier Co-op Colombard★★★A
This Co-operative bottles three Colombars (dry, off-dry and semi-sweet), all of which are very good. They have good cultivar character and do consistently well at the South African Championship Wine Show. The semi-sweet (effesoet), frequently certified Superior, is usually one of the country's outstanding, quality Colombar wines.
Roodezandt Co-op Colombar★★(★)A
A pleasant, easy-drinking wine with good Colombar nose. The 1990 is off-dry and has more complex character.
Rooiberg Co-op Colombard★★★(★)B
One of the cellar's great successes, this Wine of Origin Vinkrivier has very good Colombar nose. Over the vintages the flavour has also developed well, with slight sweetness balancing well with the wine's relatively high acid. It regularly carried the old Superior rating. The 1983 was selected for sale at the New World Wine Auction in 1990. The 1990 is developing well.
Slanghoek Co-op Colombard★★★A
This is something special in the way of Colombars and is certainly

one of the more interesting examples of the cultivar. All the vintages have outstanding cultivar character and good balance. It frequently gained Superior certification under the old system. The off-dry 1990 is right up to standard.

Soetwynboere Colombar★★(★)A

An off-dry very fruity wine at a remarkably low price.

Spruitdrift Co-op Colombar★★A

An off-dry wine with very little cultivar character but one that is pleasant enough to drink.

Swartland Co-op Colombar★★★(★)A

A fruity, full-flavoured, dry wine with definite cultivar character. The 1991 is very good quality and also good value for money – one of the Cape's best.

Swartland Co-op Off-dry Colombar★★★A

A nice off-dry wine, which is not quite as light and fresh as the dry.

Van Loveren Colombar★★★A

This is usually a pleasant, semi-sweet Colombar with very good nose and full flavour. Better than most.

Villiersdorp Co-op Colombar★★★A

An off-dry wine with good Colombar character, making nice, fruity, easy drinking.

Weltevrede Colombard★★★(★)A

This Colombar has distinctive cultivar character and the unmistakable style of the wine maker, Lourens Jonker. An off-dry wine that, for Colombar, has reasonable ageing potential, it reaches its best in about two years from the date of vintage though most will enjoy it young when it is full of cultivar character. It is a regular award winner at regional and national shows.

Woolworths Robertson Colombar★★★A

From Weltevrede. This is a very good example of the cultivar finished off-dry. A Woolworths Regional wine, it drinks very well.

Fernão Pires

Andalusia Fernão Pires (Vaalharts Co-op)★★B
A semi-sweet white wine with muscaty nose and pleasant flavour.
Bergsig Fernão Pires★★★B
This wine has definite cellar style, yet it still has the muscaty nose of the cultivar. It is finished off-dry.
De Wet Co-op Fernão Pires★★(★)A
Almost in the 'Light' category but with good flavour and pleasant semi-sweet finish. Not surprising, it is one of the cellar's more popular wines.
Douglas Co-op Fernão Pires★A
This wine has improved over the vintages, with 1991 being semi-sweet and lowish alcohol. Pleasant drinking.
Nederburg Private Bin D207★★★★B
This wine is 100% Fernão Pires, but it is not certified as such. (*See* page 128 Blended/Non-varietal Dry White Wines.)
Nuy Co-op Fernão Pires★★★B
This wine has less muscat character and is more distinctive than most wines from this cultivar. The good spicey nose, fine fruity flavour and nice long taste make for interesting drinking. Although semi-sweet, it finishes decidedly dry.
Spier Fernão Pires ★★★B
A pleasant off-dry wine with good nose and brisk finish.
Swartland Co-op Fernão Pires★★★A
In the 'Light' style, with pleasant flavour and off-dry finish.
Van Loveren Fernão Pires★★★B
Van Loveren has probably produced a commercial wine from this cultivar through more vintages than any other cellar. Since 1987, production has been considerably good. It is off-dry with good, fruity nose and tasty cultivar flavour. The 1991 is a good drinking wine. Previous vintages have been semi-sweet Late Harvests, and the 1983 and 1984, produced as Perlé wines, were very good.
Vredendal Co-op Fernão Pires★★★B
Giel Swiegers seems to be able to do unusual things with cultivars not noted for quality. With this wine he gets very good flavours and produces a good, easy-drinking off-dry wine. Good value for money.

Furmint

Bergsig Furmint★★★B
Launched as an easy-drinking, off-dry wine with faint but fine flavour, this wine is becoming consistently good and one of the cellar's special products. The 1991 has delicate nose and pleasing palate; nice drinking wine and good value for money. Best enjoyed when young.

Gewürztraminer

Altydgedacht Masquerade Gewürztraminer★★★B
Enticing nose and good fruity-flavoured wine, finished bone-dry. A good example of a dry Gewürztraminer.
Ashton Co-op Gewürtztraminer ★★A
An off-dry wine with tropical spice nose and brisk finish.
Backsberg Gewürztraminer
(*See* page 180, Noble Late Harvest.)
Bergsig Gewürztraminer★★B
A very pleasant, off-dry wine with attractive nose. (*See* page 174, Special Late Harvest.)
Boschendal Jean Garde Vineyard Gewürztraminer★★★★C
The first release comes from the 1986 vintage from the Estate's single vineyard scheme. The 1987 was far better wine, in line with the quality expected of the Cape's better Gewürztraminers. The 1988 is a little lighter and lacks the concentration of the 1987. The 1989 is slightly disappointing, but the 1990 is dry with fuller nose and better flavour. The 1990 was judged the best SA dry white wine at the International Wine and Spirit Competition in the UK and received the Cape Wine Academy trophy.
Bottelary Co-op Gewürztraminer★★★B
Throughout the 1980s a very good wine. Those of the 1990s are pleasant but lack the concentration of the earlier wines.
Bovlei Co-op Gewürztraminer★★★B
A semi-sweet wine introduced from the 1991 vintage. A good start.
Danie de Wet Gewürztraminer★★★(★)B
Dry in the style of Alsace. Good rose petal nose and nice, dry herby flavour and clean finish. First from the 1991 vintage.
Delheim Gewürztraminer★★★★(★)C
Always an interesting wine. This is one of the few South African 'traminers which can deservedly be called Gewürztraminer. Super when young, it ages with benefit. All the 1980s were super. The 1990 was a more luscious and softer wine. The 1991 is one of the better from consistently good vintages. Beautiful rose petal nose, lots of spicey and peach flavours. Good clean finish. Big alcohol will allow good ageing. South Africa's consistently best wine from this cultivar.
Die Krans Estate Gewürztraminer★★★B
The first release, from 1989 vintage, was very short on cultivar character. The 1990 is off-dry, lacked Gewürztraminer but had pretty flowery nose in its youth. The 1981 seems to have come of age – good rose petal nose and attractive, spicy flavour. Finished off-dry.
Douglas Co-op Gewürztraminer★★(★)A
New entry from the 1991 vintage. A semi-sweet and low alcohol wine with nice floral character. Good price.
Fleur Du Cap Gewürztraminer (Bergkelder)★★★★D
The first release, from the 1984 vintage, had lovely cultivar nose and delightful semi-sweet, full-flavoured taste. The next release, from the 1990 vintage, is full of rose petal nose and nice spicey flavours. A lovely off-dry wine. The 1991 is also off-dry and ranks as one of the Cape's best – a four-star wine – nose full of flowery 'come-ons' and the taste a delight of fruits and spices, with long lingering finish.
Groot Constantia Gewürztraminer★★★★C
A very good off-dry version of the cultivar. It has full Gewürz-

traminer nose with plenty of flavour. The 1991 is a great wine with all kinds of fruit flavours made more complex by a touch of botrytis. Consistently one of the country's best.

Nederburg Gewürztraminer★★★★★C
Nederburg Gewürztraminer was originally sold at the annual Auction as a delicate, semi-sweet white with true rose-petal nose. More recently it has been released as a 'special'. Twice in succession it has been awarded the trophy for best Gewürztraminer on show at the Club Oenologique International Wine and Spirit Competition, first with the 1983 vintage at the 1984 event, and then with the 1984 vintage at the 1985 event, helping Günter Brözel on his way to the Winemaker of the Year accolade. This wine has outstanding nose with full, rich flavour enhanced by the excellent sugar-acid balance. The 1985 vintage brought Günter his second Diners Club Award. The 1986 is one of the best ever – a beautiful wine. The powerful 1988 is developing very nicely. The 1989 is made in a slightly lighter style but has the potential to develop with great benefit. The 1990 has it all – intense fruit and spice, floral nose with lots of rose-petal, finished off-dry. Delicious.

Neil Ellis Gewürztraminer★★★★C
A beautiful, almost bone-dry wine in the style of Alsace. Wonderful rose-petal scents and lots of Gewürztraminer. It is developing with great benefit. No more will be released under this label.

Neethlingshof Gewürztraminer★★★★C
Originally one of the better dry versions of this cultivar in the Cape, it is finished off-dry now. The 1991 vintage brings it into the ranks of the Cape's best. A complex product with full rose-petal bouquet, aromas, and lots of lovely fruit salad flavour.

Roodezandt Co-op Gewürztraminer★★★B
Bone-dry wine, with good nose full of flowery aromas and nice clean flavours, briskly finished. The 1991 is softer and nicer.

Stellenryck Gewürztraminer★★★★C
Another of the Cape's fine Gewürztraminers. An off-dry wine, it sets off the cultivar at its best. It has lovely nose and good flavour. The only release from the 1984 vintage carried Superior certification.

Van Loveren Gewürztraminer★★★(★)B
The first release was from the 1987 vintage. This big, full-bodied wine has a high alcohol content, but is a little shy on cultivar character. The 1990 is good clean wine with floral scents.

Vlottenburg Co-op Gewürztraminer★★★B
The 1987 was beautiful rich sweet wine, certified Superior, full of flavour and character. The inexpensive 1988 is less exciting but carried Superior and appears much sweeter, as did the 1990. The 1991 is much better wine with lovely nose, good flavours and in a much better pack – four-star wine.

Weltevrede Gewürztraminer★★★★B
Consistently good wine. The 1991 is one of the best. Good rose-petal nose, nice spicy flavour and finished off-dry, yet tastes much drier. Good, brisk finish. Excellent value.

Woolworths Le Quatrieme 914W★★★★C
Part of the Woolworths' Vintage Collection: 91 indicating the vintage; 4, fourth in the range and W is for white. A beautiful Gewürztraminer from Villiera. Just off-dry, but has enough acid to balance. Delicious wine.

Zevenwacht Gewürztraminer★★★★C
The first release from the 1986 vintage was almost dry with good nose and full flavour. It has developed well in the bottle. The classy and elegant 1988 had copybook, rose-petal aroma and good off-dry flavour. The 1989 appears dry and has good nose and flavour. The 1990 is almost bone-dry with a mixture of rose-petals and tropical fruit salad on the nose. The 1991 continues the top quality in dry style. Despite the high alcohol it has lots of floral tones and spices, and full, soft flavour. Delicious wine, and one of the best.
Zonnebloem Gewürztraminer (SFW)★★★C
This wine has prominent spicy nose and good flavour. It is just off-dry and at its best when young and fresh.

Hárslevelü

Lemberg (Hárslevelü)★★★★C
Previously called Hárslevelü, this wine is now entitled 'Lemberg'. Hárslevelü has never been my favourite cultivar yet the wines from this cellar's 1990 and 1991 vintages have made me accept that wines that are not just good, but that really appeal to me, can be made from this Hungarian cultivar. The 1991 is super and elevates this to a four-star wine – the Cape's best from this cultivar. Lots of fruit on the nose, good full flavour, nice body and fresh finish. It will develop well with time.
Porterville Co-op Hárslevelü★★A
A new wine for this cellar from the 1991 vintage. It is almost semi-sweet, and is clean, fresh wine.
Swartland Co-op Hárslevelü★★A
The 1990 almost qualifies for the 'Light' category.
Van Loveren Hárslevelü★★★B
One of the better examples of this variety, which first appeared with the 1982 vintage. Consistently good each vintage. It is nowadays finished just off-dry. Reliable good drinking wine.
Vredendal Co-op Hárslevelü★★(★)A
One of the better efforts with this variety from a Co-op, this dry wine has full flavour and a somewhat sharp finish. Latest releases have good nose, herby flavour and are soft, easy-drinking wines.

Late Harvest

Aan-de-Doorns Co-op Laatoes Steen★★A
A honey-nosed wine in Late Harvest style.
Andalusia Late Vintage (Vaalharts Co-op)★(★)B
Semi-sweet Colombar and Chenel blend.
Ashton Co-op Laatoes★★(★)A
Based on Steen with other varieties giving a fruity-nosed, light-bodied, semi-sweet gentle wine.
Autumn Harvest Late Vintage★★A
A semi-sweet blend with clean, honeyed nose and soft, fruity flavour.
Badsberg Co-op Late Harvest★★A
From 1991, a delicate semi-sweet made from Steen.
Bakenskop Late Harvest (Jonkheer)★★A
A good semi-sweet white made from clean, fruity Colombar.
Barrydale Late Harvest★★A
From 1991 comes a semi-sweet wine with nice fruity nose.
Beaufort Late Harvest (Solly Kramer)★★A
This is typical of the semi-sweet style of honeyed nose Late Harvest. Like all the products in the range, it is excellent value for money.
Bergendal Wines Late Harvest★★★B
A semi-sweet white, with clean style and fresh finish.
Bolandse Co-op Late Vintage★★(★)A
Chenin Blanc semi-sweet with honeyed nose.
Bon Courage Kerner Late Harvest★★★B
The 1991 is a rich, full-bodied, semi-sweet white with lovely flavour and soft mellow taste.
Boplaas Late Harvest★★(★)B
A less than semi-sweet wine which has attractive nose and good flavour. The 1989 is particularly pleasant and the 1990 was a gold medal winner at a local show. (Still available.)
Botha Co-op Chenin Blanc Late Harvest★★A
An ordinary, semi-sweet, Late-Harvest-style wine. It won a gold medal at the local young wine show.
Bottelary Co-op Late Harvest★★A
A semi-sweet white wine, which is fairly full-flavoured and with honeyed nose.
Brandvlei Co-op Laat Oes★★A
Made from Steen, giving a pleasant, fruity, semi-sweet wine.
Breughel Late Harvest (Aroma Group)★★A
A semi-sweet white with a slightly honeyed nose and flavour coming from Steen.
Cellar Cask Premier Late Harvest (Oude Meester)★★A
A good, rich-flavoured, semi-sweet wine from Steen. Now available in cork-closed bottles.
Cellar Reserve Late Harvest (Hyperama)★★A
Semi-sweet fresh fruity wine.
Checkers Yellow Label Late Harvest★★A
Multiple blend with fruity nose and finished semi-sweet.
Clairvaux Late Harvest★★A
A soft wine from Rhine Riesling out of 1991 vintage. Semi-sweet.
Culemborg Late Harvest (Union Wine)★★★B
An ever-improving wine with good sweetness and acid balance. Very good value for money.

De Doorns Co-op Laatoes★A
A pleasant semi-sweet from Colombar.
De Leuwen Jagt Late Harvest★★★B
Attractive nose and good flavour in which the small percentage of Chardonnay in the mainly Chenin Blanc blend stands out. Not too sweet, well-made, good drinking wine.
Delheim Spatzendreck Late Harvest★★★★B
A semi-sweet wine labelled 'Late Harvest'. The name and the cheeky sparrow featured on the label reflect the lively nature of its wine maker, Michael 'Spatz' Sperling. A sample of one of his first efforts, produced when he was struggling with the techniques of wine-making, was given to a friend – and promptly evoked a simple, four-letter, agricultural assessment. Sperling vowed to make the man eat his words and eventually, after years of doggedly determined experiment, produced this splendid Late Harvest. The name he gave it is a whimsical play on words: both Michael's surname and nickname mean 'sparrow' in German; 'spatzendreck' literally translates as 'sparrow droppings' – an appropriate if not entirely sophisticated allusion to the original trial sampling. It is a semi-sweet, full-bodied wine, made nowadays from Steen, with good late harvest qualities. In 1986 the wine celebrated its 25th anniversary with an excellent 1985 vintage wine carrying Superior certification. All recent vintages are very good, luscious, full-flavoured wines with the 1991 being splendid.
Die Krans Late Harvest★★(★)A
A multiple blend of Colombar and Steen and a touch of Muscat, giving a lovely flavour and fresh, fruity nose.
Douglas Co-op Late Harvest★(★)A
Mainly Colombar with Steen and Hanepoot, finished semi-sweet.
Douglas Green Late Harvest★★(★)B
Clean, well-made, light-style Late Harvest.
Drostdy-Hof Late Harvest (Oude Meester)★★B
A nice, fruity, clean, semi-sweet wine.
Edelkeller Late Harvest★★★B
Well-made, good-tasting sweet white.
Goudini Co-op Steen Late Harvest★★(★)A
A semi-sweet white with pleasant flavour and nice fruity nose.
Goue Vallei Late Harvest (Citrusdal Co-op)★★★A
Based on Steen, with some Sauvignon Blanc and a touch of Muscat, the result is pleasant fruity wine with attractive nose and fresh finish.
Helderberg Co-op Late Vintage★★B
A clean, well-made wine where Steen dominates in its own Late Harvest style.
Huguenot Late Harvest★★(★)A
A nice, fresh, fruity, simple Late Harvest with clean finish.
Kellerprinz Late Harvest(SFW)★★A
Remarkable, not only in the volume of its sales but also because of its surprisingly good Late Harvest character. Excellent value.
Klawer Co-op Late Vintage★A
A semi-sweet Steen and Colombar blend that is pleasant tasting but lacks nose.
Kupferberger Auslese (Bergkelder)★★★C
Basically a Late Harvest Steen, it has improved in quality in recent years and now shows very good Late Harvest character.

KWV Late Harvest★★★(no price available)
An easy-drinking semi-sweet wine with appealing flavour.
Landzicht Late Harvest★★A
A multiple blend with an attractive nose. This is one of the cellar's better offerings.
Langverwacht Co-op Late Harvest★★A
A light, fruity semi-sweet Steen.
Late Harvest Steen (Groot Eiland Co-op)★★A
A pleasant, fairly neutral semi-sweet white.
Loopspruit Late Vintage★★★B
Good fruity semi-sweet white.
Louwshoek-Voorsorg Co-op Laatoes★A
A very sweet, full-bodied wine that lacks flavour.
Lutzville Co-op Laatoes★A
A fruity-nosed, semi-sweet wine, usually from Steen and the latest from Colombar.
Mamreweg Co-op Late Harvest★★A
A semi-sweet Steen with good cultivar character.
McGregor Co-op Laatoes Steen★★A
One of the more interesting Co-op semi-sweet Steens that has some Late Harvest character.
Merwespont Co-op Late Vintage★★A
A blend of equal proportions of Steen and Colombar with good, fruity nose and pleasant flavour.
Monterey Late Harvest (Western Province Cellars)★A
A soft, full, semi-sweet wine.
Montpellier Late Harvest★★B
The blend varies vintage by vintage, but it is always pleasing, light, fresh wine with fruity nose and appealing flavour.
Nordale Co-op Late Harvest★★A
A semi-sweet wine made from Steen with fine, fruity flavour.
Nuy Steen Laat-oes★★★★B
A well-made, good-flavoured wine, full of fruit and very well balanced. It makes lovely easy drinking and is best enjoyed young.
Oranjerivier Wynkelder Late Harvest★A
A Sultana-Colombar blend finished semi-sweet.
Oude Nektar Belladonna Late Vintage★★★A
Nice clean-flavoured, semi-sweet wine that, despite the name, won't poison you!
Overhex Bukettraube Late Harvest★★(★)B
A gentle, semi-sweet wine with flowery nose and soft flavour.
Overmeer Laatoes★★A
A good, clean-flavoured, semi-sweet white wine which makes pleasant, easy drinking.
Overvaal Late Harvest (Vaalharts Co-op)★★A
A blend of Steen and Chenel, finished semi-sweet.
Perdeberg Co-op Late Vintage★★A
A semi-sweet wine with attractive fruity nose and pleasing flavour.
Porterville Co-op Late Vintage★A
A semi-sweet Steen with full flavour.
Ravenswood Late Harvest★★A
A semi-sweet, low-alcohol wine with clean finish.
Rebel Late Harvest★★A
A full, semi-sweet wine.

Riebeek Co-op Late Harvest★★★A
A well-made, semi-sweet Steen with lots of flavour and well-balanced fruit.
Rietrivier Co-op Late Harvest★★A
This is quite an interesting, semi-sweet Late Harvest, blended from varying cultivars from vintage to vintage. Colombar is usually the main component with Steen and Sauvignon Blanc.
Robertson Co-op Steen Late Vintage★★★A
A good, semi-sweet Steen. The 1990s are well-made and attractive.
Romansrivier Co-op Late Harvest★★(★)A
Well-made, good-flavoured, clean, semi-sweet wine.
Roodezandt Co-op Late Harvest★★(★)A
A full-flavoured Steen of reasonable body and clean, clear finish.
Rooiberg Co-op Late Vintage★★★A
The Vinkrivier Ward provided the grapes for this semi-sweet wine. It has full nose and flavour, and a little Muscat on the nose. It is well-made wine with good Late Vintage character.
Rusthof Late Harvest (Mooiuitsig)★★A
A semi-sweet white wine with attractive Muscat nose.
Simonsvlei Co-op Late Vintage★★A
An honest, semi-sweet Steen of medium body.
Slanghoek Co-op Late Harvest★★A
A good wine with good fruity flavour.
Soetwynboere Late Harvest★★A
A nice flavoured wine finished semi-sweet.
Spruitdrift Co-op Late Harvest★★★A
A semi-sweet wine with far more Late Harvest character than most in this category. It is full-flavoured and ages reasonably well.
Swartland Co-op Late Vintage★★A
A blend which has varied unbelievably over the years. Ordinary easy-drinking Steen.
Tulbagh Co-op Late Harvest★★A
A semi-sweet white with soft feel and pleasant flavour.
Twee Jongegezellen Night Harvest★★★C
This Late-Harvest-style wine is made from grapes picked in the cool of the night, thereby retaining the delicate nuances of the grape. The multiple blend contains Steen, Sauvignon Blanc, Gewürztraminer, Rhine Riesling and even Furmint, giving a rich yet delicately flavoured, semi-sweet wine.
Valley Late Harvest (Gilbeys)★(★)A
A very pleasant, full-flavoured, semi-sweet wine with a good touch of Muscat which adds to its attraction.
Villiersdorp Co-op Late Vintage★★A
Clean, fresh wine with brisk finish.
Vinovat Late Harvest (Marcows)★A
A semi-sweet blend.
Vintner's Choice (Drop Inn) Late Harvest★★A
Pleasant semi-sweet wine with flowery nose and brisk finish.
Vredendal Co-op Late Harvest★★★A
A nice Steen-based wine with Fernão Pires giving fresh fruity wine.
Wamakersvallei Laat Oes★★A
Fruity spicy nose with good flavour finished semi-sweet.
Wellington Wynboere Laatoes★★A
A pleasant, light-bodied, semi-sweet with a bit of Muscat nose.

Welmoed Co-op Late Vintage★★A
A good, fruity Steen with nice, full flavour; touched out with 10% Gewürztraminer.
Weltevrede Therona Late Harvest★★★B
This Late Harvest is made from a locally-developed grape variety. It is clean, well-made and fruity.
Witzenberg Late Harvest Edelgoud (Oude Meester)★A
A semi-sweet, soft white wine with honeyed nose.
Woolworths Late Harvest★★(★)A
From Douglas Green Bellingham. A good semi-sweet wine which drinks easily.
Woolworths Petit Vin Late Harvest★★B
A semi-sweet white in 250 m*l* Tetrapak.

Special Late Harvest

Aan-de-Doorns Co-op Spesiale Laatoes Steen★★A
Introduced with the 1987 vintage, this is a light, delicate, easy-drinking wine. The 1989 had more botrytis than usual. The 1991 is somewhat delicate.
Ashton Co-op Special Late Harvest★★★A
The 1991 is a most attractive wine from Muscat de Frontignan, and remarkable value.
Backsberg Special Late Harvest★★★★B
A luscious, full-flavoured, rich wine with the honeyed Steen taste, which is soft and smooth across the palate. This wine has always been good and is now making the most of the more recent laws allowing higher sugars. It usually carried Superior certification. The 1989 is a blend of Steen, Muscat and Gewürztraminer. In the 1990, the Gewürztraminer certainly gives a flowery lift to the nose.
Barrydale Co-op Special Late Harvest★★★B
The 1992 is fresh-flavoured, with nice smoothness, and is good for early drinking.
Bellingham Special Late Harvest★★★(★)C
This wine, introduced with the 1983 vintage, was a step towards upgrading the Bellingham Late Harvest, in keeping with the improvement in the other Bellingham wines, and to meet the requirements of the new laws. The recent releases are Steen-based with Rhine Riesling and Sauvignon Blanc; clean tasting, brisk finish wines – not the botrytis wine of the middle 1980s.
Bergsig Bukettraube Special Late Harvest★★★B
An attractive fruity nose introduces a wine that is soft across the palate, with a pleasing, sweet taste.
Bergsig Chenin Blanc Special Late Harvest★★★B
A good, golden, rich, sweet wine. Consistently good. The 1991 and 1992 are good fruity wines with satisfying flavour and fresh finish.
Bergsig Gewürztraminer Special Late Harvest★★★★B
Well made with intense flavours of peaches and tropical fruits. It has lots of complexity, is lovely as a young wine and usually develops well. The 1992 is up to standard.
Bergsig Weisser Riesling Special Late Harvest★★★B
From the 1989 vintage came this good, semi-sweet wine with definite cultivar character. It has developed well over the year and is showing far more layers of flavour. There was no 1990 vintage. The 1991 is lovely fresh wine, even a year later.
Blaauwklippen Special Late Vintage★★★(★)B
A wine with a long success, of which 1990 seems to be the last release. The cellar is now opting for the Natural Sweet route. The 1990 is developing well. Blaauwklippen suggests serving this wine in summer, poured over crushed ice.
Bon Courage Gewürztraminer Special Late Harvest★★★★C
André Bruwer has a string of awards and championships to his name, however, the one he probably takes most delight in was the 1991 Diners Club Award for his 1989 Gewürztraminer Special Late Harvest. When the quality of Cape Special Late Harvests is so high, to be judged the best is no mean accolade. With its 11,6% alcohol and 48 g/*l* sugar balanced with 6,6 g/*l* acid, the wine has good botrytis character yet enough fruit flavour to be very attractive. The 1990 is

more elegant, with citrus and tropical fruit flavours, and the 1991 has the most enticing floral nose and is developing layers of lovely flavour in the bottle. Delicious wine.

Bon Courage Kerner Special Late Harvest★★★(★)B
Usually a good, full-flavoured wine, which has had a surprising lack of aroma, but is well balanced. The 1986 had good botrytis which added much-needed complexity. This wine is ageing with interest.

Boplaas Special Late Harvest★★★(★)B
Usually blended from late-harvested Colombar, Muscat d'Alexandrie and a little Weisser Riesling, this combination results in a most attractive nose, touched out with enough botrytis to give a fascinating complexity, yet the wine still has good, clean freshness. The 1990 appears slightly less sweet than usual, giving better elegance. This is a lovely, fragrant wine.

Bovlei Co-op Special Late Harvest★★A
A limited production from the 1988 vintage made from Steen. It is medium-bodied, well-balanced wine which is developing in the bottle. The 1990 is a pleasant semi-sweet wine, as is the 1991.

Clairvaux Co-op Special Late Harvest★★(★)B
A light but most attractive fruity nose from this Steen-based, well-balanced wine. The pleasing flavour makes easy drinking.

Delaire Special Late Harvest★★★★B
This is a delicious, full, fruity wine from the 1989 vintage. It has good botrytis with citrus and tropical fruit tones. Lovely as it is when young, it has plenty of potential to develop in the bottle. Now a non-vintage 'Selected Late Harvest' has taken its place.

Delheim Special Late Harvest★★★★B
This was excellent wine throughout the 1980s with regular Superiors. The 1989 is tremendous and really developing with great benefit. The 1990 is a slightly lesser wine, however it continues to be one of the Cape's best. The 1991 is a stunner in every respect.

De Wet Co-op Special Late Harvest★★★B
Based on Chenin Blanc with a bit of Bukettraube for spiciness, it is semi-sweet wine with enough acidity to have a brisk finish.

Die Krans Special Late Harvest★★★A
Not too sweet, this is a good wine with slight botrytis character. A blend of Steen, Colombar and some Hanepoot. The 1991 has a good tropical fruit nose.

Drostdy-Hof Adelpracht Special Late Harvest★★★C
A good example of a well-made Late Harvest Steen, it regularly carried Superior certification. The 1990 is a rich wine with good balancing acid.

Du Toitskloof Co-op Special Late Harvest★★★★B
A good, full-flavoured, Late Harvest wine, which is a regular award winner. The 1988 is particularly good with lots of flavour and a little botrytis. It is developing well. The 1989 is very good and has lots of fruity flavour. The 1990 has better botrytis with good fruit acid. The 1991 is fresh, clean wine, without botrytis.

Edward Snell Special Late Vintage★★★B
A good, clean, well-made wine with fruity nose and rich flavour.

Eersterivier Valleise Co-op Special Late Harvest★★★B
A fine Late Harvest with particularly pleasing nose. It ages well in the bottle. The 1987 is from Steen, the 1988 from Sauvignon Blanc and the more recent have strong Gewürztraminer character.

Eikendal Special Late Harvest★★★★B
The first release, from the 1986 vintage, is full-bodied and has a slight touch of botrytis. The 1988 is lovely wine with botrytis complexity and fine fruit acid. The 1989 is a lovely four-star wine, while the 1990 is bigger and better in every way – more botrytis, more nose, more flavour. It is developing with great benefit. The 1991 is attractive, but without botrytis doesn't have the complexity of 1990.
Fairview Special Late Harvest★★★(★)B
A good wine which has varied in taste over the past few vintages, but is always full of fine, fresh flavour at the time of release. Nowadays it is usually made from Steen with an occasional touch of Bukettraube and usually carries Superior certification. The 1991 is a four-star, super wine.
Fleermuisklip Spesiale Laatoes (Lutzville Co-op)★★A
From Colombar, a simple semi-sweet wine for early consumption.
Fleur du Cap Special Late Harvest (Bergkelder)★★★★B
A lovely wine with enticing botrytis character. It usually carries Superior certification and develops beautifully in the bottle. The 1987 is a delightfully fresh wine with lots of complex fruit character. The 1983 won the Cape Wine Academy Trophy for the highest scoring Cape white wine at the 1988 International Wine and Spirit Competition in London. In 1988 and 1989 it was awarded the highest possible Mondé Selection trophy, and in 1991 it gained double gold in the first South African National Bottled Wine Show. The 1989 is developing nicely in the bottle and is a lovely, stylish, elegant wine. The 1990 is yet to be released.
Goue Vallei Special Late Harvest (Citrusdal Co-op)★★(★)A
A respectable, well-balanced wine with tropical fruit and nice smooth texture is now being produced in an effort to improve the cellar's quality.
Hartenberg L'Estreux★★★★C
L'Estreux is only bottled in vintages when the cellar believes that nature has provided the style of wine that fits their quality requirement. There was no 1986, owing to a lack of botrytis. The 1987 is made from Steen that was harvested at about 30 Balling and some 30% botrytis-infested, giving delightfully attractive nose and complex flavour. It is about at its best now. The 1989 is 40% Steen with the balance made up of Gewürztraminer, Morio Muscat and others. It has a nice touch of botrytis, but not enough to cover the fresh, fruity, Muscat character. Although included in this section, it is not certified Special Late Harvest. The 1990 continues the same enticing quality. The 1991 is, to my taste, the best so far – made from no fewer than five cultivars including some botrytized Gewürztraminer giving a full range of perfumes, luscious feel and fresh finish.
Hazendal Freudenlese★★★C
This Special Late Harvest was first released from the 1982 vintage with 44 g/*l* residual sugar. Fresh and fruity when first released, it has developed well in the bottle. It carried Superior certification. The 1987 was a full-bodied wine with a hint of botrytis, and although the 1988 is a full, sweet wine, it has a rather dull nose. The 1989 and 1990 are fresher, better wines with a honey-like character.
Huguenot Special Late Harvest★★B
The only release, so far, is from the 1989 vintage. It is semi-sweet with honey hints, and is showing some age.

Kaapzicht Weisser Riesling Special Late Harvest★★★B
This wine has an attractive, flowery nose, soft texture and a clean, sharp finish.
Klawer Co-op Special Late Vintage★★A
A full-flavoured sweet wine with botrytis nose, made from Steen with the addition of Bukettraube.
Koelenhof Co-op Chenin Blanc Spesiale Laatoes★★(★)B
A well-balanced, good-value-for-money wine, which is not too sweet, yet has a nice touch of botrytis.
Lievland Kerner Special Late Harvest★★★D
Released from the 1985 vintage, it had a strange but not unattractive nose and good, full flavour which is developing well in the bottle. The 1987 is a good, full-flavoured wine with a distinctive nose and carries Superior certification. The 1989 has a full, fruity nose and good flavour which should bottle-age with benefit.
Lievland Special Late Harvest ★★★B
A blend of varieties including Weisser Riesling and Kerner, with some botrytis and good fruit on the nose, makes this wine smooth in the mouth with ripe flavours. Lovely wine.
L'Ormarins Guldenpfennig★★★(★)C
A lovely, fresh-flavoured Late-Harvest-style wine full of attractive nose and complex flavour. The sugar content does not qualify it for Special Late Harvest but the quality does. The first release came from the 1987 vintage. The 1988 has more definite botrytis and the 1989 is of the same quality. The latest release is a non-vintage blend of Gewürztraminer, Rhine Riesling and Muscat Ottonel. It has fruity nose and good botrytis, high alcohol of 13,4% and good acid.
Lutzville Co-op Spesiale Laatoes★★A
The 1991 is high-alcohol, semi-sweet wine from Colombar.
Mamreweg Co-op Special Late Harvest★★(★)B
Made from Steen, this wine has reasonable Late Harvest character, and nice softness in the mouth.
Montpellier Special Late Harvest★★★(★)B
The first release, from the 1985 vintage, was very good wine. It had good botrytis nose and lovely, fruity, semi-sweet taste from the Hárslevelü used. The 1989 is a blend of Chenin Blanc, Hárslevelü and Rhine Riesling. The blend of 1990 changes again to Bukettraube, Riesling, Sauvignon Blanc and Steen, which has a honey-like character, and is rich in the mouth with a fresh finish.
Nederburg Special Late Harvest★★★★B
South Africa's leading Late Harvest wine which has enjoyed many, many years of acclaim for its high quality. This Wine of Origin Paarl is full of sweet richness, genuinely developed from grapes allowed to age on the vine prior to pressing. In recent years it has had very good botrytis, or noble rot, character which puts it in a class of its own. With the most recent definitions of sweetness legally classifying Late Harvest wines, the Nederburg is automatically classed as Special Late Harvest and is almost always certified Superior. When allowed to age for three to four years, a luscious wine of intense depth develops, an outstanding example of an elegant and gentle botrytis wine. Eight successive vintages carried Superior before this certification was dropped. Latest releases are more complex blends of Sauvignon Blanc, Steen and topped with Gewürztraminer. The 1990 is a show-stopper!

Nederburg Weisser Riesling Special Late Harvest★★★★D
The first release of this elegant, rich, golden-textured wine came from an almost perfect 1982 vintage, which yielded a beautiful wine, released only at the annual Nederburg Auction. The 1986 vintage was sold at the 1988 Auction and the 1987 sold at the 1989 and 1990 Auctions. It is probably the best so far, but all are developing with great distinction.

Vintage	**Alcohol**	**Sugar** *g/l*	**Acid** *g/l*
1982	14,29	26,4	7,0
1986	11,6	40,9	6,1
1987	13,6	45,6	6,8

Neethlingshof Gewürztraminer Special Late Harvest★★★★B
A well-made wine from the 1984 vintage, with excellent cultivar character. It has developed beautifully in the bottle. It has, however, given way to the Noble Late Harvests.
Neethlingshof Weisser Riesling Special Late Harvest★★★★C
The maiden vintage of 1983 was a beautiful wine with complexity which can only come from botrytis and good wine-making. It has been awarded Superior certification and is developing beautifully in the bottle. It has also given way to the Noble Late Harvests.
Overhex Spesiale Laatoes★★★A
A 1990 from botrytis Steen with full flavour, in screw-top bottles.
Rheboksskloof Special Late Harvest★★★(★)C
Not available on a regular basis. The 1990 was most attractive and has developed well in the bottle.
Riebeek Co-op Special Late Harvest★★★(★)A
The 1991 is a big wine made from Rhine Riesling and with good fruit. It should develop well with over 13% alcohol.
Robertson Co-op Special Late Harvest★★★(★)B
Since 1989 it has been certified Gewürztraminer. The 1990 lacked 'gewürz', but 1991 has good rose-petal nose and is not too sweet.
Romansrivier Co-op Special Late Harvest★★★A
Recent vintages are very good – Steen-based with good botrytis character, giving full-flavoured wines that are best enjoyed young.
Roodezandt Co-op Special Late Harvest★★★A
Originally a good, fruity, well-flavoured wine with more than the usual complexity from Steen. The 1988 was particularly good. The 1989 is made from Colombar, giving a delightfully fruity, full-bodied wine, while the 1990 and 1991 are once again Steen. Good quality.
Rooiberg Special Late Harvest★★★A
The earlier vintages made from Colombar were most unusual wines. The 1988 is from Steen and has lots of good, rich flavour but no botrytis. The 1989 is made from Steen with 20% Gewürztraminer, giving good spicey/fruity flavours. It is a four-star product. The 1990 is much the same blend, but not quite as good.
Saxenburg Special Late Harvest★★★(★)B
The 1985 was the first release and was followed by the Superior 1986. The 1987 is the best release yet. It has good botrytis character, is not too sweet and has developed well. The 1991 follows in the same character.
Simondium Co-op Special Late Harvest★★A
This is light, clean wine finished semi-sweet.
Simonsig Franciskaner Special Late Harvest★★★(★)B
Generally a good, Steen-based, late-harvested wine with medium

body and rich sweetness. All vintages have been good and have aged well. The 1989 and 1990 are probably the best yet; lovely, fruity, pleasing wines at excellent value for quality.

Simonsvlei Co-op Special Late Harvest★★(★)B

The 1990 and 1991 are good wines with botrytis influence and good, brisk, fresh finish.

Spier Chenin Blanc Special Late Harvest★★★(★)C

Although only some of the 1983 releases have Superior certification, they are good wines with very definite botrytis character and a strange orange colour. They are still available from the cellar and have developed with great benefit.

Spruitdrift Co-op Special Late Harvest★★★(★)A

The original release was the 1982, and it had the distinction of being the first Olifants River wine to gain Superior certification. The 1990 from Sauvignon Blanc is nice and fruity.

Swartland Co-op Special Late Harvest★★★A

A full-flavoured, semi-sweet wine made from Steen. The 1991 has retained good Steen flavour with hints of honey.

Van Loveren Special Late Harvest★★★(★)B

Consistently good wine with recent vintages showing good Gewürztraminer. The 1991 contains a massive 14,5% alcohol, and will develop as well as all the previous vintages.

Villiera Garonne Special Late Harvest★★★★B

A pleasant, full-bodied, Steen-based wine with an attractive complexity that develops well over a year or two. One of the best.

Vlottenburg Co-op Special Late Harvest★★★A

Usually a sprightly, fruity wine with enough acid to balance the sweetness. It occasionally carries Superior certification. The 1990 and 1991 are delicious, elegant wines.

Vredendal Co-op Special Late Harvest★★A

A soft, well-flavoured wine in Late Harvest style.

Vredenheim Special Late Harvest★★(★)B

A wine with full flavour and pleasant nose, but a little unbalanced.

Welmoed Co-op Special Late Harvest★★★A

A good, full, Late Harvest wine. The 1990, from Steen, has very little nose but nice flavour, and is for early drinking.

Weltevrede Special Late Harvest★★★(★)B

Weltevrede's strength lies in their Superior liqueur wines and clearly this rich, semi-sweet Late Harvest shows that the wine maker has a feel for sweeter wines. It is a very good example of a Chenin Blanc in Late Harvest style, often touched with Gewürztraminer.

Weltevrede Therona Special Late Harvest★★★B

The first release was from the 1986 vintage. The 1987 is a delicate wine with a fine, spicey nose and sweet, pleasant flavour.

Zonnebloem Special Late Harvest (SFW)★★★(★)C

The successor to the popular Zonnebloem Late Harvest, the Special Late Harvest, was launched with the 1982 vintage and carried Superior certification. The 1989 and 1990 are complex, quiet wines.

Noble Late Harvest

Backsberg Noble Late Harvest★★★★E
To my knowledge this was the earliest Gewürztraminer made in Noble Late Harvest style. First made from the 1987 vintage, it was full-flavoured, light-coloured and packed with good character, and is one of the more elegant wines. It has developed very well. In spite of the botrytis, the 1988 still has very good varietal character; it has developed beautifully and is a lovely wine.

Bellingham Noble Late Harvest★★★★D
The first of Bellingham's limited-release wines is a 1987 Noble Late Harvest. It is a lovely botrytised wine with good raisin character and has developed beautifully with time. The 1991 vintage is full of floral fragrance from Gewürztraminer and forms part of Bellingham's French theme.

Bergsig Edel Laatoes★★★(★)D
This good, Steen-based wine, with its attractive nose and luscious palate, celebrated its maiden vintage in 1982. The 1983 vintage had 12% Bukettraube and 8% Chenel added to the blend, giving a fuller wine with more complex nose and rich flavour. Both have been awarded Superior certification. The 1984, made from Chenin Blanc, has good botrytis and complexity, and crisp finish.

Blaauwklippen Noble Late Vintage★★★★(★)C
A powerfully flavoured wine with superb botrytis character. It is ageing beautifully. Like most of the Noble Late Harvests, it is not regularly available.

Bon Courage Noble Late Harvest★★★(★)E
A very good, delicate Noble Late Harvest made from Bukettraube of the 1985 vintage. Its citrus nose has a vague resemblance to Sauternes. It needs to be consumed by now. Next release from the 1991 vintage has prominent botrytis and high acids, and should develop with interest.

Boschendal Vin d'Or★★★★D
First vintage from 1979. Made from Riesling and Steen, it was a rich, smooth wine with plenty of sugar (170 g/*l*) and good acid. It is past its best. There is now a very limited quantity of 1990 from Pinot Gris. It is unusual wine with enticing nose and full flavour. The 1991 is from Bukettraube.

Bottelary Co-op Noble Late Harvest★★★(★)D
The first release, from the 1983 vintage, has plenty of sweetness, botrytis character and honeyed flavour, making more than just pleasant sipping. It developed well over five years. The 1985 is probably at its best now and should be drunk up and enjoyed. The 1989 is, to date, the best produced and in fact the best wine from this cellar. It is made from Bukettraube and packed with fruit and botrytis – a four-star wine.

Buitenverwachting Noblesse★★★★E
This release, from the 1987 vintage, has a sugar content of 136 g/*l*, total acid of 10,3 g/*l* and alcohol of 12,3%. It is well-balanced with good botrytis and is developing well in the bottle. It won a gold medal at the International Wine and Spirit Competition in Britain in 1989. The 1991 is gorgeous wine from Rhine Riesling with botrytis and oak.

Delheim Edelspatz Noble Late Harvest★★★★★C
Vintages tasted to date were the 1979, 1980, 1981, 1982, 1984, 1987,

1988, 1989 and 1990. All were recognizable as from the same cellar, but each had its own special distinction. All have definite botrytis character and occasionally have small amounts of Bukettraube and Kerner added to the blend. The 1987 was more along the lines of a Sauternes than ever before. The 1988 and 1989 follow this line of lower sugar, resulting in a very attractive wine with good acid balance, making an excellent digestif. The 1990 is a more concentrated, very rich wine, from Bukettraube with some Steen and Rhine Riesling offering great depth of flavour. The 1991 is made from Rhine Riesling, Bukettraube with touches of Steen, Muscat and Sauvignon Blanc, and is as good as ever. Truly a delicious wine.

Die Krans Noble Late Harvest★★★(★)C

This wine was first released from the 1988 vintage. The low sugar content (60 g/*l*) makes a soft, silky wine with good fruit and botrytis layers. This is the best wine from this cellar. Plans for 1990 were thwarted by Mother Nature when the grapes that had hung on the vines for weeks after normal riching for concentrate, were blown off by strong wind before they could be picked.

Du Toitskloof Co-op Noble Late Harvest★★(★)E

Packed in 375 m*l* Bottles. Distinct pineapple nose, honey-like flavour and sweet finish.

Engeltjepipi Noble Late Harvest★★★★C

Over the years, Twee Jongegezellen have produced some remarkable Late Harvests which were not sold, but shared with friends only. The 1982 vintage was certified Superior and is a well-made, fine, gentle wine. Then at last, a small quantity of the 1983 was released to the public, followed by the 1987 vintage made in light style with less sugar than many others. This is a wine very much along the lines of a Sauternes.

Goudini Co-op Steen Noble Late Harvest★★★(★)C

The cellar's first Superior is a light-style, fruity wine with good acid balance, from the 1987 vintage. It is developing well.

Groot Constantia Noble Late Harvest★★★D

The 1984 was Groot Constantia's first attempt at this type of wine and contained 270 g/*l* sugar. The 1986 is a much better product with 180 g/*l*. It is better balanced and has good flavour. Two wines were produced in 1990, one from Rhine Riesling-Chenin Blanc blend, and a Gewürztraminer-Muscat blend. Both are very attractive wines. The 1991 was used to celebrate the 200-year anniversary of the pediment at the Groot Constantia Wine Cellar. It is a lovely wine from Sauvignon Blanc, Rhine Riesling and Chenin Blanc. At the celebratory function, Mrs Marike de Klerk, wife of the State President, was presented with a numbered bottle, number one. I had the honour of representing the SA Wine writers and was presented with bottle number two!

KWV Noble Late Harvest★★★★(★)(no price available)

This is one of KWV's best products from the 1984 vintage. It is full of botrytis but still has good, fruity flavours. The 1987 became the Cathedral Cellars export brand. Beautiful wine.

Lievland Noble Late Harvest★★★★D

The first attempt, from the 1986 vintage, has a faint botrytis nose and full, sweet flavour, but lacks finesse. The 1987 is in a totally different class, with lovely fruity flavours, not too much sweetness and a more delicate style. It is a good four-star wine. A wood-matured variation was bottled for Lievland and first shown at the Cape Winemakers' Guild Auction where it realized an average price of R125 per case of 12 x 375 ml bottles. The 1988 is a deep, rich wine. The 1989 has a much higher sugar content with full botrytis and lots of fruit, and was awarded a gold medal at the International Wine and Spirits Competition in London. The 1990 maintains the same high standard. The 1991 is more along the style of Sauternes with lower sugar, gentle botrytis and is wood-aged. The high alcohol of 14% gives beautiful glycerine sweetness. A four-star, gorgeous wine.

L'Ormarins Noble Late Harvest★★★★C

Usually sold through the Bergkelder Vinotèque scheme. The cellar contains outstanding botrytised Steens, Rhine Rieslings and Bukettraubes from various vintages and, eventually, more of these palate-confusing wines will be launched as prestige products.

Louwshoek-Voorsorg Co-op Noble Late Harvest★★A

The 1986 vintage was made from Steen with good, clean, botrytis character. The 1989 won a gold medal at the SA Show.

Nederburg Bukettraube Edelkeur★★★★D

The first vintage was the 1979, which had a very low alcohol content of only 7%, acid of 10,3 g/*l* and incredible sugar of 258,4 g/*l*. It was released only at the annual Nederburg Auction.

Nederburg Bukettraube Noble Late Harvest★★★★D

The word Edelkeur was dropped from the name of this wine for the 1983 vintage. Alcohol content is 12,3%, acid 10,6 g/*l* and sugar 152,3 g/*l*. This is beautiful wine which fills the mouth with the smallest sip and is released only at the annual Nederburg Auction. The 1986 vintage has an analysis very similar to the 1983, and was sold at the 1988 and 1989 Auctions.

Nederburg Chardonnay Noble Late Harvest★★★★(★)

A one-off allowed the production of only 54 cases of half-bottles from the 1987 vintage, containing 12% alcohol, 158 g/*l* residual sugar, and 9,7 g/*l* acid. This is an unique wine full of most unusual flavours, and developing with great distinction.

Nederburg Edelkeur★★★★★D

Edelkeur cannot be adequately described – it must be tasted. A half-bottle costs a lot of money but offers wine-lovers an experience never to be forgotten. Moreover, half a bottle is enough for six to eight people to sip in liqueur fashion at the end of a complementary meal. Made in extremely small quantities, this incomparable botrytis wine varies greatly from vintage to vintage: there is no guarantee that the elements conducive to noble rot will occur each year. Except for the very first vintage (1969), which was sold by postal auction, it is available to retailers only at the annual Nederburg Auction. It will age for many years. In accordance with the Wine and Spirit Board's regulations, special permission and supervision is required each time the wine is made. The 1987 is considered by overseas fundis to be the best ever produced. The approximate figures for the vintages in the 1970s and 1980s are as follows:

Vintage	Alcohol%	Sugar g/l	Acid g/l
1974	11,0	183	8,7
1975	12,1	133	8,9
1976	9,1	212	11,7
1977	13,1	159	10,9
1978	10,9	193	8,9
1979	10,4	190	12,5
1980	10,9	184	13,1
1981	11,5	165	12,4
1982	10,5	183	12,2
1983	11,2	195	11,1
1984	12,2	162	9,9
1985	11,6	145	10,4
1986	12,2	151	10,5
1987	11,4	159	9,1
1988	11,7	180	9,5

Nederburg Eminence Noble Late Harvest★★★★★D
The maiden vintage of this remarkable wine was the 1983. It was made from the historic White Muscadel grapes, known variously as Muscat de Frontignan (in France), Muscat Canelli (in California) and Gelber Muskateller (in Germany). The grapes were allowed to ripen to a raisin-like stage, yielding a very aromatic wine with luscious sweetness and magnificent Muscadel characteristics, totally free of botrytis. It has been produced regularly since. These later vintages show a little botrytis which adds to this fine and very attractive wine. The wine is an instant show-stopper at its pre-auction tastings and is sold only at the annual Nederburg Auction.

Vintage	Alcohol%	Sugar g/l	Acid g/l
1983	12,7	107	8,4
1984	13,2	109	7,4
1985	13,5	117	9,0
1986	13,8	101	8,1
1987	12,5	119	8,1
1988	12,5	112	7,7
1989	11,2	102	8,8

Nederburg Noble Late Harvest ★★★★C
Three vintages of this delightful wine were packed in 250 m*l* bottles with screw-tops. This is a super idea as the concentrated wine contained is an ideal amount to be shared by two. Since 1988 it has been produced in cork-closed 375 m*l* bottles.

Nederburg Riesling Edelkeur★★★★D
First produced in 1979, this wine has an alcohol content of 10,3%, acid 10,6 g/*l* and sugar 162,5 g/*l*. It has a fruit-filled nose combined with botrytis, and lovely mouth-filling flavour, well-balanced with good fruit acid. It is just for sipping and was released only at the annual Nederburg Auctions.

Nederburg Steen Noble Late Harvest★★★★(★)C
A truly great South African wine, this was first produced from the 1980 vintage, which was followed by the 1981 and 1982 vintages. It was one of the earliest wines to make use of the new Late Vintage epithet of 'noble', and is available only in limited supply. It has wonderful depth of complexity and lusciousness seldom achieved in a South African wine. It ages with great merit. The latest vintage is the 1986, which is truly magnificent.

Nederburg Weisser Riesling Noble Late Harvest★★★★★D
A distinctive wine showing clean cultivar characteristics. As with all the Nederburg Noble Late Harvests, this one is superb. It is released only at the annual Nederburg Auction.

Vintage	Alcohol%	Sugar g/*l*	Acid g/*l*
1986	13,4	139	11,8
1987	13,4	117	9,6
1989	10,0	131	10,3

Neethlingshof Rhine Riesling Noble Late Harvest★★★★★D
The first vintage from the 1990 won the General Smuts trophy for South African Champion wine at the 1990 SA Championship Young Wine Show. It is full of super citrusy and tropical fruit fragrances and flavours, all mingled with botrytis, and contains 166 g/*l* residual sugar. In 1991 the awards were reversed – the Rhine Riesling following the Sauvignon Blanc – but again a super wine.

Neethlingshof Sauvignon Blanc Noble Late Harvest★★★★D
To highlight the master's ability, this 1990 wine was the Reserve champion at the 1990 SA Championship Young Wine Show. It has a lot of sugar at 224 g/*l*, and a decidedly peachy nose with fruit salad flavours in the mouth. The 1991 SA Champion is packed with fruit and botrytis. It is a beautiful wine which should age with considerable interest.

Pick 'n Pay Noble Late Harvest★★★★D
Made under the masterful eye of Gunter Brözel in the Stellenzicht cellars from Rhine Riesling out of the 1991 vintage. South African Championship material. Super after-dinner sipping at 16,5 g/*l*.

Romansrivier Co-op Edel Laatoes★★★(★)B
A very good botrytis wine, made in 1984, from Steen. Well worth seeking out.

Roodezandt Co-op Le Grand Deluge Noble Late Harvest★★★E
A rich botrytis wine named in memory of the 1981 floods, which wrought havoc along the Breede River. Ironically, however, the floods also produced conditions conducive to noble rot, enabling this wine to be produced. It should be drunk now. The 1991 was produced 10 years after the deluge. It is rich, full wine, with botrytis and apricot flavours and packed in sensible 250 m*l* bottles.

Rooiberg Edel Laatoes★★★★C
My first introduction to this wine was from an amazing magnum – this kind of wine is usually bottled in 375 m*l* units. It was from the 1986 vintage and made from Muscat de Frontignan, which shows well, with complexity coming from some botrytis. It is not all that rich and has good acid balance. The 1988 and 1989 are lovely wines, the latter a blend of 60% Steen and 40% Rhine Riesling.

Saxenburg Noble Late Harvest★★★(★)D
A full, fruity-flavoured wine with good acid balance and most attractive nose. Now, from the 1990 vintage, comes a wine from three varieties: Chenin Blanc, Sauvignon Blanc and Weisser Riesling. It has a honeyed character with some botrytis. It was followed by an over-sweet 1991 of similar blend.

Simonsig Noble Late Harvest★★★★E
Once regular producers of very good Noble Late Harvest and now, after a long break, Simonsig has bottled 750 and 375 m*l* of 1990 vintage from Gewürztraminer. It is a stunning wine full of enticing aromas and wonderful flavours.

Simonsvlei Co-op Noble Late Harvest★★★★C
This was made from Bukettraube during the 1989 vintage and is one of the cellar's best-ever wines. It is full of fruit, spice and sweetness, and is well balanced with good acid.
Stellenzicht Noble Late Harvest★★★★E
Beautiful wine from 1991 made from Rhine Riesling with concentrated flavours, almost sweet-sour character, and clean fresh finish. It will develop well.
Van Loveren Noble Late Harvest★★★(★)B
A well-balanced, complex wine made predominantly from Weisser Riesling with a lesser amount of Steen from the 1985 vintage.
Vredendal Co-op Noble Late Harvest★★★★C
Out of the 1989 vintage from Steen comes a very good attempt. It is a soft wine with fruit salad flavours.
Weltevrede Noble Late Harvest★★★(★)C
The first release from the 1981 vintage was a most unusual wine with deep colour and good botrytis character. It had a low alcohol content and now needs to be drunk. The 1988 release from Muscat de Frontignan has 13% alcohol and about 100 g/*l* sugar. Its characteristics include good botrytis and nice fruit. It is developing well.
Woolworths Noble Late Harvest★★★★(★)
A delightful wine made by Klein Constantia for Woolworths out of the 1990 vintage from Sauvignon Blanc. The 120 g of sugar is well balanced with fresh fruit acid and good botrytis character. Nectar in 375 m*l* bottles!
Zonnebloem Noble Late Harvest (SFW)★★★★E
The most appealing pack contains a beautifully balanced, botrytis wine which is a departure in style for Cape Noble Late Harvests, and is more along the style of Bordeaux than of Germany. Light, fresh flavour led by inviting fruity aroma gives a wine which can be drunk and not simply sipped like most Noble Late Harvests. The 1983, in a gold pack, was made from Steen. The 1987, in a green pack, is certified Sauvignon Blanc. Overseas fundis believe this to be one of the Cape's best Noble Late Harvests and it is very much a five-star wine. The 1989 is again a gold label wine, made from Steen, and a lovely, luscious wine which is not quite up to the 1987 standard.

Müller-Thurgau

Uiterwyk Müller-Thurgau★★(★)B
An interesting first-release of Müller-Thurgau in the Cape, this delicate, dry wine with good potential came from the 1985 vintage. The 1986 was a good, dry white with attractive, fruity nose. The 1987 had good, fruity nose and fresh, zesty taste which is now toning down. The 1988 was a delightful off-dry wine with fruity, almost apple-like nose and very pleasing flavour. The 1989 was made along the same lines and is definitely at its best when young and fresh. The 1990 shows improved quality – it is nice and fruity, yet soft on the palate. The 1991 is fresh, off-dry wine best enjoyed in its youth.

Muscat Wines

Blaauwklippen Muscat Ottonel★★★B
This popular semi-sweet wine is most attractive and full of flavour. The 1991 appears drier, is low in alcohol, and drinks very easily.
Die Krans Muscat d'Alexandrie★★★(★)A
A delightful, semi-sweet wine with very pleasant nose and flavour. The 1991 is nice and fruity, with lots of cultivar character. This is one of the cellar's better natural wines.
Du Toitskloof Co-op Muscat d'Alexandrie★★★B
A very pleasant semi-sweet wine with good cultivar nose and pleasing flavour.
Eersterivier Co-op Muscat d'Alexandrie★★(★)B
A very good Muscat, unusual in that it is bone-dry, yet it still has all the attractive Muscat aromas and taste. Best when young.
Nederburg Muscat de Frontignan★★★(★)C
Sold only at the Nederburg Auction, this Late-Harvest-style wine has a most attractive, fine Muscat nose and seductive flavour. The last vintage to be released, the 1980, is a beautiful wine and was sold at the 1987 Nederburg Auction.
Pick 'n Pay Bouquet Blanc★★★B
Delightful wine, similar to Fragrance and produced by the same cellar – Stellenzicht. Enticing nose, off-dry, with fine Muscat flavour.
Soetwynboere Muscat d'Alexandrie★★A
A semi-sweet lightish wine from the 1991 vintage.
Spruitdrift Mario Muskaat★★(★)A
New from 1991, this is an off-dry wine with good floral nose and soft palate.
Stellenzicht Fragrance★★★C
A delightful light dry wine with most attractive Muscat nose. It contains less than 10% alcohol and is made from the table grape variety Erlihane which is a type of Hanepoot. Lovely, easy drinking.
Thelema Muscat de Frontignan★★★★B
A delightful, off-dry wine with a most attractive nose and good acid balance. Lovely, refreshing drink.

Natural Sweet

Avontuur Above Royalty★★(★)B
A sweet wine of nearly 60 g/*l* with citrus flavours. Named after one of the Estate's thoroughbred race horses.

Blaauwklippen Natural Sweet★★★B
With just over 50 g/*l* sugar and high alcohol of 13,7% this is an interesting first from the cellar in this new category, from the 1991 vintage. Good, fruity, clean, sweet wine.

Bovlei Co-op Natural Sweet★★A
This wine is not certified so it carries no vintage. It is very similar to this cellar's Special Late Harvest, and contains close to 50 g/*l* sugar but not much fruit acid. It is showing bottle age very early.

Dwarsrivier Cederberger (Cederberg Cellars)★★B
A full-flavoured Steen with lots of cultivar character, and some 75 g/*l* sugar.

Domein Doornkraal Kuierwyn Sweet Natural★★B
A lowish-alcohol wine and only 40 g/*l* sugar. A variety of grapes are used and it has pleasant Muscat nose.

Goudini Co-op K'Gou Dani★★★A
Using the Hottentot name for Goudini on this first entry into the new category from the 1991 vintage, this is a semi-sweet, honey-nosed wine from Steen with delicate flavours, in 250 m*l* bottles.

Loopspruit Goldenes Fest★★★B
This is one of the cellar's better products, made mainly from Steen, but with Muscat showing on the nose. It has a vague hint of botrytis, and nice, clean finish.

Nederburg Sauvignon Blanc Natural Sweet★★★★C
This is the first wine in this new category to be made at Nederburg. It is an elegant wine with good fruitiness and lovely flavours, free of botrytis. Alcohol is 12,2%. Residual sugar is 76 g/*l* and total acid is 6,6 g/*l*. It is in a class of its own in this category. Two-hundred cases of 12 x 375 ml were sold at the Nederburg Auction.

Overvaal Natural Sweet Table Wine (Vaalharts Co-op)★★B
This is non-vintaged wine from 1991, blended from Colombar and Chenel. It has an odd herby nose, but a pleasant soft flavour, and contains 40 g/*l* sugar and 6 g/*l* acid.

Vin de Constance Noble Late Harvest★★★★★E
When Duggie Jooste bought Klein Constantia in June 1980, it was his intention to endeavour to reproduce the great wines that made Constantia famous around the world in the 18th and 19th centuries. Muscat de Frontignan was planted specifically to try and reproduce the great wine. Five years since the first harvest and four years since Vin de Constance was put into wood, wine maker Ross Gower released the magnificent 1986 wine bottled in replica antique bottles. It contains 13,7% alcohol and 95 g/*l* residual sugar. A taste unreal. The next release, from 1987, is along the same lines.

Pinot Blanc

Landskroon Pinot Blanc★★B
From 1990 comes a light-flavoured dry white.
Van Loveren Pinot Blanc★★★B
Made from Pinot Blanc with some 20% Chardonnay blended into it and nicely oaked. Very good value for money and lovely drinking. Lots of flavour and will develop well over two to three years. High alcohol of almost 14%.
Nederburg Pinot Blanc★★★(★)C
From the 1989 vintage comes this easy-drinking, uncomplicated wine with attractive nose and pleasant flavour. Just off-dry but with enough acid to appear dryish. Lively on the palate with crisp, fresh finish. Lovely summer drinking wine at a very affordable price.

Pinot Gris

Buitenverwachting Pinot Gris Reserve★★★C
Wine from the 1989 vintage is still available. Lots of bottle age is its main interest.

Cederberg Cellars Pinot Gris★★(★)A
An off-dry white wine with a slightly perfumed nose and sweet, spicey flavour.

Drostdy-Hof Pinot Gris★★★B
Original release is fairly lacking in nose, but has a pleasant enough flavour. It is a dry wine that has a good, sharp, fresh finish. The 1990 is much better wine.

Fairview Pinot Gris★★★B
This is one of the better efforts with the cultivar, and is a bright, full-flavoured wine with a brisk finish.

Groot Eiland Co-op Pinot Gris★★★A
A dry white wine, with the first release from the 1990 vintage. It is pleasant-tasting, medium-bodied wine with some spice on the nose.

Landskroon Pinot Gris★★★B
First release from 1990 is dry and has an unusual flavour, almost like basil and thyme. A nice drink when chilled. The 1991 is on the price list, but has not been tasted.

L'Ormarins Pinot Gris★★★C
The first vintage (1985) gave a full-flavoured, off-dry wine with sufficient acid to make it taste drier. The second vintage (1986) has much the same chemical make-up with perhaps better flavours. The well-balanced 1987 was full of character. The dry 1988 was probably the best to date with good flavour and a hint of wood which made an easy-drinking wine. The 1989 has good flavour and is a nice drinking wine, as is the 1990. In keeping with the Estate's drive for extra quality, the grapes for this wine are picked at night in an endeavour to ensure more flavour in the cooler night temperatures.

Roodezandt Co-op Pinot Gris★★(★)B
The first release was from the 1989 vintage – a first for the Co-op. The 1990 has better flavour, fruitier nose and is a pleasant, gentle, dry wine. The 1991 is bigger, bolder wine, and an improvement on earlier vintages.

Spier Pinot Gris★★C
New from 1990, this is a light, dry white wine.

Uitkyk Pinot Gris★★★C
First release from the 1991 vintage comes in new-style packaging. It has a nice spicey flavour, a touch of wood, and has more body than most others.

Van Loveren Pinot Gris★★★B
The cellar's first release of this cultivar came from the 1986 vintage. With sugar content fractionally higher than that of L'Ormarins', it tasted considerably sweeter, probably because it had less flavour and possibly less acid. Nevertheless it was a pleasant off-dry wine which has developed well. The 1987 had far better cultivar character and is finished off-dry. The 1989 is a full-flavoured, well-wooded wine that makes very easy drinking. In blind tastings it has been mistaken for Chardonnay! The 1990 is bone-dry and has good flavour. The 1991 has massive 14,5% alcohol but is lacking in character. Hopefully this will develop with time.

Premier Grand Crû

Aan-de-Doorns Co-op Premier Grand Crû★★A
The composition of this wine has varied from vintage to vintage, but it is always dry with fresh, appealing nose when young.
Autumn Harvest Grand Crû (SFW)★★(★)A
A blended dry wine containing Colombar. Its good, vinous character and crisp freshness have made it a favourite of Grand Crû devotees and it is an award winner in international competitions.
Bakenskop Grand Crû (Jonkheer)★★A
A pleasant, fruity, dry blend of Colombar and Steen.
Beaufort Premier Grand Crû (Solly Kramer)★★A
An easy-drinking, dry *vin ordinaire*.
Bellingham Premier Grand Crû★★★B
The wine which gave South Africa the term 'Premier Grand Crû' more than 30 years ago. It has shown great variation of character over the decades. In line with Bellingham's entry into the top quality market, this wine has been vastly improved in character and consistency. Today it is blended from Riesling and Steen with a touch of Colombar to give good nose and flavour. It is good drinking wine.
Bovlei Co-op Grand Crû★★(★)A
An attractive, dry, refreshing wine.
Brandvlei Grand Crû★★A
An easy-drinking wine, dry yet soft, and with less acid than most.
Breughel Wines Grand Crû (Aroma Group)★★A
Light, easy, dry wine from Steen and Colombar.
Cellar Cask Premier Grand Crû★★A
A dry wine which is good value for money, and now available in cork-closed bottles.
Cellar Reserve Premier Grand Crû (Hyperama)★★A
Pleasant enough dry white wine.
Checkers Yellow Label Premier Grand Crû★★(★)B
Dry white wine with Colombar-Steen guava nose.
Culemborg Grand Crû★★A
A good-value-for-money, dry wine with good, fresh, fruity character.
De Doorns Co-op Grand Crû★★A
A dry blend of Steen and Colombar.
Drostdy-Hof Premier Grand Crû★★A
A pleasant, fruity, dry wine with more complexity than most.
Fleur Du Cap Premier Grand Crû★★★B
A good, Steen-based, crisp, dry wine, recent blends of which are being improved in complexity with Sauvignon Blanc.
Franschhoek Vallei Premier Grand Crû★★A
A blend of Sémillon, Steen and Riesling, giving a wine best drunk young to enjoy its youthful freshness. It is remarkably inexpensive.
Kellerprinz Grand Crû (SFW)★★(★)A
A sound, dry white with subtle flavour which makes a good quaffing wine. It is best enjoyed when young.
Klawer Co-op Grand Crû★★A
Always a pleasant, dry, inexpensive product. The blend varies from vintage to vintage.
Landzicht Premier Grand Crû★★A
This is predominantly Colombar, with some Hanepoot, and is pleasant when young.

Louwshoek-Voorsorg Co-op Premier Grand Crû★★A
The cellar's best seller. A dry blend based on Colombar and Steen, with some Clairette Blanche.
Lutzville Grand Crû★★★A
Screw-capped for low price, this is a nice dry wine from Steen and Colombar, which is good for early drinking.
Monterey Premier Grand Crû (Western Province Cellars)★A
A crisp, bone-dry, white wine.
Mooiuitsig Rusthof Premier Grand Crû★★A
A typical dry, Steen-Colombar blend touched out with some Muscat on the nose.
Nederburg Premier Grand Crû★★★(★)B
A delightfully light, crisp, dry wine showing that character *is* attainable in this style. The latest releases are outstanding wines. When well chilled, it is the ideal partner for oysters and other subtly flavoured seafoods.
Oranjerivier Wynkelders Premier Grand Crû★A
One of the better dry wines from these cellars. It shows good Colombar character.
Overmeer Premier Grand Crû★★A
Only in boxes, this is a crisp, quaffing wine which is good value.
Overvaal Grand Crû (Vaalharts Co-op)★A
A dry white with little character.
Porterville Co-op Grand Crû★★A
The dry blend varies but is usually Colombar and Steen. It is fruity when fresh.
Rebel Premier Grand Crû★A
A brisk, blended, dry white.
Riebeek Wine Farmers' Co-op Grand Crû★★A
One of the lighter-styled Premier Grand Crûs.
Romansrivier Co-op Grand Crû★★A
A pleasant, soft-drinking wine, blended from Steen, Colombar and Clairette Blanche.
Roodezandt Co-op Premier Grand Crû★★A
The latest releases are fresh and fruity when young.
Rooiberg Co-op Premier Grand Crû★★B
A dry white blend, full-bodied and bold.
Simondium Co-op Grand Cru★★A
New from 1991 is a big, strong Steen.
Simonsvlei Co-op Premier Grand Crû★★(★)A
Originally a light wine with a slightly fruity nose. The blend has varied over the years but is usually from Steen, and is generally a good, easy-drinking wine.
Slanghoek Co-op Premier Grand Crû★★A
This is a blend of a number of varieties, including Steen, Colombar and others. Recent vintages are possibly the most delicate of all the Premier Grand Crû wines from the Co-operatives.
Soetwynboere Co-op Grand Crû★★A
New in 1990, with vague Sauvignon Blanc character.
Spruitdrift Co-op Premier Grand Crû★★A
Recent vintages are dry, Steen-Colombar blends with good fruit and pleasant flavour. They are good value for money in screw-top bottles.
Swartland Co-op Premier Grand Crû★★(★)A
A surprisingly light, smooth wine, usually Steen-based but also

containing other varieties such as Clairette Blanche and Colombar. Always fruity, soft and dry across the palate. Easy drinking.

Valley Premier Grand Crû (Gilbeys)★★(★)A

A dry blend featuring Colombar, Sémillon and Steen, giving attractive nose as well as good fruit.

Van Loveren Premier Grand Crû★★★A

A very pleasant, light, dry blend of numerous cultivars, with a touch of Muscat on the nose, giving an above-average Premier Grand Crû.

Villiersdorp Co-op Grand Crû★★A

A bone-dry Grand Crû with nice fruity nose when young.

Vinovat Premier Grand Crû (Marcows)★A

A dry white *vin ordinaire.*

Vintner's Choice Premier Grand Crû (Drop Inn)★A

A pleasant, dry white wine with refreshing crispness.

Vlottenburg Co-op Premier Grand Crû★★A

A consistently reliable dry wine, the composition of which has varied slightly with each release.

Waboomsrivier Co-op Grand Crû★★A

New in 1990, this is a well-made, clean, dry wine with Muscat nose.

Wamakersvallei Co-op Premier Grand Crû★★★A

An unusually good Co-operative Premier Grand Crû, it is a light, uncomplicated blend with a pleasant flavour.

Welmoed Co-op Grand Crû★★(★)A

A good, clean, dry blend of mainly Steen and some Riesling, giving ample flavour and balance. This is another cellar to drop 'Premier' from its label.

Woolworths Premier Grand Crû★★B

From Gilbeys. A pleasant, fresh, easy-drinking, dry wine.

Zonnebloem Premier Grand Crû (SFW)★★★(★)B

It took many years before Zonnebloem joined the ranks of Premier Grand Crû producers, but when it did it was with an outstanding wine, full of flavour from the fruit of its Steen and Colombar blend. Delightful and refreshing when young, it ages with interest over two or three years. Latest releases are amazingly good quality for this category of wine.

Riesling – Cape

Aan-de-Doorns Co-op Riesling★★A
A good addition to the range from the 1988 vintage, with fruity nose and good, dry flavour. The 1990 and 1991 are fuller-bodied, but best when young.
Ashton Co-op Riesling★★A
Often features well on local young wine shows. Recent vintages offer delicate flavours and brisk finish.
Avontuur Cape Riesling★★★B
Unusual character, big full wine with lots of life. Best in its youth.
Badsberg Co-op Riesling★★A
This wine is dry and has fair cultivar character.
Bakenskop Riesling (Jonkheer)★★A
A fairly ordinary, dry white.
Barrydale Co-op Riesling★★(★)A
Usually fresh, fruity wine with good clean flavour.
Bellingham Franschhoek Riesling★★★B
A vast improvement on the old type of Bellingham Riesling. This is an off-dry wine with strong cultivar character. It drinks very well.
Bergsig Riesling★★★B
Regularly good, dry Riesling with softness on the palate. Good value, easy-drinking wine.
Bolandse Co-op Riesling★★★B
A regular gold medal winner at the regional shows and good value for money. It is best enjoyed when young. Recent vintages are fresh and fruity.
Bon Courage Riesling★★★B
A soundly made wine with good, fruity, Riesling character. Best enjoyed when young to savour its good, fresh flavour. Always an easy drinking wine.
Boschendal Riesling★★★C
Boschendal entered the wine-making industry in 1976 with some wines of rather dubious quality, so it is pleasing to see such a dramatic improvement in the products of this cellar. The Riesling has not been one of the Estate's fashionable wines, yet it is consistently very good. The current blends contain substantial amounts of Weisser Riesling. Recent releases are lovely wines and the addition of some Rhine Riesling gives considerably more complexity.
Botha Co-op Riesling★★B
A big, dry wine with good cultivar nose.
Bottelary Co-op Riesling★★★(★)B
This Co-operative has developed into a producer of good white wines, and the Riesling in particular has become a delightful wine with pleasing cultivar character. A friendly, easy-drinking wine, it was a regular award winner both regionally and nationally. Recent vintages are lighter-bodied, fresh and lively, and best enjoyed when young.
Bovlei Co-op Riesling★★A
Recent vintages have a full varietal nose, crisp finish and drink well when young.
Cape Vintners Members Only Riesling★★★B
Well-made dry wine from Welmoed, with good, brisk finish. Nice drinking wine.

Cederberg Kelders Cape Riesling★★A
A clean, fresh, easy-drinking dry wine.
De Leuwen Jagt Paarl Riesling★★★B
Good cultivar character, lots of fruit, soft in the mouth, crisp finish.
De Wet Co-op Cape Riesling★★★A
The first release came from the 1986 vintage. It is a regular class winner at the Worcester show, and is always good, easy-drinking wine. It is probably this cellar's best natural wine and best enjoyed when young.
Douglas Green Riesling★★(★)C
Although this is never one of the better wines from this merchant, recent releases have improved considerably. The latest vintages show more character and are soft, easy-drinking wines.
Du Toitskloof Co-op Riesling★★★B
The cellar has improved the quality of its white wines over recent years and its Riesling has become a regular award winner at the Worcester show. Recent vintages are soft, easy-drinking wines that are best enjoyed when young.
Edelkeller Riesling★★★B
Well-made Cape Riesling. Good, easy drinking.
Edward Snell Cape Riesling★★(★)B
A non-vintaged, fresh dry white with brisk finish. Best when young.
Eersterivier Valleise Co-op Riesling★★★B
This cellar consistently produces Rieslings of good value. Recent vintages are big, full wines with lots of flavour. Like most of the previous vintages, they should age well if left to develop over the next three to four years.
Fleur Du Cap Riesling (Bergkelder)★★★(★)C
A delightful Cape Riesling of sparkling, fresh fruitiness. Always good, occasionally superb, it develops well in the bottle. It is delightful when young, yet is one of the few Cape Rieslings that improves with age.
Franschhoek Vineyards Co-op Cape Riesling★★B
Light-bodied, well made, fresh, fruity dry white. Formerly bottled under the La Cotte label.
Goudini Co-op Riesling★★★A
This wine does well at local shows. It has good cultivar character and is bottled dry. Enjoy when young.
Goue Vallei Riesling (Citrusdal Co-op)★★★A
A good easy-drinking, fruity dry white.
Groot Eiland Co-op Riesling★★A
A pleasant, dry, medium-bodied wine.
Helderberg Co-op Cape Riesling★★A
Recent vintages are good, dry wines with fine, fruity, fresh finish. Best when young.
Huguenot Cape Riesling★★A
Nice, easy-drinking wine, best when young.
Kleindal Riesling★★★B
A good, dry, reliable wine with attractive cultivar character.
Koelenhof Co-op Riesling★★★B
Consistently good wine with definite cultivar nose, best enjoyed when young.
KWV Riesling★★★(no price available)
A consistent dry wine with somewhat delicate features. It is best

enjoyed when young and fresh, or after four to six years when it develops an unusually deep bottle-age character.

L'Ormarins Franschhoek Riesling★★★★C

A prolific gold medal winner, both regionally and nationally, this is a very well-made, big wine and one of the Cape's best representatives of the cultivar. The 1983 was labelled Cape Riesling; from 1986 on it is certified Franschhoek Riesling. The lovely 1989 is not quite dry. The 1990s are fresh, fruity, substantial wines – lovely when young, yet develop with a few years in the bottle.

Louwshoek-Voorsorg Co-op Riesling★A

A light, dry wine.

Mamreweg Co-op Riesling★★★A

Fruity, attractive wine, with good flavour and brisk finish. Best when young. Current production is a big improvement on the first release.

Merwespont Co-op Riesling★A

A dry white with reasonable cultivar character. Best when young.

Merwida Co-op Riesling★★A

A fairly consistent wine of pleasing style.

Nederburg Paarl Riesling★★★B

This is the successor to the wine which introduced South Africans to Rieslings of fine quality. It is usually characterized by a good varietal aroma and clean, dry finish. The various vintages are notably consistent: the firm Teutonic influence ensures a stable wine which ages with beautiful results. Always good, it has flowery nose, excellent varietal character and dry finish. Like all the Nederburg products, this is not a simple wine: it has good depth of character and, as excellent as it is on release, will age with interest for a couple of years, developing remarkable bottle bouquet.

Neethlingshof Riesling★★★C

Latest releases are clean, fresh, light-bodied wines.

Nuy Co-op Riesling★★★A

A consistently good dry wine with more complex nose than a lot of other Cape Rieslings. The 1991 is outstanding and will age with benefit. Excellent value for money.

Oude Rust Riesling (Mooiuitsig)★★A

Crisp, light, clean, easy-drinking wine.

Overhex Co-op Riesling★★B

Usually a pleasant, light, delicate dry wine, best enjoyed when young and fresh.

Perdeberg Co-op Riesling★★A

The 1990 was for early drinking. Now tired.

Riebeek Wine Farmers' Co-op Cape Riesling★★A

A good, dry wine with sound cultivar character.

Romansrivier Co-op Riesling★★(★)A

A medal-winning wine, recent vintages of which are showing very well. It is zesty, fresh and attractive, especially when young.

Roodezandt Co-op Cape Riesling★★A

This is fuller, fruity wine that makes good early drinking. The cellar offers them with a bit of age and have three vintages, but I still prefer the most recent.

Rooiberg Co-op Vinkrivier Riesling★★★(★)B

A Wine of Origin Vinkrivier, Rooiberg Riesling has good cultivar character and, because of its high acid content, ages into a most attractive wine.

Simonsig Riesling★★★B
Frans Malan, the owner of Simonsig, took the Wine and Spirit Board to court to defend his right to state '100% varietal' on his labels. He won his case and his Riesling was thus presented, but the law was subsequently changed, not allowing percentage contents to appear on labels. This law, however, changed in 1990 to permit more informative labelling. Recent vintages are dry and delicate and develop well in the bottle, as have previous vintages.
Simonsvlei Co-op Riesling★★(★)A
This light, dry wine with its good aroma has varied considerably over the years. Recent vintages are fresh and attractive, and make good early drinking.
Slanghoek Riesling★★A
Good dry wine with honest cultivar character, brisk finish, and regarded as pleasant, easy drinking.
Spier Riesling★★★B
Blended with 25% Rhine Riesling, this is good, well-flavoured dry white wine.
Spruitdrift Co-op Riesling★★A
The first release from 1991 is light bodied, fairly fruity dry wine.
Swartland Co-op Riesling★★★A
This is a wine that has improved over recent vintages. It is full-bodied, yet elegant, with good flavour and fresh finish. Best enjoyed while fairly young.
Theuniskraal Riesling★★★C
A South African Riesling of remarkably consistent quality – it is pleasant, dry and light.
Tulbagh Co-op Riesling★★A
Delicate, easy-drinking dry white.
Uiterwyk Riesling★★★B
This wine was consistently good during the 1980s and the 1990s continue the quality. It is dry, full-flavoured, with good style, and develops well in the bottle.
Uitkyk Riesling★★★C
A good, dry Riesling which has a subtle, sometimes elusive fragrance. It is best in the bloom of youth, but also ages with elegance. The vintages of the 1990s are fine, fresh, well-made wines, with good long finish.
Van Loveren Cape Riesling★★★B
A well-made, dry wine with good fruity nose and pleasant flavour. One of this cellar's lighter wines and best when young.
Vlottenburg Co-op Riesling★★★A
This is always a reliable dry white and frequent champion of the district. It has good varietal character and develops well, but it's also good for early consumption.
Waboomsrivier Co-op Riesling★★A
A dry wine which needs to be drunk early to appreciate its fullness and freshness.
Wellington Wynboere Co-op Riesling★★A
A light-style Riesling, fresh and fruity with brisk finish.
Welmoed Co-op Riesling★★★A
A regular award winner, this is a most attractive dry wine with delicate Riesling cultivar character. It is regularly one of the better Rieslings from the Co-operatives.

Weltevrede Cape Riesling★★★A
A dry, full-flavoured white wine that is one of this cellar's most attractive products and consistently one of the Cape's better wines from this cultivar.
Woolworths Cape Riesling★★★B
From Weltevrede. A good example of the cultivar which drinks well when young, although recent releases can develop with benefit.
Zonnebloem Riesling (SFW)★★★B
An easy-drinking, reliable dry wine with a touch of Sauvignon Blanc adding to the fruity nose. It develops with interest over a year or two in the bottle, but is best as a young, fresh wine.

Riesling – Emerald

Andalusia Emerald Riesling (Vaalharts Co-op)★★B
A fairly neutral off-dry white.
Roodezandt Co-op Emerald Riesling★★★A
This is an interesting dry wine from an unusual cultivar. It has good, fruity nose, firm flavour, and develops well in the bottle over a year. It doesn't keep much longer than that.

Riesling – Rhine/Weisser

Alphen De Gruchy Rhine Riesling★★★B
Part of the revamped Alphen range produced in the Kleine Zalze cellar from a wide range of vineyards in the Stellenbosch and Somerset West area. The first from the 1990 vintage was finished off-dry as is the 1991. There is good cultivar character with a touch of Gewürztraminer, making a delightful, good drinking wine.
Ashton Co-op Weisser Riesling★★★A
Consistently good semi-sweet white and regular prize winner.
Avontuur Weisser Riesling★★(★)B
First release from 1990 vintage was dry with a sharp finish. The 1991 is a better effort and drinks well.
Backsberg Rhine Riesling★★★(★)B
One of the easiest, pleasant-drinking Rhine Rieslings available at a good price and capable of developing in the bottle over a year or two.
Bergsig Weisser Riesling★★★B
The 1987 has aged into deep-flavoured intriguing wine in 1992. The 1990 and 1991 are lighter, off-dry wines with good flavour and clean finish. Probably at their best while young.
Blaauwklippen Rhine Riesling★★★B
This was first introduced in 1981 and became a regular award winner. The finish varies between just off-dry to dry. The latest releases are very attractive, with lovely bouquet and full flavour. The 1991 is finished just off-dry, is super wine and one of the best from this cultivar. It drinks well now and will develop well over two to three years, like the very good 1989.
Bon Courage Rhine Riesling★★★B
The 1987 was a most attractive off-dry wine of greatly improved quality and a local award winner. In 1992 it has developed beautifully, but now needs to be drunk. The 1988 was not released. The 1991 is fruity, off-dry and delightful when young.
Boschendal Rachelsfontein Rhine Riesling★★★(★)C
This was one of the wines launched in 1987 with the Estate's single-vineyard concept. Although it had only a little cultivar character at the time of the launch, a year later it developed much more flavour. The 1988 is a drier wine but has more cultivar character. It has developed a considerable richness, seldom found in Cape Rhine Rieslings. The 1989 and 1990 are showing good development while in the bottle.
Bottelary Weisser Riesling★★(★)B
This is usually one of the better Weisser Rieslings. The 1981 vintage was excellent, as was the 1984, although the 1983, 1986 and 1988 were also good. All developed well over two to three years. Recent vintages are off-dry, much lighter in style, and are best enjoyed in their youth.
Bovlei Ko-op Weisser Riesling★★(★)A
A full-flavoured off-dry wine for easy, early drinking.
Buitenverwachting Rhine Riesling★★★(★)C
The 1989 is a four-star wine with full flavour and lots of spice and fruit, all on a bone-dry background. The 1989 is still available and one of the Cape's best.
Cape Vintners Members Only Rhine Riesling★★★B
An easy-drinking, off-dry wine with attractive nose and fresh finish.

Chamonix Rhine Riesling★★B
An off-dry wine with somewhat faint cultivar character. The 1987 is showing some varietal character but lacks complexity and is beginning to show age.
Clairvaux Co-op Rhine Riesling★★B
The 1991 is bone-dry like the earlier vintages and best when young.
Danie de Wet Rhine Riesling★★★★C
This wine falls under Danie de Wet's own label and is not to be confused with his other wines marketed by the Bergkelder. This is a super-dry Rhine Riesling in the classical style, with lots of cultivar character. It is beautiful as a young wine but should develop with distinction over a couple of years. Unbelievably good value.
Danie de Wet Rhine Riesling Reserve★★★★C
Although labelled 'Reserve', this delightful fruity, sweetish, very Germanic wine is slightly cheaper than the dry Rhine Riesling without 'reserve'. Delicious, refreshing, invigorating wine with sweetish fruit flavours backed with a touch of botrytis. Good brisk, fresh finish. A chilled glass makes ideal 'elevenses'.
Delaire Weisser Riesling★★★★C
An attractive wine, fractionally off-dry, with good cultivar character that is developing well. The 1989 is delightful, has developed well over three years and will still go more. The 1990 ranks as one of the Cape's best: drier than before, with full cultivar character that will also develop well in the bottle. The 1991 continues the fine style.
Delheim Rhine Riesling★★★★B
A wine with a good history of being regularly one of the Cape's best Rhine Rieslings. The 1991 is excellent, with very complex nose and lots of layers of deep flavours. It is rich without being too sweet. Delicious wine.
De Wetshof Rhine Riesling★★★(★)C
First produced in 1981, this was a most impressive wine, as have been all vintages since.
Douglas Green Rhine Riesling★★★(★)C
A special release of the 1982 vintage was a delightful off-dry Superior. The 1983 was fuller and developed a distinct terpene nose within the year. Both wines developed with benefit and showed considerable complexity. They should now be drunk up. The 1984 is probably the best and has developed beautifully in the bottle. The 1986 carries Superior certification and is one of the best examples of the cultivar. A lighter wine, it is probably past its best now. The late 1980s were drier and not as attractive. The 1991 is big, rich, off-dry wine in much the same style as the mid-1980s.
Du Toitskloof Co-op Weisser Riesling★★(★)A
The first release, the 1989 vintage, came from very young vines. It is off-dry and has more Muscat character than real Weisser Riesling, and did well at local shows. The 1990 and 1991 are good, off-dry white wines.
Eersterivier Valleise Co-op Weisser Riesling★★★B
A pleasant example of this cultivar, finished off-dry, it makes good drinking wine, especially when young.
Fairview Weisser Riesling★★★A
Usually a slightly off-dry wine with aromatic nose and pleasant flavour that develops well in the bottle over a year or three. The 1991 is a lovely, aromatic off-dry wine.

Goue Vallei Weisser Riesling (Citrusdal Co-op)★★★A
The first release from the 1988 vintage was semi-sweet with good fruity nose. Since then it has improved vintage by vintage. In keeping with the cellar's determined effort to improve its quality and image, it has produced a lovely, fruity, semi-sweet wine with good flavour. The label depicts a gousblom. All the 1990s have been attractive wines at good-value prices.
Groot Constantia Weisser Riesling★★★★B
I thought this wine was first produced in 1977 and that it was the best example of Weisser Riesling yet made in the Cape. In 1987, however, I was given a 1976 to taste and now must accept that it was as good as the 1977. The wines were dry, yet full-bodied, and five-star material. The 1976 matured majestically. These earlier vintages aged magnificently over 10 or more years. Subsequent vintages were semi-sweet and pleasing, with the 1984 carrying Superior certification. The 1985 was a little subdued when released but showed very well three years later. I doubt very much that the recent wines will age as well over ten or more years, but over two to three years they have lovely cultivar character. In 1988, the 1986 showed very well. The 1987 and 1988 are very good examples with 1987 being selected by Alphen Wine of the Month Club as the best wine in its category. The 1989 is a super, off-dry Weisser Riesling, full of spice, fruit and a lovely penetrating flavour that will develop with great benefit. The 1990 continues the lovely off-dry style and full character. The 1991 is low in alcohol (under 11%) but has good acid and off-dry finish, with delightful nose and flavours. It is probably at its best when young and fresh.
Hartenberg Weisser Riesling★★★★B
A wine that seems to have got better vintage by vintage and nowadays finished off-dry with a hint of botrytis amongst the fruity, flowery aromas and good flavours. Each vintage appears to have the ability to age well over about four years.
Helderberg Co-op Weisser Riesling★★A
The 1990 and 1991 continue in the pleasant light off-dry, delicate style. Best within two years of age.
Kaapzicht Weisser Riesling★★★A
The first release, from the 1984 vintage, amounted to only 500 cases – a quantity produced most years. The 1989 is off-dry with good nose and fruity flavours. The next release will most probably be from the 1991 vintage.
Klein Constantia Rhine Riesling★★★★C
The 1986 is the first vintage released from this restored and expanded Estate. Each vintage released has had grand style and great complexity. The 1990 is stunning wine, finished off-dry and packed with deep rich flavours. These wines all develop remarkably well. Absolutely super wine and definitely Constantia at its best.
Koopmanskloof Rhine Riesling★★★C
First released from the 1984 vintage. The 1986 was released in numbered bottles carrying a neck label depicting *Erica mammosa* drawn by the Cape artist, Drexler Kyzer. Good, off-dry, pleasing wine with honest cultivar character. All develop good bottle-age.
KWV Weisser Riesling★★★(★)(no price available)
Consistently one of the Cape's better wines from this cultivar, it is finished off-dry and develops good bottle character over the years.

La Bri Weisser La Bri★★★C
First release of this attractive wine came from the 1986 vintage. It is very pleasant and easy drinking. It is marketed in an eye-catching pack, similar to that of German wines, but which fairly and boldly states on the front label 'Wine of Origin Franschhoek'. It has improved vintage by vintage, with the 1991 a decided step-up in overall quality, and should develop well over two to three years.
Lebensraum Weisser Riesling★★(★)B
The first release, from the 1987 vintage, is off-dry and has good cultivar character. The 1989 is considerably better and is also off-dry. Both are developing with interest. No release since.
Lievland Weisser Riesling★★★★B
A well-made, off-dry wine with good cultivar character, the 1986 was tremendous and recognized at the Wine Olympiad in Paris. The extremely pungent terpene nose of this extraordinary wine developed remarkable intensity – to the dislike of some people and the delight of others. The 1988 is a full-bodied and flavoured off-dry wine, packed with a complexity that has developed with benefit over the years. The 1989 is lighter than usual but a delightful product. Apparently drier, it has lots of fine flavour and good spicy-citrus nose. Tank samples of the 1990, 1991 and 1992 show wines well worth waiting for. Continually one of the Cape's more unusual but better Rhine Rieslings.
L'Ormarins Rhine Riesling★★★(★)C
This is an award-winning wine which develops well in the bottle. The 1986 was off-dry and a fine example of the fullness of flavour this cultivar can produce. The 1988, 1989 and 1990 are along the same lines with good fruit and fine flavour. They will develop well over two to four years. No 1991 release.
McGregor Co-op Rhine Riesling★★A
The 1990 is a semi-sweet with attractive nose and pleasant flavour.
Mon Don Rhine Riesling★★★B
Clean, fruity, well made, off-dry, easy-drinking wine with first release from 1991 vintage.
Montpellier Gleno Selection Rhine Riesling★★★B
Named after a section of the farm, this off-dry wine is light in style and has attractive nose.
Montpellier Tuinwingerd★★A
The wine is simply labelled Tuinwingerd with no mention of the cultivar. There is no doubt, however, that this wine is made from Weisser Riesling. The 1989 is light, off-dry and better than usual.
Morgenhof Rhine Riesling★★★B/C
The 1991 is big, full-flavoured wine with high alcohol that might age well. The first release, from the 1987 vintage, was off-dry but with such high acid that it needed years to soften. The 1988 and 1989 has developed good terpene but is now a little tired. The 1989 and 1990 are firm, fuller, fruity wines.
Nederburg Elgin Weisser Riesling★★★★D
Released from 1990 vintage under the cellar's 'Limited Vintage' label from grapes grown in the cooler Elgin area. This is lovely wine, full of enticing aromas and deep layers of flavour. It is good when young but should develop in the bottle over two to three years.
Nederburg Rhine Riesling★★★★B
A welcome addition (in 1981) to the cellar's range, this wine has

been tremendously successful in terms of public acceptance, awards and Superior certification. It was winner of the 1983 Diners Club award, and is a regular carrier of Superior certification. The 1988 was selected for SAA in 1989. An off-dry, well-flavoured wine with good cultivar character, it has enough acid to be attractive when young, yet is able to age with benefit. Vintages of the early 1990s show even better vinous qualities, and this high quality for wine produced in this quantity is remarkable. Excellent value for money.

Nederburg Weisser Riesling★★★★C

This occasionally appears on the Nederburg Auction, and is very different to the regular range wine. Decidedly dry, full of good nose and flavour, it ages with great benefit over five years.

Neethlingshof Rhine Riesling★★★(★)C

Consistently one of the Estate's better wines. The 1990 and 1991 are well-balanced, well made, off-dry wines that will repay two or three years in the bottle.

Neil Ellis Rhine Riesling★★★★C

The first release from the 1986 vintage was a very good example of this cultivar in a dry style. It has developed very well. The 1987 is off-dry and was drinking earlier and more easily than the previous vintage. The 1988 has a good character intensity in line with previous releases, and is also not quite dry. The 1989 is much drier, but just as good. Each release has developed well in the bottle. Wine is no longer bottled under this label.

Onverwacht Weisser Riesling★★B

The 1991 is better than earlier vintages. It is finished off-dry, and is pleasant, lightly flavoured wine.

Rhebokskloof Weisser Riesling★★★★B

First release from 1991 vintage is a delightfully fragrant wine finished off-dry. This is an excellent start with this cultivar for this relatively new cellar. The 1992 is a good follow-up.

Riebeek Wine Farmers' Co-op Weisser Riesling★★★A

Recent vintages are somewhat toned down compared to those of the late 1980s. Off-dry, pleasant flavoured wines, for early drinking.

Rietvallei Estate Rhine Riesling★★★C

A dry, fruity wine with good cultivar character and fresh finish.

Rooiberg Co-op Rhine Riesling★★A

This was a dry wine with good cultivar nose and full flavour, but, with the change of name from Weisser to Rhine, it has become off-dry. Despite this, the wines of the early 1990s have a relatively hard finish.

Ruiterbosch Mountain Cuvée-Rhine Riesling★★★(★)C

First release from 1989 vintage is dry and has developed well by early 1992. The 1990 is off-dry but with the same depth of fruit and flavour. The 1991 tank sample shows developing potential.

Simonsig Weisser Riesling★★★★B

Weisser Riesling has become one of the specialities of this Estate. It appeared for the first time with the 1977 vintage and was sold as a rare wine at the 1978 Nederburg Auction. It has developed with subsequent vintages – the 1979 had a good, distinct, spicey nose and slightly sweet, medium body, and aged well. It used to be available as a dry or semi-sweet wine. The latter accumulated a number of Superior certifications and had a good varietal nose followed by complex taste. It has now been discontinued. The dry was certified

Superior in 1983 while both sweet and dry versions, from the 1985 vintage, carried Superior certification. The 1983 won a gold medal at the Club Oenologique International Wine and Spirit Competition in 1985. It developed beautifully in the bottle. The 1984 (dry) was Superior and featured at the 1987 Nederburg Auction. The 1983 and the 1985 (dry) featured at the 1988 Nederburg Auction. The 1986 and 1987 vintages are both Superior. The 1988 is not as big as 1987 but has developed well. The 1989 continued the high quality style with 1990 particularly full-flavoured and fruity. These are most attractive wines that age with benefit and some of the Cape's best.

Simonsvlei Co-op Rhine Riesling★★★B

An off-dry wine with fine flavour and good cultivar nose. Excellent value for money.

Spier Weisser Riesling★★★B

From the 1989 vintage. This wine is showing some age, but has developed flavours that are very pleasant.

Stellenryck Collection Rhine Riesling (Bergkelder)★★★★C

An excellent example of this cultivar with the typically flowery yet spicey nose which distinguishes the Rhine Riesling grape. These old vintages are all developing amazingly well in the bottle, but reaching the time that they should be drunk up. No recent bottlings.

Stellenzicht Vineyards Rhine Riesling★★★C

First release from 1989 vintage has developed beautifully. The 1990 is full of varietal character, as is the 1991. Fine, off-dry, elegant wines that are super when young, but have the potential to develop well over two to three years.

Thelema Rhine Riesling★★★(★)B

The first release, from the 1988 vintage, was an excellent start. It was only fractionally off-dry and full of attractive cultivar character. It drank delightfully while fresh and zesty, and has aged with benefit. The 1989 is most attractive with full flavour, good cultivar and distinct classy style. The 1990 is as near to dry as can be. The 1991 is well made, well-balanced, off-dry wine. These are lovely wines that develop well but are very good drinking when young.

Uiterwyk Rhine Riesling★★(★)B

Originally a good, brisk, dry wine, with later vintages slightly off-dry. Clean wines with good cultivar character.

Van Loveren Rhine Riesling★★★B

A fuller-bodied wine than most made from this cultivar, and finished off-dry. The 1987 has developed beautifully and in early 1992 is delicious wine. The early 1990s are all good.

Villiera Rhine Riesling★★★★B

This wine has improved over the years: the later vintages are delightfully dry, full and fragrant. The 1984 was a winner at the 1988 Paris Wine Olympiad. The 1985 was particularly good and has developed beautifully in the bottle. The 1987 is a delightful, off-dry wine and still ageing well. The 1988, 1989 and 1990 are finished dry and are superb wines that are developing with distinction. The 1991 is off-dry and this adds to the complexity of the wine, which should develop with great distinction. The cellar is firmly established as one of the most consistent producers of fine wines from this cultivar.

Vlottenburg Co-op Weisser Riesling★★★A

This is a consistently good, off-dry wine with attractive nose and true cultivar character.

Welmoed Co-op Weisser Riesling★★★A
This is another very good wine which celebrated its maiden vintage in 1981. Modern vintages are off-dry, fruity wines that generally make good drinking.

Weltevrede Rhine Riesling★★★★A
This is an off-dry wine with good nose, touched out with a hint of botrytis which lends added attraction. The Superior 1985 developed beautifully over four to five years. The 1989 is fresh, fruity, off-dry wine with good cultivar character and was an Alphen Wine of the Month selection. The 1990 is almost dry, lovely wine. The 1991 was not as attractive when young, but it is developing well. This wine is established as consistently one of the best of the area.

Woolworths Rhine Riesling★★★★B
This is delightful as a young wine, and has the potential to develop in the bottle. It is a consistently good example of this cultivar finished off-dry, from the specialist Rhine Riesling producers, Simonsig.

Zandwijk Weisser Riesling★★C
The first release, from the 1989 vintage, is a somewhat neutral, off-dry wine. Considering that to make kosher wine the wine maker has to pasteurize the fresh juice before fermentation, the result is surprisingly acceptable. The 1990 is finished dry.

Zevenwacht Rhine Riesling★★★(★)B
A delightful wine with excellent nose and fresh, off-dry taste. It fully deserves its Superior rating. The 1985 and 1986 have been made dry and have taken time to show their best. The Superior 1985 was selected for the 1988 Nederburg Auction. The 1987 is off-dry and has the potential to develop over four or more years. The attractive 1989 is full of flavour and only just off-dry. The 1990 is the best release to date. One of the cellar's best products, it will develop well. To date, there has been no 1991 release.

Zonnebloem Rhine Riesling (SFW)★★★C
Limited quantities were released from the 1984 and 1985 vintages. Both were pleasant, off-dry wines but neither were great examples of the cultivar. Now a regular member of the range in an off-dry form, this is a reliable wine with good cultivar character. The recent vintages are good examples of well-made, true-to-cultivar wines with no dramatics.

Sauvignon Blanc

Aan-de-Doorns Co-op Sauvignon Blanc★★B
Light-flavoured, smooth, dry wine that makes pleasant drinking.
Aan de Wagenweg Blanc Fumé (Bergkelder)★★★★E
Produced in very small quantities. The first release came from the 1989 vintage and was launched early in 1990. This wine was made from grapes grown in the Stellenbosch district and was aged for six months in small oak and then in the bottle for another six months before release. It is pale in colour with good varietal nose backed by nice oak. The 1990 was the next release but there has been nothing since. The wines should develop well in the bottle through to the mid-1990s.
Alphen Le Fevre★★★★B
First release from 1990 vintage as part of the revamped Alphen range was produced in the Kleine Zalze Winery from grapes grown in Stellenbosch and the Somerset West area. Part of the blend is wood-fermented producing fine, well-flavoured wine that has been successful in tastings including the SAA selection. Good wine.
Altydgedacht Estate Sauvignon Blanc★★★B
The Estate introduced this wine to their range from the 1988 vintage. There was no 1989 vintage, but the 1990 is a good, grassy, unwooded wine with fine brisk finish, as is the 1991.
Arthur Freedburg Selection Sauvignon Blanc (Rebel)★★★B
Well-balanced, steely, dry white with good cultivar character.
Avontuur Sauvignon Blanc★★(★)C
A dry, wood-fermented wine with attractive nose and flavour though, while young, not showing much cultivar character.
Backsberg John Martin★★★★C
A wine made from Sauvignon Blanc and named after the Estate's late administrator, bottling man and even wine maker on occasion – indisputably a character and persuasive salesman. John was always against wood-aged or wood-treated white wine and Sydney Back quirkily named this wood-fermented and further wood-aged wine after him. It appears that John had no choice but to learn to appreciate this massive, full-flavoured, complex wine. The first release, from the 1985 vintage, was a stunning wine at the time. It has aged with great interest and in 1992 is still full of life. The 1986 was much the same, while the 1987 was as good but has developed far greater complexity much sooner. The 1988 is great, but worth waiting for for a few years to allow full potential to develop. The 1989 is not quite in style, but the 1990 is really super and developing well. The 1991 will be a stunner. Although there is no mention of the cultivar on the gold and black label, this wine has been included in this section as it is obviously Sauvignon Blanc. On top of all of this, it's excellent value for money.

85 ★★★★ drink. **86** ★★★★(★) ready. **87** ★★★★ drink. **88** ★★★★(★) ready. **89** ★★★(★) ready. **90** ★★★★ ready, will still develop. **91** ★★★★(★) ready, will still develop.

Backsberg Sauvignon Blanc★★★(★)B
This dry, medium-bodied wine with good varietal character was one of the earliest, if not the first, of the modern string of wines made from this cultivar. It was the South African white wine champion at the South African Championship Wine Show in 1982 and the re-

gional champion white in 1984. The amount of wood treatment has varied over the years but the experience gained shows in the 1985 release, which is probably one of South Africa's best examples of this cultivar, and it deserved five stars. The 1986 has pleasant nose and attractive flavour. The 1987 was a good dry white but lacked a little in cultivar character. The 1988 has more to offer and drank very easily when young. The unwooded 1989 is full of cultivar character and is a lovely wine, as are the 1990 and 1991.

82 ★★★★ past its best. **83** ★★★★ drink. **84** ★★★★ drink. **85** ★★★★★ drink. **86** ★★★(★) drink. **87** ★★★ drink. **88** ★★★(★) drink. **89** ★★★(★) ready. **90** ★★★(★) ready. **91** ★★★(★) ready. **92** ★★★ ready.

Badsberg Co-op Sauvignon Blanc★★A
The first release from the 1989 vintage is a pleasant enough example of this variety; subsequent vintages show an improvement. Unlike other wines of the cellar, it is closed with a cork and not a screw-top.

Bakenskop Sauvignon Blanc (Jonkheer)★A
A dry, white wine with very little cultivar character.

Barrydale Blanc Fumé★★★B/C
The 1991, made from Tradouw Valley grapes, has good cultivar character and a touch of oak background.

Barrydale Co-op Sauvignon Blanc★★B
The first release from the 1988 vintage was a fraction off-dry with very faint nose but pleasant enough taste. The 1989 is a massive wine with lots of flavour and alcohol. It is much better than the first release. The 1991 vintages are clean, fresh, well-made wines.

Bellingham Blanc Fumé★★★B/C
A new wine to this cellar from the 1991 vintage of which about 20% spent some time in small oak. It is big wine with lots of cultivar character and fresh finish. I look forward to future releases.

Bergsig Sauvignon Blanc★★B
The 1987 lacked the sharpness of the 1986 but it still made pleasant drinking and was best enjoyed while young. The same goes for the 1988 which was very light in character but made pleasant, youthful drinking. The 1989 is much the same. There was no release in 1990 but 1991 is a light, soft wine for early drinking.

Blaauwklippen Sauvignon Blanc★★★(★)B
This is consistently good wine, with the 1991 outstanding – the best since the first release from 1982 vintage: dry, full flavoured, lots of cultivar character and without any oak influence. It drinks well now but has plenty of potential for ageing.

Bloemendal Estate Sauvignon Blanc★★★(★)B
The original vintage from 1987 was a very light character wine. Since then, each vintage has shown improvement with the 1991 being full-flavoured dry wine with fig and grassy characters. The 1992 tank samples are encouraging. Good-value wine.

Bolandse Co-op Sauvignon Blanc★★B
This first and very creditable release from the 1985 vintage was dry and had a touch of wood highlighting the cultivar character. Following vintages were decidedly odd, but 1991 is lovely crisp, clean, unwooded dry wine, worthy of three stars.

Bon Courage Sauvignon Blanc★★★B
After skipping a few vintages, a fresh, clean release came from 1991. It has flowery nose and distinct asparagus flavour.

Boplaas Blanc Fumé★★★B
The 1990, 1991 and 1992 are pleasant, easy-drinking wines with good but light oak backing.
Boplaas Sauvignon Blanc★★★B
This is a nice, fresh wine with good cultivar character of a grassy style. It is an easy-drinking wine which is good value for money. From 1992 comes a crisp, fresh, good cultivar.
Boschendal Sauvignon Blanc★★★(★)C
The 1987 is an unwooded wine which was launched with the concept of making separate wines from individual vineyards. This release, from the Pierre Simon Vineyard, is a wine that develops well over two years in the bottle. The 1990 is a bone-dry, unwooded, flinty-type wine with a brisk finish. The 1991 reflects the quality of the vintage for this cultivar and is much better than earlier vintages; a touch of wood adds extra complexity – a four-star wine.
Bottelary Co-op Sauvignon Blanc★★★B
The first bottling, in 1982, showed plenty of promise, confirmed by numerous awards at the Stellenbosch show, as well as at regional and bottled wine shows. The wines have a continuity of style, with a lovely fresh character that is best enjoyed when young.
Bouchard Finlayson Sauvignon Blanc★★★C
First release from the new cellar in the Hemel en Aarde Valley, Walker Bay, made from grapes grown at Bot Rivier in 1991. This creditable start offers gentle, soft, unwooded dry wine.
Bovlei Co-op Sauvignon Blanc★(★)A
Although considerable variation vintage by vintage, this wine is usually big-bodied, bold, and better in its youth.
Buitenverwachting Blanc Fumé★★★★D
The 1986 vintage produced only 8 000 bottles of this beautiful wine. Big, rich and complex when launched, it has developed beautifully. The 1987 has been fermented and aged in good French oak, and is proving to be even better than the 1986. The 1988 is made from high-sugar, almost Late-Harvest grapes. It is a big, complex wine without the charm of the 1987. The 1989 is also a beautiful, complex wine which is full of cultivar character and highlighted by good wood. It is developing with great benefit. The 1990 and 1991 continue in impressive style. It is well worth ageing this wine to develop its full complexity.
Buitenverwachting Sauvignon Blanc★★★★D
The 1988 shows a change in style for the better. It has good cultivar nose with lots of penetrating clean flavour. It tasted very good on release and with time has developed into a fine drinking wine. The 1989 is bigger in all respects – nose, flavour, and alcohol – with a tremendous intensity of cultivar character. The 1990 is another fine wine, but the 1991 is outstanding – this big, mouth-filling wine must be one of South Africa's best.
Cape Vintners Members Only Blanc Fume★★★C
A blend of 70% wooded and 30% unwooded Sauvignon Blanc from Welmoed out of 1991 vintage. Satisfying, good drinking wine.
Cape Vintners Members Only Sauvignon Blanc★★★B
A full-flavoured, unwooded Sauvignon Blanc from Welmoed. Attractive nose, good flavour, brisk finish.
Cederberg Kelders Sauvignon Blanc★★★B
The best wine from this remote cellar. It has good, fruity nose,

good-flavoured taste and makes pleasant drinking. Recent vintages have good steely touch, good fruit and brisk finish.

Danie de Wet Sauvignon Blanc★★★(★)B

Although made by Danie de Wet, this range is not to be confused with the De Wetshof range marketed by the Bergkelder. The 1991 is well made, lovely, dry, fresh, fruity wine.

De Doorns Co-op Sauvignon Blanc★A

This cellar produces an off-dry wine that is unmistakably Sauvignon Blanc and needs a year to soften.

Delaire Blanc Fumé★★★★C

Consistently good dry wines with complex character that develops well with time.

Delaire Sauvignon Blanc★★★(★)B

Good, clean cultivar character that develops well in the bottle, yet still a nice, easy drink when young.

Delheim Blanc Fumé★★★(★)B

An ever-improving wine with 1991 partially fermented in French oak, making it more complex than previous vintages. The 1991 is a four-star wine; good drinking now with the potential to benefit with time in the bottle.

De Wet Co-op Sauvignon Blanc★★A

A dry and light-bodied wine with pleasant but sharp cultivar character. It softens after about a year in the bottle. The 1991 has a hefty 13,5% alcohol.

De Wetshof Blanc Fumé★★★(★)B

A delightfully different South African white wine: big in structure, it commands attention with a very definite character and style, although it is undeniably a Sauvignon Blanc. The more recent vintages are particularly appealing. This wine is very different from the Sauvignon Blancs of Constantia, Stellenbosch or Franschhoek.

Die Krans Sauvignon Blanc★★★A

The first release from the 1990 vintage is a very good effort. It has a nice gooseberry character which has developed over the year, and the palate has softened. The 1991 is fuller flavoured with long finish.

Dieu Donné Sauvignon Blanc★★(★)B

The 1990 is a great improvement on previous wines and is a big, high-alcohol wine. No 1991 release.

Douglas Green Sauvignon Blanc★★★C

The 1990 vintage, released in the ranges new livery, has spent three months in new French oak. Easy-drinking wine.

Du Toitskloof Co-op Sauvignon Blanc★★(★)B

Consistently good, gentle wines that are at their best in their youth.

Edelkeller Sauvignon Blanc (Marcows)★★★B

Well made, good cultivar wine, dry on the palate, fresh finish.

Edward Snell Sauvignon Blanc★★★B

A non-vintaged, good dry cultivar character in the grassy style.

Eersterivier Valleise Co-op Sauvignon Blanc★★★A

The surprise of 1984 must have been wine maker Manie Rossouw's Diners Club Award for this Sauvignon Blanc. It was a good dry wine with true Sauvignon Blanc cultivar character. The 1985 had attractive cultivar nose and good flavour, and the 1986 was a gold medal winner at the Stellenbosch show. In 1987 I said I preferred these wines when they are young. If, however, they age as well as the 1984, which was at the 1988 Nederburg Auction, then it is worth keeping a few bottles for four years. The 1984 has developed a magnificence difficult to believe unless experienced. The 1988 had big pungent cultivar character that has developed well with time. Seventy cases were selected for the 1991 Nederburg Auction. The 1989 seems to have suffered along with many others with the vintage, but this could be one of the better efforts. The 1990 is very good and developing well in the bottle. The 1991 was great as a young wine, but seems to be going through a dip in early 1992 – hopefully it will recover and develop as well as the earlier vintages.

Eikendal Sauvignon Blanc★★★(★)B

This cellar is producing better and better wine. The Sauvignon Blanc has settled into good substantial style with full body, distinctive nose and an easy drinkability.

Fairview Sauvignon Blanc Fumé★★★B

The first release, from the 1989 vintage, is a good combination of wood and cultivar. Actually wood-fermented, it is dry and has good potential. Nothing since 1989.

Fleur Du Cap Blanc Fumé (Bergkelder)★★★(★)C

The 1987 is big, serious, bone-dry, well-wooded wine full of cultivar and complexity. It is developing well in the bottle. It is packaged in the new style similar to the Chardonnay. The 1989 is very good considering the generally poor year for Sauvignon Blanc. The 1990 is a good, clean cultivar with a nice oak backing, and is developing well in the bottle.

Goedvertrouw Estate Sauvignon Blanc★★★

First release from this new Botrivier cellar from 1991 vintage. Good, fruity, unwooded, dry white with pale cultivar character and clean, fresh finish.

Goue Vallei Sauvignon Blanc (Citrusdal Co-op)★★A

Each vintage is a good example of clean cultivar character.

Groot Constantia Sauvignon Blanc★★★(★)B/C

Ten years since 1982 saw first release, this wine has varied in type, style and quality. The 1987 was outstanding and is still a fine wine. From 1989 the wines have settled into a consistent style: big, full, unwooded, generous wine, which is exciting when young, but with every potential to age.

Hamilton Russell Vineyards Sauvignon Blanc★★★★D

Originally marketed under the Grand Vin Blanc label, this is now a good representative of a well-wooded Sauvignon Blanc, with the 1983 vintage being a more complex wine than the 1982. The 1984 is a lovely, light, dry example of the cultivar, while the 1985 was the best to date when released, although the 1986 proved to be even better. Forty per cent of this vintage spent three months in small French oak, giving a complexity which is developing with time. The 1987 is yet another improvement in a very good year for Sauvignon Blanc. The vines, which were between six and nine years of age, yielded very good fruit and a wine, rare both in quality and quantity, of which only 1 500 bottles were produced. The 1988 reflects the vintage, yet it is still one of the best, with good fruit flavour but no wood. The 1989 is lovely wine but not quite up to the standard of the 1988. The 1990 is very good and will develop well. The 1991 could well be the best to date, and a beautiful wine which will develop with great distinction – one of the Cape's best. Cellar samples of 1992 show consistency.

82 ★★★★ ready. **83** ★★★★ ready. **84** ★★★★ ready. **85** ★★★★★ ready. **86** ★★★★★ ready. **87** ★★★★★ ready, will still improve. **88** ★★★★(★) ready, will still improve. **89** ★★★★ ready. **90** ★★★★ ready, will improve. **91** ★★★★(★) ready, will improve **92** ★★★★ ready, will still improve.

Hartenberg Sauvignon Blanc★★★C

The wine from the 1987 vintage had good cultivar character, but rather hard acidic finish, which softened with age. The 1988 is better. The 1989 is very good – it has lots of complex character and is ageing with benefit. The 1990 is very attractive and will probably improve in the bottle, although it is not quite up to the 1989. The 1991 is big in every way and the 1992 shows promise.

Haute Provence Blanc Fumé★★★C

The first release, from the 1989 vintage, was a very good effort with the cultivar character marrying well with the wood. The 1990 is not quite as good, but very acceptable, while the 1991 is disappointing for a year so good (in general) for Sauvignon Blanc.

Hazendal Blanc Fumé ★★★C

The first release from the 1989 vintage is fairly ordinary, but the 1990 is much better, with good cultivar character and a much brisker feel. The 1991 should be even better.

Helderberg Co-op Sauvignon Blanc★★A

The wines of the 1990s are good, clean, refreshing wines, best enjoyed in their youth. The 500 m*l* bottle is a very good idea.

Kaapzicht Estate Sauvignon Blanc★★★(★)B

A very good value for money wine. The 1991 has fine cultivar character and is full of rich aromas and flavours.

Kango Co-op Sauvignon Blanc★A

A dry, simple wine with very little cultivar character.

Klawer Co-op Sauvignon Blanc★★A

A soft, well-rounded wine in which the cultivar character is recognizable but certainly not a great feature.

Klein Constantia Sauvignon Blanc★★★★★D

New Zealand is supposed to be making the best Sauvignon Blancs in the world and Ross Gower, the wine maker at Klein Constantia, spent a few years working there after leaving Nederburg. No doubt the experience he gained, together with the magnificent fruit from this Estate, has enabled this talented man to produce such a tremendous Sauvignon Blanc. Like so many South African wines of great character, it has a high alcohol content of almost 13% and is undoubtedly one of the Cape's great wines. The wine which won the white wine championship at the 1986 Young Wine Show was also a Sauvignon Blanc from this same cellar but it has been kept for special releases, for example, the New World Wine Auction. Neither wine has had any wood-ageing as the wine maker believes that wood would detract from rather than enhance it. There was no bottling of the 1987 vintage as it was not considered up to standard and it was blended into the Blanc de Blanc. The 1988 is an even bigger wine than the 1986. It has astonishing character and will develop well over four to five years. The 1989 and 1990 continue with the great quality. The 1989, tested by British critics in the United Kingdom in 1990, was rated above the same vintage of the fabled New Zealand Cloudy Bay Sauvignon Blanc. The 1991 reflects the quality of vintage better than almost any other cellar.

Kleindal Sauvignon Blanc★★★B
A well-made dry wine with good cultivar character. The 1991 is very good wine.
Koelenhof Co-op Sauvignon Blanc★★★C
A big, dry white, with reasonable fruit and well-balanced acidity.
Koopmanskloof Marbonne Sauvignon Blanc★★★C
This new release drops the Blanc and is certified Sauvignon Blanc. It has a good asparagus flavour and a dry, flinty finish.
KWV Sauvignon Blanc★★★(no price available)
Until the 1988 vintage the wines were very lacking in cultivar character. From then on, there was a great improvement with good nose and pleasant taste. It is now a regular, good quality wine.
La Bri Sauvage de La Bri★★★(★)C
The 1987 release was outstanding. Made at the Franschhoek Vineyards Co-op from grapes grown by Michael Trull at La Bri, this wine has intense character on the nose and full-flavoured palate. Sauvage de La Bri must be the most outstanding wine to have ever come out of this Co-op. The 1988 is also good, but the 1989 is not quite up to scratch. It is better, however, than many wines produced during what was a poor year for this cultivar. The 1990 is an improvement and is developing well. The 1991 is a good four-star wine with lots of fruit, good palate and long, fresh finish.
La Cotte Sauvignon Blanc (Franschhoek Vineyards)★★(★)B
The first release, from the 1983 vintage, was an excellent wine when young. Subsequent vintages have not been quite as arresting, but the 1990, 1991 and 1992 are much better wines.
La Couronne Blanc Fume★★★C
First release from the 1991 vintage. High alcohol. This is a barrel-fermented wine, strongly flavoured with lots of oak.
La Couronne Sauvignon Blanc★★★B
This unwooded wine was first released with the 1989 vintage; it has good cultivar character and fruitiness in its youth. The 1990 is along the same lines – a nice, fresh wine.
La Couronne Sauvignon Blanc Reserve★★★(★)C
The 1990 has good cultivar character. It is a clean, dry wine that could develop well in the bottle. The 1991 is a much better wine.
La Motte Blanc Fumé★★★★D
The first release from the 1989 vintage is a beautiful elegant wine with good cultivar character and fine oak; very soft in the mouth. The 1990 is even more complex and appealing with good texture, and the 1991 is just as attractive. These wines drink very well young, yet the earliest are developing with great benefit in the bottle.
La Motte Sauvignon Blanc★★★★D
A really super Sauvignon Blanc in the bold, high fruit style. The first release from 1989 has shown good development in the bottle. The 1990 has everything the first release had and will develop with the same distinction. The 1991 is even better.
Landskroon Sauvignon Blanc★★★B
The wines of the 1990s are very attractive and good drinking products, with good cultivar and cellar character.
La Provence Blanc Fumé★★★C
This was originally Blanc Fleuri, but was forced to change to Blanc Fumé by the owners of the Fleur label. The 1990 vintage is a good, unwooded (despite the name) Sauvignon Blanc. No 1991 release.

La Provence Sauvignon Blanc★★★B
Big full wine with lots of fruity character and fresh finish.
Le Bonheur Blanc Fumé★★★★C
It is a pity that in such a good Sauvignon Blanc year there was no release from this quality cellar to celebrate the 10-year anniversary of its first Blanc Fumé release. The 1989 is promising considering the poor vintage. The 1990 is as good as ever with full, intense cultivar character and could well be called 'savage'.
Lemberg Aimée★★★★C
The 1991 is possibly the best ever and full-flavoured at an early stage. It will develop with great benefit. The label does not carry the name 'Sauvignon Blanc', but the leaf depicted is one from the cultivar. The 1992 is sure to continue the high quality of this cellar.
Les Chênes Sauvignon Blanc★★B
A pleasant off-dry white with reasonable cultivar character.
Lievland Sauvignon Blanc★★★B
A good, easy-drinking wine with attractive Sauvignon Blanc character. Always interesting. Recent vintages have good cultivar character and drink well.
L'Ormarins Blanc Fumé★★★★(★)C
A wine packed with powerful cultivar nose and flavour, touched out beautifully with good oak. This cellar has an incredibly good record of well made wine since the first release in 1982, and this Blanc Fumé is consistently one of South Africa's best. The 1989 is in the same, big style as is the 1990.
L'Ormarins Sauvignon Blanc★★★★C
The Estate's Sauvignon Blanc was the 1983 South African white wine champion. The 1984 had even more piercing character and, in early 1986, was showing very well with some bottle age. The 1988 was a delightfully fruity wine and thoroughly enjoyable when young. The 1989 is more reserved; dry and unwooded, this is a very good example of the cultivar. Not so the 1990 – a full flavoured great wine, with a strong, varietal nose. The 1991 continues the big bold style.
Lutzville Co-op Fleermuisklip Sauvignon Blanc★★A
Early drinking, fruity, soft wine with brisk finish.
Matin Soleil Sauvignon Blanc★★★C
First release from the 1991 vintage is a reasonable effort and, although without much cultivar character, it's a pleasant drink.
Mont Blois Blanc Fumé★★B
The first release from the 1989 vintage has little fruit character as the wood shows through.
Morgenhof Sauvignon Blanc★★★C
The 1986 vintage was a good first attempt giving a fresh wine with a hint of wood and reasonable cultivar character. Subsequent vintages have varied, with the 1991 showing well with crisp, fresh finish.
Mulderbosch Blanc Fumé★★★(★)C
First release from 1991 vintage from this new cellar on the Koelenhof side of the Bottelary range. A portion of the wine was oak-fermented and the lot matured in various oaks, including some American. This is a fine first effort, and comes in eye-catching strip-label bottles. Augurs well for the future.
Mulderbosch Sauvignon Blanc★★★(★)C
Full of exciting cultivar character. First release from the 1992 vintage from this new venture; lots to look forward to.

Nederburg Private Bin D229★★★(★)B
The first release came from the 1985 vintage, followed by the 1986, 1987, 1988 and 1989; all of them big, full wines with excellent fresh acidity, giving this predominantly Sauvignon Blanc blend good fruitiness and character without any wood influence. It is released only at the annual Nederburg Auction.
Nederburg Private Bin D234★★★D
This is a wood-aged Sauvignon Blanc that spent nine months in small French oak developing a strong vanilla and cultivar nose, an attractive dry flavour and deep character. It should develop well over two to three years. The 1988 was sold at the 1991 Auction and the 1989 at the 1992 Auction.
Nederburg Sauvignon Blanc★★★B
To date there have been limited releases of two vintages: the 1982 and the 1984. The wine is offered in a clear, Bordeaux-type bottle and is very much in the style of coastal Sauvignon Blancs as opposed to the inland wines of the Loire. It is dry, fresh and finely flavoured, the cultivar true, without wood influence. There was also a 1980 Sauvignon Blanc, offered at the 1983 Nederburg Auction: a fine, steely wine which drank well when young.
Neethlingshof Sauvignon Blanc★★C
Nowadays a consistently good wine with crisp, appealing, varietal character. It is well made, soundly balanced and the 1991 is particularly good.
Neil Ellis Blanc Fumé★★★★C
From the 1988 vintage came a big, rich wine with full flavour and lots of complexity of cultivar and wood. One of the Cape's best Sauvignon Blancs, it is very good and developing beautifully. The 1990 is a beautiful wine, and also one of the best. Although it is no longer produced, previous bottlings are still developing well.
Neil Ellis Sauvignon Blanc★★★(★)C
The first release from the 1986 vintage had good cultivar character and has developed well over the year. The 1987 was a more complex wine with 25% having been fermented and matured in wood. It developed well in the bottle and is worthy four-star material. The 1988 and 1989 are showing well now. (Replaced by Whitehall.)
Neil Ellis Whitehall Sauvignon Blanc★★★★★C
The first release from the 1990 vintage comes from Elgin and is a magnificent wine; a bright, brisk, flinty style with great fruit intensity. Tremendous to drink in its youth, it must certainly develop with great distinction. The 1991 is an exciting wine and set a new standard for this varietal.
Nordale Co-op Sauvignon Blanc★★A
Light dry white for easy drinking.
Nuy Sauvignon Blanc★★★B
Good introduction from the 1991 vintage. Fine varietal flavour; nice and dry – and very drinkable.
Overgaauw Sauvignon Blanc★★★(★)B
Consistently good, regular drinking wine with lots of cultivar character. Recent vintages are good, clean, well-balanced wines.
Overhex Co-op Sauvignon Blanc★★A
A light, easy-drinking dry white, first released from the 1991 vintage.
Pick 'n Pay Sauvignon Blanc★★★C
Unwooded, big, full, New World style wine. Good varietal nose, lots

of flavour and good, fresh, crisp finish. From 1989 vintage this wine is showing good bottle age. Made by Simonsig.

Pieter Cruythoff Sauvignon Blanc Reserve★★★B

The 1991 vintage is good, full-flavoured wine with steely character and fresh finish. Good value for money.

Rhebokskloof Blanc Fumé★★★(★)C

A dry, crisp wine with good cultivar character; a touch of oak helps its complexity. A well-made, easy-drinking wine.

Rhebokskloof Sauvignon Blanc

Discontinued. Replaced with Blanc Fumé.

Robertson Co-op Sauvignon Blanc★★★A

Regular quality, easy-drinking dry wine.

Roodezandt Co-op Sauvignon Blanc★★B

A two-time first for this Co-op: their 1987 vintage was their first Sauvignon Blanc and their first white wine to be wooded, and now seems to have reached its best two years after its release. The 1990 is a well-balanced wine for early drinking.

Rooiberg Co-op Blanc Fumé Sur Lie★★★(★)B

To my taste the best Sauvignon Blanc from over the mountains was the 1987 vintage of this wine. It was cask-fermented and left on its lees for five months, and then the clear wine was drawn off and bottled unfiltered. Packed with cultivar character, it showed good, tasty wood and other flavours that enabled it to develop with spectacular results. The 1989 is not as good, but the 1990 has good cultivar character backed by good wood. The 1991 is a little subdued.

Rooiberg Co-op Sauvignon Blanc★★A

A full-flavoured wine, with the 1991 having good cultivar character.

Ruiterbosch Mountain Vineyard Sauvignon Blanc★★★(★)C

A very good first attempt from the 1989 vintage from the cool mountain-side vineyard overlooking Mossel Bay. The 1990 is fine wine but the 1991 is the best release so far; a crisp, clean cultivar which will develop well.

Saxenburg Sauvignon Blanc★★★C

The 1991 is good fruity wine. The 1990 developed very quickly and should be drunk when young.

Saxenburg Sauvignon Blanc Barrel Matured★★★C+

Good cultivar wine backed with good clean wood.

Simonsig Sauvignon Blanc★★★(★)C

Always good, with recent vintages having touches of class; big, bold, flavourful wines that can be relied on to satisfy.

Simonsvlei Co-op Blanc Fumé★★★B

A full-flavoured, well-oaked Sauvignon with a slight smoky tone.

Simonsvlei Co-op Sauvignon Blanc★★★B

This cellar must be pleased at having achieved such a regularly good wine. The 1990 and 1991 are not totally dry, which gives added smoothness. A very satisfying drink.

Slanghoek Co-op Sauvignon Blanc★★A

A dry wine with reasonable cultivar character, making easy-drinking wine. The 1990 is dry and delicate.

Spier Sauvignon Blanc★★B

The first release from the 1984 vintage was very light wine. The 1985 was better, and the 1987 was a gold medallist at the Stellenbosch show. The 1988 is a soundly-made dry white wine and the 1989 is light and pleasant with a good cultivar character. No recent releases.

Spruitdrift Co-op Sauvignon Blanc★★A
A regular medal winner at local shows, this is pleasant wine which is best enjoyed in its youth.
Stellenryck Blanc Fumé★★★★C
This is an extremely good, unwooded wine which develops beautifully with two to three years of bottle-ageing. It is dry, with a high natural acidity and the distinctive flavour of grassiness and gunflint, typical of wine made from Sauvignon Blanc in the Sancerre style. The 1984 vintage was magnificent and has developed beautifully in the bottle. The 1985 also showed well. The 1987 is a lesser wine but is drinking well now, and the 1988 was selected for the 1989 SAA wine list. The 1989, 1990 and 1991 are all super wines that have developed well and at their best after two to four years.
Stellenzicht Sauvignon Blanc★★★★D
Yet to be released. This is beautiful, big dry wine packed with fresh cultivar character and has long lingering finish. Super.
Swartland Sauvignon Blanc★★★A
Introduced with the 1985 vintage, this wine showed distinct cultivar nose but had a somewhat flat flavour. It has improved since then. The 1988 was a good example of how good a Co-op can be with this cultivar, combining penetrating nose and intense flavour with medium body. The 1989 is not as good; the 1990 is not up to standard; but the 1991 is back to quality. Good value wine, best enjoyed in its youth to capture its good character.
Thelema Blanc Fumé★★★★B
The 1989 bottling for the 1990 Cape Independent Winemakers' Guild and Auction is a spectacular wine. The 1990 regular release is not quite as great, but very good all the same. A good cultivar backed with fine oak.
Thelema Sauvignon Blanc★★★★C
The first vintage from 1987 was remarkable for the intensity achieved from such young vines on this wine farm. The 1988, released for sale just after the 1989 vintage was in the cellar, is opening up into a bright, fresh, dry wine with good cultivar nose and fine flavour in the mouth. The 1989 is a super wine with very good cultivar character. Lovely as a young wine, it has the potential to develop with benefit. The 1990 is superb, and the 1991 excellent in all respects – one of the Cape's best. It is full of lovely fruit and lots of flavour, and will develop with great distinction.
Uiterwyk Estate Sauvignon Blanc★★★C
The first release from the 1988 vintage is a good example of young Sauvignon Blanc and made pleasant meal-time drinking. The 1989 is altogether better with attractive nose and good flavour; the 1990 and 1991 are much the same.
Uitkyk Estate Sauvignon Blanc★★★★B
Throughout the 1970s this was a pleasant, off-dry, Steen-based blend. In 1981, however, a considerable amount of Sauvignon Blanc was introduced, producing a delightfully dry wine. It made an excellent impression at the Club Oenologique International Wine and Spirit Competition, where it gained a gold medal. The 1986, a strict, more formal wine, carries Sauvignon Blanc on the label. With the 1991 release the 'Carlsheim' has been dropped and it is now labelled as Sauvignon Blanc – strong, full, beautiful wine with lots of development potential.

Van Loveren Sauvignon Blanc★★B
The first release came from the 1983 vintage. Nowadays this is a big wine with better cultivar character and full flavour.
Villiera Cru Monro Blanc Fumé★★★★B
A beautiful Sauvignon Blanc with good oak influence, this is a well-rounded, complex wine, that taste good on release and should develop well with time. The 1991 is stunning.
Villiera Sauvignon Blanc★★★★(★)B
The 1980 vintage was a delightful, off-dry wine with clear varietal character and drank very well when young. Subsequent vintages are bone-dry, with good cultivar character. The latest vintages have some wood influence, which adds a little more complexity without diminishing the cultivar character. The 1985 was a lovely, light wine with fine flavour and the 1986 has freshness and good character. The 1987 was delicate with a pleasant, fragrant bouquet and nice, dry flavour. It developed well over two years. The 1988 and 1989 have good characters, the 1988 being the best and worth four stars. The same can be said for the 1990. These wines are characterized by a touch of lightness seldom found in South African Sauvignon Blancs – a delightful difference. The 1991 is one of the Cape's best ever.
Villiersdorp Co-op Sauvignon Blanc★★A
The first release from the 1988 vintage was a dry white wine with reasonable cultivar nose and flavour. The next vintage is the 1990, a good, easy-drinking wine, as is the 1991.
Vlottenburg Co-op Sauvignon Blanc★★A
Good, regular-drinking wine with brisk finish.
Vredendal Co-op Sauvignon Blanc★★★A
This may not be a 'purist's' wine but it is remarkable considering its origin; a good wine and excellent value for money. The 1990 and 1991 are lighter, but still have an attractive flavour. It always amazes me how Giel Swiegers pays attention to these smaller productions despite the massive quantities this Co-op handles.
Welmoed Co-op Sauvignon Blanc★★★A
The maiden vintage was the 1981 and contained a little of everything that a wine from the Sauvignon Blanc cultivar should. Subsequent vintages have not been quite as exciting, although the mid-1980s showed an improvement. The 1990 and 1991 are particularly good.
Weltevrede Estate Blanc Fumé★★★B
Oak-ageing has helped this wine develop a better complexity of character than its unwooded partner. It is dry and tasty. The 1990 is the first release since 1987 and is followed by a very acceptable 1991.
Weltevrede Estate Sauvignon Blanc★★★B
The 1986 provided the first vintage of this cultivar from this Estate. Latest vintages are well flavoured and make good drinking.
Woolworths Blanc Fumé ★★★★B
Produced by Neil Ellis. An excellent buy – beautiful wine with plenty of cultivar character out of the 1990 vintage. Good to drink now, but with potential to develop with great benefit.
Woolworths Sauvignon Blanc★★★(★)B
A most attractive Sauvignon Blanc ready for drinking. Fresh and fruity when young, it is well worth ageing at the price. Produced by Robertson Co-op.
Woolworths Sauvignon Blanc Reserve★★★★D
An excellent wine from Klein Constantia specially blended for

Woolworths out of 1989 vintage. Less alcoholic than the Estate's label. Attractive nose, good flavour. Fine for drinking now, but has the potential to develop over three to four years.

Zandwijk Sauvignon Blanc★★C

The 1989 vintage is the first release of this kosher wine. It did not have much cultivar character, but it was a sound, pleasant wine. The 1990 is an improved product with better cultivar character.

Zevenwacht Sauvignon Blanc★★★C

The 1989, 1990 and 1991 are big, full wines packed with cultivar character and should all develop as well as the 1989 is now showing.

Zonnebloem Sauvignon Blanc (SFW)★★★B

Made in the Loire style, this wine develops well in the bottle but is also good when young. It is one of the best-drinking, dry Sauvignon Blancs in the Cape. During its relatively short career it has been selected by SAA for its wine list and picked up a number of overseas awards. It is consistently reliable. The 1990 is a bigger, bolder product with good cultivar character.

Sémillon

Boschendal Sémillon (no price or rating)
Yet to be released; full-flavoured, oaky wine.
Delheim/Lloyd Sémillon★★★(no price)
Angela Lloyd produced a small amount of Sémillon from 1989 – a good attempt with this wine which proves that there is a place for a well-made Sémillon.
Drostdy-Hof Sémillon★★★A
The 1983 vintage was introduced to the market in 1986 when it was already showing interesting bottle-age; deep and well-flavoured, it drank well. There has been no release since then. I tasted the 1983 recently, and it was in amazing condition – with deep, sage-like nose and soft, full flavour.
La Bourgogne Joie de Vivre Sémillon★★(★)B
First release from the 1991 vintage is a good effort; dry, fruity with flowery tones.
La Cotte Sémillon (Franschhoek Vineyards Co-op)★★(★)B
Consistently one of the cellar's better, well-flavoured, dry wines. The 1986 was a Paarl Show gold medal winner. The 1990 and 1991 are easy-drinking, fresh and fruity. The Co-operative also produces a semi-sweet Sémillon, which is more akin to a Late Harvest.
Le Moutonné Sémillon★★(★)B
A dry, crisp wine with good cultivar character. The 1985 vintage was the first release and the 1986 has developed well in the bottle. The 1987 is showing good bottle development and should be drunk.
Les Chênes Sémillon★★(★)B
The first release, from the 1986 vintage, is a dry white with good, clean character. The 1987 is much better wine with good fruit and flavour, and was the last release of this wine. Sémillon now forms part of C'est la Vie.

Sylvaner

Overgaauw Sylvaner★★★(★)B
A speciality of this cellar, it is always a good, interesting wine with a fresh and fine Sylvaner bouquet. Of consistent quality, it matures very well in the bottle. The 1986 was very fruity on release and in excellent condition in 1992. The 1987 and 1988 are not developing as well as the 1986 and need to be drunk up. The 1989 and 1990 are both delightful in 1992. The 1991 seems to be slightly sweeter than previous vintages but still only off-dry, lovely fresh fruity wine and delightful in its youth.

Blanc de Noir/Rosé Wines

Blanc de Noir

Aan de Doorns Co-op Blanc de Noir★★A
A semi-sweet wine made from Pinotage.
Alphen Deliana Blanc de Noir★★★B
A blend of Pinotage and Zinfandel, with latest bottlings finished dry with a good fruity nose and fresh finish. This wine is part of the Alphen revamped range made in the Kleine Zalze cellar.
Avontuur Blanc de Noir★★★B
Originally made from Pinotage. The 1991 and 1992 are fruity Pinotage-Merlot blends finished off-dry. Delightful wine, especially when served chilled.
Barrydale Co-op Blanc de Noir★★A
This interesting orange/pink wine made from Red Muscadel has a pretty nose and pleasant semi-sweet flavour, which is best enjoyed in its youth.
Beaufort Blanc de Noir★★A
A pleasant, easy-drinking off-dry wine made from Pinotage.
Bon Courage Blanc de Noir★★★B
A light, easy-drinking wine blended from Shiraz and Muscat, with the latter present in sufficiently small quantities to add interest without being obtrusive. The wine is off-dry and well balanced by the fresh, fruity finish.
Boplaas Blanc de Noir★★★B
A blend of predominantly Pinotage with Cabernet and Tinta Barocca giving intriguing nose and flavour. Finished off-dry with little more than 10 g/*l* sugar and a lowish alcohol content of 10%, it makes very easy and pleasant drinking.
Boschendal Blanc de Noir★★★(★)C
This was the first Blanc de Noir to be marketed under this name in South Africa. The maiden vintage, in 1981, was an instant success and became the drink of the fashion-conscious. The blend has varied and improved over the vintages, and now has good complex character due to the combination of Cabernet, Pinotage, Shiraz and Tinta Barocca. Usually finished off-dry (but tastes dryish), it makes very easy drinking, especially when young and chilled.
Botha Co-op Blanc de Noir★★A
Made from Cabernet and finished off-dry with some 10 g/*l* sugar content. It is pale in colour but strong in alcohol, and best enjoyed while still young.
Bottelary Co-op Blanc de Noir★★(★)A
Usually a very pleasant, crisp, off-dry wine. Like most wines of this type, it is best enjoyed while still young.
Buffelskroon Blanc de Noir (Calitzdorp Co-op)★A
Fruity and semi-sweet, this Blanc de Noir has definite Pinotage nose.
Cederberg Kelders Blanc de Noir★★★B
From Pinotage, this wine has lovely colour, a fruity nose, plenty of off-dry taste, and a good, sharp finish.
Chamonix Blanc de Noir★★C
A light-pink, light-bodied, off-dry wine with undemanding character, which drinks easily when chilled.

Culemborg Blanc de Noir★★★B
An attractive, off-dry wine with young, fruity, Pinotage character. It is excellent value for a vintage-dated wine.
De Wet Co-op Blanc de Noir★★A
Finished semi-sweet, this Blanc de Noir is unusual in that it is usually a blend of Cabernet Franc and Cinsaut. It was a class winner at the South African Championship Wine Show.
Die Krans Blanc de Noir★★(★)A
A semi-sweet wine with unusual nose, made from Pinotage.
Domein Doornkraal Tinta Bianca★★A
The first release was from the 1988 vintage and is an interesting blend of 45% Pinotage, 40% Tinta Barocca and 15% Red Muscadel, all pressed and fermented together. The 1989 was made the same way and has a most attractive orange colour. The wine is finished off-dry with a white capsule and semi-sweet with a red capsule. Both are pale, coppery-coloured wines and make easy drinking.
Douglas Co-op Blanc de Noir★★B
Very pink, easy-drinking wine made from Pinotage and finished off-dry.
Douglas Green Pinotage Blanc de Noir★★(★)B
Pleasant, fruity, off-dry wine when young.
Du Toitskloof Co-op Blanc de Noir★★★A
The blend is now predominantly Cinsaut and some 25% Ruby Cabernet. This semi-sweet, attractive, fruity wine is best enjoyed when young.
Edward Snell Blanc de Noir★★★B
A non-vintage, off-dry wine made from Pinotage.
Fairview Blanc de Noir★★★C
While earlier releases were made from Cabernet, more recent ones are from Shiraz. (There is, however, no cultivar claim on the label.) An easy-drinking, light, dry wine with good, fruity character.
Goudini Co-op Blanc de Noir★★A
An easy drinking off-dry wine made from Cinsaut.
Goue Vallei Blanc de Noir (Citrusdal Co-op)★★A
This is an unusual example in the Blanc de Noir line-up as it is made from Grenache. It is sharp-flavoured and has a fairly sharp finish which is balanced by being off-dry.
Hartenberg Blanc de Noir★★★C
Earlier wines were a blend of Cabernet and Shiraz finished dry and crisp. Later vintage-dated releases are most attractive wines, mainly Shiraz with 20% or so Zinfandel.
Helderberg Co-op Blanc de Noir★★(★)A
The first release, from the 1989 vintage, has attractive colour and nose with good Cabernet flavour. It is finished off-dry. Latest vintages have a decided cherry character.
Kango Co-op Blanc de Noir★★A
A blend of Pinotage and Muscadel with an off-dry finish, this is a delightfully fruity and attractive wine.
Klawer Co-op Blanc de Noir★★A
A low-alcohol, semi-sweet wine made from Grenache.
La Cotte Pinotage Blanc de Noir ★(★)B
Pretty, pale wine with full Pinotage nose, finished off-dry.
Landskroon Blanc de Noir★★B
The varying characteristics of the vintages have made this an inter-

esting wine. Previously made from Pinot Noir, but latest vintages are made from Pinotage and finished off-dry.

Les Chênes Blanc de Noir★★B

A product of the Franschhoek Vineyards Co-op scheme, this is made from Pinotage, giving a dryish, easy-drinking wine which is best enjoyed when young.

Lutzville Co-op Blanc de Noir★A

Made from Grenache and Carignan, this full-flavoured wine is finished semi-sweet.

Mamreweg Co-op Blanc de Noir★★A

Recent vintages from Cinsaut are pleasant, fruity, semi-sweet wines.

Morgenhof Blanc de Noir★★(★)B

Originally a light, dry wine with high acid, good Cabernet flavour and most attractive colour, it is now made from Pinotage and finished off-dry. The 1991 has a powerful 13% alcohol content.

Nederburg Cabernet Blanc de Noir★★★★C

Initially produced from the 1982 vintage, this was the first Blanc de Noir to carry a cultivar claim and to achieve Superior certification. Each subsequent vintage has been dry, elegant and gentle yet persistent with a most attractive aroma and a light but fine flavour. Best when young.

Neethlingshof Blanc de Noir★★★★C

Made from Cabernet, this wine is a touch of class, with good cultivar character. Finished dry.

Noorderkeur Vin Blanc de Noir (Loopspruit Estate)★A

A semi-sweet wine previously made from Red Hanepoot by the Loopspruit Winery, near Bronkhorstspruit in the Transvaal. Now made from Cinsaut.

Opstal Blanc de Noir★★★B

This wine has a very definite Cabernet character. The 1991 is finished off-dry and makes for easy drinking.

Riebeek Wine Farmers' Co-op Blanc de Noir★★★A

The latest release from Merlot is easy-drinking, pleasant tasting, dryish wine.

Roodezandt Co-op Blanc de Noir Muscat de Frontignan★★A

A pale wine with a lovely nose and good flavour. Available dry or off-dry.

Rooiberg Co-op Blanc de Noir★★★A

The 1983 vintage was judged champion Blanc de Noir at the South African Championship Wine Show. Made from Pinotage, it carried Superior certification. Various blends (including Cabernet, Cinsaut and Pinotage) have been made over the years. From 100% Pinotage, it is now back to being a multiple blend, finished off-dry, making pleasant drinking.

Saxenburg Blanc de Noir★★(★)C

The first release was a fairly ordinary dry wine made from Cinsaut. Subsequent releases have been much better. A Cinsaut-Pinotage blend, it has a good fruity nose and nice dry finish. It has been one of the Alphen Wine- of- the- Month selections.

Simonsig Blanc de Noir★★★B

A very pale-coloured, but fruity, dry wine made from Pinotage.

Simonsvlei Co-op Blanc de Noir★★A

An off-dry from Pinotage with good flavour. It is at its best when young and chilled.

Spier Blanc de Noir★★B
A dry, easy-drinking, light-bodied wine made from Pinotage.
Spruitdrift Co-op Blanc de Noir★★A
An easy-drinking, off-dry wine made from Pinotage.
Swartland Co-op Blanc de Noir★★★A
Originally a blend of Tinta Barocca and Pinotage, this wine is currently made only from the latter, which shows well on the nose. It is finished off-dry and is excellent value for money.
Van Loveren Blanc de Noir Muscat de Frontignan★★(★)B
This wine has a strong Muscat nose and good semi-sweet flavour. Each vintage drinks well when young.
Van Loveren Blanc de Noir Shiraz★★B
Made from Shiraz, this very pale-coloured wine has an unusual character. When chilled it makes an excellent aperitif.
Villiera Gavotte★★★(★)B
Made mainly from Cabernet and some Shiraz. A delightful, off-dry, well-flavoured wine that is regularly selected by the Wine of the Month Club against stiff opposition. To my mind, this cellar consistently produces one of the most attractive Blanc de Noirs available.
Villiersdorp Co-op Blanc de Noir★★(★)B
A pleasant, easy-drinking, semi-sweet wine made from Pinotage.
Vintner's Choice Blanc de Noir (Drop Inn)★★A
A very pleasant, off-dry, salmon-coloured wine with a good vinous nose and fresh flavour.
Vredenheim Blanc de Noir★★A
The 1989 vintage was made from Pinotage, finished dry, and now showing age.
Welmoed Co-op Blanc de Noir★★★B
An off-dry Pinotage wine of consistently good character. Well balanced and, although semi-sweet, appears drier.
Weltevrede Blanc de Noir★★★B
One of the more interesting Blanc de Noir wines – it has a fine, off-dry flavour and Muscat nose.
Woolworths Blanc de Noir★★★B
A very pleasant off-dry wine with more complex flavours than usual for a Blanc de Noir.
Zevenwacht Blanc de Noir★★★B
An attractive Pinotage, Shiraz and Cabernet blend that is finished off-dry.
Zonnebloem Cabernet Blanc de Noir (SFW)★★★C
Recent vintages are lovely when released, off-dry and best when still young. Certified Cabernet Sauvignon.

Rosé

Autumn Harvest Rosé★★B
A pleasant, easy-drinking, semi-sweet wine which has more body than most Rosés.

Backsberg Rosé★★★B
A consistently delightful, semi-sweet Rosé usually made from Pinotage and designed for early drinking. Latest release is from Pinot Noir and vintage-dated.

Bellingham Almeida Rosé★★★B
An attractive semi-sweet Rosé from Pinotage.

Bellingham Rosé Sec★★★A
In keeping with the upgrading of Bellingham products, the cellar's Rosé Sec is a good, light, fresh, fruity wine made from Pinotage, to be enjoyed when young.

Delheim Pinotage Rosé★★★★B
It used to be released annually alongside the Nouveau wines of that year, but not any longer. In the pink of its youth it is delightful wine, yet it has enough body to sustain its attractiveness 12 to 18 months later. Finished off-dry, it is one of my favourites. Very easy drinking.

De Zoete Inval Rosé Sec★B
Anything but dry, this deep-coloured wine has an unusual nose and, although soft in the mouth, leaves a strange aftertaste.

Douglas Co-op Rosé★★A
An off-dry Rosé made from Pinotage and Tinta Barocca.

Douglas Green St Clare★★★B
A Rosé made mainly from Pinotage.

Fairview Rosé D'Une Nuit★★★B
A vintage-dated wine made from Pinotage. The skins were left in contact under refrigeration – to prevent fermentation – for one night, and the result is a very pleasant, fragrant, fruity, semi-sweet wine which is best enjoyed when young.

Kellerprinz Rosanne (SFW)★★A
A well-made, semi-sweet blend with attractive, fruity nose.

Koelenhof Co-op Pinotage Rosé★★A
This is not produced every vintage, but when it does appear it has deep colour, is usually semi-sweet and makes for easy drinking.

Landzicht Bloemdal Rosé★A
A semi-sweet wine made from Pinotage.

Lanzerac Rosé★★★B
A lovely, semi-sweet Rosé, full of flavour and presented most attractively in its dewdrop-shaped bottle.

Nederburg Rosé★★★B
One of South Africa's earliest Rosés and a long-time favourite. Once again it is being sold in an attractive Italian-style bottle, the cross-hatching of which shows off its pink colour to perfection. It is Pinotage-based with the latest blends containing Gamay. It is a semi-sweet and well-flavoured wine which is best consumed in its vibrant youth. It is vintage-dated.

Nederburg Rosé Sec★★★C
The first really successful dry Rosé of good quality to gain popularity in South Africa. It has always had a hint of Cabernet, but is now a Cinsaut-Gamay blend. Delightful when young, this vintage-dated Rosé ages into a most intriguing wine over two to three years.

Noorderkeur Rose★★B
The 1990 is a semi-sweet from Cabernet, Steen and Muscat, and is now showing age.
Oranjerivier Wynkelders Rosé★★A
A pleasantly flavoured, dry Rosé. Originally made from Pinotage and Colombar, but it is now only from Pinotage.
Simonsig Rosé★★B
A semi-sweet, vintage-dated Rosé that is always reliable.
Simonsvlei Co-op Rosé★★A
A fruity, semi-sweet Rosé made from Pinotage and Chenin Blanc.
Swartland Co-op Rosé★★A
An easy-drinking semi-sweet from Pinotage and Steen.
Valley Rosé★★A
A pleasant, non-vintaged, semi-sweet Rosé.
Woolworths Rosé★★B
From Simonsig. Almost crimson in colour, this Rosé has a pleasant nose and a semi-sweet taste.

Nouveau Wines

The Nouveau wines have not been star-rated as these wines change so rapidly that it is difficult to assess them accurately.

Altydgedacht Nouveau B
1992 saw the first production of a Nouveau from this cellar. A small quantity was produced for De Oude Welgemoed Restaurant Nouveau Festival and after that it was only available at the Durbanville Tap Huis situated at the restaurant. Made in the traditional way using Gamay, this is very juicy, drinkable wine.
Backsberg Nouveau Rouge B
Again in 1992, this wine is made from Pinot Noir, although it is not certified as such. It is made by carbonic maceration giving a most attractive, easy-drinking wine in real Nouveau style. It is finished dry.
Bloemendal Nouveau B
As with Altydgedacht, the first production in 1992 was for the Welgemoed Nouveau Festival. It is made from Merlot with good deep cultivar character and is very easy drinking.
Boland Wineries Nouveau B
In 1992 this Nouveau is made from Gamay by carbonic maceration, giving a rich red wine that tastes slightly off-dry.
Buitenverwachting L'Arrivée B
This is one of the more interesting Nouveau wines which was first released in 1986 on a fun-filled festival day at Buitenverwachting. Using traditional Gamay, the wine was made by carbonic maceration. A special feature of the wine was its label and each year a competition was held among local art schools to create a colourful design. (This is, however, no longer done.) The 1987 wine was made from Merlot and was a personal favourite of mine. Since 1989 it has been made from Gamay, yielding light wine which is attractive when chilled. The 1990 was chosen by the Alphen Wine of the Month Club as their best Nouveau of 1990.
De Leuwen Jagt Nouveau Rouge B
Made by carbonic maceration from a blend of Merlot and Cabernet, this wine was produced in very small quantities for the Paarl Mountain event.
De Wet Co-op Fronte Pétillant A
A bubbly, semi-sweet Muscat de Frontignan made as a Nouveau with low alcohol.
Diemersdal Nouveau B
This comes with the same attractive and colourful label as used on the Bloemendal and Altydgedacht Nouveaus produced for the Welgemoed Nouveau Festival. It is made from Pinot Noir with lovely fresh berry flavours and is very easy to drink.
Eikendal Nouveau B
Produced for the cellar's annual Weintaufe, where each year a celebrity names the new young wine 'Jung Frau' after the mountains in Switzerland.
Fairview Gamay Noir B
One of the earliest Nouveau wines made from Gamay along the lines of a Beaujolais, using the traditional method of carbonic maceration. It is dry and full of flavour, and although made for early drinking, it

still has good character a year later. The attractive label shows Adam and Eve being led astray by the serpent with a glass of wine rather than an apple. The 1990 was chosen by The Oaks Wine Club as best Nouveau.

KWV Cape Nouveau Blanc (no price available)

Made only for export by KWV, this Nouveau is usually the first South African wine available commercially in Europe. It is made from Steen and finished off-dry.

Landskroon Nouveau Rouge B

This dry wine was made specifically for the Paarl Mountain event using Pinotage.

Romansrivier Co-op B

Annual producer of a dry red Nouveau.

Simonsvlei Co-op Nouveau B

Certified Pinot Noir, this wine has a good, fresh flavour and a nice, refreshing bite in the finish. It took only twenty-four days from picking to bottling.

Vredendal Co-op Goiya Kgeisje A

This wine was again the earliest to be certified in 1992. It is named Goiya Kgeisje (pronounced 'Goya Kaysee') which is very appropriate for what is always the Cape's 'first' Nouveau on the market. All the grapes come from vineyards where neither pesticides nor fungicides have been used and it is believed that this led to an overabundance of ladybirds which checked fungi growth. The product is a Wine of Origin Vredendal and is certified Sauvignon Blanc.

Woolworths Jeune Blanc B

From Villiera. This is an elegant dry wine with a lively crispness. The nose is fruity, with floral tones, and the palate refreshingly dry. Jeune Blanc is a blend of 30% Gewürztraminer, 30% Morio Muscat, 30% Chenin Blanc and 40% Muscat Ottonel.

Woolworths Jeune Rosé B

From Villiera. This is a blend of 44% Gewürztraminer, 36% Chenin Blanc and 20% Gamay which contributes a certain amount of Nouveau character. So successful have Woolworths been with their Nouveau wines that they introduced this semi-sweet Rosé to their range, which is now a popular, permanent feature.

Woolworths Jeunesse B

From Villiera. This is a classic Nouveau-style wine made using the maceration carbonique method. It is a brilliant red colour with striking fresh fruitiness, a hint of raspberries, full and supple on the palate. Since Nouveau wines took off, this has been one of the consistently better products. Nowadays the wine is made from 100% Gamay planted specifically for Nouveau production.

Bubblies

Méthode Champenoise Sparkling Wines

Backsberg Estate Méthode Champenoise★★★★D
Made by the *méthode champenoise*, and clearly labelled 'fermented in the bottle', this sparkling wine was launched in 1988, coinciding with Sydney Back's 50th anniversary of wine making on the property which now forms the Backsberg Estate. Showing the exceptional quality which only time can give, the 1985 vintage was made from equal portions of Pinot Noir and Chardonnay, resulting in a very good wine. The 1986 is of the same quality and has developed well in the bottle. The 1987 and 1988 are 40% Pinot Noir and the balance Chardonnay, and make nice, easy drinking. They should develop in the bottle over another two years.
Backsberg Estate Pink★★★(★)C
An off-dry *méthode champenoise* wine made entirely from Pinot Noir. Attractive colour and very appealing fruity nose, with lovely deep flavour. Delightful wine.
Barrydale Co-op Méthode Champenoise Chardonnay
Yet to be released so no price or star rating, this Co-op has on the lees in bottle a *méthode champenoise* from Chardonnay.
Blaauwklippen Barouche★★★(★)D
The first release was a blend of 90% Pinot Noir and 10% Chardonnay, resulting in a pink sparkling wine with a beautiful nose and fine flavour. It is made by the *méthode champenoise*. It was launched with the 1984 vintage and has developed well in the bottle. The 1985 was made only from Pinot Noir and developed a lovely nose and good, full, lively flavour. The 1987 is also all Pinot Noir, has good flavour and has developed beautifully. Future productions may revert to the classic Pinot Noir-Chardonnay blend.
Boplaas Pinot Noir Sparkling Wine★★★B/C
Made by the traditional *méthode champenoise* and using Pinot Noir. The 1986 has a full strong flavour and good *mousse*. The 1988 was a vast improvement, then there was a gap in production. The 1991 is a fresh, lively product with good character.
Boschendal Brut★★★★D
The first release of this decidedly dry wine was made from the 1979 vintage by the classic *méthode champenoise*. It was basically a Riesling but had good, bottle-aged character and incredibly lively, fine bubbles which gave an excellent nose. Thereafter the blend became much more interesting and over the years has contained Pinot Blanc, Pinot Gris and Pinot Noir. A limited amount of the 1980 vintage was released in numbered magnums to celebrate the 300th anniversary of the arrival of the Huguenots at the Cape. The 1984 contains Pinot Noir and a high percentage of Chardonnay. It is an excellent wine with fine nose and good *mousse*. The 1985 is made from Pinot Noir and Chardonnay, resulting in better character as ageing occurs. The 1986 is heralded as an altogether better quality product. Latest productions also carry a degorgement date: the 1988 vintage done in June 1990 and the 1989 vintage in June 1991.
Boschendal Brut Rosé★★★★E
The first release from the 1986 vintage was a delightful bubbly that

can rank with the best. It was degorged in January 1989 and this long period on the lees resulted in a wine with good body, lovely bouquet and fine flavour. The fresh, coral-pink colour comes from the high proportion of Pinot Noir that has been blended with mature Chardonnay grapes to form the *cuvée*. Champagne is only vintage-dated in outstanding years, and then only a portion of the production, as will be the case with Boschendal Brut Rosé.

Boschendal Grande Reserve★★★★D

A limited amount of this fine wine was produced to commemorate the tercentenary of the Huguenots' arrival in Franschhoek. The label states that it has been fermented in the bottle.

Boschendal Pavillion Blanc de Blancs★★★(★)D/E

First release in 1991 was a blend of Chardonnay, Riesling and Sémillon and is a delightful bubbly, not entirely dry, with decided appley character. The subsequent release was 100% Chardonnay. It is attractively packed with a label covering almost every description option: 'méthode champenoise', 'Fermente en Bouteille' and 'Sparkling Wine' plus Cuvée Brut and Blanc de Blancs.

Buitenverwachting Brut★★★★F

Vintage dated with the first release from 1988 and blended from Pinot Noir and Pinot Gris. The next release will be very different from 1989 and all Chardonnay. Very classy label and very expensive.

Charles Gerard Brut (Fairview)★★★(★)D

The original production from the 1987 vintage was so successful that twice the amount has been produced from the 1989 vintage. This wine is made from red grapes using the traditional *méthode champenoise*, the combination of which gives good character wine with fine bubbles.

Douglas Green Blanc de Noir Sparkling★★(★)C

A very pale, bottle-fermented wine with good acid and fine, but subdued, flavour. It does not age well, so enjoy it while it is young.

Grand Mousseux Grand Cuvée (SFW)★★★E

The first commercial release of a vintage dated *méthode champenoise* from this long-time favourite brand name came from the 1986 vintage, after three years on its lees. No 1987. Next release from 1988 has a lovely, yeasty aroma with fine, sustained *mousse*.

Here XVII Grand Cuvée (Bergkelder)★★★★E

Launched late in 1988 as a non-vintage, bottle-fermented bubbly with good character. It is made from Pinot Noir in the traditional *méthode champenoise*. Spending two years on the lees gives this wine a special quality. Since the release of the 1987 vintage it is certified for vintage.

JC le Roux Chardonnay Méthode Champenoise★★★(★)E

The 1984 was released possibly a little too early, but it developed into a fine wine over the years. After six years of ageing, the Chardonnay character had developed very well, probably reaching its limit of development. The 1988 is very good.

JC le Roux Pinot Noir★★★★D

Originally made from Pinot Noir of the 1984 vintage (grown on the Alto and Meerlust Estates) and fermented in the bottle, it is almost water-white but with good flavour which developed over a year or two in the bottle. The 1986 was released in 1990, giving it four years on its lees. A delicious *méthode champenoise* wine, hard to find but worth the search. In 1991 it won the Schramsberg Trophy for the best bottle-fermented sparkling wine entered in the International Wine and Spirit Competition against very stiff opposition.

Krone Borealis (Twee Jongegezellen)★★★★F

Produced in most attractive custom-built cellars from 40% Chardonnay, 40% Pinot Blanc and 20% Pinot Noir. Lovely soft *mousse* with fine flavours backed with good full yeast aromas. Attractively packaged sparkling wine.

Laurent (Onverwacht Estate)★★F+

Only 500 bottles of this bubbly were produced, the cheeky labels numbered and signed by the artist André Naudé.

L'Ormarins Jean Roi★★★★(no price available)

From the 1987 vintage, with classic Pinot Noir-Chardonnay blend and amongst the growing number where the wine has been slightly oaked before bottling. Delicious bubbly.

Nederburg Blanquette E

Released at the 1992 Auction from Chardonnay harvested in 1990. This is one of the products used to mark Nederburg's bicentenery.

Pick 'n Pay Crémant★★★(★)D

A very good value bubbly made by Villiera. It has a distinct, youthful character and is very refreshing. It will benefit with an extra year of ageing before drinking.

Pierre Jourdan Belle Rosé (Clos Cabrière)★★★★F

The 1986 was sold at the 1989 Cape Independent Winemakers' Guild Auction. Made from Pinot Noir, it has developed a lovely orange colour with distinct *méthode champenoise* character and good steady, fine bubbles. Subsequent releases are more complex and should develop with even more benefit.

Pierre Jourdan Brut (Clos Cabrière)★★★★(★)E

Clos Cabrière's original *méthode champenoise* and the traditional champagne combination of Pinot Noir and Chardonnay. This wine was released late in 1985 and was very good, commanding a grand price. Of the number of Pierre Jourdans, this one has the original blue-green label, although it does not carry a vintage date. The punt of each bottle also has a colour code: the yellow stripe indicates the 1984 Reserve vintage, the red and white stripe the 1985 and the white stripe the 1986. The 1987 has a single red mark on the edge of the punt. The 1988 and 1989 have strip labels which disappear under the punt and the 1989 vintage carries a big star on the back label, also showing the bar code for the first time. All these wines are developing beautifully and there is no doubt that specializing is worthwhile. The Brut is also available in Magnum bottles.

Pierre Jourdan Blanc de Blancs (Clos Cabrière)★★★★F

Made only from Chardonnay. A delightfully light, frothy wine with crisp, fresh flavour. Not produced with every vintage. The dark label makes the gold stand out richly.

Pierre Jourdan Cuvée Reserve (Clos Cabrière) ★★★★F

The yellow label is of the same blend as the blue-green label, however it spends four years or more on the lees in the bottle before being disgorged, giving more complex character and deeper flavours. A super wine.

Pierre Jourdan Extra (Clos Cabrière)★★★★F

With the paler blue label and the words 'Fermenté en Bouteille' below Pierre Jourdan. Originally known as Brut Sauvage. Good bottles are stunning.

Pongrácz (Bergkelder)★★★★D/C
Named after Desiderius Pongrácz, a Hungarian aristocrat who settled in the Cape after fleeing his country of birth when it was overrun by the Bolsheviks. He was a viticulturist and produced two books on the subject and, although a controversial personality, was always an absolute gentleman. He died after a tragic motor accident in 1985. The wine, a *méthode champenoise*, was especially prepared by countryman and colleague Julius Lazlo and is a classic blend of 75% Pinot Noir and 25% Chardonnay. It is a fraction off-dry with a most attractive 'French' nose, making light, easy drinking. This is a well-flavoured bubbly with fine creamy *mousse*. It is splendidly packaged and there's no mistaking the value for money price.
Simonsig Kaapse Vonkel★★★★D
This sparkling wine is made by the traditional *méthode champenoise*, which was reintroduced to the Cape by the wine maker, Frans Malan, with the first vintage in 1971. Originally a Steen-based wine which was produced each alternate vintage, it is currently produced each year. It has grown in character and contains increasingly more Pinot Noir and Chardonnay with each vintage. The 1982 and the 1984 both rated four stars and the 1985 turned out to be a very acceptable bubbly. There was no 1986 but the 1987 represents a total change of style in that it uses just the classic Champagne grapes, Pinot Noir and Chardonnay. This results in a good, mouth-filling wine with creamy *mousse* and yeasty character. It developed very well as has the 1988. The next release is a very fine 1989 that is developing with perhaps the best potential so far.
Villiera Tradition de Charles de Fère★★★★D
An unusual partnership – between Villiera Estate and the Frenchman, Jean Louis Denois – led to the creation of this sparkling wine. Both red and white grapes were used in its production, the result of which is a splendid, refreshing wine which is improving all the time. Excellent value for money, it is constantly one of South Africa's better *méthode champenoise* wines. The latest releases contain increasing amounts of Pinot Noir, along with the Chenin Blanc and Pinotage. From 1990 onwards Chardonnay will be included. In keeping with the traditions of Champagne, this cellar's main production is not vintage-dated. However, to give an indication of age, the 1985 release has an unmarked punt. The 1986 has a round red sticker, the 1987 yellow, the 1988 blue, the 1989 orange and 1990 red. This consistently good wine is one of my favourites.
Villiera Tradition de Charles de Fère Reserve★★★★(★)E
Some 50 cases are sold at each of the annual Cape Independent Winemakers' Guild Auctions. The wine is never less than three years on its lees and is disgorged just shortly before the Auction. This is a delicious bubbly that improves with each release as the cellar perfects its techniques and introduces more of the classic varieties to the blend. It is a bubbly well worth seeking out.
Villiera Tradition Prestige Cuvée
Still to be released, and the chances are that it will be South Africa's best *méthode champenoise*.
Villiera Tradition Rosé★★★(★)C
A dry Rosé made from Pinot Noir in the *méthode champenoise*. Two and a half years on the yeast and three months on the cork before release gives this pink-coloured bubbly full flavour and aftertaste.

Woolworths Méthode Champenoise★★★★C
From Villiera. Unbelievably good value for money. A fine *méthode champenoise* wine.

Non-méthode Champenoise Sparkling Wines

Aan de Doorns Co-op Sparkling Wine★★A
A blend of Pinotage and Chenin Blanc resulting in a pink semi-sweet wine. Not much to recommend other than its low price.
Badsberg Co-op Sparkling Wine★★B
Predominantly from Steen with fruity, foamy *mousse.*
Barrydale Co-op Demi-sec Sparkling Wine★★B
The original blend had nice nose and pleasant flavour from Hanepoot and Sauvignon Blanc. Since the 1990 vintage it has 60% Colombar and 20% each Sauvignon Blanc and Muscat, with enough acid to counter the sweetness. Tank-produced with good consistent bubble.
Beaufort Cuvée Brut (Solly Kramer)★★B
A good bubbly with pleasant nose and light flavour – excellent value for money.
Beaufort Cuvée Doux (Solly Kramer)★★B
A sweet bubbly which will appeal to wedding-reception caterers.
Bellingham Blanc de Noir Sparkling Wine★★★C
A pleasant, pale-pink, dry sparkling wine which has improved since it was launched. Though this product is now culled, the older bottles are rather nice.
Bellingham Brut★★★C
An extra-dry wine which usually has good bottle-age on the nose. Later blends have some Sauvignon Blanc and Chardonnay.
Bellingham Brut Vintage Rosé★★★★C
The 1989 vintage of this Pinotage-based wine was launched late in 1990 in its own specially-produced bottle. It has an attractive, fruity nose, is full-flavoured with a hint of sweetness on the palate, yet finishes nice and dry. The 1990 has a decided strawberry flavour and appears drier.
Bellingham Gold★★★C
A delicious and most unusual Special Late Harvest from Chenin Blanc with fine foamy *mousse*. Full of flavour, it would appeal to the sweet-toothed and yet the bubbles tend to hide the sweetness. A glass or two well-chilled makes an excellent aperitif.
Bergsig Painted Lady ★★(★)B
The bright pink label depicts the *Gladiolus carneus*, commonly known as the Painted Lady. This is a peach-coloured, semi-sweet Blanc de Noir made from Pinotage.
Bolandse Co-op Demi-sec Sparkling Wine★★B
A tank-produced bubbly from Sauvignon Blanc. Now sweeter but still with good cultivar character.
Bon Courage Chardonnay Vin Sec★★(★)B
A well-balanced off-dry bubbly with good cultivar character.
Boplaas Pinot Noir Sparkling Wine★★★B/C
Made by the traditional *méthode champenoise* and using Pinot Noir. The 1986 has a full strong flavour and good *mousse*. The 1988 is even better. This wine will give way to a tank-produced product while the Nels develop new cooler climate vineyards where they will grow Pinot Noir and Chardonnay specifically for a *méthode champenoise* wine.
Boplaas Sparkling Wine (Sweet)★★B
A pleasant-flavoured sweet wine with a consistent stream of bubbles for easy drinking.

Botha Co-op Sparkling Wine★★B
A Steen-based, semi-sweet bubbly with clear finish.
Bottelary Co-op Vin Sec★★(★)B
This is a tank-produced bubbly from equal quantities of Sauvignon Blanc and Steen. It tastes drier than most of the Co-op bubblies.
Bovlei Co-op Dry Sparkling Wine★★B
A tank-produced bubbly with the blend changing through the years. The latest production is mainly Steen with honeyed nose.
Bovlei Co-op Semi-sweet Sparkling Wine★B
A sweet Chenin Blanc produced by the tank method.
Carnival Vin Sec/Vin Doux (Spar)★★B
Multiple blends in which Muscat shows on the nose. Good *mousse*. Sec is off-dry; Doux is sweet.
Chamonix Courchevel Cuvée Brut★★C
This sparkling wine is produced by the tank method, using the traditional South African blends of Steen and Clairette Blanche. The label bears a remarkable resemblance to the famous Korbel Natural of California.
Chamonix Courchevel Demi-sec★★C
A sweeter version of the above.
Checkers Semi-sweet Sparkling Wine★★B
A sweetish blend of a number of cultivars giving attractive fruity nose and full flavour.
Chevalier Sparkling Wines (Prestige Cellars)★★B
An off-dry and a sweet wine sparkler under Vin Sec and Vin Doux labels. Clear wines from multiple blend.
Cinzano Spumante (Gilbeys)★★★B
A very popular, sweet, sparkling wine with Muscat nose and good flavour. It deserves to be the biggest single brand in the market.
Cinzano Tiziano★★★C
Cinzano's entry into the sweet red bubbly segment. Delightful, easy-drinking and full of flavour. Attractively packaged.
Citrusdal Co-op Rosé Sparkling ★★★B
A Rosé bubbly made from Grenache and finished semi-sweet.
De Doorns Co-op Sparkling Wine★B
A semi-sweet, tank-produced bubbly made from Sauvignon Blanc.
Delaire Joie de l'Air★★★C
This is a semi-sweet, fruity, tank-produced bubbly made from Weisser Riesling. Attractive nose and good flavour. Easy drinking.
Delheim Pinot Noir Rosé Brut★★★B
The first release from the 1986 vintage was a bright-coloured wine with lots of fresh fruit and full flavour. The 1988 was a better wine, with good yeasty character complementing the fruit of the cultivar. Since 1989 it has settled into a consistently good character bubbly.
De Wet Co-op Cuvée Brut★★★B
Made from Sauvignon Blanc. Dry and refreshing.
De Wet Co-op Vin Doux★★B
Low-alcohol, semi-sweet, with pleasant muscat nose and flavour.
Die Krans L'Enchanté★★★B
This is an off-dry, pretty pink wine made from Pinotage. Served chilled, it makes pleasant, easy drinking.
Domein Doornkraal Tickled Pink Vonkelwyn★★★B
A Blanc de Noir sparkling wine made from Red Muscadel, Tinta Barocca and Pinotage. It has a very pleasant nose and satisfying

semi-sweet taste and for an extra R2,00 you can have the bottle gift-wrapped with a pink ostrich feather.

Douglas Green Cuvée Brut★★(★)C
A refreshing, sparkling wine which is not as dry as the label suggests.

Douglas Green Demi-sec Sparkling★★C
A semi-sweet and fruity-flavoured sparkling wine.

Du Toitskloof Sparkle★★★B
A semi-sweet bubbly with better balance of acid than most Co-op bubblies. Made from Muscat varieties it is an attractive wine in an attractive pack. Sparkle replaces Dagbreek.

Edward Snell Brut★★B
A Steen-based, dry, easy-drinking, fruity bubbly.

Eikendal Vineyards Duc de Berry C'est si Blanc Brut★★C
A non-vintage, off-dry, tank-produced bubbly made from Steen and Sauvignon Blanc. Its pleasant fruitiness makes easy drinking.

Eikendal Vineyards Duc de Berry C'est si Blanc Demi-sec★★C
The same wine as above, but with a semi-sweet finish.

Enchante Sparkling Wine (Heritage Wines)★★(★)B
An off-dry bubbly with Muscat nose that tastes sweeter than the analysis would suggest. Not to be confused with the established pink bubbly produced by Die Krans.

5th Avenue Cold Duck (SFW)★★★B
Another very popular, medium-sweet pink bubbly with an intriguing flavour not found in any other South African sparkling wines.

Franschhoek Vineyards Co-op Sauvignon Blanc Brut★★(★)B
This Sauvignon Blanc is better than most from this variety. It is dry, yet fruity, and is highly alcoholic (nearly 13%).

Franschhoek Vineyards Co-op Sparkling Wine★★B
Composition varies with the vintage. Originally a semi-sweet wine, highly acidic Colombar, then a toned-down blend of Chenin Blanc and Weisser Riesling. Now a pleasant, fruity wine from Sémillon and Colombar. A tank-produced wine.

Goue Vallei Vin Doux (Citrusdal Co-op)★★B
This wine is made from a blend containing Sauvignon Blanc, Hanepoot and Steen. It is produced in the tank and finished semi-sweet. It has a softer bubble than other Co-op sparklers.

Grand Mousseux Extra Brut (SFW)★★★C
A good-quality product, drier than most popular South African sparkling wines. It has become even drier in recent years but has kept its good flavour. Its quality is reflected by consistent success in overseas competitions, including the annual Club Oenologique International Wine and Spirit Competition. If you can find any – buy and enjoy as it has now been discontinued.

Grand Mousseux Grand Rouge (SFW)★★★★C
This Cabernet-based, semi-sweet bubbly launched in 1990 has already developed a popular following. It makes an excellent wine to accompany a sweet course at the end of a meal.

Grand Mousseux Spumante (SFW)★★★C
This sparkling wine has good Muscat nose and decidedly fresh flavour, and sufficient acid ensures that it does not taste as sweet as it really is.

Grand Mousseux Vin Doux (SFW)★★(★)C
At one time South Africa's favourite bubbly, and still very popular. A well-made, medium-sweet wine full of flavour.

Grand Mousseux Vin Sec (SFW)★★(★)C
An off-dry sparkling wine with good flavour.
Grand Provence Cuvée Doux (Union Wines)★★★C
A semi-sweet sparkling wine with attractive character.
Haute Provence Brut★★(★)B
A dry bubbly from a blend of Sauvignon Blanc and Sémillon. Very fizzy with nice nose, though a little neutral on the palate.
Helderberg Co-op De Heldere Vonkel Brut★★(★)B
This pale-pink, off-dry wine is made from Pinot Noir. It has a good flavour and a light-bodied, crisp finish.
Helderberg Co-op De Heldere Vonkel Demi-sec★★(★)B
Following the success of their Brut, the cellar introduced this Sauvignon Blanc-based bubbly. Not too sweet, not over-gassy, it is soft, pleasant, uncomplicated wine.
Here XVII Souverein (Bergkelder)★★★C
Regarded as one of South Africa's prestige sparkling wines, Here XVII's character has improved in recent times, giving it a good nose and an off-dry taste – more appealing to many consumers than the drier bubblies.
Jac Canard Spumante (OK House brand)★★★B
A lovely, fresh, sweet bubbly with good Muscat nose, blended from Colombar, Steen and White Muscadel.
Jac Canard Vin Sec (OK House brand)★★B
An off-dry blend of Cape Riesling, Chenin Blanc and Sauvignon Blanc, none showing on the nose or palate. Full, vigorous bubble.
Jac Canard Vin Doux (OK House brand)★★B
A semi-sweet Steen with fruity nose, good clean flavour, and very vigorous bubble.
JC le Roux La Chanson (Bergkelder)★★★C
A ruby red bubbly that is sweet, but with enough acid not to be cloying and a low alcohol level of only 8,2%. It makes very easy drinking with good bubbles, attractive fruity nose and full, satisfying flavour. Like all JC le Roux wines, it is most attractively packed.
JC le Roux Le Domaine (Bergkelder)★★★C
A lovely flavoured, Spumante-style wine made from Muscadel and Sauvignon Blanc, it has the finest bubbles and good, clean character, with very low alcohol of only 7,5%. It is very popular.
JC le Roux Sauvignon Blanc (Bergkelder)★★★C
A most unusual, dry sparkling wine made from Sauvignon Blanc. It might not be everyone's idea of flavour for a bubbly, but it certainly is a good wine and adds an extra dimension to the market. The wine is vintage dated.
Jean Le Riche Vin Doux (Simonsig)★★★B
A non-vintage, inexpensive semi-sweet bubbly launched in 1990. It is a blend of some four varieties of which the Muscat gives most attractive nose. A fresh, clean wine with good, lively bubble.
Jean Le Riche Vin Sec (Simonsig)★★★B
A drier version of the above wine.
Jean Pierre Marcé (Gilbeys)★★★C
A most attractively packaged, off-dry bubbly which has very good *mousse* and pleasing flavour. It drinks very easily.
Klawer Co-op Vonkelwyn Demi-sec★★(★)B
This sweet, tank-produced bubbly is made from Muscat Ottonel in the Spumante style.

Klawer Co-op Vonkelwyn Sec★★B
A dry, gassy, tank-fermented wine from Sauvignon Blanc.
KWV Mousseux★★(★) (no price)
KWV produce a Mousseux Blanc Brut, Mousseux Blanc Demi-sec and a Mousseux Rouge. They are all pleasant wines and match most commercially available products.
KWV Cuvée Brut★★(★) (no price)
The pack bears a strong resemblance to a commercially-available product but the content is a give-away. Not quite a Brut but with a sweetish aftertaste, it is easy-drinking, uncomplicated wine.
Laborie Sparkling Blanc de Noir (KWV)★★★C
A sparkling wine made by the tank method. Usually lively and refreshing when young. The 1989 is showing bottle age.
La Valle Vin Doux (Reserve) (SFW)★★★C
Inexpensive but soundly-produced bubbly with pleasant nose and sweet taste.
Loopspruit Winery Bosveldvonkel★★B
In 1989 this cellar introduced two bubblies: one is off-dry and pale pink, made from Hanepoot and Steen and coloured with Cinsaut, the other is semi-sweet and the Cinsaut is left out. Both are tank produced. In 1991 the wines carried a special Bles Bridges label for Valentine's Day.
McGregor Co-op Demi-sec★★★B
This is a tank-produced bubbly, from Rhine Riesling, which is fruity and fresh with consistent bubble.
Merwida Co-op Cuvée Brut★B
An off-dry, tank-produced bubbly from Sauvignon Blanc.
Michelle Vin Doux (Klawer Ko-op)★★B
A light-coloured red made mainly from Red Muscadel and a touch of Colombar. Nice bubbly for the sweet palate.
Montagu Muscadelboere Sparkling★★B
An unusual bubbly from White Muscadel produced to commemorate the cellar's 50th anniversary.
Mont D'Or (Drop Inn)★★(★)B
The Mont D'Or name was originally a Benny Goldberg House brand. Now it is available throughout the Drop Inn group in the Cape. The bubblies are made by the Rooiberg Co-op.

Brut: a good clean wine made from Sauvignon Blanc.
Vin Sec: an off-dry, fuller wine from Rhine Riesling.
Vin Brut: a semi-sweet with lots of flowery nose.

Nederburg Kap Sekt★★★★C
Produced originally for export to Germany where, to qualify for the appellation 'Sekt', this wine has to be aged for at least one year. In 1992 the 1987 vintage is still available, indicating that this wine has good bottle bouquet, especially after having at least six to nine months lees contact before bottling. It appears not to be dry, yet has a sugar dosage of less than 10 *g/l*. The 1981 vintage was introduced to the local market in 1982 and showed excellent character after bottle-ageing. In fact, all the vintages have been good and develop beautifully. While the Superior certification existed, at least one bottling of each vintage carried Superior. The 1986 has been very good, the 1987 is developing well, and the 1988 is very good. The 'German' style will begin to disappear as from 1990 as small quantities of Chardonnay are introduced.

Nederburg Première Cuvée Brut★★★(★)C
South Africa's most outstanding sparkling wine made by tank-fermentation. When young and fresh, it has a vitality and appeal all of its own. Its high acid is refreshing and allows it to age with great attraction; a character seldom obtained in South African sparkling wines.
Nederburg Première Cuvée Doux★★★(★)C
Produced originally for export, and now available locally, this is an absolute delight for those with a sweeter tooth.
Nuy Co-op Sparkling★★★B
A delightful, fresh, off-dry bubbly made from Sauvignon Blanc.
Onverwacht Estate Savoire Brut★★(★)B
A dry sparkler without much finesse.
Overvaal Doux (Vaalharts Co-op)★★★B
A semi-sweet bubbly made from Colombar and Hanepoot.
Papillon Brut (Van Loveren)★★★B
Of the three Papillons the Brut has the most enticing nose, made in tank from Sauvignon Blanc and Muscat de Frontignan. The latter shows well on the nose. Attractive butterfly label.
Papillon Demi-sec (Van Loveren)★★(★)B
A multiple blend of Colombar, Pinot Blanc and Muscat de Frontignan. The almost guava-like nose is attractive and the flavour is drier than most labelled Demi-secs.
Papillon Doux (Van Loveren)★★B
A sparkling wine of orange-pink colour with tropical nose; semi-sweet taste with hints of Muscat.
Paul Bonnay Rouge (Pick 'n Pay)★★B
This is an easy-drinking, good-flavoured, sweet bubbly made from Pinotage and Merlot.
Paul Bonnay Vin Sec (Pick 'n Pay)★★B
A complex blend giving a fruity, off-dry sparkler.
Paul Bonnay Vin Doux (Pick 'n Pay)★★B
A semi-sweet, Steen-based bubbly.
Rebel Vin Doux ★★B
Semi-sweet with vigorous bubble.
Rebel Vin Sec ★★B
An off-dry, fruity bubbly.
Renee Charbon (Marcows)★★B
A Vin Sec and a Vin Doux for the Marcows chain.
Riebeek Co-op Sparkling Brut★★★B
A good-flavoured, off-dry bubbly made from Sauvignon Blanc with good, brisk *mousse*.
Riebeek Co-op Sparkling Demi-sec★★★B
A semi-sweet bubbly from multiple blend of Muscat-flavoured wines. Pleasant, easy drinking for the sweet palate.
Rietrivier Co-op Vonkelwyn★★B
Easy drinking sweet wine from Sauvignon Blanc and Colombar.
Romansrivier Co-op Vin Doux★★B
A well-made, semi-sweet wine with good clean character.
Romansrivier Co-op Vin Sec★★B
It seems sweeter than the name would suggest. Made from Sauvignon Blanc.
Roodezandt Co-op Sparkling Wine Brut ★★B
A dryish blend of Sauvignon Blanc, Pinot Gris and Gewürztraminer with fresh flavour heightened by the bubbles.

Roodezandt Co-op Sparkling Wine Demi-sec★★(★)B
The same as above, finished as a semi-sweet bubbly with attractive nose and flavour.
Rooiberg Co-op Brut★★★B
This is another dryish Sauvignon Blanc-based sparkling wine. It has good fruit and massive *mousse*.
Rooiberg Co-op Chardonnay Brut★★★★B
Probably South Africa's first carbonated Chardonnay. Very acceptable, lots of bubble and good flavour.
Rooiberg Co-op Chardonnay Demi-sec★★★(★)B
Not as flavourful as the above, but just as bubbly and finished semi-sweet.
Rooiberg Co-op Vin Doux★★★★B
A very attractive nose coming mainly from Gewürztraminer. A rich, fruity wine with soft, slow bubbles.
Rooiberg Co-op Demi-sec★★(★)★B
A semi-sweet sparkling wine with a fine bubble, rather pleasant nose and good clean taste.
Rubele Demi-sec (Waboomsrivier Co-op)★★★B
A semi-sweet pink bubbly from Pinotage and Cinsaut.
Santino Spumante (Robertson Co-op)★★★B
A triple blend in which the Muscat shows well on the nose, it is semi-sweet, full of bubble with nice fruity flavour.
Simonsvlei Vin Sec★★★B
An off-dry bubbly with good clean nose, fine bubble and very satisfying flavour.
Simonsvlei Vin Doux★★★B
Very definitely a Muscat in the semi-sweet, Spumante style. Good, fine bubble and clean finish.
Slanghoek Co-op Vonkelwyn★★★B
Produced to celebrate the Co-op's new cellar. Clean, semi-sweet wine with decided Sauvignon Blanc nose and good flavour.
Soetwynboere Vonkelwyn★B
This carbonated, semi-sweet bubbly contains a strange blend of Sauvignon Blanc and Hanepoot which gives it a pleasing fizz.
Spier Spumante★★★B
The Spumante style of bubbly is ever-increasing in popularity, so it is not surprising to see Spier introduce one to their range of many bubblies. Better than their average, it has the most amazing bright yellow colour with flowery nose and good sweet flavour. The 6,6% alcohol makes for easy drinking.
Spier Vin Doux and Vin Sec★★C
Two very similar wines made from Steen by the tank method.
Spruitdrift Demi-sec★★★B
A blend of three cultivars: Colombar, Hanepoot and Steen. Semi-sweet, with citrusy flavours and lots of bubble.
St Felix Vineyards Tamay (Rhebokskloof)★★★★C
Light, pleasant, easy-drinking, off-dry bubbly. The fruity nose suggests a much sweeter wine, however the finish is pleasantly dry.
St Louis Cold Duck (Gilbeys)★★C
An interesting, sweetish Rosé bubbly with good flavour.
St Pierre (Vinimark)★★B
A Vin Sec and a Vin Doux are both clear, well-made products with plenty of fizz.

Swartland Co-op Cuvée Brut★★★B
This is a dry, tank-produced sparkler from Sauvignon Blanc.
Swartland Co-op Demi-sec★★(★)C
An inexpensive, semi-sweet bubbly with pleasant nose and flavour.
Swartland Co-op Vin Doux★★B
Muscatty-nosed sweet, well made bubbly with good fizz.
Symphony (Gilbeys)★★★C
A very pale pink bubbly for those with a sweeter tooth. Discontinued.
Tulbagh Co-op Demi-sec★★B
Fresh, sweet, pink bubbly made from Pinotage that gives good nose to an otherwise simple wine.
Tulbagh Co-op Vin Sec★★B
A pleasant off-dry sparkler.
Val du Charron Brut (Wamakersvallei Co-op)★★B
Clear, well-made dryish vintage dated bubbly.
Valentine Sparkling Wine Cerise (Huguenot)★★B
A sweetish red bubbly, with attractive nose and pleasant flavour.
Valentine Sparkling Wine Vin Doux (Huguenot)★★B
Pleasant semi-sweet white bubbly.
Vredendal Co-op Vonkelwyn Blanc Fumé★★★B
The strong cultivar character and vigorous bubbles make this semi-sweet carbonated wine taste drier than it actually is.
Welmoed Co-op Cuvée Brut★★★B
A dry bubbly with packaging that makes you suspect that you've seen it somewhere before.
Welmoed Co-op Sec★★★B
An easy-drinking, off-dry bubbly made from Steen.
Woolworths Vivezza Brut★★★B
Good, clean, finely-bubbled sparkler.
Woolworths Vivezza Dry★★★B
A pleasant, well-made, off-dry bubbly with good fruity flavour, it drinks very easily. From Gilbeys.
Woolworths Vivezza Sweet★★★B
This is a good, semi-sweet, Spumante-style bubbly which is excellent value for money. From Gilbeys.
Woolworths Vivezza Blanc de Noir★★★C
Pleasant, fruity, dry wine with fine bubbles.

Perlé Wines

Ashton Co-op Pétillant Blanc★★(★)A
A semi-sweet white blend, predominantly Colombar with a nice attractive nose coming from small amounts of Bukettraube, Gewürztraminer and Weisser Riesling. This seems rather a lot to go into a relatively inexpensive wine but it has obviously worked as it is the cellar's best seller.
Autumn Harvest Crackling (SFW)★★(★)A
An enormously popular, semi-sweet Perlé which, when chilled, has a very pleasant, fruity nose accentuated by the pétillance. It is a refreshing, lively wine that has gathered a string of international awards, including gold medals at The Monde Selection and the Club Oenologique International Wine and Spirit Competition.
Botha Co-op Perlé★★A
A blend with Colombar, finished semi-sweet, with gentle bubbles.
Capenheimer (SFW)★★★A
This is the oldest Perlé on the market and holds premier position. With its off-dry effervescence and clean, fruity flavour, it makes a very refreshing wine. It is also a winner of international awards.
Culemborg Diamanté Crystal Blanc Perlé★★★A
A semi-sweet Perlé with good Muscat nose and Steen flavour.
Culemborg Diamanté Perlé Blanc de Noir★★★A
This Perlé has a pretty pink colour and gives a nice fresh bubble; semi-sweet in flavour. It is made from Pinotage from which it gets slightly more flavour than most Perlés.
De Doorns Co-op Perlé Blanc★A
A somewhat ordinary semi-sweet from Chenin Blanc and Colombar.
De Doorns Co-op Perlé Rosé★A
A full pink semi-sweet made from Pinotage.
Domein Doornkraal Kuierwyn Perlé★★A
The same as the semi-sweet Kuierwyn from this cellar, only with bubbles, and therefore sold in Perlé bottles with screw-tops.
Grünberger Spritziger (Bergkelder)★★★B
This Perlé wine, attractively presented in a green, tower-type bottle, is, according to the label, produced by the *charmat* process, which is usually associated with the more expensive sparkling wines. It has excellent fine bubbles which continue to rise long after the bottle has been opened. It has a very refreshing, off-dry finish and a slight Muscat nose with lovely Steen flavours.
KWV Musanté★★(★) (no price available)
A semi-sweet Perlé with Muscat nose.
KWV Pétillant Blanc★★ (no price available)
A pleasant, clean, off-dry wine with a fresh finish.
KWV Pétillant Rosé★★ (no price available)
It always seems to have more bubble than most Perlés; a very pleasant off-dry wine.
Loopspruit Muxandre★★A
Under its new name, which comes from Muscat d'Alexandrie, this wine is an improvement on the previous Perlé. It is light in flavour and bubbles, and makes a pleasant off-dry wine in comparison with the previous semi-sweet and very ordinary product.
Merwespont Co-op Morlé★★★A
This Co-op has produced some interesting Perlés in the past and this

latest addition maintains the interest. A third Mario Muscat and the balance Sauvignon Blanc gives most attractive nose to this full-flavoured, semi-sweet wine. Not too fizzy.

Mooiuitsig Wynkelders Bonperlé A

A semi-sweet, white Perlé.

Onverwacht Estate Pétillant Rosé★★B

An off-dry, pink wine from the 1989 vintage that had a nice flavour and refreshing bubble – it is now getting very tired.

Original Paarl Perlé (Oude Meester)★★A

This wine does not necessarily come from the Paarl region. It is a very popular, semi-sweet, white Perlé.

Perlé Dali (Groot Eiland Co-op)★★A

The same blend as Honigtraube, which is Bukettraube and Ferdinand de Lesseps, which is very apparent with the bubbles. It is named after the painter and has a label to match.

Perlino Perlé★★A

Popular in parts of the country, this wine has an attractive Muscat nose and is finished semi-sweet.

Saxenberg Perlé Pére Francis★★★B

An attractive, refreshing Blanc de Noir made from Pinotage and finished off-dry.

Soetwynboere Co-op Perlé Hopewell★A

A semi-sweet Perlé made from Steen grown on Hopewell farm. Though discontinued, there are still a few bottles around.

Sprizzo (Union Wine)★★A

Delightful semi-sweet Muscat with soft bubbles.

Valley Frizzanté (Gilbeys)★★★A

A well-packaged Perlé with good flavour from the Chenin Blanc and Clairette Blanche blend. Refreshing appeal when well chilled.

Wagenboom Perlé (Waboomsrivier Co-op)★★B

A semi-sweet white Perlé from Steen with lots of bubble and better taste than nose.

Fortified Wines

Muscat Wines

Aan-de-Doorns Co-op Muscat d'Alexandrie★★★B
A reliable, rich, full, sweet dessert wine. The 1977 vintage was outstanding, though subsequent vintages have been lighter-bodied and more delicate. This is apparent in all recent releases, including the 1989, which are delicate but well flavoured. These wines are enjoyable when released and need no ageing.
Aan-de-Doorns Co-op Muskadel★★★B
The first release from 1990 is a full-flavoured, rather spirity product.
Agterkliphoogte Co-op Muscadel★★A
Usually fairly spirity wine, yet light in character. Amazing colour.
Apex★★(★)B
Under this label are various well-made fortifieds including Mustelle. Good, inexpensive Muscadels.
Ashton Co-op Hanepoot★★A
A light, sweet wine with good flavour.
Ashton Co-op Rooi Muskadel★★★★A
A bright red, full-flavoured, fruity wine that tastes like raisins. Delicious when released.
Ashton Co-op Wit Muskadel★★★A
Golden-coloured, smooth, good Muscat, fresh finish. A well-made, lightish wine with clean flavours.
Backsberg Hanepoot★★★C
This vintage-dated wine is a delicious, fresh, full, sweet Hanepoot with a hint of tropical fruit in the nose. The 1987 and 1989 have the most attractive nose and very good flavour. The consistency continues with the 1990 and 1991. They will develop well with time.
Badsberg Hanepoot★★★★B
This cellar produces an excellent, full, sweet and golden Hanepoot: a remarkable wine that has gained numerous awards at regional and national shows. It is also a consistent gold medal and trophy winner at the South African Championship Wine Show, and has carried Superior certification for almost every vintage since 1974 until the superior system was dropped.
Barrydale Co-op Hanepoot Jerepiko★★(★)B
A full-flavoured Hanepoot from 1991.
Barrydale Co-op Red Muscadel Jerepiko★★B
A pale-coloured, full, sweet wine from 1991 of subdued character.
Bergsig Sweet Hanepoot★★★B
This has a strong Hanepoot nose, with full, sweet Muscat flavour. The 1991 is a lovely wine and sports an original label in an otherwise very boringly labelled area.
Bolandse Co-op Hanepoot Jerepiko★★B
A good, sweet, full, alcoholic Hanepoot.
Bolandse Co-op Muscadel★★★B
Pale-coloured with good Muscat flavours and smoothly sweet.
Bon Courage Red Muscadel Jerepiko★★★★B
The 1984 carries Superior certification and is a clean, full-flavoured Muscadel. The next release, from the 1988 vintage, is delicate in style, yet intense in flavour. It was followed by a beautiful 1989.

Boplaas Bonaparte Red Dessert★★★(★)B
Again a Tinta Barocca-Muscadel blend but not quite as sweet as the Red Dessert. No recent release.
Boplaas Red Dessert★★★B
A delicious sort of portish wine with Muscat; being a fortified blend of Tinta Barocca and Muscadel.
Boplaas Sweet Hanepoot★★B
The 1987 was a full, sweet wine lacking fruit. The 1988 has a good Muscat nose and a full, sweet flavour. The 1990 is considered the best in the past ten years.
Boplaas White Muscadel★★★★B
This Wine of Origin Klein Karoo is a deep yellow, full-bodied, sweet wine with lots of intense Muscadel character. The 1991 is splendid.
Botha Co-op Soet Hanepoot★★★A
A full, sweet, award-winning Hanepoot.
Bovlei Co-op Soet Hanepoot★★★A
This Co-op produces good quality red and white sweet Hanepoots.
Brandvlei Co-op Soet Hanepoot★★A
A full-bodied Hanepoot and a consistent gold medal winner.
Calitzdorp Co-op Hanepoot★★A
A dark-coloured, full-bodied dessert wine.
Calitzdorp Co-op Jeripiko★★A
Same as the Hanepoot but not certified.
Calitzdorp Co-op Muskadel★★A
This Co-op produces both Red and White Muscadels which are deep-coloured, full, sweet dessert wines.
Clairvaux Co-op★★A
The Co-operative produces both red and white Jerepigos which have substantial wood character.
De Leuwen Jagt Muscadel★★★(★)C
The 1990 and 1991 are good, old-style, sweet, delicious wines.
De Wet Co-op Muscats★★(★)B
This Co-op produces a good, full, sweet Hanepoot and a lighter-styled, sweet Red Muscadel.
Die Krans Estate★★★(★)B
This cellar produces a good, honest range of vintage-dated fortified wine including the 'Heritage' collection.
Die Poort★★A
The cellar produces good Hanepoots, Muscadels and an interesting white Port made from Muscat de Hambourg.
Domein Doornkraal Hanepoot★★★A
The 1989 has a smooth, light, raisin character.
Domein Doornkraal Muscadel★★(★)A
The 1989 release is garnet-coloured, with a somewhat alcoholic character and good Muscat fruit and raisin character from showing.
Domein Doornkraal Pinta★★★B
This wine takes its name from its blend of Pinotage and Tinta Barocca, and is a rich, sweet dessert wine.
Douglas Co-op★★A
The Co-operative produces fortified Muscat d'Alexandrie, fortified Rooi Muskadel and a fortified Sultana.
Durham (Union Wine)★★C
The three wines available in this new range are Muscats: Hanepoot, Marsala and Sultana.

Du Toitskloof Co-op Hanepoot Jerepigo★★★B
This Co-op produces good, award-winning dessert wines which are full-bodied and sweet.
Du Toitskloof Co-op Red Jerepigo★★★(★)B
A very sweet red, raisin-like wine made from Cinsaut.
Du Toitskloof Co-op Soet Hanepoot★★★B
The 1985 vintage carried Superior certification and 27 cases were offered at the 1988 Nederburg Auction. It was the Worcester Show Champion Hanepoot and won a gold medal at the South African Championship show. It is a very sweet, full-flavoured wine with plenty of fruit. The 1986 also carries Superior certification. The 1990 is excellent.
Eersterivier Valleise Co-op Hanepoot★★★B
A lighter-styled, grape-flavoured sweet aperitif.
Fairview Sweet Red★★★(★)B
Good value, fortified Shiraz; deep, rich and lovely.
Franschhoek Vineyards★★B
A lightly-flavoured white fortified.
Goudini Co-op Soet Hanepoot★★★★B
Previously called Muscat d'Alexandrie. A regular medal and trophy winner at local and national shows, it is always full and sweet, with plenty of fruit flavour. Wines such as this one deserve to be better known. The 1988, 1989, 1990 and 1991 are all very good. The latest release has far more complexity than earlier ones.
Goue Vallei (Citrusdal Co-op)★★B
The Co-operative produces full, sweet dessert wines ranging from Hanepoot Jerepigo through full, sweet Steen Jerepigo to sweet red wine. The Hanepoot Jerepigo also has the Gousblom on its label. The Wit Jerepiko is a local show award winner. The Rooi Jerepiko is made from Pinotage. The three-star 1988 (South African Champion Non-Muscat Jerepigo) was a beautiful, deep wine; the 1989 much lighter. The Wit Muskadel is pale in colour and of the lighter style, but still a lovely wine.
Groot Eiland Co-op Hanepoot Soetwyn★★(★)B
A regular medal winner at local shows and occasionally at national shows. A good, smooth wine with a fair amount of Hanepoot flavour.
Groot Trek Red Jeripigo (Vredendal Co-op)★★★★B
Excellent wine from Tinta Barocca. Rich, red and fruity.
Helderberg Co-op Jeripiko★★★B
Good Gold Medal wine at local and national young wine shows. For those who want a change from Muscat, this is the wine.
Huguenot Wines★★(★)A
This cellar sells very acceptable Soet Hanepoot, Wit Muskadel and Wit and Rooi Jeripiko.
Huguenot Wines★★(★)B
This cellar produces a Nagmaalwyn and a Nektar which are good, clean, well-flavoured fortified wines.
Jonkheer Farmers' Winery★★A
This winery markets a range of good fortified Muscats under the brand names of Melita and Myrtella, of which the Red Muscadel is perhaps the best. Their 1985 White Muscadel was the South African Championship Fortified Muscat.
Kango Co-op★★A
This Co-op makes a range of Muscadels and Hanepoots.

Klawer Co-op★★B
The Co-operative produces both red and white Muscadels and a good Halfsoet Hanepoot.
Koelenhof Co-op Hanepoot★★B
A good, golden Hanepoot.
Koelenhof Steen Jeripiko★★★B
A full sweet wine with more than average fruitiness on the nose and nice fresh finish.
KWV★★★★(★)D
Releases include the 1953 Muscadel Jerepigo, 1963 White Muscadel Jerepigo, 1969 Hanepoot Jerepigo and 1968 Jerepigo Liqueur wine. In 1987 the KWV released the 1973 Hanepoot Jerepigo to succeed the 1969. It was a Wine of Origin Breede River, full, luscious and very satisfying. All are Superior.
La Cotte Sweet Hanepoot (Franschhoek Vineyards)★★B
A very sweet, golden-coloured dessert wine.
Landzicht★★A
The Co-operative produces a full, sweet Hanepoot and a fortified Sultana. It also makes a less sweet Hanepoot called Morddré.
Libertas White Muscadel (SFW)★★(★)A
Consistently good, full, sweet, inexpensive wine.
Lombards Sweet Hanepoot★★A
A very popular, good, golden Hanepoot.
Loopspruit Winery★B
Fortified Hanepoots are produced at this winery in the Transvaal.
Louwshoek-Voorsorg Co-op Muscat d'Alexandrie★★★B
Consistently and deservedly certified Superior, this full, sweet Hanepoot is well worth locating.
Lutzville Co-op Hanepoot★A
A full-bodied, smooth, very sweet fortified Hanepoot.
McGregor Co-op Muscadel★★★A
This Co-op produces both red and white Muscadels. The red is remarkable wine with deep flavours and amazing amber colour.
Mamreweg Co-op Hanepoot★★A
A deep, dark, rich, sugary wine with full Hanepoot flavour.
Merwida Co-op Hanepoot★B
A full, sweet dessert wine.
Monis Moscato★★★(★)C
Everything a good, clean red Muscat should be; a Wine of Origin Breede River Valley which is invariably Superior.
Mons Ruber Estate Hanepoot Jerepigo★★(★)B
The local young wine champion: a strong, big, sweet wine.
Mons Ruber Estate Muscadel Jerepigo★★★A
A light-style wine with lovely Muscat nose and delicious flavour. When slightly chilled, it makes an excellent aperitif.
Mons Ruber Estate Red Jerepigo★★★(★)B
From this tiny Klein Karoo Estate comes a deep, rich wine. Muscat whiffs arise from the nose while the full, sweet flavour is complex, but not dominated by Muscat. It is a distinctly different drink.
Montagu Muskadelboere Co-op Rooi Muskadel★★★A
A good example of a full, sweet red Muscadel. Bottled young, it has a delightful nose and fresh flavour.
Mont Blois White Muscadel★★★★(★)C
A consistent award winner at home and abroad, this rich, delicious,

golden-coloured dessert wine is the classic of Robertson Muscadels. It might develop in the bottle but is so good when released that I think that's the time to enjoy it. There's a 1985 and 1987.

Mooiuitsig Wynkelders★★★A

In the true tradition of the Bonnievale Ward, this cellar produces a range of good fortified wines: White Muscadels, Hanepoots, Jerepigos, Marsalas, and Bonwins (Muscadel liqueur wines).

Multana★★★B

A red and a white Muscadel are produced under this label. Well-made, clean, good Muscat flavours.

Muratie Amber★★★D

A vintage-dated, fortified Hanepoot which has a considerable following. Latest releases are very good Muscat.

Nordale Co-op Red Muscadel Jerepigo★★★★A

A beautiful, rich wine full of raisins on the nose.

Nuy Red Muscadel★★★★★C

One of the best sweet Red Muscadels made in South Africa: light, not full-sweet, and showing the Hanepoot character at its best. A consistent award winner at regional and national shows, it has twice been judged champion Muscat at the South African Championship Wine Show and every vintage carries Superior certification. It is regularly sold at the Nederburg Auction.

Nuy White Muscadel★★★★C

This has the same high quality as the Nuy Red but it does not quite achieve the latter's peak. Nevertheless, it is a regular medal and class winner at regional and national shows. It was not only winner of 1988 Diners Club Award with the 1985 vintage but runner-up with the 1983. It is regularly sold at the Nederburg Auction.

Opstal Volsoet Hanepoot★★(★)A

A golden, rich, full-sweet Hanepoot of very good character.

Oranjerivier Wynkelders★★A

The cellar produces a range of Hanepoots, Jerepigos and Muscadels.

Overhex Co-op Muscadels★★★B

This Co-op has pleasant, light-styled red and white Muscadels.

Overvaal (Vaalharts Co-op)★★(★)B

Under this label are very acceptable Jeripigos and Hanepoots.

Paddapoot (Paddagang Vignerons)★★C

A full, sweet, fortified Hanepoot which makes for easy sipping.

Perdeberg Muscat d'Alexandrie★★A

Full, sweet Muscat fortified wine.

Porterville Co-op Jerepigos★A

Good, sweet, white and red Hanepoots.

Riebeek Wine Farmers' Co-op★★A

This Co-operative makes two Jerepigos, a red from Pinotage and a full, sweet Hanepoot, which is the better of these two fine wines.

Rietvallei Rooi Muskadel★★★★(★)B

A sweet fortified wine of the kind every South African should try as an alternative to after-dinner Port – it's excellent. The wine is vintage-dated and is a Wine of Origin Robertson. The 1985 and 1987 are particularly attractive. It was always Superior and is really what this cellar does best.

Robertson Co-op Baron Du Pon Red Muscadel★★★★B

The 1986 Red Muscadel is bottled in magnums and carries Superior certification. Only when this cellar produces an exceptional wine will it carry the Baron Du Pon label. The only other fortified wine has been a 1985 Colombar.

Robertson Co-op Soet Muskadel★★★A

A different kind of Muscadel, delicate, soft and very well-balanced. It deserves to be better known.

Roodezandt Co-op★★★★B

This Co-operative excels in its fortified Hanepoots and Muscadels. Its Muscat d'Alexandrie, Soet Hanepoot and White Muscadel are all outstanding examples of four-star wines: all regularly carry Superior certification and are consistent award winners.

Roodezandt Co-op Hoopsrivier Red Muscadelle★★★B

This vineyard's fine, full, sweet, red dessert wine achieved Superior certification with its 1981, 1982 and 1984 vintages. The 1986 is just as good, while the 1987 and 1989 are a little lighter.

Rooiberg Co-op Jerepiko Red Muscadel★★★★B

A deep-red Muscadel which is always reliable. It is a regular gold medal winner at local and national shows. The 1986 was outstanding.

Rooiberg Co-op White Hanepoot★★★B

A delightful, golden dessert wine with very good Hanepoot character. It is a consistent award winner; frequently certified Superior.

Rooiberg Co-op White Jerepiko★★★(★)B

The 1986 is truly worthy of its Superior certification. It is a big, full, sweet, Muscat-flavoured wine. The 1987 and 1988 are not of the same quality, but the 1989 is again Superior and is every bit as good as the 1986. The 1990 is the best for several years.

Simondium Hanepoot★★B

Good flavoured, full, sweet wine.

Simonsvlei Co-op Hanepoot★★★B

The Co-operative is a regular award winner with this full, sweet, pale gold Hanepoot. It regularly carries Superior certification.

Simonsvlei Co-op Humbro★★★B

Made from Muscat de Hambourg grapes, this full, sweet red dessert wine has very good Muscat flavour and is a regular award winner at the South African Championship Wine Show.

Slanghoek Co-op Soet Hanepoot Jerepigo★★★(★)B

A dessert wine with very good Hanepoot character and golden colour. The 1980, 1982 and 1984 vintages carry Superior certification. The first bottling from 1988 was certified Superior; at subsequent bottlings the Superior was dropped.

Soetwynboere Co-op★★★(★)B

Situated in the Montagu region, this Co-operative specializes in making rich, fruity, fortified wines, including Muscadels, Hanepoots and Jerepigos.

Southern Cape Cellars★★★(★)(various prices)

This is a wholesale operation set up by Boplaas to market a range of select and rare Cape wines. Initial releases are various Muscats carrying the label adorned with the rare mountain flower, *Golden Mimetes*.

Spier Mistelle★★C

A fortified blend of Steen and Hanepoot.

Spruitdrift Co-op Muskadel Jerepiko★★★(★)A

An award-winning, full-flavoured wine.

Spruitdrift Co-op Sweet Hanepoot★★★(★)A

Sampling is like eating raisins. This is a regular award winner.

Swartland Co-op★★★B
The Co-operative makes a range of award-winning fortified wines, including Hanepoots, Jerepigos and Ports.
Tulbagh Co-op★★B
This cellar produces good Hanepoots and Jerepigos.
Van Loveren Red Muscadel★★★(★)B
Delicious, well-made Muscadel with attractive, almost rose, colour. Winner of local awards and an Oaks Club selection.
Villiersdorp Co-op Hanepoot Jerepigo★★B
A full, sweet, golden dessert wine.
Vlottenburg Co-op Hanepoot★★(★)B
A full, sweet fortified wine with good cultivar character. The 1983 was a super four-star wine. Recent vintages are good (uncertified) wines in screw-top bottles.
Vlottenburg Co-op Muscat de Hambourg★★(★)B
Previously called Vin Doux Noir, this is an unusual, full, sweet, red dessert wine made from Muscat de Hambourg.
Vredendal Co-op★★★(★)A
The Co-operative makes a very good range of full-bodied, fortified wines, including Muscadels, Hanepoots, Marsalas and Jerepigos.
Waboomsrivier Co-op Hanepoot★★★A
A full, sweet Hanepoot.
Wamakersvallei Co-op Hanepoot Jerepigo★★A
A full, sweet, white Hanepoot.
Wellington Wynboere Co-op Hanepoot Jerepigo★★A
A full, sweet, white Hanepoot.
Welmoed Co-op★★★A
Another Co-operative which makes a range of good fortified wines, including sweet Hanepoot.
Weltevrede Estate Muscat de Hambourg★★★★C
A beautiful, light, red dessert wine with fine cultivar character. It regularly carries Superior certification.
Weltevrede Estate Rooi and Wit Muskadel★★★C
These are delicate fortified wines with good cultivar character.
Weltevrede Oupa se Wingerd Red Muscadel★★★★C
To my knowledge the only 'single vineyard' fortified wine in the Cape. The label honours Weltevrede's founder, Klaas Jonker. This is a deep, rich, red wine which was SA Champion Muscat at the National Young Wine Show.

Ports

Aan-de-Doorns Co-op Port★★B
Made from Tinta Barocca and without any wood influence at all. It is not suitable for ageing.
Allesverloren Port★★★★D
A consistently and highly successful Port with many Superior certifications and young wine show medals and trophies to its credit. It is made predominantly of Tinta Barocca, with the balance comprising Souzão, giving a deep, rich, ruby Port which ranks among the best in the Cape. It usually carried Superior. It is vintage-dated with the latest being 1984.
Apex Port★★(★)B
Pleasant, inexpensive, ruby-type Port.
Bergsig Port★★B
A young Port made from the fruit of old vines including Cinsaut and various Port varieties and sometimes Cabernet, all contributing to the good flavour. The 1989 is now available.
Bertrams Ruby Port★★★C
A Wine of Origin Boberg Port which drinks very easily and which carries Superior certification. It is closed with a cork.
Blaauwklippen Port★★★(★)D
The 1982 release had good Pontac content, in marked contrast to its Zinfandel-based predecessors. There is great depth of colour, and good flavour from the blend and from wood-ageing. The 1983 and the 1984 are both wines of interest. The 1985 and 1986 are apparently less alcoholic than the previous vintages and are made in the old style with Zinfandel and Pontac from bush vines. The 1987 and 1988 are drier and slightly less alcoholic, but again made from Zinfandel and Pontac. All vintages are developing well and are worth laying down.
Bolandse Co-op Port★★(★)B
This is the first release of a vintage Port from 1986 made from Pinotage. It is a good, rich wine with a nice, dry finish. A quantity of this Port was held back for release in magnums in 1990. The slightly drier 1988 is good and fruity with berry flavour – a nice attempt. The 1989 SA Champion non-Muscat is made from Pinotage and Tinta Barocca. The 1990 is good, smooth, but not too sweet.
Boplaas Ruby Port★★★C
A very pleasant, young Port with good, full flavour – not vintaged, but with good character.
Boplaas Vintage Reserve Port★★★★(★)E
This cellar has produced excellent Ports over a number of years and, after a good run of medals and awards, achieved South African Champion status in 1986. The flagship wine comes from selected barrels and is now bottled with a distinctly Portuguese-style label in an imported Portuguese Port bottle. It is only available from the Estate. The 1987 was again the SA Champion and considered to be one of the finest Ports ever produced at Boplaas, if not in South Africa. There will be no release of the 1988, but the 1989 is the best ever and is the first Port to which I have given five stars. Sales are limited to six bottles per person at R30,00 each from the Estate. I look forward to future vintages.
Boplaas Vintage Port★★★★D
This Port is sold with the traditional Boplaas label, and has the

Boplaas pedigree of awards behind it. Since 1988 it has been bottled at under two years of age and so will benefit from long ageing (ten years or more) in the bottle. The 1989 and 1990 are gorgeous examples of Port.

Boplaas White Port★★★B

An off-dry Port with good flavour. Pleasant aperitif when chilled.

Botha Co-op Portwyn★★A

A well-wooded Port made entirely from Cabernet.

Bottelary Co-op Port★★B

Made from Pinotage, this Port has good fruity nose and sweet finish. It is no longer certified.

Brandvlei Co-op Port★★A

A well-made wine made from Cinsaut.

Calitzdorp Co-op Port★★A

This used to be a young fortified wine from Shiraz and Pinotage, but the 1988 was made from Cabernet. It has no wood influence and needs time to develop. The 1990 is a Pinotage-Cabernet blend and the 1991 a Merlot-Pinotage blend.

Clairvaux Co-op Port★★B

Made from Tinta Barocca, and certified as such, it is intended for relatively early consumption.

Die Krans Port★★★(★)B

A blend in which Pinotage dominated, giving a light, fruity Port with good wood character. Nowadays it is a more typical Port which is made with a higher percentage of Tinta Barocca and then aged in wood for a year before bottling. The 1986 has good character and is not as sweet as many other Ports. The 1988 is predominantly Tinta Barocca with 20% Pinotage – a very good wine. The 1990 is a decidedly better effort.

Die Krans Vintage Reserve Port★★★★C

The 1990 was so good, a selection of the best was bottled as 'Reserve'. Only Tinta Barocca was used.

Die Poort Port★★★A

This is a 1984 wood-matured Port made from Pinotage.

Domein Doornkraal Port★★A

The first release came from the 1987 vintage. It is a good, strong, yet complex wine that could develop well. The 1988 was a gold medal winner at the South African Championship Wine Show. The 1989 is full-flavoured, fruity and dryish. Like all the wines of Domein Doornkraal, this one has an innovative label: all the pertinent information is silk-screened directly onto the bottle, which causes some frustration for label collectors like me!

Douglas Green Ports★★★C

Douglas Green produce a range of inexpensive, good-value-for-money Ports. Their 1963 Port, however, is in a different class altogether. It has good, tawny, wood-aged character and is a four-star wine. In 1988 they introduced a non-vintage white Port which, when chilled, makes a good aperitif.

Durhams Finest Old Port (Union Wine)★★C

A lightish sweet wine on the dry side, made from Tinta Barocca.

Du Toitskloof Co-op Port★★★B

A pleasant, light-bodied wine, made from Cinsaut. The 1986, however, is a wood-matured wine with good Port character. The 1990 shows some potential after a year in wood and could develop well.

A Wine of Origin Goudini, it was an award winner at the local show. The 1989 is aging well.
Goue Vallei (Calitzdorp Co-op)★★★B
Good tawny type, not as sweet as most.
Groot Constantia Port★★★(★)C
The first release from 1984 is a good style, not too sweet, from Tinta Barocca and Shiraz. It is developing well in the bottle as is the 1986.
Helderberg Co-op★★★B
This wine from the 1989 vintage won the Young Wine Show Gold Medal. The 1990 also received gold awards. It will age well, and is a blend of Tinta Barocca and Cinsaut.
Huguenot Port★★(★)A
Two nice ports, one labeled Invalid and one Tawny.
Jonkheer Farmers' Winery★★B
This cellar produces a fresh, young Invalid Port and a nutty, wood-aged Old Port.
Kango Co-op Port★★A
Made from Tinta Barocca and Cabernet, this is a dryish, spirity wine. The 1990 is entirely from Tinta Barocca.
Koelenhof Co-op Port★★B
A full, sweet, spirity Pinotage Port aged in oak.
KWV 1948 Port★★★★D
Released in 1987 in both 750 m*l* bottles and in magnums, this Wine of Origin Boberg is a tawny, wood-aged Port, bottled to celebrate Paarl's tercentenary. The 750 m*l* bottle is a unique, oval shape, specially designed for the occasion. It is ready for drinking now.
KWV Bartolomeu Dias 1963 Port★★★★D
To commemorate the rounding of the Cape 500 years before, the KWV launched a 1963 wood-aged Port early in 1988. Available in magnums, this flavourful wine drinks well now, but has the potential to develop further in the bottle.
KWV Crusted Vintage Port★★★★(★)(no price available)
A bottling from the 1963 vintage was matured in the bottle for 16 years to enable the crust to form. In 1990 it has developed extremely well and it is a pity that this has not been done more often.
KWV Tawny 1956 Port★★★(★)D
A Wine of Origin Boberg. This Port, certified Superior, is smooth across the palate and full of wood-aged flavour, but lacks the complexity of a bottle-aged Port. It drinks very easily.
La Cotte Red Port (Franschhoek Vineyards Co-op)★★B
A fairly ordinary Port made from Tinta Barocca and Cinsaut.
Landskroon Port★★★★C
A regular medal and trophy winner at regional and national shows, this distinctive wine was, in its earlier vintages, made from Tinta Barocca, Cinsaut and Alicante Bouschet. It is not as sweet as most local Ports and is a little more chewy than most. It is vintage-dated. The 1978 developed with interest in the bottle over five years, and other vintages should do the same. The 1983 is worth trying; the 1985 promises to be good. The 1986, however, could be the best. Since 1988 Cinsaut has been dropped from the blend and comes in a dumpy Port bottle. It is a good wine that will develop well.
Merwida Co-op Port★B
Equal proportions of Cabernet and Pinotage make up this full-bodied dessert wine.

Monis Collector's Port★★★★C
Excellent, old, wood-aged Port, vintage-dated 1948, of which three issues have been made. Their labels reproduce rare old South African stamps. A special edition was produced for the Johannesburg centenary, with labels carrying portraits of renowned Rand personalities of the past. The last release is from the 1961 vintage and features six different labels, each showing pieces of artillery used by both sides in the South African War. The Superior Tawny Port was made from Souzão, Cinsaut, Tinta Barocca and Cabernet Sauvignon.
Monis Special Reserve Port★★★(★)C
A dry, ruby-styled Port from Cabernet, Cinsaut and Tinta Barocca.
Monis Very Old Mature Port★★★(★)C
One of the most respected and oldest names in fortified wines. For years Monis have sold a product called Vintage Port, which, as good as it was, was certainly not a Vintage Port. It is now renamed Very Old Mature Port, which describes more accurately this 10 – 15 year old, wood-matured Port of good character and excellent value.
Mons Ruber Port★★★B
Good, dryish Ports from the 1990s, made from Cabernet.
Mooiuitsig Wynkelders★★A/B
This cellar produces a range of Ports under various names such as Fine Old, Old Tawny and Old White.
Morganhof Port★★★(★)C
From 1988 comes a good attempt from Pinotage and Tinta Barocca. Good fruit, dryish aftertaste.
Muratie Port★★★E
This blend of Cinsaut and various Port varieties is in line with the cellar's over-all style. It has a faithful following. The 1990 and 1991 are a totally different style made from Port varieties and bottled early. It should develop well.
Nederburg Port★★★★★(no price available)
A very rare wine, always given away, never sold. It is light and fruity, and completely different from any other South African wine. Beg, borrow or steal a bottle: it'll be worth the experience.
Overgaauw Port★★★★E
This Port, made from various cultivars, has been wood-aged for two years and then bottled in the true Vintage Port style. It develops well but needs many years in the bottle to reach its full potential. The 1976 is good in 1990. The 1981 is similar and keeps Overgaauw among the forerunners in South African Vintage Port production. The 1983 is very Portuguese in style. Overgaauw is making serious Port.
Riebeek Wine Farmers' Co-op Port★★★B
A light but attractive Port made in the 1982 vintage from a number of Port varieties. It has been reserved for release in 1992 to celebrate the cellar's golden anniversary. This cellar also makes a regular Port. The 1987 and 1989 are from Shiraz.
Romansrivier Port★★(★)B
This limited release in magnums is a blend of vintages from 1981 and 1984, and is made from a number of varieties including Cabernet, Pinotage and Tinta Barocca. It is a Wine of Origin Breede River. The 1987 from Tinta Barocca is pale, light, oaky and dryish.
Rooiberg Co-op Port★★★(★)A
This 1985 Port replaces the previous Pinotage-based Port. Made from equal portions of Tinta Barocca and Souzão and fortified with

three-year-old brandy, it was wood-aged in small oak for a year. The result is a good, rich, concentrated wine with lots of fruit and a firm, dry finish. The 1986 and 1987 were made along similar lines. The 1988 had 20% Cabernet Franc added to give unusual dimension.

Rustenberg Port★★★(★)C

The 1984 is the first release, made from predominantly Souzão with some Cabernet, giving a big, rich Port which is developing beautifully in the bottle. The next release, from the 1987 vintage, is made along the same style.

Santys Invalid Port★★B

A good, inexpensive, tawny Port.

Santys Old Ruby Port★★★(★)B

A fruity, flavourful, wood-aged Port from Port varieties and Cinsaut.

Sedgwicks Government House Port★★★B

One of South Africa's oldest Port labels; it is much respected, popular and inexpensive, and has good character.

Simonsvlei Co-op Port★★★(★)E

A limited release from 1983, blended from Cinsaut, Shiraz and Tinta Barocca. It was aged for a year in small wood and will need a further five to seven years in the bottle to smooth out. A good attempt. The next release from the 1986 vintage is much better.

Spier Port★★C

The 1983 Pinotage Port is a great improvement on earlier releases and the powerful 1984 continues the trend. The 1986 and 1987 are now available.

Swartland Co-op Port★★(★)A

A very young, full, grape-flavoured Port. Mixed with lemonade, it makes a delicious summer drink.

Vergenoegd Estate Port★★★C

Although it was made from Tinta Barocca, this wine is not as big and rich as most South African Ports. The 1986 was the first release. The 1987 is sold in tall, high-shouldered bottles and comes with a separate stopper cork so that once you have pulled the cork you can reseal the bottle. The next release was from the 1988 vintage and will be followed by the 1989.

Villiersdorp Co-op Port★★(★)B

A blend of Pinotage and Tinta Barocca giving full, sweet wine with pleasant flavour.

Vredendal Co-op Port★★★A

An interesting young Port made from almost equal parts of Carignan, Cinsaut, Grenache, Pinotage and Tinta Barocca, all of which produce a most unusual nose and character. It will need time to integrate and should develop a depth of complexity.

Waboomsrivier Co-op Port★★(★)A

A blend of Cinsaut and Tinta Barocca, aged for two years in wood and then kept for two years in the bottle before being released. This produces a good, rich flavour that could develop with age.

Welmoed Co-op Vintage Port★★★C

The wood-aged 1983 Port made from Tinta Barocca has developed very well in the bottle. The 1985 is much the same. The 1989 is the next release.

Sherries

South Africa produces very good Sherries, the more expensive brands being very similar in quality, varying only in name, through a range of styles and sweetness, for example:

Dry: Often termed 'pale dry', because these are the lightest of the Sherries in terms of colour. These are usually bone-dry, in the tradition of the Spanish *finos*, or have, at the most, the smallest fraction of sweetness. Delicately flavoured, these Sherries make the best aperitifs when served chilled.
Medium, Medium-dry, or Medium-sweet: Sherries thus labelled vary widely in degree of sweetness, depending on the individual brand name's particular market. Usually they are of the Spanish *oloroso* style: golden, with good bouquet and lovely flavour.
Full Cream: Usually the darkest-coloured and the sweetest of the finer Sherries, they are of the Spanish *amoroso* style and at one stage were known as 'East Indian Walnut' or 'Old Brown'.
Old Brown: In South Africa, Old Brown Sherries are a category on their own, usually inexpensive, deep in colour and full of flavour.
Golden Sherries: Another category peculiar to South Africa. Such wines are usually sweet and full of flavour, but bear very little resemblance to classic Sherry. They are survivors of a bygone age in this country when fortified wines ruled supreme and unfortified wines were hardly known.

Because of these broad similarities, I have not described individual wines in any detail, except in a few instances where some outstanding or unusual aspect has invited further comment. The following list does not reflect the full range of sherries on the market and relates only to those I have tasted during the past two years.

Bertrams★★★★C
The sherries from this merchant are also certified Superior; the range is Santa Petra Pale Dry, Medium Dry, Medium Cream and Full Cream and Premier Reserve Fine Old Pale Cream.

Boschendal 'Ronnie van Rooyen' Vintage Sherry (1977)★★C
This Wine of Origin Paarl was made by Ronnie van Rooyen in 1977; none has been made since. It is something of a curiosity as Sherries are not normally vintage-dated; the traditional method of Sherry making in a solera involves the slow blending of Sherries from many vintages, young wines being added to older. A collector's item.

Douglas Green★★★★B
The 'Flor' Sherries from Douglas Green are well known and include the Extra Dry (No 1), Medium (No 3) and a Full Cream.

Drostdy (Oude Meester)★★★★B
The Drostdy Sherries are all Wines of Origin Tulbagh and are certified Superior. The range is Pale Dry, Medium and Full Cream.

Eekay Old Brown (EK Green)★★A
Inexpensive, sweet, 'Old Brown' style.

Goue Vallei (Citrusdal Co-op)★★★B
This Co-op markets a range of Pale Dry, Medium Cream and Old Brown Sherries.

KWV Very Old Medium Dry and Medium Cream★★★★C
A Wine of Origin Boberg and certified Superior.

KWV Very Old Sherry★★★C
Sold in the KWV's new long-necked bottle, this Medium Cream Sherry was released in 1988. A very good wine, it carries Superior.
Monis★★★★C
Monis Sherries are certified Superior. The range is Pale Dry, Medium Cream and Full Cream.
Monte Vista (Mooiuitsig)★★B
In addition to the popular Old Brown Sherry this merchant also makes Pale Dry, Medium Dry and Medium Cream Sherries.
Santys Walnut Old Brown (Gilbey)★★A
A good quality, Old Brown style.
Sedgwicks Old Brown★★★A
By far the market leader in terms of the Old Browns.
Ship Sherry (SFW)★★A
A surprisingly good product that is the friend of South Africa's commercial deep-sea fisherfolk. In Port Elizabeth alone, more than a million cases are sold each year.
Van der Stel Club Sherry (Oude Meester)★★A
Inexpensive, well-made, sweetish Sherry.

Other Fortified Wines

Brulpadda (Paddagang Vignerons)★★D
This sweet, Porty wine carries my favourite label in the Paddagang range of wines. Very pleasant when young, the wine will no doubt improve with time.

Die Krans La Difference★★★B
A well-flavoured fortified Steen.

Domein Doornkraal Kaptein★★★A
A blend of some Pinta (Pinotage and Tinta Barocca) and Muscadel produces a most unusual wine which is full of flavour and character.

Domein Doornkraal Majoor★(★)A
A full-flavoured Steen Jerepigo.

Fairview Full Sweet Sémillon★★★B
An unusual fortified wine made from Sémillon. Served ice-cold, it makes a fine substitute for a sorbet between the courses of a dinner. The 1980 vintage has a most attractive grapey character.

Goudini Co-op Red Dessert★(★)A
A 1987 fortified sweet Pinotage. It has an attractive nose but lacks flavour and is a little watery in the mouth.

Goue Vallei Jerepigo (Citrusdal)★★★A
This national champion from the 1988 vintage has good, clean aroma and fine flavour. Made from very ripe Pinotage and fortified with wine spirit, it should develop with time in the bottle.

Kango Co-op Golden Jerepiko★★★★B
A super fortified Steen and a regular award winner. One of the best non-Muscat fortifieds.

Kango Co-op Red Jerepigo★★A
Made from Tinta Barocca; an interesting variation.

Louwshoek-Voorsorg Co-op Nectar de Provision★★★B
First release from the 1987 vintage. This Co-op produced a fortified wine typical of the Cognac region where it is called Pineau des Charentes. In other parts of France similar products are called Amistelle. This one is made from fully ripe Colombar and fortified with brandy. It is aged for two years in oak and should be served chilled. Next release from the 1991 vintage.

Mons Ruber Bonitas★★A
Another white dessert wine, somewhat smoother than the Regalis.

Mons Ruber Elegantia★★B
A full-flavoured, red dessert wine.

Mons Ruber Regalis★★B
Initially this was a spirity, hot, white dessert wine, not without character. It has developed into a smooth, easier-drinking wine with unmistakable Hanepoot character.

Perdeberg Co-op Cinsaut Liqueur Wine★★A
A good, light, Port-style, fortified wine made from Cinsaut.

Vaalharts Co-op★★A
Interesting fortified wines from this Co-op include Andalusia Jerepigo made from Pinotage and Andalusia Erlihane, which is the first fortified wine from the cross between Hanepoot and Queen of the Vineyards table grape varieties.

Welmoed Co-op★★★(★)B
This Co-op produces interesting red dessert wines, made previously from Shiraz and now from Tinta Barocca.

Stop Press

Belcher Blanc de Blanc★★★B
From the 1991 vintage comes a good-character blend of Cape Riesling, Chenin Blanc and wooded Colombar. Dry wine, with good, fruity finish.

Belcher Bouquet Blanc★★★B
A multiple blend from 1992 with fruity nose and pleasant flavour, finished semi-sweet.

Belcher Noble Late Harvest★★★(★)E
Well-botrytised wine that has been in French oak, giving it extra dimension. The 1992 vintage has good nose and full flavours.

Belcher Non-méthode Champenoise
This attractive new cellar produces a sweet and a dry sparkler, both from 1992.

Belcher Riesling Special Reserve★★★(★)C
A wood-fermented Riesling with good nose and lots of flavour. Two vintages are available – the 1991 and the 1992.

Belcher Sémillon★★★B
A good example of this cultivar. Clean, fresh, good grassy nose and flavour from 1992 vintage. Nice, dry finish.

Belcher Stein★★★B
An off-dry, good-tasting blend from Chenin Blanc and Colombar. From 1991 vintage. Good drinking wine.

Les Monts Malverne (Clos Malverne)★★★B
A very attractive, good value for money wine of mainly Pinotage (around 70%), Cabernet and Sauvignon Blanc (yes – Sauvignon Blanc!). Fruity, dry and easy to drink.

Listing of Wines According to Star Rating

(npa) = no price available

Bordeaux Blends

★★★★★

Delheim Grand Reserve E
Fairview Merlot Reserve E
Glen Carlou Classique E/F
Kanonkop Auction Reserve F
Kanonkop Paul Sauer E
Meerlust Rubicon E
Overgaauw Tria Corda E
Rozendal C
Rustenberg Gold E
Rust-en-Vrede E
Warwick Trilogy E
Welgemeend C
Zevenwacht E

★★★★(★)

Backsberg Klein Babylonstoren D
Bertrams Robert Fuller E
Clos Malverne Auret Reserve F
Glen Carlou Les Trois D
L'Ormarins Optima Reserve F
Vriesenhof Kallista C
Woolworths Cabernet Sauvignon-Merlot D

★★★★

Avontuur Avon Rouge C
Avontuur Baccarat D
Boplaas Grand Vin Rouge D
Buitenverwachting Grand Vin E
Cape Vintners Members Only Grand Reserve D
Clos Malverne Auret E
Delaire Barrique D
Eikendal Classique D
Fairview Charles Gerard Reserve C
Groot Constantia Gouveneurs Reserve E
Hamilton Russell Vineyards Premier Reserve E
Kloofzicht Alter Ego E
La Motte Estate Cabernet Sauvignon E
La Motte Millenium D
Meerlust Red D
Nederburg Private Bin R109 E
Neil Ellis Reserve Selection D
Overgaauw D C Classic D
Talana Hill Royale E
Vergenoegd D
Villiera Estate Crû Monro D
Welgemeend Douelle C
Woolworths Grand Rouge C
Woolworths Le Cinquieme D
Woolworths Le Premier D

Cape Traditional Blends

★★★★★

Nederburg Private Bin R103 E

★★★★(★)

Nederburg Private Bin R115 E
Rustenberg Dry Red C

★★★★

Nederburg Edelrood C
Roodendal Reserve C
Rozendal C
Vaughan Johnson's House Red C
Warwick Femme Bleue E

Dry Red Blends

★★★★

Altydgedacht Tintoretto C
Hemel-en-Aarde Valley Vin Rouge C
Overgaauw Overtinto B

Cabernet Franc

★★★★

Warwick Cabernet Franc D

Cabernet Sauvignon

★★★★★

Beyerskloof Cabernet Sauvignon F
Blaauwklippen Reserve Cabernet Sauvignon D
Kanonkop Cabernet Sauvignon E
Klein Constantia Cabernet Sauvignon E
Meerlust Cabernet Sauvignon E
Nederburg Auction Cabernet Sauvignon E

Stellenryck Cellarmaster's Choice E
Stellenryck Collection Cabernet Sauvignon E
Thelema Cabernet Sauvignon E
Vriesenhof Cabernet D

★★★★(★)

Backsberg Cabernet Sauvignon C
Bellingham Cabernet Sauvignon C
Blaauwklippen Cabernet Sauvignon E
Fleur Du Cap Cabernet Sauvignon D
Glen Carlou Cabernet Sauvignon E
Le Bonheur Cabernet Sauvignon E
Middelvlei Cabernet Sauvignon D
Nederburg Paarl Cabernet E
Overgaauw Cabernet Sauvignon D
Rustenberg Cabernet Sauvignon E
Stellenryck Historic Wine Museum Cabernet Sauvignon 1975 E
Uitkyk Carlonet E
Vergenoegd Cabernet Sauvignon C
Warwick Cabernet Sauvignon D/E
Zonnebloem Cabernet Sauvignon C

★★★★

Allesverloren Cabernet Sauvignon C
Alphen Cabernet Sauvignon C
Alto Cabernet Sauvignon E
Bertrams Cabernet Sauvignon C
Bloemendal Estate Cabernet Sauvignon D
Cape Vintners Members Only Cabernet Sauvignon D
Clos Malverne Cabernet Sauvignon E
Delheim Cabernet Sauvignon C
Fairview Cabernet Sauvignon B
Fairview Reserve Cabernet D
Fleur du Cap Oak Collection D
Goedvertrou Cabernet Sauvignon E
Groot Constantia Cabernet Sauvignon C
La Motte Estate Cabernet D
Landskroon Cabernet Sauvignon C
Lievland Cabernet Sauvignon D
L'Ormarins Cabernet Sauvignon E
Neil Ellis Vineyard Selection Cabernet Sauvignon C
Oude Libertas Cabernet Sauvignon B
Rhebokskloof Cabernet Sauvignon D
Rozendal Colour Label Magnums D
Rustenberg Cabernet Sauvignon Reserve F
Rust-en-Vrede Cabernet Sauvignon E
Simonsig Cabernet Sauvignon C
Stellenzicht Cabernet Sauvignon D
Welgemeend Cabernet Sauvignon C
Woolworths Vintage Cabernet Sauvignon C
Zevenwacht Cabernet Sauvignon D

Merlot

★★★★(★)

Villiera Merlot D

★★★★

Boschendal Jean de Long Merlot Auction Reserve E
Buitenverwachting Auction Reserve E
Cape Vintners Members Only Merlot D
Delheim Merlot (not for sale)
Fairview Merlot Reserve D
Fleur du Cap Merlot C
Glen Carlou Merlot E
Meerlust Merlot D
Overgaauw Merlot C
Warwick Merlot E
Warwick Special Reserve 1987 (No price – auctioned)
Woolworths Le Deuxieme 902R E

Pinotage
★★★★★
Kanonkop CIWG Pinotage E
★★★★(★)
Simonsig Pinotage Reserve E
★★★★
Fairview Pinotage Reserve C
Fleur Du Cap Pinotage C
Kanonkop Pinotage C
Lanzerac Pinotage (npa)
Meerendal Pinotage C
Nederburg Auction Pinotage
Oude Libertas Pinotage F
Rheboksklo of Pinotage D
Simonsvlei Co-op Pinotage C
Zonnebloem Pinotage B

Pinot Noir
★★★★★
Hamilton Russell Pinot Noir E
Hamilton Russell Vineyards Pinot Noir Reserve F
★★★★
Blaauwklippen Pinot Noir C
Bouchard Finlayson Pinot Noir E
Glen Carlou Pinot Noir E
Nederburg Pinot Noir C
Rustenberg Pinot Noir C
Woolworths Pinot Noir C

Shiraz
★★★★(★)
Nederburg Shiraz C
★★★★
Allesverloren Shiraz C
Backsberg Shiraz C
Bellingham Shiraz D
Bertrams Shiraz E
Delheim Shiraz B
Fairview Reserve Shiraz C
Groot Constantia Shiraz C
Hartenberg Shiraz E
Klein Constantia Shiraz D
La Motte Estate Shiraz D
Landskroon Shiraz C
Lievland Shiraz D
L'Ormarins Shiraz E
Paradyskloof Roodewyn A
Pick 'n Pay Shiraz C
Rust-en-Vrede Shiraz E
Simonsig Shiraz D
Vergenoegd Shiraz C
Zonnebloem Shiraz C

Blended/Non-varietal Dry White Wines
★★★★(★)
Fairview Charles Gerard Reserve C
★★★★
Chant de Nuit A
Klein Constantia Blanc de Blanc C
Nederburg Prelude C
Nederburg Private Bin D207 B
Stellenzicht Grand Vin Blanc C
Stellenzicht Heerenblanc C
Woolworths Le Troisieme 913W
Zonnebloem Grand Soleil C

Blended/Non-varietal Off-dry/Semi-sweet White Wines
★★★★(★)
Nederburg Private Bin S354 D
★★★★
Fairview Bouquet Fair B
Nederburg Private Bin S312 C
Nederburg Private Bin S333 C
Twee Jongegezellen Schanderl C

Chardonnay
★★★★★
Hamilton Russell Vineyards Chardonnay Reserve F
Klein Constantia Chardonnay F
Talana Hill Chardonnay F
Thelema Chardonnay D
★★★★(★)
Backsberg Chardonnay D
Glen Carlou Chardonnay E
Hamilton Russell Vineyards Chardonnay E
Overgaauw Chardonnay D
Simonsig Chardonnay C
Vriesenhof Chardonnay D
★★★★
Aan de Wagenweg Chardonnay E
Bellingham Reserve Chardonnay E
Boschendal Chardonnay E
Bouchard Finlayson Chardonnay E
Buitenverwachting Chardonnay E

Danie de Wet Chardonnay D
Danie de Wet Chardonnay Bateleur E
Danie de Wet Chardonnay Bon Vallon C
Danie de Wet Chardonnay Clos de Roche C
Delaire Chardonnay E
Delheim Chardonnay D
De Wetshof Estate Finesse D
Eikendal Chardonnay D
Graham Beck Wine of Madeba Chardonnay C
John Platter Chardonnay D
Louisvale Chardonnay E
L'Ormarins Chardonnay D
Mondial Chardonnay E
Neethlingshof Chardonnay E
Nederburg Auction Chardonnay D
Nederburg Chardonnay D
Neil Ellis Chardonnay D
Pick 'n Pay Chardonnay C
Rustenberg Chardonnay Reserve E
Van Loveren Chardonnay E
Weltevrede Estate Chardonnay D
Woolworths Chardonnay C
Woolworths Chardonnay (unwooded) C

Colombar(d)

★★★★

Nuy Co-op Colombard A

Fernão Pires

★★★★

Nederburg Private Bin D207 B

Gewürztraminer

★★★★★

Nederburg Gewürztraminer C

★★★★(★)

Delheim Gewürztraminer C

★★★★

Boschendal Jean Garde Vineyard Gewürztraminer C
Fleur Du Cap Gewürztraminer D
Groot Constantia Gewürztraminer C
Neil Ellis Gewürztraminer C
Neethlingshof Gewürztraminer C
Stellenryck Gewürztraminer C
Weltevrede Gewürztraminer B
Zevenwacht Gewürztraminer C

Hárslevelü

★★★★

Lemberg C

Late Harvest

★★★★

Delheim Spatzendreck Late Harvest B
Nuy Steen Laat-oes B

Special Late Harvest

★★★★

Backsberg Special Late Harvest B
Bergsig Gewürztraminer Special Late Harvest B
Bon Courage Gewürztraminer Special Late Harvest C
Delaire Special Late Harvest B
Delheim Special Late Harvest B
Du Toitskloof Co-op Special Late Harvest B
Eikendal Special Late Harvest B
Fleur du Cap Special Late Harvest B
Hartenberg L'Estreux C
Nederburg Special Late Harvest B
Nederburg Weisser Riesling Special Late Harvest D
Neethlingshof Gewürztraminer Special Late Harvest B
Neethlingshof Weisser Riesling Special Late Harvest C

Noble Late Harvest

★★★★★

Delheim Edelspatz Noble Late Harvest C
Nederburg Edelkeur D
Nederburg Eminence Noble Late Harvest D
Nederburg Weisser Riesling Noble Late Harvest D
Neethlingshof Rhine Riesling Noble Late Harvest D

★★★★(★)
Blaauwklippen
Noble Late Vintage C
KWV Noble Late Harvest (npa)
Nederburg Chardonnay
Noble Late Harvest (npa)
Nederburg Steen
Noble Late Harvest C
Woolworths
Noble Late Harvest
★★★★
Backsberg
Noble Late Harvest E
Bellingham
Noble Late Harvest D
Boschendal Vin d'Or D
Buitenverwachting Noblesse E
Engeltjepipi
Noble Late Harvest C
Lievland Noble Late Harvest D
L'Ormarins
Noble Late Harvest C
Nederburg Bukettraube
Edelkeur D
Nederburg Bukettraube
Noble Late Harvest D
Nederburg
Noble Late Harvest C
Nederburg Riesling Edelkeur D
Neethlingshof Sauvignon
Blanc Noble Late Harvest D
Pick 'n Pay
Noble Late Harvest D
Rooiberg Edel Laatoes C
Simonsig Noble Late Harvest E
Simonsvlei Co-op
Noble Late Harvest C
Stellenzicht
Noble Late Harvest E
Vredendal Co-op
Noble Late Harvest C
Zonnebloem
Noble Late Harvest E

Muscat Wines

★★★★
Thelema Muscat
de Frontignan B

Natural Sweet

★★★★★
Klein Constantia
Vin de Constance
Noble Late Harvest (npa)
★★★★
Nederburg Sauvignon Blanc
Natural Sweet C

Riesling – Cape

★★★★
L'Ormarins
Franschhoek Riesling C

Riesling – Rhine/Weisser

★★★★
Danie de Wet Rhine Riesling C
Danie de Wet
Rhine Riesling Reserve C
Delaire Weisser Riesling C
Delheim Rhine Riesling B
Groot Constantia
Weisser Riesling B
Hartenberg
Weisser Riesling B
Klein Constantia
Rhine Riesling C
Lievland Weisser Riesling B
Nederburg Elgin
Weisser Riesling D
Nederburg Rhine Riesling B
Nederburg Weisser Riesling C
Neil Ellis Rhine Riesling C
Rhebokskloof
Weisser Riesling B
Simonsig Weisser Riesling B
Stellenryck Collection
Rhine Riesling C
Villiera Rhine Riesling B
Weltevrede Rhine Riesling A
Woolworths Rhine Riesling B

Sauvignon Blanc

★★★★★
Neil Ellis Whitehall
Sauvignon Blanc C
★★★★(★)
L'Ormarins Blanc Fumé C
Villiera Sauvignon Blanc B
★★★★
Aan de Wagenweg
Blanc Fumé E
Alphen Le Fevre B
Backsberg John Martin C
Buitenverwachting
Blanc Fumé D
Buitenverwachting
Sauvignon Blanc D
Delaire Blanc Fumé C

Hamilton Russell Vineyards
Sauvignon Blanc D
Klein Constantia
Sauvignon Blanc D
La Motte Blanc Fumé D
La Motte
Sauvignon Blanc D
Le Bonheur Blanc Fumé C
Lemberg Aimée C
L'Ormarins
Sauvignon Blanc C
Neil Ellis Blanc Fumé C
Stellenryck Blanc Fumé C
Stellenzicht Sauvignon Blanc
Thelema Blanc Fumé B
Thelema Sauvignon Blanc C
Uitkyk Estate
Sauvignon Blanc B
Villiera Crû Monro
Blanc Fumé B
Woolworths Blanc Fumé B
Woolworths
Sauvignon Blanc Reserve D

Blanc de Noir

★★★★

Nederburg Cabernet
Blanc de Noir C
Neethlingshof Blanc de Noir C

Rosé

★★★★

Delheim Pinotage Rosé B

Méthode Champenoise Sparkling Wines

★★★★(★)

Pierre Jourdan Brut E
Villiera Tradition de Charles
de Fère Reserve E

★★★★

Backsberg Estate
Méthode Champenoise D
Boschendal Brut D
Boschendal Brut Rosé E
Boschendal Grande Reserve D
Buitenverwachting Brut F
Here XVII Grand Cuvée E
JC le Roux Pinot Noir D
Krone Borealis F
L'Ormarins Jean Roi
Pierre Jourdan Belle Rosé F
Pierre Jourdan
Blanc de Blancs F
Pierre Jourdan
Cuvée Reserve F
Pierre Jourdan Extra F
Pongrácz D/C
Simonsig Kaapse Vonkel D
Villiera Tradition de
Charles de Fère D
Woolworths
Méthode Champenoise C

Non-méthode Champenoise Sparkling Wines

★★★★

Bellingham Brut
Vintage Rosé C
Grand Mousseux
Grand Rouge C
Nederburg Kap Sekt C
Rooiberg Co-op
Chardonnay Brut B
Rooiberg Co-op
Vin Doux B
St Felix Vineyards Tamay C

Muscat Wines

★★★★★

Nuy Red Muscadel C

★★★★(★)

KWV D
Mont Blois
White Muscadel C
Rietvallei Rooi Muskadel B

★★★★

Ashton Co-op Rooi
Muskadel A
Badsberg Hanepoot B
Bon Courage
Red Muscadel Jerepiko B
Boplaas White Muscadel B
Goudini Co-op
Soet Hanepoot B
Groot Trek Red Jeripigo B
Nordale Co-op
Red Muscadel Jerepigo A
Nuy White Muscadel C
Robertson Co-op Baron Du
Pon Red Muscadel B
Roodezandt Co-op B
Rooiberg Co-op Jerepiko
Red Muscadel B
Weltevrede Estate
Muscat de Hambourg C
Weltevrede Oupa se Wingerd
Red Muscadel C

Ports

★★★★★

Nederburg Port (npa)

★★★★(★)

Boplaas Vintage Reserve Port E
KWV Crusted
Vintage Port (npa)

★★★★

Allesverloren Port D
Boplaas Vintage Port D
Die Krans
Vintage Reserve Port C
KWV 1948 Port D
KWV
Bartolomeu Dias 1963 Port D
Landskroon Port C
Monis Collector's Port C
Overgaauw Port E

Sherries

★★★★

Bertrams C
Douglas Green B
Drostdy B
KWV Very Old Medium Dry
and Medium Cream C
Monis C

Other Fortified Wines

★★★★

Kango Co-op
Golden Jerepiko B

Index

Wines printed in *italics* are available but have not been assessed.
(npa) = no price available